Economic Methodology, History and Pluralism

Economic Methodology, History and Pluralism: Expanding Economic Thought to Meet Contemporary Challenges pays tribute to Emeritus Professor Sheila Dow (University of Stirling, Scotland). This volume focusses on the contributions of Dow to economic methodology, pluralism and the history of economic thought. These explorations serve to underpin her ideas and theories on macroeconomics, banking and money.

Bringing together an impressive panel of contributors, the chapters in this work examine Dow's writings on structured pluralism and schools of thought, meanings of open and closed systems, reflections on the relationship between economics and other sciences (both social and natural), the methodology of behavioural economics, as well as the political economy of the Scottish school of thought. The book challenges the foundations of the mainstream economics paradigm in a novel and holistic manner, seeking to advance thinking across Dow's favoured discipline.

The essays in this collection provide thought-provoking reading for advanced students and scholars of economic methodology, the history of economic thought, heterodox economics and political economy. The book will also be valued by the economics profession at large, as it contains important elements and ideas concerning ethics, methodology and tolerance within economics as a discipline and as a profession.

Ioana Negru is a Reader in Economics at 'Lucian Blaga' University of Sibiu. She is the co-editor of *The Ethical Formation of Economists* (2019, with Wilfred Dolfsma) and of *The Gift in the Economy and Society: Perspectives from Institutional Economics and Other Social Sciences* (2020, with Stefan Kesting and Paolo Silvestri). She has been a member of the Skidelsky Committee for improving the economics curriculum worldwide.

Penelope Hawkins is Senior Economist in the Debt and Development Finance Branch, within the United Nations Conference on Trade and Development (UNCTAD). Her research focusses on public and private country debt, development finance, illicit financial flows and financial inclusion. Previously, as the founder and Managing Director of Feasibility (Pty) Ltd, she undertook leading research projects in the financial sector in South Africa and advised policy makers and regulators in southern and eastern Africa.

Routledge Studies in the History of Economics

Classical Economics, Keynes and Money
Edited by John Eatwell, Pasquale Commendatore and Neri Salvadori

Global Commerce in the Age of Enlightenment
Theories, Practices, and Institutions in the Eighteenth Century
Jesús Bohorquez

Metaphors in the History of Economic Thought
Crises, Business Cycles and Equilibrium
Edited by Roberto Baranzini and Daniele Besomi

Liberalism and the Philosophy of Economics
Tsutomu Hashimoto

An Economic Philosophy of Production, Work and Consumption
A Transhistorical Framework
Rodney Edvinsson

The Early History of Economics in the United States
The Influence of the German Historical School of Economics on Teaching and Theory
Birsen Filip

Economic Methodology, History and Pluralism
Expanding Economic Thought to Meet Contemporary Challenges
Edited by Ioana Negru and Penelope Hawkins

Monetary Economics, Banking and Policy
Expanding Economic Thought to Meet Contemporary Challenges
Edited by Penelope Hawkins and Ioana Negru

For more information about this series, please visit: www.routledge.com/series/SE0341

Economic Methodology, History and Pluralism

Expanding Economic Thought to Meet Contemporary Challenges

Edited by
Ioana Negru and Penelope Hawkins

Routledge
Taylor & Francis Group
LONDON AND NEW YORK

First published 2023
by Routledge
4 Park Square, Milton Park, Abingdon, Oxon OX14 4RN

and by Routledge
605 Third Avenue, New York, NY 10158

Routledge is an imprint of the Taylor & Francis Group, an informa business

British Library Cataloguing-in-Publication Data
A catalogue record for this book is available from the British Library

Library of Congress Cataloging-in-Publication Data
Names: Negru, Ioana, 1974- editor. | Hawkins, Penelope Anne, 1965- author.
Title: Economic methodology, history and pluralism : expanding economic thought to meet contemporary challenges / edited by Ioana Negru and Penelope Hawkins.
Description: Abingdon, Oxon ; New York, NY : Routledge, 2023. | Series: Routledge studies in the history of economics | Includes bibliographical references and index.
Identifiers: LCCN 2022026429 (print) | LCCN 2022026430 (ebook) | ISBN 9780367695675 (hardback) | ISBN 9780367695682 (paperback) | ISBN 9781003142324 (ebook)
Subjects: LCSH: Dow, Sheila C. | Economists—Scotland—Biography. | Economics—Methodology. | Economics—Psychological aspects. | Neoclassical school of economics.
Classification: LCC HB103.D7 A3 2023 (print) | LCC HB103.D7 (ebook) | DDC 339.092 [B]—dc23/eng/20220711
LC record available at https://lccn.loc.gov/2022026429
LC ebook record available at https://lccn.loc.gov/2022026430

ISBN: 978-0-367-69567-5 (hbk)
ISBN: 978-0-367-69568-2 (pbk)
ISBN: 978-1-003-14232-4 (ebk)

DOI: 10.4324/9781003142324

Typeset in Bembo
by codeMantra

Ioana Negru would like to dedicate this volume first to her family and second to Simone and Kathy: they have helped her become a better person.

Contents

Tables

Box

About the editors

Penelope Hawkins is Senior Economist at the Debt and Development Finance Branch of the United Nations Conference on Trade and Development (UNCTAD). Her research focusses on public and private debt, development finance, illicit financial flows and financial inclusion. Previously, as the Founder and Managing Director of Feasibility (Pty) Ltd, she undertook leading research projects in the financial sector in South Africa and advised policy makers and regulators in southern and eastern Africa.

Ioana Negru is Reader in Economics at the 'Lucian Blaga' University of Sibiu, Romania. She has been a practicing Lecturer for 24 years and has been a Member of the Skidelsky Committee for improving the economics curriculum worldwide. She is the Co-editor of *Ethical Formation of Economists* (2019, with Wilfred Dolfsma) and of *Gift in Economy and Society* (2020, with Stefan Kesting and Paolo SilvestrI).

Contributors

Victoria Chick is Emeritus Professor of Economics at University College London. She has written articles and books on money, the economics of Keynes and methodology, including a book on Keynes's *General Theory*. She is a Life Member of the Post-Keynesian Economics Society and the Association of Heterodox Economists and is an Advisor to Rethinking Economics.

Jennifer Churchill is Senior Lecturer in Economics at UWE, Bristol, United Kingdom.

Paul Dalziel is Professor of Economics and Deputy Director of the Agribusiness and Economics Research Unit (AERU) at Lincoln University, New Zealand. He is a Fellow of the Regional Studies Association.

John B. Davis is the Author of *Keynes's Philosophical Development*, *The Theory of the Individual in Economics* and *Individuals and Identity in Economics*, and co-author with Marcel Boumans of *Economic Methodology: understanding Economics as a Science*, and Robert McMaster of *Health* Care *Economics*.

Robert W. Dimand, a Graduate of McGill and Yale universities, is a Professor of Economics at Brock University, St. Catharines, Ontario, Canada. His books include *The Origins of the Keynesian Revolution* (1988), *The Routledge Handbook of the History of Women's Economic Thought* (ed. with Kirsten Madden, 2018), *Irving Fisher* (2019) and *The Elgar Companion to John Maynard Keynes* (ed. with Harald Hagemann, 2019).

Stavros A. Drakopoulos (PhD, Stirling) has served academic appointments at the Universities of Glasgow and Aberdeen. He is currently Professor of Economics, National and Kapodistrian University of Athens; he has published 66 papers in journals and edited books, as well as five books.

Peter E. Earl is an Honorary Associate Professor of Economics at the University of Queensland, Australia. His latest book is *Principles of Behavioral Economics: Bringing Together Old, New and Evolutionary Approaches* (Cambridge University Press, 2022).

John Hart retired as an Associate Professor of Economics at the University of KwaZulu-Natal in 2014, before joining the department of economics, the University of South Africa from 2015 to 2019, with which he is currently affiliated for research purposes.

Geoffrey M. Hodgson is Emeritus Professor of Management, Loughborough University London, UK. The author of more than 20 books and more than 200 academic articles, he is also Editor-in-Chief of the *Journal of Institutional Economics*. His personal website is at www.geoffreymhodgson.uk.

Jesper Jespersen, Dr. Scient. Adm., is Emeritus Professor of Macroeconomic Theory, History and Methodology at Roskilde University, Denmark.

Tony Lawson is a British Philosopher and Economist. He is Professor of Economics and Philosophy in the Faculty of Economics at the University of Cambridge. He is a Co-editor of the *Cambridge Journal of Economics*, a former Director of the University of Cambridge Centre for Gender Studies and Co-founder of the Cambridge Realist Workshop and the Cambridge Social Ontology Group. Lawson is noted for his contributions to philosophical issues in social theorising, most especially to social ontology. His books include *Economics and Reality* and the *Nature of Social Reality.*

Robert McMaster is a Professor of Political Economy in the Adam Smith Business School at the University of Glasgow. Prior to joining Glasgow, Robert was a Senior Lecturer in Economics at the University of Aberdeen. He has held various visiting positions in the United States and Europe. He co-edited the *Review of Social Economy* from 2005 until 2018.

Maria Pia Paganelli is a Professor of Economics at Trinity University. She works on Adam Smith, David Hume and 18th-century monetary theories. She wrote, among others, *The Routledge Guidebook to Adam Smith's Wealth of Nations* (Routledge 2020).

Christopher Torr is a Research Fellow in the Department of Economics, College of Economic and Management Sciences, at the University of South Africa, Pretoria.

Foreword

John E. King

Emeritus Professor, La Trobe University

These two splendid volumes contain many fine expositions and critical reviews of Sheila Dow's superb writings on monetary economics and the methodology of political economy. A quarter of a century ago, when she was writing the 'Preface' to the revised second edition of *The Methodology of Macroeconomic Thought*, Dow welcomed the fact that there was 'now a much greater willingness among economists in general, and methodologists in particular, to contemplate a range of schools of thought with different methodological foundations'. But, she continued, 'this willingness has often gone too far. By reacting against the previous situation, in which methodology's role was to establish rules for best practice, many went to the other extreme of attempting to avoid judgement altogether'. She could not agree with these writers that merely describing the methodologies of different schools of thought was sufficient in itself. In the first edition of the book, she had 'approached description as a necessary first step towards more constructive debate', in the hope that this would initiate 'reasoned argument, based on a mutual understanding of the methodological foundations of different approaches to economics'.

'The point of *Macroeconomic Thought*', Sheila continued, 'was thus not that, in economics or in methodology, anything goes'. On the contrary, she hoped that methodological awareness would serve as 'a basis for constructive debate'. She herself had one specific and very important proposition to defend. Her own position was 'non-dualistic', based on the firm belief that 'there is a range of methodologies, each with its own set of appraisal criteria'. However, some of her readers had 'interpreted my approach dualistically: either there are universal appraisal criteria or there are none'. This was quite wrong, for Dow was instead arguing that 'tolerance and understanding are required among methodologists as well as among economists, but that neither precludes reasoned argument between those with different perspectives. It is through such reasoned argument that knowledge progresses' (Dow 1996, pp. ix–x).

Many of the crucial elements in Dow's approach to methodology were derived from her reading of Keynes, who in his *Treatise on Probability*

> . . . was grappling with how in practice people overcome the problem of induction; that is, the problem that past observations are never sufficient

> to establish the truth of a proposition, as future observations may show it to be false. Keynes was thus concerned with how reasonable grounds for belief may be established in such circumstances, as the basis for action.
>
> (Dow 2002, p. 165)

The general theory of probability that Keynes developed 'encompassed quantitative probability as a special case', so that 'each judgement as to probability . . . is held with greater or lesser confidence depending on the weight of evidence' (*Ibid.*, p. 165). This differed sharply from 'the demonstrative certainty of classical logic', which 'required that the system under study be finite, and that the elements of the relations under study be atomic' rather than organic (*Ibid.*, p. 166). The application of mathematics to economic problems required that this was the case in the real world. Keynes

> . . . did not argue against the use of mathematics *per se*. He favoured mathematical argument where appropriate to the subject matter. But its use could not be universally justified, and care should therefore be taken to distinguish those contexts in which it was justified from those in which it was not justified
>
> (*Ibid.*, p. 166)

Sheila concluded by agreeing with the fundamentalist Post Keynesian methodological interpretation of Keynes, which shared his 'vision of the economy as being organic, requiring an emphasis on (irreversibly evolving) institutions, behaviour and knowledge', and emphasising 'uncertainty (as non-quantifiable risk), irreversible historical time, and money as an integral factor in capitalist economies' (*ibid.*, p. 172).

She had made the same points in a seminar presentation at the University of Lancaster in 1988 that aroused my dormant interest in economic methodology, and again in January 1993 when I interviewed her for what would become a chapter in *Conversations with Economists* (King 1995, pp. 153–67). Actually, 'interview' is the wrong word. It was a very stimulating conversation, in which we talked about methodology, monetary theory and monetary policy, and the relationship between Post Keynesian economics, the mainstream and other heterodox schools of thought. I got off to a rather poor start, asking Sheila if her principal interest had been in monetary economics at the outset, with her involvement in methodology developing out of that. 'No', she replied, 'they were parallel developments. I was interested in them as separate subjects, and it was only later on that I appreciated the significance of methodology for the way we did monetary economics' (King 1995, p. 153).

In fact, her first book was on the theoretical and policy questions that arise in a monetary economy, the co-authored and very aptly titled *Money Matters* (Dow and Earl 1982). Her position on these important issues has always been very simple, and in my view entirely correct: money is *not* neutral, and a monetary economy cannot be analysed 'as if' it were a barter economy.

Following on from this, Sheila has always endorsed the Post-Keynesian analysis of endogenous money, which denies that the money supply is (as the mainstream assumes) exogenously determined. As she told me in our conversation, Keynes himself had assumed endogenous money in much of his mature work, except in the *General Theory*, where he treated the supply of money not as exogenous but rather as *given* (King 1995, p. 159). This, she continued, was an example of his intuitive use of the Babylonian method (on which, see below). But the banking system had changed a great deal since the 1930s, so that 'the money supply wasn't endogenous to the same extent as now when Keynes was writing' (*Ibid.*, p. 160).

Some of Sheila's work on monetary questions has been co-authored with her good friend Victoria Chick, whose

> work on the stages of banking development is a really important contribution to the endogeneity debate, in showing how the nature of endogeneity has changed as banking systems have developed, and how its force has in fact increased over time.
>
> (*Ibid.*, p. 160)

Another important influence on her understanding of money and finance has been Hyman Minsky, and in our conversation she described her approach to financial crises as 'very Minskyian' (*Ibid.*, p. 161). Although the supply of money is endogenous, it is not perfectly accommodating, as is inevitably demonstrated in periods of financial instability by the phenomenon of credit rationing. Sheila was able to apply her thinking on all these matters to provide a detailed and convincing analysis of the global financial crisis of 2008–2009 (see, for example, Chick and Dow, 2012).

Returning to questions of the economic method, she told me that Post-Keynesians had taken a greater interest in methodology than their mainstream colleagues, especially since the early 1980s. 'I feel quite strongly that the way one defines Post Keynesianism is methodological', she said, 'and that's why I've always thought it was important to be quite explicit about methodology' (King 1995, p. 154). The essence of Post-Keynesian methodology, Sheila suggested, was its commitment to methodological pluralism. This had been misunderstood by some critics, including Bruce Caldwell, with whom she had debated these issues in an early issue of the *Review of Political Economy* (Caldwell 1989; Dow 1990). Caldwell had not understood that

> . . . there's a difference between methodological pluralism, which is the methodologist being aware of and respecting a variety of different methodologies, and theoretical pluralism, which is that an economist would not take a position on using a particular method or not . . . it's actually a coherent methodological position to choose a particular range of methods united by a vision of some sort. . . . It's not a matter of dilettantism or eclecticism, it's quite consciously choosing a range of methods as the best

> way of going about understanding a very complex system, rather than specifying one set method which everybody has to adhere to.
>
> (*Ibid.*, pp. 155–6)

And this did not preclude the use of formal methods, so that mathematical modelling and econometric techniques could be employed legitimately in some contexts:

> since Post Keynesian methodology involves using a range of methods, it's quite legitimate to use a closed model to deal with one part of the system, as long as you're quite happy to open it up to incorporate other parts of the system which have been dealt with using other methods, possibly.
>
> (*Ibid*, p. 156).

When I asked Sheila where she stood on Paul Davidson's claim that the world is inherently non-ergodic, she demurred. 'My view is that the world is in general organic', she told me, 'which is a more general case than non-ergodic, and uncertainty is endemic, and yet there are parts of the economic system which are sufficiently stable that we can actually treat them as if they were atomic or ergodic'. She regretted the tendency to conflate uncertainty with instability:

> I think that there is a tremendous amount of stability in the system, and Keynes's epistemology shows that in a variety of contexts we develop conventions and habits to deal with uncertainty, and this is what provides stability in the system.
>
> (*Ibid.*, p. 157)

After some discussion of the Post-Keynesian criticisms of Friedmanite and New Keynesian thinking on the economics of money, we turned to the question of the relationships between Post-Keynesians and other heterodox schools. This was a period (the early 1990s) when relations between the Sraffians and the Post-Keynesians were rather strained, and Sheila was keen to affirm her belief that there was no necessary incompatibility between the two schools. I soon realised that she was more tolerant than many other Post-Keynesians of the use of long-run equilibrium prices as centres of gravity. 'It is a perfectly coherent methodological position to say that one uses different methods for different purposes, and that one doesn't have to stick to one exclusively' (*Ibid.*, p. 163). She was saddened by the acrimony that had sometimes arisen between the different non-mainstream groups:

> So to me methodology is still the key: if only Post Keynesians could fully understand Keynes's epistemology and the scope for using different methods . . . we could save ourselves a lot of bother and get on with more constructive things than arguing.
>
> (*Ibid.*, p. 164)

We concluded our conversation by discussing the relationship between Post-Keynesians, institutionalists and behavioural economists. Sheila adopted the view that Keynes's epistemology was also relevant here, since his 'analysis of conventions and habits and so on is quite fundamental to the way we theorise as well as the way individuals behave. I think that could be fed into institutionalism quite constructively' (*Ibid.*, p. 165). She suggested, too, that behavioural economics might be useful in developing what was then the relatively undeveloped area of Post-Keynesian microeconomics.

So, I learned from my conversation with Sheila that economic methodology was both very interesting and very important; that there were major differences within the profession on the way(s) in which these questions might be approached; and that Post-Keynesian economists needed to take all this very seriously. When I came to write my *History of Post Keynesian Economics*, I drew on her work on the major methodological changes that had accompanied the Keynesian revolution in macroeconomic theory, noting how Keynes's defence of 'the case for ordinary reasoning was strengthened by the restrictions that uncertainty placed on human knowledge' (Dow 1991, p. 138, cited by King 2002, p. 183). Uncertainty was also central to the theory of liquidity preference, I noted, following Sheila. 'Why hold an asset yielding a zero return, unless you doubt your ability to predict the yield of other, competing forms of assets?' (King 2002, p. 183).

I also outlined the reasons for her endorsement of an 'open-systems' view of methodological questions, which she associated with Richard Feynman's 'Babylonian approach' to science more generally, and to physics in particular (Feynman 1965; cf. King 1995, pp. 155, 159). This 'involved a break with the Cartesian-Euclidian mode of thought, which developed closed systems of necessary truths from self-evident axioms'. Sheila agreed with Feynman that this did not entail the acceptance of postmodernism, and therefore rejected

> the 'dual' of Cartesian-Euclidian thinking, which denied the very possibility that we can ever obtain knowledge . . . proposing instead a sort of Hegelian synthesis of Cartesian-Euclidian and non-Cartesian-Euclidian ways of thinking, in which knowability was treated as a matter of degree.
> (King 2002, p. 196)

As Sheila explained, Babylonian methodology favoured 'open-system thinking',

> . . . where not all the constituent variables and structural relationships are known or knowable, and thus the boundaries of the system are not known or knowable. This is the province of fuzzy mathematics, with indeterminate boundaries of sets. . . . It is also the province of non-classical logic, where logical relations are applied to uncertain knowledge; this logic is variously known as ordinary logic or human logic, as exemplified by Keynes's . . . probability theory. If reality is understood as an open

> system, then scope is allowed for free will, for creativity, and for the indeterminate evolution of behaviour and institutions.
>
> (Dow 1996, p. 14)

Her critical comparison of the macroeconomic methodologies of different schools of thought led her to conclude that only the Post-Keynesians were consistently Babylonian, whereas mainstream economists were unqualified Cartesian-Euclideans, and that this had led them to take very different positions on such important issues as 'the need for microfoundations, the role of equilibrium theory, the modelling of expectations and the treatment of money' (King 2002, p. 197). Sheila quite rightly maintained that these Babylonian ideas had much in common with the underlying principles of 'critical realism', a methodological position set out very clearly by Tony Lawson (1997), which many Post-Keynesian economists were actively supporting by the turn of the century (Dow 1999, cited by King 2002, p. 200).

References

Caldwell, B.J. 1989. 'Post-Keynesian methodology: an assessment', *Review of Political Economy*, 1(1), pp. 43–64. https://doi.org/10.1080/09538258900000004

Chick, V. and Dow, S. 2012. 'On causes and outcomes of the European crisis: ideas, institutions and reality', *Contributions to Political Economy*, 31, pp. 51–66. doi:10.1093/cpe/bzs006

Dow, S.C. 1990. Post Keynesianism as political economy: a methodological discussion', *Review of Political Economy*, 2(3), pp. 345–58. https://doi.org/10.1080/09538259000000033

Dow, S.C. 1991, April. Review of A. Carabelli, *On Keynes's Method* (London: Macmillan) and R.M. O'Donnell, *Keynes: Philosophy, Politics and Economics* (London: Macmillan), *Economics and Philosophy*, 7(1), pp. 132–9. https://doi.org/10.1017/S0266267100001024

Dow, S.C. 1996. *The Methodology of Macroeconomic Thought: A Conceptual Analysis of Schools of Thought in Economics*. Cheltenham, UK and Northampton, MA: Edward Elgar.

Dow, S.C. 1999, Fall. 'Post Keynesianism and critical realism: what are the connections?', *Journal of Post Keynesian Economics*, 22(1), pp. 15–34. https://doi.org/10.1080/01603477.1999.11490225

Dow, S.C. 2002. 'Keynes, Post Keynesians and methodology', in S.C. Dow and J. Hillard (eds), *Post Keynesian Econometrics, Macroeconomics and the Theory of the Firm*. Cheltenham, UK and Northampton, MA: Edward Elgar, pp. 162–75.

Dow, S. and Earl, P. 1982. *Money Matters: a Keynesian Approach to Monetary Economics*. London: Martin Robertson.

Feynman, R. 1965. *The Character of Physical Law*. Cambridge, MA: MIT Press.

King, J.E. 1995. *Conversations with Post Keynesians*. Basingstoke: Macmillan.

King, J.E. 2002. *A History of Post Keynesian Economics since 1936*. Cheltenham and Northampton, MA: Edward Elgar.

Lawson, T. 1997. *Economics and Reality*. London: Routledge.

Introduction

Sheila Dow as a visionary economics scholar

Professor Sheila Dow was born in Dumfries, Scotland, on 16 April 1949; she was brought up in Scotland as a 'daughter of the manse' (her father was a Church of Scotland minister). She met her husband and co-author, Alistair (Alexander), at St Andrews University where she studied Pure Mathematics and Political Economy. Professor Sheila Dow started writing academic papers in 1978 while a PhD student, following employment at the Bank of England and the Government of Manitoba. She holds a PhD in Economics from the University of Glasgow; the title of her thesis was 'Money and Real Economic Disparities between Nations and between Regions', and it was supervised by Professor Tom Wilson. Her career was mostly based at the University of Stirling, but she has managed to keep up Canadian connections, most recently as a current Adjunct Professor at the University of Victoria. Her interest in economics started with the fields of macroeconomics, monetary policy and theory, and money and banking, but it is scientific methodology and pluralism that underpinned her own research agenda.

There is no doubt that within the academic and economic community Sheila Dow has been the most consistent economist in advocating pluralism in economics, in most of its forms: methodological, epistemological and theoretical, and, above all, pluralism in economics education. Sheila Dow is a leading scholar in economic methodology, philosophy of economics, and history of economic thought, and has influenced the first Post-Keynesian economists in accepting the significance of these matters, followed by other groups of heterodox economists (Institutionalists, Feminists, Ecologists, and so on). Despite Bruce Caldwell (see 1982 *Beyond Positivism*) mentioning the concept of methodological pluralism (later refined as critical pluralism, see 1988 and 1994) for the first time in the context of economic methodology, Professor Sheila Dow deserves the credit for developing pluralism as a 'mode of thought', for any economist who wishes to interpret the economy as an open, complex, and evolutionary system.

The emergence of Blaug's (1980) *Methodology of Economics* dramatically contributed to the birth of a sub-discipline in economics, that of economic methodology. In the context of the methodological disarray in economics during the 1970s and 1980s, Sheila Dow understood the limitations of the

DOI: 10.4324/9781003142324-1

method and methodologies of mainstream economics and the importance of understanding and explaining alternative schools of thought and how they can contribute, with separate economic solutions, toward solving different economic problems and phenomena. One of the first major contributions brought by Sheila Dow is the category of a 'school of thought', which she equates with that of a 'paradigm' in the Kuhnian sense (where a paradigm is a possible direction of research shared within an academic group or a community). To this, we can add with confidence the awareness of difference and tolerance exhibited towards the existence of different schools of thought through her conceptualization of pluralism in economics. In her 1985 book (reprinted and updated in 1996), Dow introduces a discussion of schools of thought in Macroeconomics (such as Mainstream Economics, Post-Keynesian Economics, Austrian Economics, and Marxian economics) where she argues that the differences amongst them are *methodological* in nature. Through her comparative work on various approaches, Sheila Dow recognizes that there are no evident 'empirical grounds for theory appraisal'. Sheila Dow alongside other scholars such as Bruce Caldwell (1982, 1988, 1994) and Samuels (1997, 1998) stress the need for tolerance for enabling progress in economics as a discipline and grounded in epistemic complexity, recognizing the uncertainty within the social and economic realm. The complexity of the real economic world renders impossible the certainty of economic knowledge. Sheila Dow adds another dimension to this debate, by advancing pluralism as a 'Babylonian mode of thought' and an analysis based on open-closed systems that characterizes mainstream and heterodox economics. The final steppingstone in Dow's intellectual and conceptual thinking around pluralism is her 2018 piece, 'Is Pluralism Scientific?' where she asks whether supporting pluralism compromises economics. Her argument illustrates that without pluralism we cannot have reliable knowledge, 'evidence-based inquiry', and 'critical thinking'.

Sheila Dow was educated as a historian and here she shares with the economist Frederic Lee a common background and heritage. This can explain the orientation towards empirical and grounded research as an input to economic policy-making. But where Sheila differs is that her motivation for research into the philosophy of science (and economics) is its application to economics and the real world, hence her intellectual flexibility and capacity to produce conceptual economics. Professor Sheila Dow has always shown respect and tolerance for students and colleagues and is herself an epitomization of pluralism, the outcome of her background and education. She remembers her first class in economics, that of capital theory where she was taught from a historical perspective, with a focus on the Scottish School of Political Economy. More precisely, she was taught economics with reference to methodology, mathematics, and history and not through a rigid categorization of these disciplines (ISRF interview 2017). She is a 'system maker' rather than a 'system taker' and one of the meta-theories that underpinned her work on pluralism was the debate around open-closed systems of thought. Regardless of the problem at hand, pluralism and the awareness of different approaches allows space for communication and porous boundaries of schools of thought. Preoccupied throughout her professional life by the development of 'modes of thought', that is, the Cartesian-Euclidean versus the 'Babylonian' mode of thought (inspired by Feynman's Babylonian Mathematics), she argued that an economist cannot be pluralist unless she/he holds a certain conception of open economic systems in opposition to the axiomatic and closed systems that characterize mainstream economics. This opens the multiple possibilities for methodology and methods and the recognition of various types of knowledge. But pluralism must be structured, and it does have boundaries; hence, we need to recognize its development through the existence of a diversity of schools of thought in economics (Dow, 2004). When it comes to pluralism in teaching economics, she accepts the difficulties of teaching economic courses based on different schools of thought and maintains that what is essential for students is to instill 'a new way of thinking', which is critical, pragmatic, and innovative, and that no single approach can deliver the 'truth' within the economics discipline. The best way forward is to enable students to contest 'received truths and knowledges' and develop an open mindset.

Under the influence of DeMartino (2011), the conversations amongst economists that involved professional ethics mushroomed in the literature. Professor Sheila Dow (2013, 2016a, 2016b) also engaged with the problematic nature of ethics and the professional ethics of economics and economists. As is known, economists do not have professional ethics, unlike many disciplines. Economists engage with policy-makers based on their academic ideas and theories and for mainstream economists, the discipline is a technical one that is seen as not needing any ethical values or ethical judgments. Dow (2013, 2016b) discusses the possibility of a code of ethics for the profession, taking a pluralist stance and argues that the principle of pluralism overrides the three principles that lead to the relationships between economists: 'put social interest before personal interest', 'pursue and state the truth', and 'do no harm'. Dow (2013, 2016a, 2016b) argues that the mainstream's vision of economics is not one of plurality or pluralism and thus any attempt to draw a code with precise obligations and duties for economists might be dangerous, prescriptive, and monist. Dow (2013, p. 28) concludes, even if a professional code of ethics could be constructive for the discipline:

> . . . the main conclusion is that pluralism itself should be the focus of our discussion of ethics. It is pluralism that distinguishes heterodox economics and it is pluralism which makes detailed codes of ethics problematic. Other principles included in a code of ethics should therefore be understood and applied in the spirit of the principle of pluralism.

In the context of the economic and financial crisis, numerous economists had not shown any modesty in recognizing the limitations of their models and insisted that economics is a technical judgment. Dow (2016a) takes this idea and reflects on it with the aid of the Scottish School of Political Economy, and especially David Hume, for whom economics is a moral science, a part of moral philosophy; its conceptual framework comprises values, value judgments, and conventions, all intertwined with ethics. In other words, ethical values are embedded in both mainstream and heterodox economics and economists should assume moral responsibilities regarding the models they use and the content of their teaching. Professor Dow (2016a, p. 4) states:

> Rather than retreating into an unsustainable defense that economics is scientific and therefore free of ethical considerations, economists should aim to rebuild trust in the profession by accepting that more robust knowledge will arise from addressing the ethical content of the subject and opening it up to debate. The professional ethic of tolerance of different approaches is critical. But non-mainstream economics, with its openness to addressing ethical issues, needs to be recognised by the mainstream as economics.

This second volume of the 'Essays in the Honor of Sheila Dow' – *Economic Methodology, History and Pluralism: Expanding Economic Thought to meet Contemporary challenges* – is organized around the major contributions of Professor Sheila Dow for the betterment of economics, that is, pluralism and economic methodology, ethics in economics, and her interpretation and analysis of the Scottish School of Political Economy.

In 'The Relation of Neoclassical Economics to other Disciplines: The case of Physics and Psychology', Stavros Drakopoulos combines the history of economic thought and economic methodology by arguing that neoclassical economics that mirrored physics since its inception has neglected the engagement with psychology and a deep and rigorous analysis of human nature. Drakopoulos analyzes the interest in psychology exhibited by classical economists and continued by marginalist economists such as Jevons, Edgeworth, and Wicksteed until the 'Paretian turn' in economics that stopped the interaction with psychology. This turn has been made to the detriment of the analysis of agency within the discipline that causes current problems such as recognizing the contributions of behavioral economics to understanding and explaining human nature. Drakopoulos reflects on the mathematization of economics that continued with economists such as Hicks, Samuelson, von Neumann, and Friedman, who used mathematical formalism and physics tools to build economic knowledge to separate economics from the psychological foundations promoted by Scottish political economists (D. Hume, A. Smith). The author subscribes to Dow (2002, pp. 170–5) while describing the influence of positivism on economics, which implies a rejection of ethical judgment and normativity in economics. In parallel, non-mainstream economists have remained open to psychological influences in their analysis of agency via Thorstein Veblen, John Maynard Keynes, and Herbert Simon.

In 'Sheila Dow's open system methodology', John Davis discusses the durable foundations of pluralism in economics by Professor Dow through her contribution to open-system thinking in economics and the debate of open-closed modes of thought. Davis uses an argument based on identifying the milestones in the conceptual evolution of her understanding of pluralism and open-system thinking starting with Dow's 1997 piece (in Salanti and Screpamti 1997), followed by the concept of structured pluralism (Dow 2004) through the existence of schools of thought and then the contribution to the debate on an open-closed system with colleague and friend Victoria Chick (Chick and Dow 2005). The last section on Sraffa adds a new dimension, with economists contributing towards the methodological and epistemological foundations of pluralism. The current contribution of Sheila Dow, that of a conception of pluralism in need of open-system theorizing and foundations, will be hopefully continued by younger scholars, in both mainstream and heterodox economics.

In 'Categorisation, criticism, and pluralism in context. Open and closed systems and the project of mathematical modelling in modern economics', Tony Lawson illustrates his debate with Sheila Dow on not only the open-closed system thinking in economics, but also the role and significance of the use of mathematical formalism in economics. Particularly, Lawson discusses the differences between himself and Sheila Dow as a differentiation in how the categories of open-closed systems are defined and utilized. For Lawson, the differences between mainstream and heterodox economics are ontological in nature. Lawson insists that the debate with Dow is not about the orientation of pluralism in economics; on the contrary, Dow's project has been clarificatory in nature ('how the terms are used') whereas Lawson's is of an explanatory type ('how economics is done'). Both Lawson and Dow have used these categories for discussing and understanding why economists have failed to provide useful insights in the past 60 or 70 years, with Lawson also being preoccupied by the insistence on the wasteful diversion of mathematical modeling in mainstream economics. Lawson's work brings forward the naivete within the discipline and the obsession with the view that economics is scientific, with the use of mathematical modeling seen as essential for its epistemology. Lawson (in this volume, p. 66) argues: 'So, the *a priori* insistence on these methods is not only problematic in itself as a barrier to pluralism and inclusivity but also an obstacle to the discipline providing insight. I have sought to make this situation more readily apparent'.

With Geoffrey Hodgson's 'Dualism revisited', we obtain a third-party view of the debate between Dow and Lawson regarding the dualism of the 'modes of thought' in economics: the Cartesian-Euclidean mode of thought that characterizes mainstream economics, and the Babylonian mode of thought, proposed by Dow since her 1985 book on macroeconomic schools of thought as an alternative. These two modes of thought embody atomism and dualism for the mainstream Cartesian-Euclidean view versus an organicist view (inherited from Keynes), which proposes theorizing from a complex, open, and evolving reality. Dow (1990, p. 143, cited in Hodgson, this volume, pp. 69–85) explains the essence of dualism:

> Dualism is the practice of organizing thought by means of all-encompassing mutually inclusive categories, with fixed meanings. It is a particular means of imposing order on ideas, or on perceptions of reality, or indeed of drawing distinctions (as between ideas and reality, for example).

Dow has seen dualism as the outcome of 'rigid conceptualization' and has advocated the correspondence between theory and reality via the Babylonian approach or the non-dualist view of the world, instead. Hodgson challenges the views espoused by both Dow and Lawson: despite having realist theoretical assumptions, theories still fall short of mirroring reality. Theories are partial and fallibilistic tools of understanding reality and building knowledge that do not always correspond with the economic and social reality. Hodgson proposes a hybrid approach for these modes of thought and abandoning the necessary correspondence between theory and reality, arguing for a defense of a 'fuzzy taxonomic dualism'. Hodgson agues for the need of a taxonomy of categories and conceptual precision that might ensure the 'survival of non-dualist approaches'.

In 'Naturalism and the new challenge to Sheila Dow's schools-of-thought approach to economics', John Hart discusses views from the philosophy of science, how these trends have impacted the economic methodology, and what are the consequences of such methodological changes on Dow's approach of schools of thought and pluralism. Hart investigates the dominance of positivism in mainstream economics and its demise following the emergence of a post-Quinean naturalist approach that has become the new dominant paradigm in the Anglo-American philosophy. Scientific naturalism presupposes a certain kind of realism and monism, and we can equate it with scientism that 'provides the only true picture of nature'. John Hart, in this volume (pp. 86–105), contends that scientific naturalism presupposes a certain kind of realism and monism, that can be equated with scientism. Hart points to claims made by naturalism that it is the only guide to answering methodological questions and that the methods for social sciences need to be the same as for natural sciences. Post-Quinean naturalists are 'enthusiastic empiricists' that drive the 'empirical turn in economics' and argue that both heterodox and orthodox economists should accept the influence of natural sciences. Finally, Hart suggests that scientific naturalism threatens Dow's approach to pluralism and schools of thought in economics.

In 'Infinite Regress Problems and the Methodologies of Behavioural Economics', Peter Earl, and engaging with Dow (2013), dedicates time to bridge Old Behavioral Economics (OBE) with New Behavioral Economics (NBE) through an analysis of decision heuristics and the infinite regression problem; the outcome of such a project is 'Homo Heuristicus', which implies socially-acquired rules and conventions (within OBE) and dysfunctions and deviations (from the rational behavior within NBE), which could be a progressive method for understanding human nature from a holistic behavioral perspective.

In 'Should equilibrium be abandoned by heterodox economists'? Victoria Chick advocates an interesting debate around the differences between equilibrium as a concept and equilibrium as a method, arguing that the use of equilibrium is not compatible with heterodox economics. As Chick states (in this volume), the equilibrium method is the procedure of finding the solution of the system in a static model, but not focusing on the forces that bring the system to a rest. This is called the 'Equilibrium Theory' by Chick and Casertra (1997) whereas Vercelli's illustration is that of a 'pure equilibrium method'. Chick considers that the equilibrium method can be useful if 'embedded in a dynamic framework', but she argues against the definitions of equilibrium that result in mathematical solutions and market clearing. Chick is not completely against abstraction and pure static systems, with the understanding of the limitations of mathematics that cannot distinguish between equilibrium and disequilibrium. Chick recommends the dismissal of general equilibrium on the basis of Knightian uncertainty, which is a core principle in various heterodox schools of thought, including Post-Keynesian Economics, being incompatible with the assumptions of heterodox economics.

In 'Dow, Keynes and the Pragmatic Tradition: More in common?', Jennifer Churchill draws on the similarities and overlaps between Institutional Economics and Post-Keynesian Economics via pragmatism, when it comes to their vision of uncertainty in economics. Churchill explains why Dow (1985) does not include a portrayal of Institutionalism in her macroanalysis of schools of thought in economics and the consequences that ensue from this 'dismissal of pragmatism' that grounds Institutional Economics. Pragmatism as a school is pluralistic in nature, advancing propositions such as all knowledge is fallible and the means and ways to reach the 'truth' are quite diverse in science. Many institutionalist economists recognized in pragmatism a philosophy that allowed them the use of scientific induction and that theories are value-laden; also the significance of conventions, habits, rules, and institutions. Churchill argues that Dow neglects pragmatism that influences other Post-Keynesian economists, with unfortunate consequences: less engagement between these two schools and the insistence on a certain view of science such as verificationism that is considered by Dow to be a narrow view of science. In Churchill's terms, pragmatism is a philosophy that should not be ignored as it aims for 'human flourishing'.

In 'Keynes in Transition: The Economic Possibilities for our Grandchildren', Jesper Jespersen catches the intellectual evolution of John Maynard Keynes, from his mainstream mode of thought in *Treatise on Money* to this essay 'The Economic Possibilities for our Grandchildren' and the phase of writing *The General Theory*. This essay displays a long-term view of human challenges and issues and Jespersen states that because policy-makers cannot foretell the future with precision, they can, at least, implement economic policies that can minimize 'irreversible consequences of uncertain events'. Jespersen argues that, in this essay, Keynes is 'mid-stream', searching the economics for a 'good society' guided by truth, beauty, and love that serve as a rationale for actions to the detriment of a macroeconomy driven by greed, money, and self-interest. The same transition for Keynes exists between his macroeconomic system (the influence of his mentor Alfred Marshall) and his social thinking. According to Jespersen, this has been a lifelong interest for Keynes, that of macroeconomic methodology and agency, in conditions of uncertainty. Only after his 1932 'A Monetary Theory of Production' he was able to reconcile his vision of a good economy, ethical individual behavior, and solid macroeconomic principles. Despite these principles, Keynes was prudent regarding a realistic transition of human nature from greed to beauty and truth, even when economic problems were solved. The main motivation for his skepticism was related to capitalism and the capital accumulation problem, the root of 'rational behavior', and the traditional conventions to be followed in society.

Continuing the preoccupation for moral individual behavior and ethics in economics, Paul Dalziel develops Dow's ideas regarding the ethics of/in economics and her views on a professional code of ethics for economists. Dalziel contributes to the ongoing conversation on professional ethics and the codes of practice in the discipline. In economics, there is a lot of econogenic harm done through economic policies on an everyday basis and a lack of humility regarding the limitations of existing models and tools that economics offers to economies and societies (see also Colander 2016). The existent diversity of approaches and schools of thought in economics makes Dow suggest that a professional code for economists that contains certain values might run counter pluralism and discriminate other groups of economists. The important questions regarding the responsibilities of economists towards the society go beyond the principles enshrined in the AEA Code of professional conduct, with a narrow focus on economic research and freedom of speech. As a conclusion, professionals need to understand and address ethical issues in economics as economic actions and policies affect individual well-being and raise ethical questions.

The last part of this volume is dedicated to Sheila Dow as a historian, educated in the Scottish Enlightenment tradition. In 'Sheila Dow as historian of economic thought: The Scottish political economy tradition', Robert McMaster discusses the achievements of Sheila Dow in the history of economic thought and in bringing back into debates the tradition of Scottish philosophy and political economy. McMaster commences his chapter with a description of the Scottish Enlightenment tradition as a new paradigm or 'mode of thinking' and as a tradition that generated 'scientific insights'. Dow and Dow (2013, 2014) and Dow et al (1997) argued that the Enlightenment exhibited different forms in Europe: in France, the emphasis was on Cartesian rationality and deductive reasoning; in England, there was an association with empiricism; and finally, in Scotland, knowledge was derived from experience and context mattered for any scientific analysis. Dow (2009) defines the main aspect of the Scottish tradition as being the focus on practical issues in a historical context. McMaster concludes that the Scottish tradition of political economy emerges out of the Enlightenment and is focusing on philosophy and method/methodologies, history, and context, whereas agency and structure are seen to be interdependent.

Chris Torr's 'The conditions under which Adam Smith's invisible hand operate' presents the concept of the invisible hand used by Adam Smith in *The Wealth of Nations* (1776) intertwined with the Hayekian approach of economic and social order (own link), spontaneous or planned, and the institutions that are necessary to sustain a spontaneous order and markets in any society (e.g., property rights). The Smithian analysis first refers to individual selfish actions that can promote beneficial outcomes for society, and to the merchants and traders who can bring societal gain. Despite the controversy related to the greed and self-interest of traders, Smith accepts that even the merchants can contribute to the public good of one society. Torr utilizes the conclusions of Mittermaier and states: 'For the invisible hand to operate, economic action needs to take place in an environment in which the monopolistic practices of merchants and manufacturers are not permitted'. Torr analyzes Mittermeier's classification between dogmatic marketers and free marketers, where the distinction is that of an invisible hand behind the Invisible Hand, that is, whether markets need to have deliberately planned institutions to support them or whether markets can at all times be spontaneous.

In 'Mary Theresa Rankin: A Monetary Economist in the Scottish Tradition of Political Economy', Robert K. Dimand highlights the personality and work of Mary Theresa Rankin, a progressive Scottish economist who has been very active on matters of monetary policy and money in Scotland and has revolutionized the way in which academic women were accepted in the higher education system, as writers and economic commentators, and even as contributors to economic policies. A pupil of Shield Nicholson, she was involved in numerous debates in *The Scotsman*, even with Keynes, and she carried along the monetary theory and opinions in the Edinburgh tradition. Dimand captures the reasons for her marginalization as a woman academic in the Scottish higher education system and a staunch critic of the more prominent ideas of Keynes and Hawtrey. Dimand concludes in this volume: 'As a woman in Scottish economics, as an upholder of the Scottish tradition of political economy, and as a monetary economist in Scotland, Rankin's career displayed parallels with the career and contributions of Sheila Dow although taking an utterly different attitude to Keynes's revolution in monetary economics'.

In 'David Hume as a Scottish Political Economist', Maria Pia Paganelli builds on Dow (2009) to argue that David Hume is a philosopher and a political economist who operates in the 18th-century economic and social context and this makes him quite different from Friedman or Lucas when it comes to money, money supply, and monetary policy, but fit for the 18th-century economic expansionary Scottish situation. Thus, context matters. Hume [(1752) 1985] argues that the cure for an 'encrease in the money supply' implies an increase of inflation and money prices and the only way to impede these events from taking place is deflation via hoarding money. Paganelli concludes that Hume's ideas are only appropriate for 18th-century Scotland, dominated by mercantilism, and that trade is important to achieve prosperity in a country.

Although I have never formally been her student, Sheila Dow's personality and research have influenced my vision of economics and of economic methodology. In her role as a mentor for doctoral students and early career scholars, she has made an impact on generations of economists. Above all, she has made economists aware that method and science are truly essential for any economist.

References

Blaug, Mark (1980), *The Methodology of Economics or How Economists Explain*, Cambridge: Cambridge University Press.

Caldwell, Bruce J. [(1982) 1994], *Beyond Positivism. Economic Methodology in the Twentieth Century*, London: George Allen and Unwin.

Caldwell, Bruce J. (1988), 'A Programme for Economic Methodologists – Methodological Pluralism', in Neil de Marchi (ed.), *The Popperian Legacy in Economics*, Cambridge: Cambridge University Press, pp. 244–52.

Chick, Victoria and Caserta, M. (1997), 'Provisional Equilibrium and Macroeconomic Theory', in Phillip Arestis, Gabriel Palma and Malcolm C. Sawyer (eds.), *Markets, Unemployment and Economic Policy*, London and New York: Routledge, pp. 223–37.

Chick, Victoria and Dow, Sheila C. (2005), 'The Meaning of Open Systems', *Journal of Economic Methodology*, 12(3), pp. 363–81. Reprinted in Dow Sheila C., *Foundations for New Economic Thinking*, Basingstoke: Palgrave Macmillan, 2012, 178–96. https://doi.org/10.1080/13501780500223585

Colander, David (2016), 'Creating Humble Economists: A Code of Ethics for Economists', in George F. DeMartino and Deirdre McCloskey (eds.), *The Oxford Handbook of Professional Economic Ethics*, p763. https://doi.org/10.1093/oxfordhb/9780199766635.013.040

De Martino, G (2011), *The Economist's Oath: On the Need for and Content of Professional Economic Ethics*, Oxford: Oxford University Press.

Dow, Sheila C. [(1985) 1996], *Macroeconomic Thought: A Methodological Approach*, Oxford: Basil Blackwell. https://doi.org/10.1017/S0266267100000833

Dow, Sheila C. (1990), 'Beyond Dualism', *Cambridge Journal of Economics*, 14(2), June, pp. 143–57. https://doi.org/10.1093/oxfordjournals.cje.a035123

Dow, Sheila C. (1997), 'Methodological Pluralism and Pluralism of Method', in Andrea Salanti and Ernesto Screpanti (eds.), *Pluralism in Economics*, Cheltenham: Edward Elgar, pp. 89–99.

Dow, Sheila C. (2002), *Economic Methodology: An Inquiry*, Oxford: Oxford University Press.

Dow, Sheila C. (2004) 'Structured Pluralism', *Journal of Economic Methodology*, 11(3), pp. 275–90. https://doi.org/10.1080/1350178042000252965

Dow, Sheila C. (2009), 'Hume and the Scottish Enlightenment: Two Cultures', *Revista de Economia*, 35, pp. 7–20. https://doi.org/10.5380/re.v35i3.16948

Dow, Sheila C. (2013), 'Codes of Ethics for Economists: A Pluralist View'. *Economic Thought*, 2 (1), pp. 20–29. http://et.worldeconomicsassociation.org/article/view/65

Dow, Sheila C. (2016a), 'Economics and Ethics'. *ISRF Bulletin*, 11, pp. 10–14. https://issuu.com/isrf/docs/isrf_bulletin_issue_xi

Dow, Sheila C. (2016b), 'Codes of Ethics for Economists, Pluralism and the Nature of Economic Knowledge', in George F. DeMartino and Dierdre McCloskey (eds.), *The Oxford Handbook of Professional Economic Ethics*, Oxford: Oxford University Press, pp. 750–64. https://doi.org/10.1093/oxfordhb/9780199766635.013.041

Dow, Sheila C. (2018), 'Pluralist Economics: Is It Scientific?', in S. Decker, W. Elsner and S. Flechtner (eds.), *Advancing Pluralism in Teaching Economics: International Perspectives on a Textbook Science.* Routledge Advances in Heterodox Economics, 39. Teaching Economics in the 21st Century, Berlin, Germany, 26.11.2015–28.11.2015. London: Routledge, pp. 13–30. https://www.routledge.com/Advancing-Pluralism-in-Teaching-Economics-International-Perspectives-on/Decker-Elsner-Flechtner/p/book/9781138037625

Dow, Allister, Sheila C. Dow and Alan Hutton (1997), 'The Scottish Political Economy Tradition and Modern Economics', *Scottish Journal of Political Economy*, 44, pp. 368–83. https://doi.org/10.1111/1467-9485.00065

Dow, Allister; editors: Kobil Ruziev and Nicholas Perdikis (2013), 'Economic Development in the Scottish Enlightenment: Ideas as Cause and Effect', in K. Ruzlev and N. Perdikis (eds.), *Development and Economic Reform in Emerging Economies*, SCEME Studies in Economic Methodology, 2, Pickering and Chatto: London, pp. 7–22.

Dow, Allister and Dow, Sheila. C. (2014), 'Scotland', in Vincent Barnett (ed.), *Routledge Handbook of the History of Global Economic Thought*, Routledge: London, pp. 38–47.

Hume, David [(1752) 1985]. *Essays, Moral, Political, and Literary*, Indianapolis: Liberty Fund.

Mittermaier, Karl (2019), 'The Invisible Hand and Some Thoughts on the Non-Existent in What We Study'. *Journal of Contextual Economics*, 139, pp. 135–58. https://doi.org/10.3790/schm.139.1.135

Mittermaier, Karl (2020), *The Hand behind the Invisible Hand. Dogmatic and Pragmatic Views on Free Markets and the State of Economic Theory.* Bristol: Bristol University Press. https://library.oapen.org/handle/20.500.12657/40100

Samuels, Warren J. (1997), 'The Case of Methodological Pluralism', in Andrea Salanti and Erbesto Screpanti (eds), *Pluralism in Economics*, Cheltenham: Edward Elgar, pp. 67–79.

Samuels Warren J. (1998), 'Methodological Pluralism', in John B. Davis and D. Wade Hands and Uskali Maki (eds.), *The Handbook of Economic Methodology*, Cheltenham: Edward Elgar, pp. 300–3.

Smith, Adam [(1776)1987], *The Wealth of Nations*, London: Penguin.

1 The relation of neoclassical economics to other disciplines

The case of physics and psychology[1]

Stavros A. Drakopoulos

Introduction

Since the emergence of the classical school, the scientific ideal of the physical sciences has been a constant influence on the economic theory and its method. Examples of this influence can be found in the works of many leading classical economists. The classical physics model of science became more prevalent with the appearance of Marginalism. The economic thought of F. Y. Edgeworth, V. Pareto, and I. Fisher shows that this trend continued with early neoclassical economics (Mirowski, 1989). The core components of contemporary mainstream methodology are also clearly influenced by the classical physics scientific method. The dominance of mathematical formalism, the conception of economics as a positive science, the complete separation of moral questions from the purpose of economics, and the emphasis on prediction are indications of the influence of physics (Dow, 2002).

Similar to the case of physics, classical economists were very open in incorporating psychological elements into economic discourse. The relevant works of authors such as J. Bentham, Adam Smith, N. Senior, J. Cairnes, James, and John Stuart Mill are indicative examples in this regard (Drakopoulos and Katselidis, 2019). The openness toward psychology continued with prominent marginalist economists such as W. S. Jevons, F. Y. Edgeworth, and P. Wicksteed, who were eager to draw from psychological ideas found in earlier authors (Goodwin, 2016). Importantly, the incorporation of psychological ideas into the economic theory laid the ground for the emergence of the systematic subjective theory of value, which was mainly based on the specific framework of psychological hedonism.

In general, and up to the beginning of the 20th century, there was almost no methodological objection regarding the incorporation of ideas from psychology into economic theories. After this period, however, a major conceptual change in economics took place and this is also known as the *Paretian turn* (Bruni and Sugden, 2007). This conceptual change, initiated mainly by Vilfredo Pareto and completed in the first decades of the 20th century by J. Hicks, R. Allen, and P. Samuelson, attempted to expunge all psychological

DOI: 10.4324/9781003142324-2

notions from the economic theory (Lewin, 1996; Frey and Benz, 2004; Hands, 2010). The subsequent application of the rational choice theory to most areas of economics, such as the public choice theory and labor economics, completed the *Paretian turn* of mainstream economics (Bruni and Sugden, 2007; Muramatsu, 2009).[2] On the contrary, non-mainstream economists continued to incorporate ideas from psychology, such as those indicated in the works of T. Veblen, J. M. Keynes, T. Scitovsky, H. Simon, and others (Earl, 1990).

Thus, although both physics and psychology had exerted a significant and continuous influence on the development of economic thought, the *Paretian turn* effectively halted any interaction with psychology. In addition, the previous observations can be used in order to assess the significant resistance of the contemporary neoclassical economic theory to accept the findings of the new behavioral economics (Earl, 2016). Therefore, the history of the relationship between the two subjects mentioned earlier and economics can lead to some potentially useful observations concerning the nature of contemporary neoclassical economics. It will be argued that the relationship between neoclassical economics and psychology is greatly determined by a specific conceptual framework with certain methodological features.

Accordingly, this chapter starts with a brief discussion of the history of the influence of physics on economic thought and continues with an examination of the presence of psychological ideas in leading classical, marginalist, and early neoclassical economists. The Section "The emergence and the completion of the *Paretian Turn*" discusses the emergence and the completion of the *Paretian turn*, which effectively severed the ties between economics and psychology. The Section "Methodological issues" focuses on some methodological issues arising from the previous discussion; namely, it discusses the negative neoclassical stance toward the rise of behavioral economics and the role of the influence of physics and formalism in determining the current methodological position of neoclassical economics toward psychological findings. The chapter concludes with a final section.

Physics as the ideal model of scientific inquiry

Classical political economy

During the 18th century and especially the 19th century, the great success of the physical sciences in explaining and predicting a wide range of physical phenomena gave these fields of study enormous status among the academic community and also among the general public. Thus, it is not surprising that the physical science ideal was present even in the writings of many classical economists. In Adam Smith's *History of Astronomy*, the Newtonian system is viewed as the basic conceptual framework for the understanding of the natural world. In Smith's view, the Newtonian method should be followed in every science, regardless of whether moral or natural (Smith, 1983, pp. 126–34; see also Raphael, 1989; Schliesser, 2005). Another major classical economist, J. B. Say, distinguishes between descriptive sciences (e.g., botany and natural history) and experimental sciences (e.g., chemistry and natural philosophy). Descriptive sciences arrange and accurately designate the properties of certain objects. Experimental sciences unfold the reciprocal action of substances on each other or, in other words, the connection between cause and effect. (Say, 1803, pp. 17–18). Political economy belongs to the experimental sciences, because it demonstrates "the manner in which events take place in relation to wealth" (Say, 1803, p. 18).

Jeremy Bentham, the founder of utilitarianism and a major source of inspiration for subsequent economic thought, strongly argued that the principle of utility could serve in social science the role that gravity plays in Newton's model of the physical universe (Gordon, 1991, pp. 251–3). In the same spirit, A. Comte provided the methodological justification for a unified social science. In Comte's positivism, social sciences should study social phenomena in the same way that Astronomy, Mechanics, and Biology study astronomical, mechanical, and biological phenomena (Bourdieux et al., 2018). Comte's philosophy of positivism had a substantial influence on the views of many post-Ricardian authors concerning the nature and scope of economics. For instance, John Cairnes places Political economy in the same class of sciences with Mechanics, Astronomy, Optics, Chemistry, and Electricity, and, in general, all those physical sciences that have reached the "deductive stage" (Cairnes, 1875, p. 35).

J. S. Mill provided one of the first detailed analysis of the method of Political economy. Although Mill advocated a separate methodological approach for social sciences, the influence of Bentham and Comte is present in his methodological discussion. Mill believes that the physical sciences such as Astronomy are exact sciences whereas the social sciences such as Economics are inexact sciences. According to Mill, economics is a science but it is not as exact as the physical sciences (Hausman, 1992, pp. 123–33). It is clear that the physical science ideal is present in his extensive analysis of the state and the method of economics as a science (see also Hollander, 2012).

In general, the physical sciences were viewed by many classical economists as the method that the new science of Political economy should follow. It should be pointed out, though, that they did not adopt the mathematical formalism of physics or astronomy in the study of economic phenomena.

Marginalism and early neoclassical economics

The emergence of Marginalism in the 1870s can arguably be described as a scientific revolution in the history of economic thought (e.g., Mirowski, 1984; Screpanti and Zamagni, 2005; for an opposite view, see Blaug, 1972; Meek, 1972). The conceptual shift toward the subjective theory of value, the emphasis on demand-based analysis rather than on supply-based analysis, the systematic use of mathematics, and the central role of the model of Homo

Economicus are the main elements that characterize the marginal school of economic thought. In spite of all these fundamental changes, the scientific ideal of the physical sciences was a key common methodological element with the classical school. In fact, the endeavor to imitate the methods of physics became much more apparent with the emergence of the marginalist school. Further, the appeal to the physical sciences provided the methodological justification for the increased use of mathematics observed in most marginalist works.

One of the founders of the school, W. S. Jevons states that the theory of economy presents a close analogy to the science of statical mechanics (Jevons, 1871, p. viii). The same thesis is also presented in his subsequent "Principles of Economics," where economic laws are conceived as universally valid and similar to those of the physical sciences (Jevons, 1905, p. 198). During the same period, L. Walras' General Equilibrium Theory is the best example of the application of the mathematical method in economics. Walras predicts that mathematical economics will rank with the mathematical sciences of astronomy and mechanics (Walras 1874 [1965], p. 47, 48; see also Turk, 2012). Although he did not advocate the use of mathematics in economics, C. Menger believed that economics can be as exact a science as the physical sciences (Menger, 1879 [1963], p. 218).

With the establishment of the marginalist school, the scientific ideal of physics was quite explicit in the writings of leading marginalists. In particular, F. Y. Edgeworth's main work titled *Mathematical Psychics: An Essay of the Application of Mathematics to Moral Sciences* (1881) represents the height of the physics emulation in the history of economic thought. It also sets the basis for the methodological justification of the use of mathematics in social sciences and especially in economics.

According to Edgeworth, the first argument supporting the employment of the methods of mathematical physics to social science is based on the assumption that every social phenomenon is the concomitant of a physical phenomenon. For instance, pleasure is the concomitant of energy (Edgeworth, 1881, p. 9). Given the close connection between energy and pleasure, it is easier to accept the maximization principle as a fundamental concept in economics. The second important reason for the application of mathematics to economics is the quantitative nature of the discipline. Edgeworth argues that the lack of precise numerical data and exact functional relations in economics is not an obstacle to the application of mathematical methods. He mentions the example of hydrodynamics where the available data are similar to the economic data (Edgeworth, 1881, pp. 4–5).

The next figure who contributed to the formation of current ideas about the method in economics was Irving Fisher, who is considered one of the most important promoters of Marginalism in the United States. For many historians, Fisher accomplished the most thoroughgoing mathematization of the marginalist theory (Breslau, 2003; Zouboulakis, 2003). The systematic introduction of mathematics into the economic theory was a conscious methodological position of imitating the methodology of classical physics. As an illustration of the correspondence between physical and economic phenomena, Fisher built an elaborate hydraulic machine with pumps and levers, thus enabling him to visually demonstrate how the equilibrium prices in the market adjusted in response to changes in demand or supply (Fisher, 1892; Tobin, 1985).

Phillip Wicksteed's approach to economics combines the physics methodological ideal with the use of mathematics, albeit not to the same extent as observed in Jevons' and Walras' works. For instance, he compares the analysis of total and marginal utility with the projection of a body upward at a given velocity (Wicksteed, 1888, pp. 2–15). In his other major work, Wicksteed (1910) continues stating the numerous analogies from physics, clearly implying that physics is the ideal model of scientific explanation.

Physics and neoclassical economics

After the strengthening of the physics ideal in the works of Edgeworth and Fisher, the increased formalization of economics continued in the seminal works of J. Hicks, R. Allen, P. Samuelson, and J. von Neumann. Their main endeavor was to construct a mathematical economic theory so as to make it as "scientific" as the hard sciences. Hicks and Allen provided a formal model of the demand theory that was essentially based on marginalist concepts but was cast in a mathematical framework (Hicks and Allen, 1934). After a few years, Samuelson's *Foundations* (1947) was also observed to be full of mathematical methods and tools used in physics. Samuelson adopted a conscious methodological stance to model economic analysis to physics. Influenced by the physicist Edwin Bidwell Wilson, Samuelson believed that economics could use the same mathematics as physics without resting on the same empirical foundations and certainties (Samuelson, 1998, p. 1376; Backhouse, 2015).

During the same period, John von Neumann's work further promoted the development of mathematics in neoclassical economics. Similar to those mentioned earlier, he also advocated and strongly endorsed the use of the methods of physics for solving economic problems (von Neumann and Morgenstern 1944, pp. 3–7). In his writings, physics is always the benchmark for the state and the status of economics and he is confident that the achievement of the scientific status of physics is attainable and only a matter of time (von Neumann and Morgenstern, 1944, p. 4).

In one of the most influential essays on economic methodology, Milton Friedman (1953) reinforces the intellectual tradition of physics as a scientific ideal. In this essay, it is suggestive that Friedman also uses the analogy of the physical sciences in his effort to construct the methodological basis of positive economics. In his view: "Positive economics is, or can be, an 'objective' science, in precisely the same sense as any of the physical sciences" (Friedman, 1953, p. 4).

The essay is full of analogies between economics and physics (Friedman, 1953, pp. 4, 5, 10, 32, 36). Although Friedman's essay has been the subject of extensive criticism (see for instance, Mäki, 2009), it still shapes current perception concerning the method of neoclassical economics.

In general and by the middle of the previous century, neoclassical economics had reached a high degree of formalism by employing mathematical methods and tools from physics (see also Ingrao and Israel, 1990; Weintraub, 2002). Nowadays, neoclassical economists do not explicitly refer to physics as their methodological ideal. The physics-based conceptual tools of neoclassical analysis are taken as given and as fundamental components of the neoclassical theory. Still, one can find influential works where the reference to physics is done intentionally in order to emphasize the scientific nature of economics. E. Lazear writes:

> Economics is not only a social science, it is a genuine science. Like the physical sciences, economics uses a methodology that produces refutable implications and tests these implications using solid statistical techniques.
> (Lazear, 2000, p. 99)

After stressing that the concept of equilibrium is central in economics as is also the case in the physical sciences, Lazear argues that economics is superior to other social sciences because "among social scientists, only economists insist on a physical-sciences-style equilibrium as part of the analysis" (Lazear, 2000, p. 101).

Psychological ideas in economics discourse

Contrary to the relationship between economics and the physical sciences, the interaction between economics and psychology depicts many episodes in the history of both fields. Since the 18th century, economists have usually founded their own economic theories on some principles and ideas about human nature; accordingly, economics has not been independent from psychological foundations. In fact, both before and during the marginalist revolution, major authors attempted to infuse psychological ideas and concepts into economics and explicitly argued for the necessity of psychological reasoning. As will be explained later in a more detailed manner, these authors adopted many significant behavioral and psychological assumptions with respect to economic activities, paving the way for future developments such as the emergence of behavioral and psychological economics.

Classical political economy

Adam Smith's thought can be placed within the framework of the Scottish Enlightenment tradition. In this conceptual framework, the view of science (which developed mainly under the influence of Hume) was that the study of human nature should be central. Thus, Political economy was understood in terms of philosophy and history, and also it was not seen as separable from the other emerging social sciences (Dow et al., 1987, pp. 371–3). Hence, it is not surprising that Adam Smith's *Theory of Moral Sentiments* (1759) dealt extensively with the psychological aspects of choice.[3] It is also well-known that in the *Wealth of Nations*, he regarded self-interest and self-love as the fundamental motives behind human motivation and action. However, in his *Theory of Moral Sentiments*, by recognizing the plurality of human incentives, he emphasized the pleasure of mutual sympathy (Smith, 1759/1976, p.4). Smith's interest in the influence of emotion and sentiment on socio-psychological motivation "foreshadows a number of areas in modern behavioral economics, particularly models of social influence" (Baddeley, 2013). Further, what is now referred to as "psychological" was Adam Smith's explanation for the motivation for science and the spread of ideas (Dow, 2010).

The strong tradition of analyzing the psychological elements of human nature continued in the work of Jeremy Bentham. With the spread of Bentham's utilitarianism, the hedonistic psychology entered economic thinking in a systematic manner. Bentham places pain and pleasure at the center of human action, which is the basic principle of psychological hedonism (Bentham, 1823, p. 1). He states: "They [pleasure and pain] govern us in all we do, in all we say, in all we think: every effort we can make to throw off our subjection, will serve but to demonstrate and confirm it" (Bentham, 1823, p. 1). The influence of Bentham's thought on subsequent economists was great. The first economists to be influenced by his ideas were the representatives of the late period of the classical school. Nassau Senior, James and John Stuart Mill, and J. E. Cairnes were the most renowned classical economists who followed the basic principles of Bentham's utilitarianism.

N. Senior was very conscious of the psychological bases of economic behavior. He stressed that in order to explain economic behavior, we should first examine the various principles and motives that shape human economic action. According to Senior, "the desire for wealth" is considered the fundamental human motive, since it is "the cornerstone of the doctrine of wages and profits, and, generally speaking, of exchange. In short, it is in Political economy what gravitation is in Physics" (Senior, 1836, p. 28; see also Karayiannis, 2001).

James Mill, influenced by Hume, Hartley, and Thomas Brown and also by associationist psychology, argued that the mind is made of only sensations and ideas that are held together by contiguity (Mill, 1829/1869). Similarly, "for Mill, the mind consisted of mental elements held together by the laws of association; therefore, mental experience was as predictable as physical events" (Hergenhahn, 2009, p. 154). Further, both James and John Stuart Mill were influenced by Bentham's utilitarian principles. It is indicative that J. S. Mill describes Political economy as a moral or psychological science and defines it as "the science relating to the moral or psychological laws of the production and distribution of wealth" (Mill, 1844, pp. 129, 133).

Apart from the major authors discussed so far, the psychological bases of economic behavior were a subject that captured the interest of many other significant figures of the classical school. R. Whately, M. Longfield, T. Banfield, R. Jennings, and J. Cairnes were some of those figures (see Drakopoulos and Katselidis, 2019).

Psychological ideas in marginalists and early neoclassicals

As discussed earlier, a subjective theory of value followed by the gradual formation of a model of individual economic behavior (Homo Economicus) was a key characteristic of the marginal school. The shift toward a utility-based theory of value did not emerge in vacuum, but it was clearly connected to the psychological ideas found in many classical and pre-marginalist economists. In Marginalism, the concept of marginal utility was central to the theory of value along with the selfish maximization of pleasure or satisfaction. Most leading marginalists explicitly acknowledged the philosophy and psychology of Benthamite hedonism as their main influence. In this respect, the incorporation of ideas from other intellectual areas was considered methodologically valid and desirable.

One of the protagonists of the first marginalist generation, W. S. Jevons openly admits the influence of utilitarianism in the introduction of his main work when he states: "I have no hesitation in accepting the Utilitarian theory of morals" (Jevons, 1871, p. 27). Further, Jevons' well-known definition of economics in terms of the calculus of pleasure and pain indicated his emphasis on psychological sensations. In a similar vein, Walras conceived all landowners, workers, and capitalists as pleasure maximizers (Walras, 1874 [1965], pp. 42–3). Finally, Menger believed that the objective of economic research was to discover those laws governing market phenomena that can be traced back to their ultimate genetic determinants in a human's physiological, psychological, and social nature (Jaffe, 1976, p. 522).

In his attempt to construct a theory of "psychophysics," F. Y. Edgeworth was keen to incorporate psychological ideas into economic analysis. Similar to Jevons' work, psychological hedonism was the underlying framework in Edgeworth's most important work (Edgeworth, 1881). Edgeworth viewed psychological phenomena as a legitimate field for the application of mathematical tools, like, for instance, his willingness to link "hedonic calculus" in psychophysics to "utilitarian calculus" in economics. The aim of a unified science of physical and mental phenomena can be found in his notion of "psychophysics" (for a detailed discussion, see Drakopoulos and Katselidis, 2015).

Wicksteed's main methodological concern was to construct an economic theory free from non-scientific elements. His misgivings about the obvious role of hedonism in marginalist formulations led him to deliberately downplay the hedonistic underpinnings of Marginalism (see Drakopoulos, 2011). However, he supported the methodological view of incorporating findings from psychology into economics: "the psychological law that dominates economics dominates life" (Wicksteed, 1894, p. 780). Moreover, he believed that all psychological considerations that bear upon the production and distribution of wealth must be included in economics if it is to become a positive science (Wicksteed, 1894). It must be emphasized here that for Wicksteed, psychology was a legitimate scientific discipline, and he therefore saw no obstacle to economics using its concepts and findings.[4]

The emergence and the completion of the *Paretian Turn*

Edgeworth's work can be viewed as the peak of the interaction between economics and ideas from psychology after the marginalist revolution. However, in the closing decades of the 19th century when the second marginalist generation of economists emerged, the influence of positivism as the dominant scientific philosophy became much more prevalent (Dow, 2002). One of the basic tenets of positivism was that the enormous success of the physical sciences meant that their scientific methodology should also be followed by the other disciplines (methodological individualism). The application of the methodology of physical sciences to economics called for the rejection of all normative, ethical, or metaphysical elements (for a discussion, see Mirowski, 1989; Dow, 2002, pp. 170–5). Due to the influence of positivism, psychological elements were also considered as value-laden and, therefore, unacceptable for the corpus of economic theory (see also Coats, 1976; Lewin, 1996). The important consequence of this methodological stance was that many leading economists of the period became indifferent—or even hostile to the findings of other social sciences, and especially to psychological theories.

Vilfredo Pareto was extremely influenced by the prevailing positivist scientific philosophy. His methodological ideal for the discipline of economics was that it should be a mathematical science, a part of the natural sciences such as physiology and chemistry (Pareto, 1896, p. 21). In the spirit of positivism, this required that economics should be freed from any philosophical or psychological notions that hamper the application of the positivist methodology.[5] In the same conceptual tradition, Pareto believed that the construction of the fictional model of the economic human was adequate for satisfying the needs of the economic theory, thus clearly implying that psychological findings are not necessary (Pareto, 1907 [1971]; see also Bruni and Guala, 2001; Bruni, 2010).

Similar to Pareto, Fisher was against the inclusion of psychological concepts in economics. Fisher considered psychology as a "soft" subject not worthy of consideration by the "hard" science of economics. In this sense, the following statement is indicative: "But the economist need not envelope his own science in the hazes of ethics, psychology, biology and metaphysics" (Fisher, 1892 [1965], p. 23).

The negative attitude toward psychology was further promoted by L. Robbins' influential methodological work in which he supported the view that psychology ought to be kept out of economic analysis (Robbins, 1932, pp. 83–4). Regarding the theoretical developments, Pareto's and Fisher's anti-psychology stance resulted in the reformulation of the consumer theory as an allegedly psychology-free theoretical construction. The reformulation was completed in the works of Hicks, Allen, and Samuelson, and mainstream economics expelled (at least nominally) any psychological and sociological notions found in earlier marginalist writings (see also Bruni and Sugden, 2007; Hands, 2010). For instance, the main intention of Samuelson's revealed preference theory was to dismiss the alleged psychological concepts of the utility theory (Samuelson, 1938, 1947). The tendency to ignore concepts and findings from other social sciences, and especially from psychology, continued in the post-war era. This was also strengthened by the rise of logical positivism—the modern version of 19th-century positivism—which became very popular among the vast majority of mainstream economists (Redman, 1993). The influential paper by Stigler and Becker (1977), where they claimed that the preference theory can free economics of any need to turn to other disciplines such as psychology, is a representative example of this trend.

The new concept of psychology-free economic rationality would also form the basis of the general equilibrium model that emerged during the same period (Arrow and Debreu, 1954; Arrow and Hahn, 1971). The extension of economic rationality in the form of the axiomatic expected utility theory in the works of John von Neumann, Oscar Morgenstern, and Leonard Savage was also observed in the spirit of independence of any psychic state (von Neumann and Morgenstern, 1944; Savage, 1954). In the middle of the 20th century, Milton Friedman's (1953) essay on economic methodology can also be viewed as an effort to shield the rationality assumption from criticism mainly originating from psychological research (see also Düppe, 2011). In Friedman's opinion, psychological assumptions were largely irrelevant to the validation of theories (see also Sent, 2004; Muramatsu, 2009).[6] These developments completed the *Paretian turn* of mainstream economics. Although for a long period in the history of economic thought economists were open to incorporating ideas and concepts from both physics and psychology, the establishment of mainstream economics severed the ties to psychology.

Methodological issues

Psychology and behavioral economics

The *Paretian turn* was largely responsible for the break in the long tradition of the interaction between economics and psychology within the framework of mainstream economics. However, non-mainstream economists continued to draw upon psychological concepts, also as a part of the criticism of the standard model of economic rationality. Thus and long before the emergence of behavioral economics as a distinct discipline, Herbert Simon criticized the mainstream model of "Homo Economicus" from a psychological viewpoint. By focusing on the behavioral and cognitive processes of humans making decisions, Simon argued that the conception of the economic human as a lighting calculator of costs and benefits is unrealistic. The important repercussion of Simon's approach was the challenge of the established model of economic rationality (Simon, 1955, 1979).[7]

Apart from undermining the standard approach to economic rationality, Simon's work provided the stimulus for a further examination of the psychological basis of economic behavior. Thus, in the late 1970s, the theoretical and empirical validity of neoclassical economic rationality, as expressed in the expected utility theory, started to be questioned further by psychologists Daniel Kahneman, Amos Tversky, and Paul Slovic (Kahneman and Tversky, 1979; Kahneman, Slovic and Tversky, 1982). These works are considered to have provided the stimulus for the emergence of new behavioral economics (as opposed to old behavioral economics stemming mainly from the work of Simon). New behavioral economics can be viewed as a systematic attempt toward the revival of psychological ideas in economic analysis (Sent, 2004). Kahneman and Tversky's approach had a strong orientation toward psychology, and many key ideas found in new behavioral economics were stimulated by psychological literature. Notions such as reference dependence, loss aversion, adaptation, endowment effects, and framing effects are commonplace in modern behavioral economics (see Rabin, 2002). For instance, Ernst Fehr and Klaus Schmidt acknowledge that their work concerning fairness is connected to the relevant psychological theories: "Our theory is motivated by the psychological evidence on social comparison and loss aversion" (Fehr and Schmidt, 1999, p. 856). Further, some of the more recent models originating from the new behavioral economics draw on explicitly from findings from neuroscience and cognitive psychology (e.g., Camerer, Loewenstein and Prelec, 2005; for a detailed discussion, see also Muramatsu, 2009).

It has to be noted, though, that the new behavioral economics does not challenge the standard model of economic rationality. Instead, "the realism of the psychology underlying economic analysis will improve the field of economics on its own terms—generating theoretical insights, making better predictions of field phenomena, and suggesting better policy" (Camerer and Loewenstein, 2004, p. 3). In the same vein, R. Thaler rejects the notion that behavioral economics was a revolution in economics and instead views it as one part of the growing importance of the empirical work in economics (Thaler, 2016). In general, though, the new behavioral economics represents the main manifestation of the current revival of the interaction between economics and psychology.

The legacy of the **Paretian Turn**

Regardless of the increasing presence of new behavioral economics, the negative attitude toward importing psychology into economics is still prevalent among neoclassical economists. A number of arguments have been suggested against the "psychology inclined" behavioral economics. One view asserts that behavioral findings that undermine the standard model are of little interest, since they correspond to deviations from the rational behavior; therefore, they only describe the mistakes that the individual can make during this process of "rationalisation" (Binmore, 1999). Another approach rejects the criticism of the rational choice theory by lab experiments conducted by behavioral economists. According to this view, "there are many reasons to suspect that these laboratory findings might fail to generalize to real markets" (Levitt and List, 2008, p. 910). Further, it is suggested that agents behave far more selfishly in natural settings than in lab experiments (Levitt and List, 2008, p. 909).

The leading neoclassical economist David Levine focuses on the methodological foundations of behavioral economics. Levine strongly rejects the criticism of the standard theory by behavioral economists. He argues that the connection of behavioral economics to psychology and neuroscience is doomed to fail because the goals of psychologists and economists are different, and this has implications for importing ideas from psychology into economics (Levine, 2012, p. 125). In the same vein, the distinguished philosopher of economics Don Ross argues that economics and psychology are fundamentally distinct disciplines with different methodologies; therefore, he "rejects the call voiced by some behavioral economists for a revolution in the main methodology of economic modelling and data analysis" (Ross, 2014, pp. 19–20). In general, and in spite of the rise of new behavioral economics, there are strong objections by neoclassical economists to incorporate psychological research into the economic theory.

Physics, formalism, and psychology

A number of specialists in economic methodology have maintained that the physics-based mathematical method has become the dominant ideology in the economics academy (e.g., Elster, 2009; Lawson, 2012). In particular and according to Tony Lawson, this ideology consists of " . . . the extraordinarily widespread and long-lasting belief that mathematical modelling is somehow neutral at the level of content or form, but an essential method for science, underpinning any proper or serious economics" (Lawson, 2012, p. 17). In the case of the relationship between economics and psychology, the stance of neoclassical economics toward psychology is still shaped by the *Paretian turn*. One can argue that the *Paretian turn* was the result of the consolidation of mainstream economic methodology: the physics ideal and the ensuing mathematical formalism provided the methodological framework for the establishment of the rational choice model.[8] Due to the legacy of the *Paretian turn*, this model is conceived as having no psychological basis, thus isolating neoclassical economics from any meaningful interaction with psychology.

Within this framework, one can understand better the failure of Simon's psychological approach to influence the standard economic theory (see also Dow, 2010). Similarly, the empirical challenge of experimental results supplied mainly by new behavioral economists has failed to make substantial inroads into the neoclassical theory (see also Rabin, 2002). As Sheila Dow notes:

> The empirical results of experimental economics at times seem to falsify key elements of pure theory in mainstream economics. Yet, amending theory in order to take this into account, particularly with input from psychology, has run up against the strictures of mathematical formalism.
> (Dow, 2013, p. 27)

The firmly established conviction of the psychology-free economic theory can also be seen as an explanation of the relative failure of the new behavioral economics to infuse psychological concepts into the neoclassical economic theory. This is despite the fact that the new behavioral economics does not challenge the basic tenets of the standard model of economic rationality (Sent, 2004). The established methodological framework can also explain the denial to consider the rich contributions of psychological insights of many leading non-mainstream economists. The examples of T. Veblen, J. M. Keynes, T. Scitovsky, and H. Simon are indicative (for discussions see Fiori, 2011; Pugno, 2014; Goodwin, 2016). The common methodological point of these heterodox approaches is the rejection of the standard model of economic rationality. The abandonment of this narrow framework inevitably allows the presence of psychological notions. As Sheila Dow aptly observes:

> But if we depart from the formal requirements of models of optimization subject to constraints, then a richer notion of psychology, and an integration of cognitive and emotional factors, are possible.
> (Dow, 2010, p. 260)

In sum, the epistemology of neoclassical economics is the key for understanding its negative attitude toward psychological ideas.

Concluding comments

The history of the relationship between physics and economics indicates that since the inception of the classical school, physics has exercised a very significant influence on the formation of the economic theory and the method involved. The height of this influence was reached with the emergence of Marginalism and of early neoclassical economics. The gradual dominance of mathematical formalism, the conception of economics as an exact, positive science, the positive-normative distinction, and the emphasis on prediction cannot be comprehended without taking into consideration the influence of classical physics. As was observed, the contemporary neoclassical economic theory and method still acknowledge their intellectual affinity to the physical sciences.

On the contrary, the history of the relationship between economics and psychology has followed a different route. The willingness of classical economists to incorporate psychological ideas was evident. The same observation can be made about the founders of Marginalism who often appealed to psychology in order to support the subjective theory of value and also to build a theory of individual economic behavior. Early neoclassicals such as Edgeworth and Wicksteed were also supporters of drawing from psychology. However, the course changed with the emergence of the *Paretian turn*. Initiated mainly by Pareto and completed in the first decades of the 20th century, psychological ideas were deemed to be unnecessary for the economic theory. The expulsion of psychology was completed by the influential works of Samuelson and Friedman.

Thus, the relatively long tradition of drawing from psychology came to a halt with the establishment of mainstream economics by the mid-20th century. Psychology was increasingly viewed as being subjective and ambiguous and, therefore, unscientific. In contrast, physics continued to be held in high esteem and was viewed as a methodological model for economics. The rise of behavioral economics (and especially of the new behavioral economics), with its strong psychological bent, did not end the isolation of economics from psychology. The contemporary neoclassical economic theory is still very reluctant to allow psychological findings in the core of the theory. The main reason for this is the dominant methodological framework that is still largely shaped by the lasting influence of the classical physics ideal. Our discussion indicates that the relationship between mainstream economics and physics ultimately constrained its interaction with psychology.

Notes

1 The author wishes to thank Professor Yannis Venieris and an anonymous referee for their useful comments and suggestions.
2 The terms "mainstream" and "neoclassical economics" were identical at the time of the *Paretian turn*. However, recent literature differentiates between the two, with neoclassical economics being a part of, but not exhausting, mainstream economics, which now includes, in addition to neoclassical economics, experimental economics, new behavioral economics, game theory, etc. (Colander et al., 2004; Davis, 2006; Morgan 2016).
3 Among the features of the Scottish political economy tradition as summarized in Dow (1987) was the recognition of the sociological and psychological aspects of theory appraisal.
4 It is interesting to note that John Neville Keynes' writing during the same period also has a positive attitude toward psychology. In his view, political economy "presupposes psychology just as it presupposes the physical sciences" (Keynes, 1890, p. 46).
5 For an extensive discussion, see Drakopoulos (1997).
6 Friedman's negative stance toward psychology was also the basic reason for his rejection of Duesenberry's "psychology based" consumption function (Mason, 2000).
7 Hayakawa and Venieris (1977) provide an early example of how satisficing behavior can be applied to the consumer theory.
8 It should be noted here that since the mid-20th century, the meaning of the term "formalism" has been associated with the triumph of form over substance rather than the mere use of mathematics (Blaug, 1999). In addition, its modern use has to do with the increasing influence of the axiomatic approach in economics as was also the case in the field of mathematics (Ingrao and Israel, 1990; Weintraub and Mirowski, 1994). For an analysis of the changing meaning of the TEM formalism, see Milonakis (2017).

References

Arrow, K. and Debreu, G. (1954) "Existence of an equilibrium for a competitive economy", *Econometrica*, 22: 265–290. https://doi.org/10.2307/1907353

Arrow, K. and Hahn, F. (1971) *General Competitive Analysis*, San Francisco: Holden-Day. ISBN 13: 9780816202751

Backhouse, R. (2015) "Revisiting Samuelson's Foundations of economic analysis", *Journal of Economic Literature*, 53(2): 326–350. https://doi.org H0.1257/jel.53.2.326

Baddeley, M. (2013) *Behavioural Economics and Finance*, London and New York: Routledge. https://doi.org/10.4324/9780203104514

Bentham, J. (1823) *An Introduction to the Principles of Morals and Legislation*, Oxford: Clarendon Press.

Binmore, K. (1999) "Why experiment in economics?", *The Economic Journal*, 109: F16–F24. http://www.jstor.org/stable/2565582

Blaug, M. (1972) "Was there a marginal revolution?", *History of Political Economy*, 4(2): 269–280. https://doi.org/10.1215/00182702-4-2-269

Blaug, M. (1999) "The formalist revolution or what happened to orthodox economics after World War II", in R. Backhouse and J. Creedy (eds.), *From Classical Economics to the Theory of the Firm*, Cheltenham: Edward Elgar. ISBN: 978 1 84064 146 2

Breslau, D. (2003) "Economics invents the economy: mathematics, statistics, and models in the work of Irving Fisher and Wesley Mitchell", *Theory and Society*, 32: 379–411. https://doi.org/10.1023/A:1024480118264

Bruni, L. (2010) "Pareto's legacy in modern economics. The case of psychology", *Revue européenne des sciences sociales* (European Journal of Social Sciences), XLVIII-146: 93–111. https://doi.org/10.4000/ress.759

Bruni, L. and Guala, F. (2001) "Vilfredo Pareto and the epistemological foundations of choice theory", *History of Political Economy*, 33: 21–49. https://doi.org/10.1215/00182702-33-1-21

Bruni, L. and Sugden, R. (2007) "The road not taken: how psychology was removed from economics, and how it might be brought back", *The Economic Journal*, 117: 146–173. https://doi.org/10.1111/j.1468-0297.2007.02005.x

Bourdieux, M., Pickering, M. and Schmaus, W., (eds.), (2018) *Love, Order & Progress, The Science, Philosophy and Politics of Auguste Comte*, Pittsburgh: University of Pittsburgh Press. ISBN-10: 0822945223

Cairnes, J. (1875) *The Character and Logical Method of Political Economy*, London: Macmillan.

Camerer, C. and Loewenstein, G. (2004) "Behavioral economics: past, present and future", in C. Camerer, G. Loewenstein, and M. Rabin (eds.), *Advances in Behavioral Economics*, Princeton, NJ: Princeton University Press, pp. 3–51. ISBN: 9780691116822

Camerer, C., Loewenstein, G. and Prelec, D. (2005) "Neuroeconomics: how neuroscience can inform economics", *Journal of Economic Literature*, XLIII(March), 9–64. https://doi.org/10.1257/0022051053737843

Coats, A. W. (1976) "Economics and psychology: the death and resurrection of a research program", in S. Latsis (ed.), *Method and Appraisal in Economics*, Cambridge: Cambridge University Press, pp. 43–64. https://doi.org/10.1017/CBO9780511572203

Colander, D., Holt, R. and Rosser, J. (2004) "The changing face of mainstream economics", *Review of Political Economy*, 16(4): 485–499. https://doi.org/10.1080/0953825042000256702

Davis, J. (2006) "The turn in economics: neoclassical dominance to mainstream pluralism?", *Journal of Institutional Economics*, 2(1): 1–20. https://doi.org/10.1017/S1744137405000263

Dow, S. (1987) "The Scottish political economy tradition", *Scottish Journal of Political Economy*, November, pp. 335–348. https://doi.org/10.1111/1467-9485.00065.

Dow, S. (2002) *Economic Methodology: An Inquiry*, Oxford: Oxford University Press. ISBN: 9780198776123

Dow, S. (2010) "The psychology of financial markets: Keynes, Minsky and emotional finance", in D. B. Papadimitriou and L. Randall Wray (eds.), *The Elgar Companion to Hyman Minsky*, Cheltenham: Edward Elgar Publishing, pp. 246–262. ISBN: 978 1 84720 849 1

Dow, S. (2013) "Formalism, rationality, and evidence: the case of behavioural economics", *Erasmus Journal for Philosophy and Economics*, 6(3): 26–43. https://doi.org/10.23941/ejpe.v6i3.149

Drakopoulos, S. A. (1997) "Origins and development of the trend towards value-free economics", *Journal of the History of Economic Thought*, 19: 286–300. https://doi.org/10.1017/s1053837200000821

Drakopoulos, S. A. (2011) "Wicksteed, Robbins and the emergence of mainstream economic methodology", *Review of Political Economy*, 23: 461–470. https://doi.org/10.1080/09538259.2011.583837

Drakopoulos, S. A. and Katselidis, I. (2015) "From edgeworth to econophysics: a methodological perspective", *Journal of Economic Methodology*, 22(1): 77–95. https://doi.org/10.1080/1350178x.2014.1003579

Drakopoulos, S. A. and Katselidis, I. (2019) "Classical and pre-marginalist ideas on the relationship between economics and psychology", *History of Economic Ideas*, 28(1): 43–63. https://doi.org/10.19272/201906101003

Düppe, T. (2011) "How economic methodology became a separate science", *Journal of Economic Methodology*, 18(2): 163–176. https://doi.org/10.1080/1350178X.2011.580196

Earl, P. E. (1990) "Economics and psychology: a survey", *Economic Journal*, 100: 718–755. https://doi.org/10.2307/2233656

Earl, P. E. (2016) "The evolution of behavioural economics", in R. Frantz et al. (eds.), *Handbook of Behavioural Economics*, London, Routledge, 5-17. ISBN 1138821144

Edgeworth, F. Y. (1881) *Mathematical Psychics: An Essay of the Application of Mathematics to Moral Sciences*, London: Kegan Paul.

Elster, J. (2009) "Excessive ambitions", *Capitalism and Society*, 4(2): 1–30. https://doi.org/10.2202/1932-0213.1055

Fehr, E. and Schmidt, K. (1999) "A theory of fairness, competition and cooperation", *Quarterly Journal of Economics*, 114: 817–868. http://www.jstor.org/stable/2586885

Fiori, S. (2011). "Forms of bounded rationality: the reception and redefinition of Herbert A. Simon's perspective", *Review of Political Economy*, 23 (4): 587–612 https://doi.org/10.1080/09538259.2011.611624

Fisher, I. (1892) [1965] *Mathematical Investigations in the Theory of Value and Prices*, New Haven, CT: Yale University Press.

Frey, B. and Benz, M. (2004) "From imperialism to inspiration: a survey of economics and psychology", in J. Davis, A. Marciano, and J. Runde (Eds.), *The Elgar Companion to Economics and Philosophy*, Cheltenham and Northampton, MA, 61–83. ISBN 184064964X

Friedman, M. (1953) "The methodology of positive economics", in *Essays in Positive Economics,* Chicago, IL: University of Chicago Press, pp. 3-43. https://doi.org/10.1086/290980

Goodwin, C. (2016) "Economics and psychology: why the great divide?", *History of Political Economy*, 48 (suppl. 1): 71–169. https://doi.org/10.1215/00182702-3619250

Gordon, H. S. (1991) *The History and Philosophy of Social Science*, London: Routledge. https://doi.org/10.4324/9780203423226

Hands, D. W. (2010) "Economics, psychology, and the history of consumer choice theory", *Cambridge Journal of Economics* 34 (4): 633-648. https://www.jstor.org/stable/24232076

Hausman, D. (1992) *The Inexact and Separate Science of Economics*, Cambridge: Cambridge University Press. ISBN-10: 0521425239

Hayakawa, H. and Venieris, Y. (1977) "Consumer interdependence via reference groups", *Journal of Political Economy*, 85: 599–615. https://doi.org/10.1086/260585

Hergenhahn, B. R. (2009), *An Introduction to the History of Psychology*, Sixth edition, Belmont, CA: Wadsworth Cengage Learning. ISBN10: 0495506214

Hicks, J. and Allen, R. G. D. (1934) "A reconsideration of the theory of value", *Economica*, 1: 52–76. https://doi.org/10.2307/2548749

Hollander, S. (2012) *John Stuart Mill on Economic Theory and Method: Collected Essays III*, London: Taylor and Francis. ISBN 0415142369

Ingrao, B. and Israel, G. (1990) *The Invisible Hand: Economic Equilibrium in the History of Science*, Cambridge and London: The MIT Press. ISBN-13: 978-0262090285

Jaffe, W. (1976) "Menger, Jevons and Walras de-homogenized", *Economic Inquiry*, 4: 511–524. https://doi.org/10.1111/j.1465-7295.1976.tb00439.x

Jevons, W. S. (1871) *The Theory of Political Economy*, London: Macmillan.

Jevons, W. S. (1905) *The Principles of Economics*, London: Macmillan.

Kahneman, D. and Tversky, A. (1979) "Prospect theory: an analysis of decision under risk", *Econometrica*, 47: 263–291. https://doi.org/10.2307/1914185

Kahneman, D., Slovic, P. and Tversky, A. (1982) *Judgment under Uncertainty: heuristics and biases*, New York: Cambridge University Press. https://doi.org/10.1017/CBO9780511809477

Karayiannis, A. D. (2001), "Behavioural assumptions in Nassau Senior's economics", *Contributions to Political Economy*, 20: 17-29. https://doi.org/10.1093/cpe/20.1.17

Keynes, J. N. (1890) [1917] *The Scope and Method of Political Economy*, New York: Macmillan.

Lawson, T. (2012), "Mathematical modelling and ideology in the economics academy: competing explanations of the failings of the modern discipline?", *Economic Thought*, 1 (1): 3–22. http://et.worldeconomicsassociation.org/issues/2012-1-1/

Lazear, E. (2000) "Economic imperialism", *Quarterly Journal of Economics*, 115(1): 99–146. https://doi.org/10.1162/003355300554683

Lewin, S. (1996) "Economics and psychology: lessons for our own day from the early Twentieth Century", *Journal of Economic Literature*, XXXIV: 1293–1323. https://www.jstor.org/stable/2729503

Levine, D. (2012) *Is Behavioral Economics Doomed? The Ordinary versus the Extraordinary*, Cambridge: Open Book Publishers. ISBN: 978-1-906924-92-8

Levitt, S. D. and List, J. A. (2008) "Homo economicus evolves", *Science*, 319 (5865): 909-910. https://doi.org/10.1126/science.1153640

Mäki, U. (2009) (ed.), *The Methodology of Positive Economics: Reflections on the Milton Friedman Legacy*, Cambridge: Cambridge University Press. https://doi.org/10.1017/CBO9780511581427

Mason, R. (2000) "The social significance of consumption: James Duesenberry's contribution to consumer theory", *Journal of Economic Issues*, 34: 553–572. https://www.jstor.org/stable/4227586

Menger, C. (1879) [1963] *Problems of Economics and Sociology*, transl. by F. Nack, Urbana: University of Illinois Press.

Meek, R., (1972) "Marxism and Marginalism", *History of Political Economy*, 4: 2. https://doi.org/10.1215/00182702-4-2-499

Mill, J. (1829/1869) *Analysis of the Phenomena of the Human Mind*, London: Longmans Green Reader and Dyer.

Mill, J. S. (1844) *Essays on Some Unsettled Questions of Political Economy*, London: John W. Parker

Milonakis, D. (2017) "Formalising economics: social change, values, mechanics and mathematics in economic discourse", *Cambridge Journal of Economics*, 41: 5, 1367–1390. https://doi.org/10.1093/cje/bex045

Mirowski, P. (1984) "Physics and the 'marginalist revolution'", *Cambridge Journal of Economics*, 8: 361–379. https://doi.org/10.1093/oxfordjournals.cje.a035556

Mirowski, P. (1989) *More Heat than Light: Economics as Social Physics, Physics as Nature's Economics* Cambridge: Cambridge University Press. https://doi.org/10.1017/CBO9780511559990

Morgan, J. (2016) (ed.) *What Is Neoclassical Economics?*, London and New York: Routledge. ISBN 9781138962095

Muramatsu, R. (2009) "The death and resurrection of 'economics with psychology': remarks from a methodological standpoint", *Revista de Economia Politica,* 29 (1): 62–81. https://doi.org/10.1590/S0101-31572009000100004

Pareto, V. (1896) *Corso di Economia Politica* [Cours d'Économie Politique]. Torino: Unione Tipographico-Editrice Torinese.

Pareto, V. (1907) [1971] *Manual of Political Economy*, transl. by A. Schwier, London: MacMillan. ISBN: 0678008817 9780678008812

Pugno, M. (2014) "Scitovsky's The Joyless Economy and the economics of happiness", *European Journal of the History of Economic Thought*, 21: 278–303. https://doi.org/10.1080/09672567.2012.683028

Rabin, M. (2002) "A perspective on psychology and economics", *European Economic Review*, 46: 657–685. https://doi.org/10.1016/S0014-2921(01)00207-0

Raphael, D. (1989) *Adam Smith*, Oxford University Press, Oxford. ISBN 9780192875587

Redman, D. (1993) *Economics and the Philosophy of Science*, Oxford: Oxford University Press. ISBN 9780195082746

Robbins, L. (1932) *An Essay on the Nature and Significance of Economic Science*, London: Macmillan.

Ross, D. (2014) *Philosophy of Economics*, New York: Palgrave Macmillan. ISBN 978-1-137-31875-6

Samuelson, P. (1938) "A note on the pure theory of consumer's behaviour", *Economica*, 5: 61–71. https://doi.org/10.2307/2548836

Samuelson, P. (1947) *Foundations of Economic Analysis*, Cambridge, MA: Harvard University Press. ISBN 9780674313033

Samuelson, P. (1998) "How 'Foundations' came to be", *Journal of Economic Literature*, 36(3): 1375–1386. https://www.jstor.org/stable/2564803

Savage, L. (1954) *The Foundations of Statistics*, New York: John Wiley and Sons. https://doi.org/10.1002/nav.3800010316

Say, J.B. (1803) *Treatise on Political Economy*, English edition, New York: A. M. Kelley (1964).

Schliesser, E. (2005) "Some principles of Adam Smith's Newtonian methods in the Wealth of Nations", *Research in the History of Economic Thought and Methodology*, 23 (Part 1): 33–74. https://doi.org/10.1016/S0743-4154(05)23002-X

Screpanti, E. and Zamagni, S. (2005) *An Outline of the History of Economic Thought*, Oxford: Clarendon Press. https://doi.org/10.1093/0199279144.001.0001

Senior, N. W. (1836) *An Outline of the Science of Political Economy*, London: Clowes and Sons.

Sent, E.-M. (2004) "Behavioral economics: how psychology made its (limited) way back into economics", *History of Political Economy*, 36: 735–760. https://doi.org/10.1215/00182702-36-4-735

Simon, H. (1955) "A behavioral model of rational choice", *Quarterly Journal of Economics*, 69 (1): 99–118. https://doi.org/10.2307/1884852

Simon, H. (1979) "Rational decision making in business organizations", *American Economic Review*, 69 (4), 493–513. https://www.jstor.org/stable/1808698

Smith, A. (1759/1976) *The Theory of Moral Sentiments*, edited by Raphael, D. D. and Macfie, A. L., Oxford: Oxford University Press. ISBN: 0865970122 9780865970120

Smith, A. (1983) *Lectures on Rhetoric and Belles Lettres*, edited by J. C. Bryce, The Glasgow Edition of the Works of Adam Smith.

Stigler, G. and Becker, G. (1977) "De gustibus non est disputandum", The *American Economic Review*, 67: 76–90. https://www.jstor.org/stable/1807222

Thaler, R. (2016) "Behavioral economics: past, present and future", *American Economic Review*, 106 (7): 1577–1600. https://doi.org/10.1257/aer.106.7.1577

Tobin, J. (1985) "Neoclassical theory in America: J. B. Clark and Fisher", *American Economic Review*, 75 (6): 28–38. https://www.jstor.org/stable/1914327

Turk, M. (2012) "The mathematical turn in economics: Walras, the French mathematicians, and the road not taken", *Journal of the History of Economic Thought*, 34 (2): 149–167. https://doi.org/10.1017/S1053837212000156

von Neumann, J. and Morgenstern, O. (1944) *Theory of Games and Economic Behaviour*, Princeton: Princeton University Press.

Walras, L. (1874)[1965] *Elements of Pure Economics*, transl. by W. Jaffe, London: Allen and Unwin. https://doi.org/10.4324/9781315888958

Wicksteed, P. (1888) *The Alphabet of Economic Science*, London: Macmillan.

Wicksteed, P. (1894) "Political economy and psychology", in: *The Common Sense of Political Economy and Selected Papers and Reviews on Economic Theory*, L. Robbins (Ed.) London: Routledge, 1933.

Wicksteed, P. (1910) *The Common Sense of Political Economy and Selected Papers and Reviews on Economic Theory*, Vols. 1 & 2, L. Robbins (Ed.) London: Routledge.

Zouboulakis, M. (2003) "L' équation des échanges de Fisher et la loi de Boyle. Les limites de l'analogie physique en économie", *Économies et Societés*, 33(12): 2191–2206.

2 Sheila Dow's open systems methodology

John B. Davis

Introduction

Among her many accomplishments as a scholar and an economist, Sheila Dow has pioneered open systems thinking as a form of methodological argument and as an important foundation for pluralism in economics. She contrasts open systems with closed systems, argues that the history of economics can be explained in terms of how its contributors have reasoned in terms of the former or the latter, and uses this framework to evaluate the development of economics as a specific type of social science explanation. This achievement needs to be appreciated, not only as giving added depth to our thinking about economics and the economic world, but also as demonstrating an especially thoughtful understanding of modern society. Under the pressure to specialize in our different domains of life, it becomes less and less common that we acquire the larger understanding of the world that helps us organize and understand the increasing diversity of things that people are able to be and do. Dow's work stands out as a particularly important counterweight to this and offers us a valuable and positive view of a world that is open to diversity and human flourishing.

This chapter discusses Dow's methodological contribution to open systems thinking and pluralism in economics, and how her views developed over the course of her career. The first section reviews the origins of her thinking in connection with her distinction between Cartesian/Euclidean and Babylonian thinking in the history of economics. The second section moves to a further development of her views regarding open and closed systems in her 2002 book *Economic Methodology* and in her "structured pluralism" conception that emphasizes the role of schools of thought in the history of economics. The third section discusses the influential 2005 paper co-authored with Victoria Chick, "The Meaning of Open Systems," that differentiates their view of open systems from that of Tony Lawson and the critical realists. The fourth section then focuses on an issue that emerges as central to Dow's and Chick's view and critique of critical realism: the relationship between models and theorizing and how the latter determines boundaries upon the former. While doing so, it discusses how Piero Sraffa used the open-closed

DOI: 10.4324/9781003142324-3

distinction earlier in the 1930s to provide a similar understanding of such boundaries and the relationship between models and theorizing. The fifth section briefly summarizes and comments on Dow's contribution to open-closed systems thinking and pluralism in economics.

The foundations of Dow's distinction between open and closed systems

As a macroeconomist, monetary theorist, and historian of economics, Dow originally set out her distinction between open and closed thinking in economics as a distinction between the Cartesian/Euclidean mode of thought and the Babylonian model of thought in her book on methodological thinking in the history of macroeconomics – a book later re-published in a revised expanded edition with added discussions of her subsequent thinking about economic methodology (Dow, 1985, 1996). In 1985, when the book first appeared, economic methodology was only beginning to be seriously investigated by historians of economics, and Dow's book did much to change this. By the early 1990s, however, economic methodology had become an important field within the history of economics (later to become an independent one altogether). At the same time, under the influence of different heterodox economics approaches, there were also the beginnings of debates about the nature of pluralism and its role in economics. Especially important as a turning point in this latter regard was a conference on pluralism and economic methodology in Bergamo, Italy, in 1994, later published as *Pluralism in Economics: New Perspectives in History and Methodology* (Salanti and Screpanti, 1997). Dow made an important contribution to the conference in advancing an argument for methodological pluralism, one specifically grounded in an open systems epistemology and ontology (Dow, 1997).[1] In part, her argument reflected a broad change in thinking among economic methodologists at the time, away from a prescriptive, theory appraisal approach to economic methodology, as associated with the thinking of Karl Popper, Imre Lakatos, and Thomas Kuhn, toward a more descriptive approach to methodology that focused on the range of different forms of methodological reasoning in economics. However, by this point, Dow had also come to believe that the contrast she had made in her 1985 book between Cartesian/Euclidean and Babylonian modes of thought had been misunderstood, and thus she was determined to re-issue the book in revised form to remedy this.

The 1985 book contrasted the Cartesian/Euclidean mode of thought, framed dualistically in terms of dichotomous categories, particularly as associated with neoclassical economics, with a nondualist Babylonian mode of thought, particularly as associated with Keynesian and classical economics as the means of distinguishing between closed and open types of methodological reasoning. On the one hand, this could be misinterpreted to mean that a Babylonian mode of thought was simply an alternative to the Cartesian/Euclidean mode of thought lacking its own independent form of thinking. On the other hand, the Babylonian mode was at risk of being seen as synonymous with the idea that "anything goes" – a common criticism at the time of arguments associated with calls for pluralism in economics. In Dow's 1996 revised and expanded edition of her 1985 book, then, she added an entirely new chapter, "Modes of Thought in Economics," to the original book to clear up such misconceptions. Babylonian thought was not inspired by a rejection of Cartesian/Euclidean thought, but it rather constituted in itself a holistic type of thought that emphasizes uncertainty and a pragmatic "knowing how" type knowledge.[2] Indeed, Babylonian thought had its own long history not only in the philosophy of science but also in the philosophy of economics. Dow, in fact, took the term from J. M. Keynes, who had used it in his biography of Newton (Keynes, 1933). Keynes, then, was intent on placing Newton in a long history of thinking in the philosophy of science that dated from the ancients but wanted to bring the term into more modern usage.[3]

As Dow later pointed out (2012), the term "Babylonian," as Keynes understood it, was largely forgotten until Mark Stohs recalled Keynes's use of it in connection with a discussion of the latter's concept of uncertainty. As Stohs put it, on this conception "there is no single logical chain from axioms to theorems; but there are several parallel, intertwined, and mutually reinforcing sets of chains, such that no particular axiom is logically basic" (Stohs, 1983, 87). Essentially in a world of uncertainty, we cannot reason from some single set of axioms to all possible consequences, because in an uncertain world there are no required starting points to our thinking. Rather, we must always reason in terms of multiple possibilities and indeed in terms of possibilities that may conflict with one another. Uncertainty, Dow wished to emphasize, was central to a Babylonian mode of thought, and moreover had a key expression in Keynes's thinking itself. As a Post-Keynesian, Dow thus saw the Keynes connection as central to advancing a type of methodological thinking alternative to the Cartesian/Euclidean mode of thought, one that reinforced the deep differences between mainstream and heterodox economics, and one to which we will return to below.

Further, the Keynes connection undercut another criticism of open systems thinking and pluralism associated with the "anything goes" idea. That notion is a pure expression of relativism, and its expression suggested a basis for favoring the Cartesian/Euclidean mode of thought. One always has to assume some things, so the argument would go, in order to explain anything. However, far from avoiding all assumptions whatsoever, Keynes made many important claims (such as concerned the nature of income determination, households' propensity to consume, liquidity preference, etc.), but he had also organized these ideas around his uncertainty idea. Thus, it was not a matter of making no theoretical commitments at all – "anything goes." It was a matter of an open systems type of reasoning that one employed in regard to how one organized one's theoretical commitments.

The Babylonian mode of thought accordingly required a more sophisticated kind of thinking than is involved in simply following out the deductions that a set of assumptions allowed as if explanations of the world itself worked in the neat manner of logic. One always needed to examine complex arrays of potentially conflicting possibilities that the world constantly threw up, and the only way this could be done is by following out these competing paths that the economy might follow, evaluating their likelihood relative to one another in terms of the circumstances at hand. The Babylonian mode of thinking, therefore, is not the dual of the Cartesian/Euclidean mode of thought as an "anything goes" idea, but it is rather based on an entirely different epistemology and ontology. In the simplest language, as Dow saw, it sees the world and knowledge as open, not closed, and builds one's reasoning around this.

For Dow, of course, Keynes's concept of uncertainty is fundamental to economics and distinctive of Post-Keynesian economics. Accordingly, placing this in the language of economic analysis, she would hardly say that Keynes and Post-Keynesianism treat all variables as endogenous. Rather, what variables are endogenous and what variables are exogenous depends on the purposes of the analysis being undertaken. This is all the more the case in economic environments that are evolving and rapidly changing. Thus, these clarifications of her original views not only answered critics of open systems and pluralism but also prepared her to further deepen her thinking about open systems. Dow went on to do this in her well-known book *Economic Methodology* and with her 2003 International Network of Economic Method (INEM) Distinguished Lecture, in which she advanced a "Structured Pluralism" view of the role of schools of thought in the history of economics.

Economic Methodology and "structured pluralism"

In 2002, Dow published *Economic Methodology: An Inquiry*, which became a leading textbook in economic methodology.[4] One thing distinctive about the book as a text is that unlike most economics textbooks it does not present economics as having followed a single path of development with only one correct understanding of its history. The history of economics is instead shown to exhibit many different sorts of explanations and arguments, all of which cannot be reduced to a single narrative. Methodologically speaking, then, we can neither dismiss some approaches out of hand for having made some sort of fundamental mistake, nor disregard some ideas because they seem to have marked out pathways of thinking alternative to dominant or more influential views. Different sorts of explanations are seen as having been motivated by different interpretations of historical problems and thereby serve different explanatory functions. Dow, consequently, rejects the naive historiographical view that history is transparent and determinate because it is past, and rather recognizes that our understanding of history, and also the history of economics itself, continually evolves as we investigate it in the present.

This sensibility, moreover, is clearly grounded in her open systems thinking. History never follows the proverbial "royal road" because there are always competing concerns and possibilities regarding how things may play out. Accordingly, different types of explanations may well be self-contained or closed to one another, but all, nonetheless, occupy the same complex world, and so taken together make up a history that is open. Dow is clear about what this means for understanding economic methodology at the outset of the book:

> The fact is that methodology is not the finger-wagging exercise which many mistake it for. While over twenty years ago there was more emphasis on interpreting rules for good science, to apply them in economics, now there is much more engagement with economics itself. Much of modern methodology in fact simply aims to build up a methodological account of what economists do.
>
> (Dow, 2002, vii)

And indeed, economists do many different sorts of things, reflecting the range and diversity of insights and assumptions that we find historically in economic reasoning.[5]

How, then, should a text on economic methodology be organized? A "royal road" model would proceed chronologically, setting out a succession of historical accomplishments that added up show how one ought to reason at any point in time about the nature of explanation in economics, and that over time have produced an ever-improving knowledge of the economy.[6] Along the way, mistaken views are always set aside, so that the history of economics and our understanding of what good explanations in economics involve seamlessly advances. This "progress" view of science, of course, is a popular one. However, professional historians, including historians of economics, generally recognize that history exhibits a more irregular development, that what was thought important sometimes turns out not to have been important and what was thought unimportant sometimes turns out to have been important, such that different paths of development often compete with one another over extended periods of time and there is no single history. In short, thinking about what we learn from the past is a complicated matter that requires an open mind and a willingness to question established ideas. Indeed, the idea that history records "progress" over time can be contested as well.

Dow, indeed, captures this thinking in the way her *Economic Methodology* – appropriately subtitled *An Inquiry* – is organized. It begins with a chapter discussion of the state of economics, including how it may be perceived by the public: "Where is Economics going?" Given that there are no definitive answers to this question, this chapter is followed by two chapters that also appropriately signal the open-endedness of economics: "Some Theoretical Issues" and "Some Empirical Issues" (note they are also only "some" issues). The book then goes on with two chapters that inquire about the nature of economics: "The Scope and Purpose of Economics" and "Progress in Economics." These are followed by chapters that emphasize the epistemological and ontological types of methodological concerns that economics addresses: "Understanding Economics" and "Understanding the Economy." The closing chapter returns to and reinforces the issues theme: "Issues for Methodology and Economics."

Thus, *Economic Methodology* is not only an *Inquiry* investigating the nature of explanation in the history of economics, but also, in rejecting conventional pedagogical approaches, organizes students' learning itself as an *Inquiry*. Perhaps Dow would comment, "how else can students investigate the history of economics?"

In contrast, Dow's "Structured Pluralism" paper, presented as the Distinguished Lecture at the 2003 INEM conference at the University of Leeds, speaks to knowledgeable historians and methodologists of economics. Here, she begins by picking up the thread from the Bergamo pluralism conference, asserting that "people interested in economic methodology seem to be, in a broad sense, ready to endorse one kind or another of 'pluralism'" (2004, 275).[7] At the same time, she finds it "curious" that this seems to have been accompanied by a "growing reluctance to refer to schools of thought in economics" since in her view this would seem to have been "one of the most obvious modes of pluralism within economics since the 1960s" (*Ibid.*).[8] Schools of thought, she suggests, seem to have become a secondary category, where the primary foundation for pluralism (for example, for critical realists, she adds) has simply become the open-closed distinction. Dow finds this paradoxical. That different schools of thought exist and co-exist would seem to be an important aspect of pluralism. Thus, she took the occasion of her Lecture to ask, "whether there is a continuing role for categorisation according to schools of thought in economics within methodological pluralism" (*Ibid.*, 276).

Her argument regarding schools of thought is historical – they are a relatively recent phenomenon resulting from increasing differentiation, or fragmentation, of ideas within both orthodox and heterodox economics since the 1960s. Describing this in terms of the paradigm thinking of Thomas Kuhn (1970), she associates this development with the notion that different approaches or schools are incommensurable with one another in the sense that communication between them is difficult, if possible at all. In effect, different paradigms, or schools of thought, employ different languages that are not easily translated into one another. This, however, could have unfortunate implications for methodological pluralism, since if schools are relatively isolated from one another and thus reluctant to communicate, rather than exhibit a positive state of affairs, then methodological pluralism might be understood as authorizing an anarchic "anything goes" in multiple arenas. For Dow, this calls for serious reflection upon what pluralism is and what it entails.

To begin, then, she believes that it is helpful to distinguish, following Salanti (1997), between pluralism as an ethical principle and pluralism as an epistemological principle.[9] This is not only helpful but also creates a tension. The ethical grounds for pluralism – whether a diversity of approaches should be recommended – tend to enjoy general support as a sort of live-and-let-live principle of tolerance, whereas the epistemological grounds – that there are different types of explanations in economics – are in often dispute since one manifestation of there being different schools of thought is that their proponents are often inclined to believe that they alone have the correct epistemological approach. This stance would not only be at odds with a pluralist vision of economics but could also place ethical pluralism at risk. Thus, we have a dilemma between what pluralism can reasonably be taken to involve and that schools of thought have become increasingly characteristic of a more fragmented, post-1960s economics. What, then, is Dow's response?

In the first place, she adopts a more moderate Kuhnian sort of view in holding that communication between schools is possible despite the difficulty involved. That is, she modifies Kuhn's incommensurability principle. Second, she rejects the idea that within schools of thought "anything goes." Indeed, different approaches in economics still share concepts and forms of reasoning that constrain economists' arguments, so it is obviously not the case that "anything goes." Third, she agrees with Warren Samuels (1998) that even if we cannot produce epistemological "metacriteria" to adjudicate between different schools' epistemologies, the existence of different schools of thought points to the boundaries between them where reasoned debates about differences are possible. That is, the boundaries between different schools of thought identify where communication is possible – a communication that combines agreement regarding where differences between schools of thought lie and disagreement regarding their justifications. Dow, then, had previously characterized her view as a "modified pluralism" (Dow, 1997) or as a "moderate pluralism" (Dow, 2002). Here, she replaces these terms with the term "structured pluralism" to capture the idea of an economics that is open to different approaches with communication between different schools at those points that they identify as determining their differences from one another.

This, consequently, creates an agenda for investigating the status and nature of pluralism in economics associated with how schools manage the boundaries between themselves and other schools. As with the boundaries between countries, there are different strategies and behaviors that one can adopt toward one's neighbors. Evaluating these different strategies and behaviors then becomes central to how we assess the status and nature of pluralism in economics. Thus, should schools of thought (like countries) adopt a relatively intolerant posture toward one another reflected in an unwillingness to communicate regarding the boundaries between them, then we ought to characterize those schools as relatively closed, and should this be true of most schools of thought, then economics altogether ought to be characterized as relatively closed. Alternatively, should schools of thought (like countries) adopt a relatively tolerant posture toward one another reflected in a willingness to communicate regarding the boundaries between them, then we ought to characterize those schools as relatively open, and economics altogether ought to be characterized as relatively open. In this way, the open-closed distinction takes on a new duty. It is not the sole means of understanding pluralism in economics, with schools of thought reduced to a secondary category status. Rather, the open-closed distinction and schools of thought are understood in terms of each other, and therefore as together providing the basis on which economics can be, or fail to be, methodologically pluralist.

Dow, thus, goes on to lay out two parallel lists of six points, each pertaining to the characteristics of schools of thought that influence whether they are and economics is closed or open.[10] I reproduce these two sets of characteristics as a single list of opposed characteristics in Table 2.1.

Methodological pluralism, then, involves embracing the latter, open systems side of these six points. In effect, proponents of different schools of thought recognize from their interaction with other schools that their own school's commitments and assumptions are always subject to re-evaluation. They need not abandon those commitments and assumptions but need to see them as programs of investigation that are always subject to change and modification. This posture describes an economics structured around schools in a pluralist way – a structured pluralism.

As a final comment, it is important to see the influence that Keynes has had on Dow's thinking. As she puts it: "Keynes's epistemology developed on the basis of an ontology of open social systems with all the characteristics outlined above" (Dow, 2004, 284).[11] Thus, though Keynes did not use the language of pluralism or open systems in the ways these ideas have developed in the post-war period, for Dow he was an important forerunner of these ideas, especially in the key role that his concept of uncertainty plays in his economics. In effect, how Keynes combined epistemology and ontology made his economic analysis open to history and communication with other schools of thought. He did not, in Dow's view, prioritize ontology and economics' ontological commitments over its epistemological reasoning. This,

Table 2.1 Characteristics of open and closed schools of thought

1. All variables can be identified in a system; it may not be possible to identify all variables in a system.
2. The boundaries of a system can be specified (and whether variables are exogenous or endogenous can be determined); the boundaries are semi-permeable (and the classification of variables may not be fixed).
3. Only exogenous variables affect the system; there may be omitted variables whose effects on the system are uncertain.
4. Relations between variables are known or random; there is imperfect knowledge regarding relations between variables.
5. The components[a] of the system are independent and atomistic; interrelationships between agents exist and may change.
6. The structure of relationships between a system's components is known; this structure may be imperfectly known and/or may change (structure and agency are interdependent).

a Components refers to types of agents, such as individuals and firms.

however, is exactly what she charges that critical realists have done in making ontological commitments the primary determinant of whether an economic approach or school of thought is open or closed. "It is this binary classification (open/closed) of ontology which is most significant for critical realism" (Dow, 2004, 285). Accordingly, I turn to Dow's (and Chick's) evaluation of critical realism and open systems in the following section.

Chick and Dow on open systems and critical realism

"The Meaning of Open Systems" (Chick and Dow, 2005) was presented at the 2004 INEM meetings at the University of Amsterdam, and it built upon and further developed both authors' previous thinking about open systems. They began by noting that because the terminology of openness and closure had been used in a variety of ways, it is important to begin by stating how it applied to systems. A system, then, is "an organized or connected group of objects" or a "set of correlated principles, ideas, or statements belong to some department of knowledge or belief" (364). On both levels, whether referring to objects and/or ideas, systems (a) vary in degree of completeness (the extent to which things within them are connected), (b) mutability, and (c) in their relations with what lies outside of them as systems (366). An open system, consequently, is one in which certain specific conditions hold, on the one hand, as "applies to characteristics of perceived reality" and, on the other hand, as applies to "theories about reality" (*Ibid.*). I have reproduced these two sets of conditions in a slightly simplified form in Table 2.2.

Table 2.2 Conditions for open systems

Real world systems
i. The system is not atomistic (outcomes cannot be inferred from actions or agent interactions may change).
ii. Structure and agency are interdependent.
iii. Boundaries around and within the system may change (structures may evolve, connections between structures may change, and structure-agent relations may change).
iv. Particular social structures are embedded in larger structures, and boundaries are generally permeable.
Implications for theoretical systems
i. There may be important omitted variables and/or their effects on the system may be uncertain.
ii. The exogenous-endogenous classification of variables may be neither fixed nor exhaustive.
iii. Connections and/or boundaries between structures may be imperfectly known and may change.
iv. There is imperfect knowledge of the relations between variables and relationships between them may not be stable.

Closed systems, then, exist where all these conditions fail. In contrast, there are degrees of openness in open systems, whereby some but not all these conditions may hold, such that open systems can be said to fall on a spectrum of openness depending on how many of them hold (Mearman, 2005).[12]

A further, important complication, Chick and Dow emphasize, is that subsystems may exist within systems, and relatively closed subsystems may exist within otherwise open systems. Following Keynes's point that one sometimes keeps the features of a system that contains a subsystem "at the back of one's head" (Keynes, 1936, 297–8), in focusing on a given subsystem one may provisionally ignore the aspects of reality that are associated with the larger system that contains it – a method known as abstraction. This practice breaks down if the (sub)system in question is taken to be complete in itself and lacking the wider effects potentially acting upon it – a method known as idealization. For example, New Classical Economics is closed in this sense in that though it incorporates expectations, no room is left for such things as exogenous shifts in expectations. Thus, the larger system that Keynes would argue that is kept "at the back of one's head" and that contains the New Classical subsystem is ignored. The model is simply closed.

For Chick and Dow, then, Keynes's case exists where subsystems' boundaries are effectively permeable, thereby allowing a range of investigations regarding how different aspects of the system influence a subsystem's performance. A useful way to think of this is to associate subsystems with models and systems with theories. Theories, then, can be open and models can be provisionally closed. This understanding is important to Chick and Dow's view of critical realism's treatment of the open and closed distinction.

Critical realism, especially as developed by Tony Lawson, identifies closed systems by their reliance on event regularities and open systems by their absence (Lawson, 1997, 2003). Reality, he argues, corresponds to the latter circumstance. The world is open in the sense that event regularities are rarely obtained. It follows that since economic models describe the relationships between variables that are seen to be regular and repeated, models assume event regularities, and therefore are *per se* closed. That is, once formulated, their boundaries cannot be permeable in the Keynes sense described above. Indeed, for Lawson, this is reflected in the fact that in economics models are typically formalized and given mathematical representation. The use of mathematics in economics itself is accordingly seen as involving a commitment to closed systems thinking in the sense that the determinacy that mathematical representation involves implies an event regularity view of the world.

Clearly then, Chick and Dow's analysis is quite different since they allow that subsystems formulated as models can be seen as only provisionally closed when they are contained in larger systems, or theories, taken to be open. What they require for this is that those subsystems' boundaries are permeable, meaning that they can be interpreted in such a way as to allow different aspects of the system containing them to influence their performance. Lawson denies that subsystems' boundaries are permeable when they possess an event regularity nature. Chick and Dow agree that if a model/subsystem is fully closed in the idealization sense, then the relevant boundaries are impermeable and this is incompatible with an open systems thinking. But they do not see event regularities as implying this. Indeed, an event regularity can be consistent with open theoretical systems as they understand them. Their example is Keynes's income-consumption relationship, where numerous features affecting that relationship are held in the background. Accordingly, they allow that economic models can be formalized and mathematical, even if this means they represent event regularities, and still associated with an open systems thinking.

The difference between them, then, comes down to how the event regularities are understood. Dow and Chick are clear about this. For Lawson, they note, the open and closed distinction is entirely an ontological matter: "Lawson gives priority to ontology" (Chick and Dow, 2005, 370). In contrast, in their view, the issue is a matter of "the relationship between theorizing and reality" (*Ibid.*) – as reflected in their two lists in Table 2.2. They give considerable attention to this relationship in the third section of their paper, but without going into this discussion in detail we can say that the issue for them is what a theory's structure implies about the relationships that one models, including in event regularity form. In their view, focusing on event regularities *per se* tells us nothing about "the relationship between theorizing and reality" or whether an open theory structure is associated with event regularities or not. In effect, there is no simple connection between event regularities and the conditions for open systems. The latter, then, should be our focus, not event regularities, when we ask whether open systems theorizing applies in any given case.

The third section of their paper, then, focuses on the nature of the boundaries that theories adopt in the models they advance. For Chick and Dow, boundaries are "in general semi-permeable and mutable" (373), and how theorizing proceeds in economics involves a wide range of choices regarding the treatment of boundaries. Thus, mainstream economics treats boundaries as hard and impermeable. Critical realism essentially rejects the concept of boundaries on the grounds that all reality is said to be open so that boundaries must create "distortions" in the representation of reality. Theory should, thus, always be constructed as ontologically open. Chick and Dow, in contrast, differentiate schools of thought according to how they conceptualize the boundaries of models in their theories. Models are embedded in theoretical systems, but how this occurs varies according to the economist's commitment to openness. In the case of mainstream economics, if a theory is defined in terms of its models, that theory is closed. Many economists, however, are less narrow, employ an open systems framework, and differ in regard to how they set boundaries on their models. This explains, then, why there are different schools of thought in economics. It also demonstrates a key foundation for pluralism in economics. Pluralism has its basis in how economists differ in their understanding of "the relationship between theorizing and reality."

This presupposes not only that reality is open (as Lawson argues), but also that its modeling gets provisionally closed according to the economist's understanding of that reality. I turn, then, in the final section of this chapter to the issue of how boundaries can be understood in connection with the related ideas that Sraffa developed on this subject.

Sraffa on open and closed systems

Sraffa is known for his famous *Production of Commodities by Means of Commodities* (Sraffa, 1960), but the thinking that led to that book began much earlier in the 1920s and 1930s. One important text that illustrates this, which in his view constituted an important turning point in his development of his later thinking, is his 1931 unpublished "Surplus Product" (Sraffa, 1931). There Sraffa refers to a problem that his method for determining commodity values produced when incorporating his key concept of surplus products. I have discussed this manuscript elsewhere in some detail (Davis, forthcoming, 2018, 2012b), and here I focus on how Sraffa used the open-closed distinction to argue that the boundary between production and distribution is essentially open and closed at the same time. This view, I suggest, is an early contribution to the same thinking about open and closed systems in regard to the models and theories laid out in the last section and thus a further basis for pluralist thinking in economics.

The problem that Sraffa thought his approach encountered was as follows. He believed that a commodity's value is determined by the commodities used up in its production – a classical cost of production approach. In an economy that produced a surplus, however, the value of the surplus was determined by both the commodities that made it up, which capitalists consumed, and also, accordingly, their willingness to withdraw circulating capital from production in order to engage in luxury consumption. The idea that a commodity's value is determined in a cost of production way involves a natural science, objectivist (or physicalist) sort of explanation that Sraffa favored (Davis, 2012b), but the willingness idea instead involves a subjectivist sort of explanation. This was a problem for Sraffa's intended rehabilitation of a classical political economy that he sought to build around a theory of commodity value alternative to the neoclassical subjectivist theory of prices.

How, then, Sraffa resolved this dilemma was by adopting an open-closed analysis of the relationship between the system of commodity values and how distribution acted on that system. Explicitly using open-closed language, he maintained that commodity production constituted a "closed system" that was acted on by causes external to that "closed system" associated with the distribution of the surplus. Referring to that "closed system" as the "economic field," he concluded that

> There must be a leak at one end or the other: the 'closed system' is in communication with the world.

Here, "the world" refers to distribution, which reflected the historical and social conflict over the shares of wages and profits in national income. He then added:

> When we have defined our 'economic field', there are still outside causes which operate in it; and its effects go beyond the boundary.
>
> (D3/12/7: 161 (3–5); quoted in Kurz and Salvadori, 2008, 268)

What I suggest is especially relevant to the discussion of boundaries and open and closed thinking in the last section, then, is how Sraffa describes this "communication" in terms of the way "outside causes" associated with distribution "operate *in*" the "economic field" and produce "effects that go *beyond* the boundary" created by "the economic field" (my emphases). This two-way movement across this boundary both modifies commodity values from what would be the case were there no surplus (the subsistence economy) and enters into determining the respective values of wages and profits. This implies that the "economic field" is both relatively closed – because commodity values are still determined primarily in the cost of production terms – and yet, at the same time, open to what lies "outside" it – since the distribution of the surplus influences commodity values. This is also captured metaphorically by Sraffa's idea that there is somehow a "leak" in the "closed system" determining commodity values.

Thus, Sraffa adopts open-closed thinking and also makes the boundaries between his "closed system" (the "economic field") and what lies outside it (distribution) permeable. He can be seen as having done this, because he sees (i) the "economic field" operating like a system subject to his cost of production model of that system, and (ii) distribution as being determined by a range of historical and social factors that permit different theories of how the shares of wages and profits are produced. That is, Sraffa's use of the open-closed distinction parallels that presented in the last section as formulated by Chick and Dow in terms of models and theories, and it thus constitutes an earlier understanding of the role of the method of abstraction in view of the relationship between models and theories. His later *Production of Commodities by Means of Commodities*, I believe, retains this conception, despite the fact that there he does not refer to the open-closed distinction. It seems fair to say, then, that the book is successful in its rehabilitation classical political economy's cost of production theory of value as an alternative to the neoclassical account, in part because of this methodological strategy. Indeed, the way in which production is both closed and also open to distribution provides a quite different view from how in the neoclassical supply-and-demand, general equilibrium model the distribution of income and commodity prices is jointly determined. There, as reflected in the closed modeling approach of mainstream economics, everything is subsumed in the model, models and theories are not differentiated, and the world plays no role in economic life apart from its idealization in the model.

Concluding remarks on Dow's open systems thinking and pluralism in economics

The goal of this chapter was to examine Dow's thinking about the open-closed distinction and its relationship with her commitment to pluralism in economics. As she has repeatedly noted, pluralism has many meanings, an implication of which is that without a clear understanding of what it involves we run the risk of defenses of pluralism being ineffective. Thus, what she has done is: we should seek to ground our understanding of pluralism in a particular methodological framework, namely, one developed in terms of the open-closed distinction. Of course, one might say that this only compounds the problem of explaining pluralism because that distinction can be used in multiple ways as well. For Dow, this, consequently, entailed sorting out that distinction in a clear way as well. It should be noted, however, that in this regard she had a key prior intuition about what pluralism in economics involves that guided her toward how she believed an open-closed account of pluralism needed to be developed. That prior intuition was that throughout its history there have existed schools of thought in economics whose differences are central to explaining how economics has developed historically – her conception of "structured pluralism." The hard work, then, was getting from this intuition to an account of what the open-closed distinction involves in economics. The result of years of reflection on pluralism and her important collaboration with Chick was their influential "The Meaning of Open Systems" paper where they systematically worked out how models could be provisionally closed and yet open to competing theories – as reflected in competing schools of thought – based on what, as Keynes put it, one kept "at the back of one's head" when one worked out any particular determinate analysis.

My argument in the last section that Sraffa worked with a similar methodological conception had two purposes. First, I hoped to begin to make the case that the open-closed analysis that Dow and Chick advance has earlier antecedents in similar methods of reasoning employed in classical political economy. From this perspective, Sraffa's rehabilitation of classical political economy can be seen as involving both the recovery of a type of economic theory and also a method of reasoning that can be interpreted in open-closed terms. Second, looking forward, my view is that linking our contemporary open-closed thinking to the method of reasoning in classical political economy, because it emphasized how institutional, historical, and social factors determine how economies function, may help motivate the development of an economics in the future that is pluralist and open in its attention to those factors. A modern political economy, it seems, would need to rely upon the same type of reasoning. In any case, my view then, is that Dow has made a significant contribution to both purposes in giving the idea of a pluralist economics durable methodological foundations. Of her many contributions, here she leaves others the opportunity to continue building on these foundations to advance economics' practice and commitment to pluralism.

Notes

1 Warren Samuels also made an important but different argument for methodological pluralism at the conference based on his "matrix approach to meaningfulness" (Samuels, 1997; also cf. Samuels, 1998, and on Samuels' methodological pluralism, Davis, 2012a).

2 Dow has given special credit to Brian Loasby for this emphasis on "knowing how" as central to economic reasoning.

3 Keynes asserted of Newton:

> [h]e was the last of the magicians, the last of the Babylonians and Sumerians, the last great mind which looked out on the visible and intellectual world with the same eyes as those who began to build our intellectual inheritance rather less than 10,000 years ago.
>
> (Keynes, 1972, 364)

4 Beginning in 2002, I taught this book for a number of years at the University of Amsterdam in an introductory course in economic methodology.

5 Moreover, economists also do funny things, as Dow shows while opening the book with "insider" jokes about economists (2002, 1–3). This may seem to some a frivolous way to begin, but the jokes she presents function as ironic comments on economists' methodological thinking. In my experience of teaching the book, these jokes succeed in stimulating students to think critically about the arguments they will review in the book, and not just take them as a given "truth" – precisely an open systems approach to learning.

6 The "royal road" model is often referred to as the "Whig" interpretation of history. A notable critic of this interpretation was Mark Blaug (1990). I discuss the development of his thinking and critiques of mainstream economics historiography in Davis (2013).

7 She also cites, as a supporting voice for pluralism in economics, Wade Hands' then recently published, comprehensive survey of "new economic methodology" (Hands, 2001).

8 One important manifestation of this development, she notes, was the emergence of a grouping of some 40 international organizations under the label the International Confederation of Associations for Pluralism in Economics (ICAPE).

9 This is a distinction, Dow notes, that Warren Samuels also makes (Samuels, 1997, 1998).

10 These six points are also set out in Dow (2002, 139–140) and paraphrased in Chick (2004).

11 That is, Dow's second list for an open systems economics.

12 Though complete openness is incompatible with a "system" being recognized as a system.

References

Blaug, Mark (1990) "On the Historiography of Economics," *Journal of the History of Economic Thought* 12 (1): 27–37. https://doi.org/10.1017/S1053837200006088

Chick, Victoria (2004) "On Open Systems," *Revista de Economica Politica* 24 (1): 3–16. https://doi.org/10.1590/0101-31572004-1638

Chick, Victoria and Sheila Dow (2005) "The Meaning of Open Systems," *Journal of Economic Methodology* 12 (3): 363–81. https://doi.org/10.1080/13501780500223585

Davis, John (2021) "Openness as a Methodological Principle of Sraffa's Economic Thinking," in A. Sinha, ed., *A Reflection on Sraffa's Revolution in Economic Theory*, London: Palgrave Macmillan: 135–154.

Davis, John (2012a) "Samuels on Methodological Pluralism in Economics," *Research in the History of Economic Thought and Methodology* 30A: 121–36.

Davis, John (2012b) "The Change in Sraffa's Philosophical Thinking," *Cambridge Journal of Economics* 36 (6): 1342–56. https://doi.org/10.1093/cje/ber016

Davis, John (2013) "Blaug on the Historiography of Economics," in Marcel Boumans and Matthias Klaes, eds., *Mark Blaug as an Historian and Methodologist of Economics*, Cheltenham: Elgar: pp. 195–215.

Davis, John (2018) "Sraffa on the Open vs. 'Closed Systems' Distinction and Causality," *Research in the History of Economic Thought and Methodology* 35B: 153–70. https://doi.org/10.1007/978-3-030-47206-1

Dow, Sheila C. (1985) Macroeconomic Thought: A Methodological Approach, Oxford: Blackwell. Reprinted in a revised and extended version as *The Methodology of Macroeconomic thought: A Conceptual Analysis of Schools in Economics*, Cheltenham: Elgar, 1996.

Dow, Sheila C. (1997) "Methodological Pluralism and Pluralism of Method," in Salanti and Screpanti, eds., *Pluralism in Economics: Theory, History and Methodology*, Cheltenham: Elgar: pp. 89–99.

Dow, Sheila (2002) *Economic Methodology: An Inquiry,* Oxford: Oxford University Press.

Dow, Sheila (2004) "Structured Pluralism," *Journal of Economic Methodology* 11 (3): 275–90. https://doi.org/10.1080/1350178042000252965

Dow, Sheila C. (2012) "Babylonian Mode of Thought," in J. E. King, ed., *Elgar Companion to Post Keynesian Economics*, Cheltenham: Elgar: pp. 15–19.

Hands, D. Wade (2001) *Reflection without Rules: Economic Methodology and Contemporary Science Theory*, Cambridge: Cambridge University Press.

Keynes, J. M. (1933) "Newton the Man," in Keynes, *Essays in Biography*, reprinted in Keynes, *Collected Writings* vol. X, London: Macmillan for the Royal Economic Society, 1972: pp. 363–74.

Keynes, J. M. (1936) *The General Theory of Employment, Interest and Money*, London: Macmillan.

Kuhn, Thomas (1970) *The Structure of Scientific Revolutions*, Chicago, IL: University of Chicago Press.

Kurz, Heinz and Neri Salvadori (2008) "Representing the Production and Circulation of Commodities: on Sraffa's Objectivism," in H. Kurz, L. Pasinetti, and Salvadori, eds., *Piero Sraffa: The Man and the Scholar*, London: Routledge: pp. 249–277.

Mearman, Andrew (2005) "Sheila Dow's Concept of Dualism: Clarification, Criticism and Development," *Cambridge Journal of Economics* 29: 1–16.

Salanti, Andrea (1997) "Introduction," in Salanti and Screpanti, eds., *Pluralism in Economics: New Perspectives in History and Methodology*, Cheltenham: Elgar: pp. 1–10.

Salanti, Andrea and Ernesto Screpanti, eds. (1997) *Pluralism in Economics: New Perspectives in History and Methodology*, Cheltenham: Elgar.

Samuels, Warren J. (1997) "The Case for Methodological Pluralism," in Andrea Salanti and Ernesto Screpanti, eds., *Pluralism in Economics: Theory, History and Methodology*, Cheltenham: Elgar: Edward Elgar: pp. 67–79.

Samuels, Warren J. (1998) "Methodological Pluralism," in J. Davis, D. W. Hands, and U. Mäki, eds., *The Handbook of Economic Methodology*, Cheltenham: Elgar: pp. 300–303.

Stohs, Mark (1983) "'Uncertainty' in Keynes' General Theory: a rejoinder," *History of Political Economy,* 15(1): 878–91.
Sraffa, Piero (1931) "Surplus Product," D3/12/7, August, Wren Library, Trinity College, Cambridge.
Sraffa, Piero (1960) *Production of Commodities by Means of Commodities*, Cambridge: Cambridge University Press.

3 Categorisation, criticism and pluralism in context

Open and closed systems and the project of mathematical modelling in modern economics

Tony Lawson

Introduction

Sheila Dow, as much as any modern economist of whom I am aware, has consistently promoted pluralism and inclusiveness in the context of the practices of modern economics. Although I too support these goals, I have, nevertheless, also felt a need to combine them with making critiques of the emphasis that modern economists place on the methods and practices of mathematical modelling. Dow, true to her goals, has been rather more tolerant and inclusive of such practices, and indeed has been somewhat questioning of my criticisms of the modelling emphasis.

Underpinning our differences on these matters is a contrast in the way that she and I form and/or utilise categories. Dow is especially critical of how I have introduced, or adopted specific interpretations of, the categories of *open and closed systems*. Her view is that in doing so I draw distinctions overly sharply or dualistically, necessarily rendering the approaches to economics either oppositional or exclusive. This, it is suggested, is clearly inconsistent with any project of pursuing greater pluralism and inclusiveness overall.

Here, though, I shall suggest that the noted manner of proceeding is after all undertaken in a project that is concerned with the furtherance of pluralism and inclusiveness in the economics discipline. I recognise that Dow and I do approach the forming and/or utilising of categories like open and closed systems differently. But this primarily reflects differences not in the overall goals regarding promoting pluralism and inclusiveness but in the strategies adopted in pursuing them. These strategies, in turn, reflect our contrasting assessments of the nature of the situation in which we find ourselves and specifically those aspects of it that most warrant attention. Let me explain.

Dow and categorisation

I start with a reminder of Dow's opposition to manner in which I have introduced and/or employed certain categories in the context of modern economics. Although Dow questions whether various specific

DOI: 10.4324/9781003142324-4

classifications I have put forward are illuminating, her primary focus, as I say, is seemingly actually on the purpose of classifications in my thinking.[1] The way I form categories, according to Dow, suggests an undesirable inclination to differentiate rather than connect (this being the 'key defining feature' of the 'age of representation', whereas in the previous, seemingly to be preferred, 'age of resemblance' the emphasis was on making connections).[2]

Of course, some classification is unavoidable. Dow recognises this. However, to the extent that categories must be put forward, the preferred goal, it seems, is to make connections, which entails employing only terms with meanings that are fluid or evolving, with any distinctions made being 'porous and vague'. I am criticised for delineating categories in ways that are too clear, consistent, precise or absolute.

Thus, in a recent article where I advance a conception of *neoclassical economics*, Dow observes:

> Lawson (2013, p. 13) does note that there can sometimes be virtue in 'loose' use of terminology ('(lexical) ambiguity'). Nevertheless the purpose of the article is to offer a clear, consistent category of neoclassical economics for general application. [. . .]
>
> He aims for precision in his definition of neoclassical economics on the grounds that a loose use of the term has inhibited understanding.
>
> (Dow, 2016, pp. 105–6)

This seeking of precision, according to Dow, is the mark of dualistic thinking that is typical of mainstream contributors, and she would expect me to proceed differently:

> This precision of categorisation is a characteristic of the dualistic thinking typical of mainstream economics (Dow, 1990); Lawson seeks to introduce a tripartite division to replace the orthodox-heterodox dual, but the critique of dualism can apply equally to three: 'all-encompassing, mutually-exclusive categories with fixed meanings' rather than two.
>
> (Dow, 2016, p. 106)

> As an open-system thinker, we would expect Lawson to employ categories in the sense of the age of resemblance, i.e. categories which are vague, evolving and whose boundaries may shift over time.
>
> (Dow, 2016, p. 106)

Dow, here as elsewhere, appears most critical of the notions of open and closed systems that I defend, and the manner in which I deploy them in identifying various groupings:

> The key distinction for Lawson is between theorising, which is consistent with open-system social reality, and orthodox theorising, which is only

> consistent with a closed-system reality (which Lawson, as a heterodox economist, argues is a fiction). The open-system/closed-system classification is treated as an absolute, i.e. taxonomic; only once the distinction (with its methodological implications) is recognised, as Lawson advocates, will economics conform to a heterodox-orthodox duality. The distinction is maintained by Lawson (2004) in response to the argument that differences between heterodox schools of thought derive from (open system) ontological differences within a non-dualistic structure (Dow, 2004).
>
> (Dow, 2016, p. 107)

And also:

> [In seeking to categorise neoclassical economics Lawson does propose new boundaries …] But the classification of these boundaries is anything but vague – it is crystal clear in the distinction between a closed-system ontology and an open-system ontology. Further it is a new classification which, rather than being mutable, can be applied across the history of heterodox economics as well as orthodox economics.
>
> (Dow, 2016, p. 106)

Dow does also draw her own distinction between open and closed systems, but it is one that by design is not dualistic or 'absolute', but vague, shifting and inclusive:

> The closed-system/open-system distinction need not in fact be dualistic. Chick and Dow (2012 [2005]) consider closed and open systems in non-dualistic terms by setting out the conditions, which all have to be met by a closed system, while there is a range of possibilities for systems to be open because any one condition (or combination of conditions) has not been met.
>
> (Dow, 2016, p. 106)

Finally, Dow acknowledges that the foregoing criticism of my approach does not carry over to the manner in which I differentiate amongst or within heterodox traditions, where the open closed distinction is not employed:

> Nevertheless, while Lawson aims for philosophical precision with respect to the definition of heterodox economics as a whole, he employs non-taxonomic categorisation in his treatment of schools of thought within heterodox economics, defining them in a loose, open-ended way in terms of 'ontological commitment'.
>
> (Dow, 2016, p. 107)

So, Dow's criticism relates primarily to the particular manner in which I have used the open system/closed system distinction. Specifically, because I have used this distinction to characterise the mainstream-heterodox divide, and more recently have included neoclassicism as a subclassification in the same categorical system, it is on these aspects of my thinking that Dow mainly focuses.

In all this, Dow's critical commentary is respectful and clearly reflecting the goals of inclusiveness and pluralism. This, I hope, is an appropriate occasion to engage with Dow on the issues she raises.

Category formulation

Before explaining why I suppose that proceeding in the manner I have is not after all inconsistent with the pursuit of pluralism and inclusiveness, I should first indicate something of my own orienting philosophical presuppositions. Dow appears to write at times as if it were a generality that drawing distinctions is worse than making connections. I believe instead that it all depends on context. Specifically, I see nothing wrong with drawing distinctions, so long as the delineations drawn both (1) capture distinctions in the world, that is, that, as philosophers like to say, cut nature at its joints and (2) are useful to us in pursuing reasonable projects.

The former – realist – criterion, of course, rests on an assessment that reality is *not* an undifferentiated homogeneous mass but comprises a variety of kinds of things that are organised in various ways – in large part, a result of evolutionary processes (see Lawson, 2019, chapter 7). The second – usefulness – criterion rests on the assessment that there is no *unique* way to fasten on to natural distinctions even if correctly uncovered, and so we carve reality up in ways (at those 'joints') that are the most beneficial to us. Where relevant, I have elsewhere suggested that this means, as a moral principle, seeking ways of 'carving' that most facilitate the generalised flourishing of human (if amongst other) beings (see Lawson, 2019).

The point for now is that whether the categories determined ought to be more or less connecting depends on context. This is especially clear in the practices of non-social or 'natural' science, as in the way (non-social) natural kind categories are usually formed. Thus, categories like water and copper are delineated to include *only and all* items with a specific common chemical composition. It is useful to us to do so. But in other cases, it is more useful to proceed differently. In fact, in carving up the non-social realm, classifications can be formed by both (1) *making connections* between substances with *different* chemical compositions; and (2) *drawing distinctions* within substances with *identical* chemical compositions.

As an example of (1), of *making connections* between substances with *different* chemical compositions, the kind referred to as *jade* is made up of different substances, each with their own chemical compositions (in fact, the substances that have been counted as jade have varied at different times and places in the course of human history). Currently, the term '*jade*' is applied to two different rocks made up of different silicate minerals that are also known as nephrite and jadeite. The former consists of the calcium- and magnesium-rich amphibole mineral actinolite and has the chemical formula $Ca_2(Mg, Fe)_5Si_8O_{22}(OH)_2$; the rock called jadeite is composed almost entirely of jadeite, a sodium- and aluminium-rich pyroxene mineral with composition $NaAlSi_2O_6$.

As an example of (2), of *drawing distinctions* within substances with *identical* chemical compositions, charcoal and diamonds are, for practical reasons, usually treated as different kinds, even though both are forms of carbon and so have an identical chemical composition. Even in the case of water, it might have turned out to be the case that in delineating it, those involved had lumped H_2O together with the substance we call 'hard water', which has a different chemical composition.

The point is that the delineations made involve both making connections and drawing distinctions in ways that depend on both the nature of reality and the usefulness of any categorical scheme to human well-being.

The same strategy, I suggest, is warranted when we come to the social realm, and more specifically to drawing categories amongst groupings in the economics academy. That is, we can with reason form categories in line with differences and connections *that already exist* and also do so in ways that that appear the most useful to our general well-being.

Deciding which is the most useful or beneficial way to make delineations in a specific context, of course, is a matter over which researchers can legitimately disagree. Dow reveals herself to be a realist in the sense indicated (e.g., Dow, 1990, p. 146). So, our differences turn on how we believe categories are the most usefully drawn, which, in turn, depends both on our assessments of the situation and on the precise reasons for drawing category delineations one way rather than another. Specifically, I want to suggest that our adopting contrasting strategies of category formation and usage in the relevant context reflects differences (*not* of orientations to pluralism but) of assessments about how outcomes consistent with pluralism are best achieved.

Specifically, whilst Dow's concern has been to clarify a situation of debate in modern economics, my concern has been to explain the failure of academic economics to provide much, if any, insight into social reality for the past 60 or 70 years. That is, Dow's project has been primarily clarificatory in nature, whereas mine has been primarily explanatory. Dow has been concerned first of all with how terms are used, whereas I have been centrally concerned with how economics is done. If a focus on categories like open and closed systems and their use has been essential to Dow's contribution, I could easily have managed without employing them. In the project I have pursued, they arise contingently in addressing the explanation of the discipline's malaise uncovered. It is because of the contrast in our objectives that Dow has employed terms like open and closed systems in being inclusive and making connections, whilst I have ultimately employed them in making criticisms and in emphasising distinctions. Let me elaborate and defend these assessments.

Differing objectives

Dow, as I say, has long sought to clarify ongoing debates. Thus, when turning to notions of open and closed systems specifically, Dow has sought to explore the different meanings that might be attributed to such expressions, with a view to clarifying economic debate where these expressions might be employed.

Thus, in an abstract to an initial paper on the topic, co-authored with Victoria Chick, Dow writes:

> The purpose of this paper is to address issues of meaning that arise in this particular discourse, with a view to clarifying both conflicts in usage and the underlying issues involved. We explore the different meanings of openness and closure extant in the literature, as applied at the ontological and epistemological levels, focusing on our own use of the terms in relation to that which prevails in neoclassical economics on the one hand and to the use made of them by Tony Lawson and other critical realists on the other.
>
> (Chick and Dow, [2005] 2012, p. 363)

And shortly into the main text, Dow and Chick repeat:

> The purpose of this paper is to tease out these differences in meaning and, more important, the underlying methodological approaches that account for these differences. This exercise is offered as a contribution to clarifying the debate.
>
> (Chick and Dow, [2005] 2012, p. 363)

In pursuing their classificatory endeavour, the method adopted by Chick and Dow is to use the *Oxford English Dictionary* to determine the traditional meanings of the terms with which they are concerned, and then to narrow down the possibilities for economics specifically, by way of employing the criterion of being 'closest to what an economist usually means'.[3] It is the employment of this latter criterion, of course, that ensures that any interpretation of categories employed is maximally inclusive.

In contrast, I have at no stage been concerned with clarifying the uses of categories by others. Rather, I introduced various terms only where they were thought to provide a useful shorthand in the context of the explanatory project undertaken and insights achieved. In this, to repeat, I could easily have proceeded without using the expressions open and closed systems, or any others standing in their place, to achieve my aims; I used the noted expressions, always defining my intended meanings in context, simply for matters of analytical convenience.

My starting point, to repeat, was an assessment that the discipline of economics has failed to contribute much, if anything, by way of explanatory insight over a long period. Of course, many others were adopting a similar view, including many prominent contributors within the discipline. Most, moreover, observed that the decline in the discipline's ability to generate explanatory insight, and relevance, was associated with the growing emphasis on the methods of mathematical modelling.

Thus, as long ago as 1981, for example, Wassily Leontief, himself a modeller as well as a Nobel Memorial prize winner, observed that 'Page after page of professional economic journals are filled with mathematical formulas leading the reader from sets of more or less plausible but entirely arbitrary assumptions to precisely stated but irrelevant theoretical conclusions' (Leontief, 1982, p. 104). A few years earlier, the prominent econometrician Edward Leamer had acknowledged that 'The opinion that econometric theory is largely irrelevant is held by an embarrassingly large share of the economics profession' (Edward Leamer 1978, p. vi). At the time, Mark Blaug was writing books on methodology to try and defend the practices of mathematical modellers despite their seeming continuing inability to provide insight. Eventually, even he gave up, concluding,

> Modern economics is sick. Economics has increasingly become an intellectual game played for its own sake and not for its practical consequences for understanding the economic world. Economists have converted the subject into a sort of social mathematics in which analytical rigour is everything and practical relevance is nothing.
>
> (Mark Blaug, 1997, p. 3)

If the growing emphasis on mathematical modelling has long been recognised as associated with a declining ability of the discipline to provide insight, the immediate puzzle as I saw it was to explain why this emphasis on mathematical modelling had not only not been abandoned but also actually continued to increase. Indeed, the emphasis on such modelling, despite the latter's failings, has so increased that, currently, the project of mathematical modelling is the discipline's most dominant. In fact, its proponents now insist that mathematical modelling is the only way to do economics and have used their dominance to abrogate the rights and obligations of academic economics departments to the advantage of their own mathematical project. Most especially and obviously, they have sought to make contributions to such modelling on the basis of all appointments, promotions, core journals, lecture courses, etc. This being so, it has seemed entirely reasonable to me to distinguish, and refer to, this specific project as the *current mainstream*, and to seek to explain its dominance in the face of its accompanying explanatory failures.

Why the mathematical emphasis?

If this question seemed pressing to me, the only explanation I could ever find of the emphasis on modelling is an extraordinary naïvety that prevails the discipline. There has long existed, and still exists, a sort of awe of mathematicians accompanied by a shared belief that the sorts of modelling methods used are somehow explanatorily neutral, that reliance on the methods of modelling cannot possibly be a reason for any failings of the discipline to provide insight. If the models so far created are not up to the job, it is only a question of time before an appropriate one will be uncovered.

More specifically, it is widely held that economics should be scientific; that mathematics is essential to science; that explanatory 'scientific' successes will arrive for the project in due course, so long as the project is not derailed; that the reason some economists fail to model is simply because they lack the skills; that allowing non-mathematicians into the discipline will lead to dumbing down, ultimately resulting in the exclusion of modelling; that non modellers are to be viewed as cranks (in the manner it is supposed that non-social scientists view astrologers or numerologists, etc.); and so on.

These views not only persist but are also increasingly adopted even amongst those who style themselves as non-mainstream or 'heterodox', as I come to below. What is wrong with them? The most basic error, of course, lies in supposing that any method or tool or approach is neutral and relevant to all conditions. It is equivalent to insisting that a hammer be used for all household and garden jobs prior to knowing the specific tasks to be undertaken, and so trying to use the hammer even, say, where the task is to cut the grass, wash clothes, or enter a house. And this insistence in the case of mathematical modelling is interpreted as being scientific.

Science though, at least as practiced in the non-social realm, is not about (its participants do not insist upon) using mathematics (or any other method) for *every* task; its practitioners rather seek to ensure that the methods used are appropriate to any task, given the latter's nature. Determining the natures of the task and of the object of study is the role of ontology. And a feature of the rising emphasis on mathematical modelling that struck me when I first entered the economics discipline was the lack of ontological scrutiny. There just seemed to be a widespread belief that there was no need for it, as the reliance on the methods of mathematical modelling could not be inappropriate.

So, it seemed important to me to indicate that the sorts of mathematical modelling methods that economists like to employ are just as restricted in their usefulness as any others. As it happens, it was easy enough to show that the conditions under which these methods are useful are limited and, in fact, rarely occur in the social domain, so that the explanatory failures of the past 60 years can, indeed, be seen to be the result of the modelling emphasis. It was merely an aid to rendering this argument clear, in so explaining the malaise of the discipline, that I introduced the categories of open and closed systems, formulating them in the manner I did. Let me very briefly explain.

The limits of mathematical modelling in modern economics

Simply put, first, the sorts of conditions or social configurations under which the methods employed by mathematical modellers standing a chance of providing insight are those that manifest event regularities or correlations. Second, where economists wish to theorise, the constraint of doing so in a fashion consistent with formulations of event regularities necessitates the positing of entities that are of the nature of isolated atoms. Atomistic entities are just those that in condition X always act to the same effect Y. Isolation ensures that when an occurrence of X triggers the atoms, nothing interferes to prevent Y from being actualised. Social configurations that take the form of worlds of isolated atoms are those that modellers must rely on occurring.

The problem for economic modellers is simply that social reality is found to be of a nature that these two conditions of modelling success rarely occur, even in approximation. First, event regularities of any interest are almost entirely absent. Second, the latter near absence is easily explained by the property of social reality consisting everywhere of phenomena that are relationally constituted (and so non-isolatable) and processual/transformational in nature (and so being far from atomistic), amongst other things.

Here, I stress that the feature of all social phenomena of being relationally constituted (employers constituted in relation to employees, teachers to students, etc.) is not only not well approximated by the requirement/assumption of isolation, but also the latter is effectively the antithesis of relational constitution. Similarly, the processual nature of social phenomena (due to their dependence in constitution on human transformation practices) is again a feature that is not only not well approximated by the requirement/assumption of being atomistic in nature, but also again the latter is effectively its anthesis.

It is only at this point, as I say, that the categories of open and closed systems enter the picture in my own contributions. They are introduced simply for convenience, and specifically, in the case of the expression *closed system*, in order to be able to refer easily to all social configurations that are able to support event regularities. But the exclusionary and dualistic scenario of modern economics that is thereby in part expressed by the label did not derive from the label's introduction but rather explained it. The specific category was introduced precisely to help focus attention on dichotomous aspects of the situation of the economics academy that had *already long existed*, stemming from the exclusionary orientation of those that insist on identifying economics with methods of mathematical modelling.

I earlier suggested that, because of its overwhelming dominance in the modern economics academy, the project of mathematical modelling warrants being recognised as the discipline's *current* mainstream. Mainstream and *orthodox* are interchangeable terms of course. Heterodox just means a group rejecting one or more *doxa* or supposed 'truths' of the orthodoxy or mainstream. Elsewhere, I have argued that the emphasis on modelling methods is the only such 'truth', the only commonality of all contributions to this mainstream (Lawson, 2006; Slade-Caffarel, 2018). So, it is the only 'truth' to be rejected by any heterodoxy. Clearly, there must be reasons for this rejection, with the most obvious one being that social phenomena are the most obvious one being that social phenomena are of a nature that mathematical modelling methods are largely irrelevant to their analysis. Elsewhere, I have indicated that this is, indeed, a presupposition that is common to those that at the time styled themselves as heterodox.

This being so, it also seemed reasonable first to *identify* or categorise those that at some level interpret social reality in terms of configurations that do not easily support event regularities (required for the mainstream to have any relevance) as *heterodox*, and, second, to label the configurations themselves as systems that are *open*.

Such a strategy of categorising can be criticised on numerous grounds. But I am not sure whether the lack of pluralism or failure to be inclusive are amongst them. The point of the strategy was simply to focus attention on the (very particular) sorts of conditions required if the sorts of methods that mainstream economists insist upon are to stand a chance of providing insight. It is the rarity of these conditions in the social domain that *explains* the widespread and continuing failures of these methods. So, the *a priori* insistence on these methods is not only problematic in itself as a barrier to pluralism and inclusivity but also an obstacle to the discipline providing insight. I have sought to make this situation more readily apparent.

I maintain, then, that our different paths stem not from the different orientations to pluralism, inclusiveness, or even, I think, to understandings of the point of categorising, but to contrasting assessments of objective thought that are the most deserving of critical attention.

The problem worsens

I might add that the situation that I sought to highlight when first introducing the noted notions of open and closed systems currently deserves even more critical attention. The reliance on using the methods of mathematical modelling seems to me to be more widespread now than ever.

Especially significant in this respect is that, in some quarters at least, the emphasis on modelling is increasingly prosecuted in the name of heterodoxy. I have analysed this trend elsewhere (Lawson, 2017) and suggested that a determining factor is precisely a situation where the practices of mathematical modelling have been dominant for such a significant period now that, for various generations of economists, modelling appears as a common-sense activity. So, its relevance is hardly questioned in a serious way, with explanations of the discipline's failings attributed automatically and unthinkingly to specific substantive errors rather than to the modelling emphasis itself.

There are two aspects to this pursuance of modelling styled as 'heterodox' that warrant comment.

First, there is the inconsistency of those who recognise that social reality conforms to configurations that I refer to as *open* but fail to recognise that the employment of various (mathematical modelling) methods requires, if these methods are to be useful, that social reality is everywhere *closed*. This is an inconsistency (of ontological presuppositions) that elsewhere I have suggested warrants being recognised as the fundamental inconsistency of the economics discipline (Lawson, 2021). Of course, it was precisely in order to capture it that Veblen introduced the label *neoclassical economics* (see Lawson, 2013, 2021; Pratten, 2022). That is, the label *neoclassical economics* was coined by Veblen to express the mixture of ontological awareness (in holding visions of openness) combined with methodological naïvety (in persevering with methods that presupposed closed systems). For Veblen, the use of the latter sorts of methods was interpreted as *classical*, whilst the maintaining of a vision of openness *at the same time* was captured by adding the prefix *neo*. So, the problem is not a new one. The point is that it not only lives on but is also seemingly increasing found. Currently, the correlates of *classical* and *neo* (as Veblen employed these terms) include *economic modelling* and *heterodox*. Hence, I have pointed to the irony involved where 'heterodox' modellers, who unwittingly sustain this mismatch, use the term *neoclassical economics* as a term of derision in referencing others (again see Lawson, 2013, 2021; Pratten, 2022).

Second, a yet more concerning aspect of this modelling turn is an increase in the number of those who *in the name of heterodoxy* are insisting that the methods of mathematical modelling be accepted by all, including students. Cases of this seem to figure especially prominently amongst a section of modern post-Keynesians. I am even aware of the departments that style themselves as heterodox in orientation, that have turned down job applicants simply because they do not employ economic models in their research (and sometimes even because they do not use some 'right sort' of modelling). This group is seemingly the most naïve and, because it is responsible for students who are concerned enough to seek relevance, it is potentially the most harmful of all.

The argument made by this latter 'heterodox' group for supposing that their modelling activities are somehow different from other forms of mathematical modelling is that they make different assumptions and/or their models produce typically more radical or thought-to-be realistic conclusions. Given, of course, that a generalised construction of economic models necessitates that a relational processual world is everywhere (mis) represented as one composed of systems of isolated atoms, requiring 'assumptions' that are knowingly gross distortions of reality, any results achieved by these heterodox modellers are necessarily (and are easily seen to be) as irrelevant as any others (see e.g., Lawson, 2021).

Meanwhile the sort of ontological analysis required to recognise all this is essentially absent from the modern discipline, so that with mathematical modelling practices accommodated automatically, in an *a priori fashion*, it appears as if there is no need for the ground clearing contribution of such (ontological) enquiry. Attempting to redress this situation, I contend, is not only warranted but also, for the sorts of reasons outlined, not at all inconsistent with the goals of pluralism and inclusiveness.[4]

Final comments

In sum, Sheila Dow has done much to advance the cause of pluralism and inclusiveness in the academic discipline of economics. In the course of doing so, she has criticised the particular manner in which I (and others) interpret and use categories like open and closed systems, suggesting that it results in, or at least encourages, groupings that are somewhat dualistic and exclusionary in nature. However, I have suggested that this is not so. The point is that the categories, as I have used them, have been designed precisely to express/reference dualistic and exclusionary social processes and groupings *that already exist and have long done so*. The categories have been introduced to express a longstanding dualism in the world, not to create one. And my goal in so employing these categories was not thereby to perpetuate the underlying (dualistic, non-inclusive) situation *as it is found* but to facilitate a critique of it and thereby help expedite a quite different scenario in which the distinctions now drawn are (for the purposes of facilitating critique) no longer of much use. As such, I believe it reasonable to consider the project described as standing not in opposition to, but playing a part in, the endeavour of rendering academic economics a more pluralistic inclusive activity.

Notes

1 Dow writes:

> There is a substantive question as to whether the boundaries Lawson sets up by his categorisation are illuminating or whether they gloss over the possibility of other categorisations (such as theoretical content [. . .]). But we focus here on the prior question as to the function and implications of classification itself, which applies also to the previous two-way classification (see further, Mearman, 2012).
>
> (Dow, 2016, p. 107)

2 According to Dow:

> The urge to classify is the key defining characteristic of what Foucault (1991 [1966], 1992 [1969]) called the classical episteme, or the age of representation. Classification arose from a separation (atomisation) of elements of what had previously, in the age of resemblance, been understood as parts of an organic whole (Vigo de Lima, 2010). While in the age of resemblance knowledge was drawn from history and the emphasis was on connections, in the age of representation knowledge was regarded as universal and the emphasis was on distinctions; the resulting taxonomies were based on resemblance within categories, but distinctions between them.
>
> (Dow, 2016, p. 105)

3 Thus, in starting by seeking a definition of the notion of system they write: 'Let us start with the concept of "system". The *Oxford English Dictionary* offers many variants, of which the following are closest to what an economist usually means' (Chick and Dow, [2005] 2012, p. 364).

4 What, it might be asked, are we to make of all this? How specifically, might we best move forward in a pluralist and an inclusive fashion? It is clear from the

forgoing discussion that a likely necessary condition of overcoming the problems of academic economics allows ontology a (its traditional – see Lawson, 2019) ground clearing.

References

Blaug, Mark (1997) *Ugly Currents in Modern Economics*, Options Politiques, September, 3–8.

Chick, V. and Dow, S. ([2005] 2012) The meaning of open systems. *Journal of Economic Methodology* 12(3): 363–81. Reprinted in Dow S. (ed.) *Foundations for New Economic Thinking: A Collection of Essays*. London, UK: Palgrave Macmillan, pp. 178–96. https://doi.org/10.1080/13501780500223585

Dow, S. (1990) Beyond dualism. *Cambridge Journal of Economics* 14(2): 143–58. Reprinted in *Foundations for New Economic Thinking*. London, UK: Palgrave Macmillan, 2012, pp. 52–71.

Dow, Sheila. (2016) Neoclassicism, critical realism, and the Cambridge methodological tradition, in Jamie Morgan (ed.) (2016).

Foucault, M. (1991 [1966]) *The Order of Things*. London, UK: Routledge.

Foucault, M. (1992 [1969]) *The Archaeology of Knowledge*. London, UK: Routledge.

Lawson, T. (2004) Reorienting economics: On heterodox economics, themata and the use of mathematics in economics. *Journal of Economic Methodology* 11(3): 229–240. https://doi.org/10.1080/1350178042000258536

Lawson, T. (2006) The nature of heterodox economics. *Cambridge Journal of Economics* 30(4): 483–505. https://doi.org/10.1093/cje/bei093

Lawson, T. (2013) What is this 'school' called neoclassical economics? *Cambridge Journal of Economics* 37(5): 947–83. Also published in Jamie Morgan (ed.) (2016), pp. 30–81. https://doi.org/10.1093/cje/bet027

Lawson, Tony (2017) What is wrong with modern economics, and why does it stay wrong? *Journal of Australian Political Economy* 80: 26–42.

Lawson, Tony (2019) *The Nature of Social Reality: Issues in Social Ontology*. London and New York: Routledge.

Lawson, Tony (2021) Whatever happened to neoclassical economics? *Revue de Philosophie Économique* 22 (1).

Leamer, Edward E. (1978) *Specification Searches: Ad hoc Inferences with Non-Experimental Data*. New York: John Wiley and Sons.

Leontief, Wassily (1982) Letter in *Science*, 217: 104–7.

Mearman, A. (2012) 'Heterodox economics' and the problems of classification. *Journal of Economic Methodology* 19(4): 407–24. https://doi.org/10.1080/1350178X.2012.742201

Morgan, Jaime (ed.) (2016) What Is *Neoclassical Economics? Debating the Origins, Meaning and Significance*. London and New York: Routledge.

Pratten, Stephen (2022) Veblen, Marshall and neoclassical economics. *Journal of Classical Sociology* 1–26. https://doi.org/10.1177/1468795X211068999

Slade-Caffarel, Yannick (2018) The nature of heterodox economics revisited. *Cambridge Journal of Economics* 43(3): 527–39. https://doi.org/10.1093/cje/bey043

Vigo de Lima, I. (2010) *Foucault's Archaeology of Political Economy*. London, UK: Palgrave Macmillan.

4 Dualism revisited

Geoffrey M. Hodgson

Beyond dualism – towards Babylon

Sheila Dow has made extensive and innovative contributions to the methodology of economics. For her, many of the differences between mainstream economics and its critics hinged on methodological issues. For example, she saw a 'Cartesian/Euclidian mode of thought' as underlying 'much of mainstream economics', concluding that 'mainstream methodology and theory is predominantly dualistic' (Dow, 1990, pp. 143, 155).

In a major book on methodology, Dow (1985) proposed 'Babylonian' thinking as an alternative. Dow (1990, p. 143) saw two 'particular features of Cartesian/Euclidian thought' as 'atomism and dualism'. The critical spotlight of her 1990 essay is on dualism. That focus is shared here, where I reflect on some of the issues involved. I find her essay as fascinating now as I did in 1990. I propose to revisit it in the light of subsequent learning and debate.[1]

Dow (1990, p. 143) explained *dualism* in the following terms:

> Dualism is the practice of organising thought by means of all-encompassing mutually-exclusive categories, with fixed meanings. It is a particular means of imposing order on ideas, or on perceptions of reality, or indeed of drawing distinctions (as between ideas and reality, for example). Dualism has been endemic to a particular stream of Western thought since the Platonic distinction between mind and matter. In classical logic, it appears as the principle of the excluded middle: given a category x, any entity must fall either into the category x, or into the category non-x.

Dow (1990, p. 146) briefly connected dualism to the idea of a closed system: 'A Cartesian/Euclidean theoretical system is a closed system … i.e. Cartesian/Euclidean thought is dualistic'. By contrast, the 'Babylonian mode of thought' is an attempt 'to theorise about a complex reality, but one which does not aim at a complete, closed, theoretical structure'. However, she did not elaborate on what she meant by openness or closure in the context. No

DOI: 10.4324/9781003142324-5

theory is 'complete' in the sense that it covers everything or is immune to revision. So, what precisely is meant by a 'complete' or 'closed' theory?

In her account, Dow saw *dualism* as primarily an error of rigid categorisation, with logical, methodological and epistemological implications. She also raised ontological issues, with her insistence that there must be some 'correspondence' between theory and reality (Dow, 1990, pp. 146–7). Hence, if reality is 'open' and 'non-dualistic', then theory also must be 'open' and '-non-dualistic'. I shall return to these issues of ontology and to this presumed correspondence below.

Dow fully accepted the need to use categories in rigorous thought. She noted that if the argument against dualism is turned against itself, it too must rest on a binary distinction between dualism and non-dualism. To be against dualism suggests the (dualist) existence of a non-dualism. The only ways out of this logical tangle seem to be either to abandon the critique of dualism or to make exceptions to it. This dilemma was raised but not further elaborated in Dow's 1990 essay.

Nevertheless, Dow found a respectable philosophical lineage for her critique. She noted Hegel's dialectical thinking, where categories obtain some meaning through a consideration of their opposites. She also built on the work of Thomas Kuhn (1962). He had argued that the meanings of some crucial scientific concepts and terms change as scientific paradigms develop in the light of arguments and evidence. Dow also noted the 'process philosophy' of Alfred North Whitehead (1929, 1938), which tackled the problem of dealing with dynamic changes and processes. She also cited the school of intuitionist logic, which argues against the law of the excluded middle and insists that there must be a third category – *undefined* or *undecided*. It is not always possible or reasonable to categorise in terms of x or not-x.

Among economists, Dow cited John Maynard Keynes as an exemplar of non-dualistic thought. She noted the influence of Keynes and Whitehead on one another, and their shared intellectual debt to G. E. Moore. Dow (1990, pp. 147–50) pointed to Keynes's concepts of uncertainty, probability and 'animal spirits' as crucial illustrations of 'Babylonian' thought.

In her 1990 paper, Dow also referred to my early work on institutions (Hodgson, 1988). She noted that, instead of a unidirectional causation from individuals to institutions, I argued (as I do now) for 'causation running in either direction' (Dow, 1990, p. 155). However, note that this is an ontological claim (concerning causation) rather than a matter of epistemology or categorisation.

In her 1990 paper, Dow did not develop her rebuttal of dualism into a warning against the over-extensive or inappropriate use of mathematics in economics. She did not then associate mathematics per se with dualism. A critique of the inappropriate use of mathematics in economics appeared shortly afterwards, in Tony Lawson's (1997) work. Later below, I shall consider whether opposition to dualism limits the use of mathematics.

Critical realism and the ontological turn

Dow's essay on dualism was published shortly before the ontological and realist turn in the methodology of economics. This was led by Tony Lawson (1997), Uskali Mäki (1992, 2001) and others. Lawson's contribution builds on the 'critical realism' of Roy Bhaskar (1975), to which Dow (1999, 2002) expressed strong sympathy, alongside occasional criticism (Chick and Dow, 2005). It is useful to revisit Dow's (1990) essay in the light of the subsequent ontological turn and rise of critical realism.

Dow argued that there must be some correspondence between theory and reality. She saw reality as 'non-dualistic', hence the mission of the 'Babylonian approach . . . is to construct theory in a non-dualistic manner in order to promote correspondence with reality' (Dow, 1990, p. 146). Here, she added to her prevailing view of 'non-dualism' in terms of epistemology or taxonomy, to make the ontological claim that economic reality is itself 'no-dualistic' and that theory must 'correspond' to reality and hence be 'non-dualistic' too.

Both Dow and Lawson emphasised that the real world is complex and open, and that its future evolution is uncertain (in the Keynesian sense). However, Lawson adopted an atypical definition of openness and closure. Lawson (1997, p. 19) followed Roy Bhaskar's (1975, p. 70) odd characterisation of a closed system 'as one in which a constant conjunction of events obtains.' This event-level definition is at variance with an emphasis on ontological fundamentals and with the prevailing definitions of openness and closure in systems theory, where a 'system is closed if no material enters or leaves it; it is open if there is import and export and, therefore, change of the components' (Bertalanffy, 1950, p. 23). The meanings of the concepts of openness and closure are, thus, controversial (Mearman, 2006; Pratten, 2007; Fleetwood, 2017).[2]

Perhaps taking a cue from Dow (1990), Lawson also required some sort of correspondence between theory and reality. Lawson (2003, p. 22) suggested that theory must '"fit" with reality'. He assumed, but made no argument, that the ontological characteristics of reality (such as complexity and openness) must be adequately reflected somehow in the theory. But this assumption has no automatic warrant: theory and reality are different things. The ideal that theory and reality should 'fit' or 'correspond' is clearly unachievable in anything more than a highly limited sense. Making such correspondence a goal would make any theory fall short.

The claim that the real world is complex, open or uncertain does not imply that any theory we use to analyse the real world must be complex, open or uncertain. Theory and reality are different ontological spheres. Theories are not and cannot be templates of reality, even if it is important that their assumptions resemble reality in some way. Theories are firstly attempts to understand parts of reality, which, in turn, may help us intervene in practice.

Lawson (1997, 2003) based his critique of mathematical formalism in economics on an ontological mismatch between formal models and reality. Because (economic) reality is generally 'open' (in his sense), theory must be 'open' too. Mathematical models are 'closed'. Hence, for him, they are appropriate in 'rare' cases only.

But in the following passage, Lawson (2003, p. 12) implied a different criterion – that of practical instrumentality rather than correspondence with reality. He wrote: 'Few people . . . would attempt to use a comb to write a letter ... or a drill to clean a window'. Of course, we use a pen to write a letter and a clean cloth to clean a window. However, the ontology of pens is very different from that of letters, and there is also a big ontological difference between clean cloths and dirty windows.

I agree with Lawson's implicit claim that theories are intellectual and practical instruments. There are different versions of instrumentalism, some of which are opposed to philosophical realism. But some versions of pragmatist instrumentalism, notably that of John Dewey (1938), do not undermine the claim that a real world exists outside our perceptions. Dewey (1910) and Dewey and Spaulding (1911) supported a form of philosophical realism. Pragmatism upholds the fact that scientific claims are appraised by their practical consequences, thereby establishing their veracity and value. Hence, theories are primarily instruments for a practical understanding of the real world. I shall return to the question of instrumentalism later below.

Crucially, there is nothing in Lawson's instrumental, appropriateness-of-tools argument that rules out using closed models to help to understand an open reality. He failed to establish that the openness of the real world requires us to adopt a theory that is 'open' in some sense.

Unrestricted openness in a theory may be impossible. Whether mathematical of verbal, all theories involve a degree of abstraction, isolation or closure – that is, some things must be left out of the picture (Mäki 1992, 1994). Lawson (1997, p. 236) accepted part of this, but he attempted to force a distinction between 'isolation' and 'abstraction', depending on whether the omissions are 'temporary' or not. This distinction is spurious, because all theories can move on as a science develops, and hence potentially *all* omissions have a temporary nature. Even if a theorist rejects the need to make the theory more comprehensive, that does not make the omission permanent. Other researchers can fill gaps. The evaluation of a theory should not depend on whether the theorist intended at some stage to relax a restrictive assumption. That would be judging the personality of the theorist and not the suitability of the theory.

Lawson focused on the limitations of econometrics. But he neglected the heuristic roles of many other formal models, which are not designed to predict but to identify and isolate the possible causal mechanisms that form part of a more complex system. Heuristics can be useful without necessarily making adequate predictions or closely matching existing phenomena (Sugden, 2000). Their purpose is to illustrate a plausible segment of a whole causal story, without necessarily giving an adequate or complete explanation of the whole phenomena to which they relate. Consequently, there is a role here for a (closed) formal theory, despite the complexity and openness of the world.

In sum, we must challenge the inference of both Dow and Lawson that if reality is open (in some sense), non-dualist, or whatever, then the theories that are used to analyse reality must also be open or non-dualist. It is neither possible nor desirable that a theory should mirror reality in such a manner. Dow and Lawson provided no argument for the proposition that ontological characteristics in reality should somehow be incorporated or reflected in a good theory. Even if we are concerned that theoretical assumptions should be as realistic as possible, this does not mean that a theory can be a mirror of reality. Theories are instruments for understanding and practical engagement: they are not, and cannot be, reflections.

Dow's (1990) critique of dualism dovetailed with Lawson's (1997, 2003) version of critical realism. But the contestable claims of the latter provide an opportunity today to look back at her dualism argument with fresh eyes. First, although there is little discussion of ontological dualism in her 1990 paper, I wish to revisit this issue, as well as of dualism in epistemology and taxonomy. But if the above argument is correct, then there is no clear reason as to why non-dualism in reality (whatever that means) would imply non-dualism in theory or taxonomy.

Ontological non-dualism? Examples from physics and biology

A number of possible kinds of non-dualism could be considered. First, because of uncertainty or whatever, *epistemological* non-dualism accepts that we can never know whether every entity is an x or a non-x. Second, *taxonomic* non-dualism would reject the project of classifying everything as an x or a non-x, accepting that some entities may be hybrids, or in transition between types, or whatever. With taxonomy, the root difficulty is not simply epistemic: it is that some things do not fit in or out of chosen categories. Third, *ethical* non-dualism would reject the idea that all acts or intentions are either wholly good or wholly evil. Fourth, there is *ontological* dualism. Dualism and non-dualism each come in at least four main types.

Several possible versions of ontological non-dualism may be considered. The most obvious case of ontological non-dualism is where things are an x and a non-x at the same time. In another case, we might reject a dichotomy between x and y because x and y were mutually constitutive or causally interactive. Is this ontological non-dualism too? Do claims that some phenomena are a hybrid mixture of x and y amount to ontological non-dualism? Ostensibly, there are different types of ontological non-dualism.

Dow (1990, p. 144) referred to quantum physics, which is replete with strong examples of ontological non-dualism. Quantum particles such as light (photons) are both waves and particles. Quantum particles can simultaneously be in two places. They can also be in multiple different states (e.g., radioactive versus decayed) at the same time, until they are observed. This gave rise to

Schrödinger's famous thought experiment of a cat that is simultaneously both alive and dead. Ontological dualism is defeated.

The bizarre world of quantum physics causes us to reflect once again on the role of mathematics in dealing with complex (or non-dualistic) phenomena. Quantum insights are often highly counter-intuitive and difficult to understand using verbal reasoning. Theories in quantum physics are developed through the use of mathematics. Quantum physicists think through their mathematical models. Through the use of probability functions and other mathematical devices, these models are capable of capturing (non-dualist) ideas such as simultaneous multiple states. Occasionally, these models throw up conjectures that are potentially observable in reality, such as the existence of Hawking radiation of the Higgs boson particle. Mathematics can represent non-dualist phenomena and relate to the real world.

There are possible ontological and taxonomic challenges to dualism from biology. Consider the herring gull and the lesser black-backed gull, both of which are common in Northern Europe (Ridley, 1985, p. 5). In that location, they are different species that do not interbreed. The herring gull focusses and moves west, looking for its cousins. Crossing the North Atlantic, we find them in Canada, then across the Bering Strait, into Siberia, and further westwards through Russia. At each step, their appearance has slightly changed. By the time we reach Northern Europe again, the same bird has become the lesser black-backed gull. By tiny increments, one species has turned into another. In Europe, the lesser black-backed gull meets its very distant herring gull relatives. But they are different species and they do not interbreed. This is an unusual case of cumulative variations within a geographically extended population. Is ontological dualism defeated again?

The example in the previous paragraph is a case of what is called a *ring species* (Mayr, 1942). There are a few other claimed examples, including a warbler, a salamander and spurge plants. Some of these examples are disputed. Though rare, ring species spatially illustrate what might happen in time when new species are formed. One species turns into another.

This is primarily a challenge to taxonomic rather than ontological dualism. In these cases, there is no warrant to classify everything as an x or a non-x because there is no non-arbitrary place to draw a line of separation. Taxonomic dualism is challenged by the evolutionary origin of different species. Species x evolved into a non-x. How did an x parent give birth to a non-x offspring? When did this occur? Attempts to classify organisms as species x or non-x are confounded by the problem that the criteria for x or non-x seem arbitrary. We cannot carve reality at the joints because there are no obvious joints to carve, or there is a large number of tiny undistinguished joints, making the choice arbitrary. These ontological circumstances confound taxonomy. But unlike quantum particles in physics, the ontology here is not dualist. The bird is either a Siberian gull or not a Siberian gull. The middle is excluded.

Consider another illustration from biology. A species is standardly defined as a population of organisms that can reproduce with one another and that are reproductively isolated from other populations (Mayr, 1942). But the problem of identifying and defining species has not been fully resolved (de Queiroz, 2005). Focussing on reproduction is complicated by the fact that living things reproduce in a variety of different ways, and a species definition that works for one set of organisms can be problematic for others. There are important cases where members of different species can hybridise in special environments and produce fertile offspring. More and more examples of hybridisation have been uncovered by DNA analysis, particularly but not exclusively among plants. In practice, multiple definitions of species and ways of demarcating them are still prevalent in biology. A firm consensus is lacking.

Some ways of demarcating species involve statistical assessments of similarity, particularly regarding DNA. Note once more the use of mathematics in some attempts to help gain understanding of a complex and open reality. In sum, for any one organism, or group of organisms, the identification of its species can be taxonomically or epistemologically problematic.

Compare these examples from biology with those from quantum physics. Quantum physics provides the strongest challenges to ontological dualism. We presume that a cat is either dead or alive – it cannot be both. Quantum physics challenges that duality, not because of the fuzzy boundary between life and death, but for more fundamental ontological reasons.

By contrast, the examples from biology given above are of a different nature. Take the examples of ring species. In Northern Europe, we find both herring gulls and the lesser black-backed gull. In Siberia, we find something in between the two. Ring species are on a continuum. Moving around the ring, we find individuals combining different degrees of x and y. There are many other populations that vary in time or space from mostly-x to mostly-y individuals, not necessarily with a time and place where they co-exist.

Crucially, variation along a spectrum, from x to y, is different from not being x or non-x, or not being y or non-y. Every individual in the global population (such as of herring gulls and lesser black-backed gulls) combines amounts of x and y. On our journey around the globe, everything we observe is either (x and/or y) or not (x and/or y). (Of course, being not (x and/or y) is equivalent to being not-x and non-y.) In these instances, ontological dualism is re-instated. Extended ontological gradations create a massive taxonomic problem. But the ontological reality in these cases are continua of co-existing characteristics. Ontologically, it is an issue of mixing x and y, not of simultaneously being x and non-x. Although it has ontological foundations, the challenge to dualism from biology is largely taxonomic rather than ontological.

Ontological non-dualism? Examples from the social sciences

The ontological discussion of examples from biology in the preceding section provides a warning about the possible misidentification of ontological non-dualism. This section shows that this problem is highly relevant in the social sciences.

For example, following Ronald Coase (1937), Oliver Williamson (1975) originally proposed a dichotomy between markets and firms (or 'hierarchies'). Then, Williamson (1985, p. 83) became 'persuaded that transactions in the middle range are much more common'. For Williamson (1991, p. 271), hierarchies (or firms) became 'a continuation of market relations by other means'. Instead of the firm-market dichotomy, he adopted a firm-market continuum. Some authors have criticised the conceptual underpinnings of this argument, but that is beyond the point (Hodgson, 2002, 2015; Gindis, 2009, 2016). The continuum argument has given rise to a literature on firm-market 'hybrids' (Ménard, 1996, 2004, 2022).

If the arguments by Williamson and others were valid, would this be a challenge to dualism? The case is redolent of the problem of identifying species in biology. If every organisational form can mix elements of market and hierarchy, then that is not a challenge to ontological dualism. Every form is *either* a hierarchy and/or market, or *not* a hierarchy and/or market. The challenge is not ontological but taxonomic. Where on the continuum do markets end and firms begin? Or is every form a firm-market hybrid?

There are other possible hybrids in the social world. Law can be understood as a hybrid combination of custom and statute. It has been argued similarly that money is sustained by both spontaneous interaction and the state (Hodgson, 2015). The *impurity principle* takes this hybridity further, by arguing that every socio-economic system must rely on at least one structurally dissimilar subsystem to function. Here, hybridity is more than accidental. It is essential for the system to cope with change and survive (Hodgson, 1984, 1988, 2015). But hybridity, whether incidental or necessary for survival, is not necessarily a challenge to ontological, taxonomic or epistemic dualism. A (necessary) mixture between x and y does not negate everything being an x or a non-x. It does not necessarily raise epistemic or taxonomic problems either.

As noted above, Dow (1990, p. 155) cited my observation of causal interaction between individuals and institutions. The fact that x and y interact is not a challenge to ontological dualism. It does not overturn the claim that everything is either x or non-x (or y or non-y). It is not necessarily a threat to taxonomic dualism either. Individuals and institutions interact, but they are different things (Archer, 1995). Epistemic dualism is also unscathed. Despite their interaction, it is possible to ascertain the difference between individuals and institutions. Hence, Dow was wrong to use my claim of causal interaction as an example to undermine dualism.

A stronger claim is that individuals and institutions are mutually constitutive (Hodgson, 1988, 2004). In other words, each plays a necessary part in helping to form and constitute the other. Human individuals evolve in social units and each such individual is formed through structured interactions with others. We learn a language and other vital social rules. These make up institutions. In turn, institutions themselves evolve partly through the interactions of individuals. But although this mutual constitution of different entities is a stronger claim than causal interaction, it does not offer a stronger challenge to dualism. Individuals and institutions are still ontologically different. It is not a challenge to taxonomic or epistemic dualism either.

There is an approach in social theory and the philosophy of the mind that is known as the dual aspect theory. It was deployed in attempts to deal with the mind-body problem. In this context, both Herbert Spencer and Thomas Henry Huxley adopted dual aspect formulations, seeing the physical and mental phenomena as different manifestations of the same underling substance (Hodgson, 2004, p. 228). This was an attempt to overturn the mind-matter dualism of René Descartes and others. But note that these dual aspect formulations did not overturn ontological dualism in general terms. Descartes claimed that everything was matter or not matter (and mind was not matter). In contrast, dual aspects theorists claimed that all phenomena were manifestations of the same underlying stuff. Although everything is made up of this stuff, each particular entity is still an x or a non-x.

The dual aspect theory also appears in attempts to deal with the problem of social structure and individual agency in social theory. For example, the sociologist Charles Horton Cooley saw society and the individual as different aspects of the same thing (Hodgson, 2004, pp. 227–8). Much later, the sociologist Anthony Giddens (1984) developed his structuration theory and the notion of 'duality of structure'. Giddens regarded agent and structure as a duality where both human subjects and social institutions are jointly constituted in and through recurrent practices, and where no element has ontological or analytical priority over the other. Structure and agency are mutually and symmetrically constitutive of each other. As Ian Craib (1992, pp. 3–4) put it in his commentary on Giddens, structure and agency are not treated as 'separate and opposing things in the world or as mutually exclusive ways of thinking about the world' but as 'simply two sides of the same coin'. But for reasons given above, this version of the dual aspect theory is not a challenge to ontological dualism. The fact that f and g are different aspects of x does not overturn the claim that everything is an x or a non-x.

The dual aspect treatment of agency and structure is challenged by a stream of thinkers, including Auguste Comte, Karl Marx, George Henry Lewes, Thorstein Veblen and Émile Durkheim, plus the modern critical realists Margaret Archer and Roy Bhaskar. They have all stressed that we are born into a world of institutions that are not of our making. Hence, there is a temporal asymmetry: although structures depend for their existence on *groups* of individuals, for each *single* individual, some structures precede agency. Although people can change and be changed by social structures, they do not choose or create the structures and institutions into which they are born. Agents and structures are not different *aspects* of the same things or processes but *different entities* (Archer, 1995; Hodgson, 2004, pp. 34–6, 180–1).

In ontological terms, the insistence that 'structure and agency are different things' is no more dualistic than dual aspect claim that they are different sides of the same coin. Humans and elephants are different species, but they are both classed as members of the mammal clade. Factories and houses have different natures and purposes, but they are all buildings. Houses used for manufacturing purposes, as well as a dwelling, present a problem of classification, as with other hybrids; however, that problem is taxonomic. Ontologically, everything is still either a house or a non-house, or either a factory or a non-factory, or either a house-factory or not a house-factory. Ontological dualism survives.

Drawing the threads together, we must conclude that outside quantum physics it is difficult to find convincing cases of ontological non-dualism. The ontological non-dualism declared by quantum physics is a major source of our puzzlement. We are perplexed by the biological and social worlds too, but not for the same ontological reasons. In these cases, our understanding is baffled by change, variation, fuzzy boundaries and complexity, not because biological or social entities defy the law of the excluded middle.

The limitation of ontological non-dualism to the quantum level has a further consequence. If social *ontology* is dualistic, then what does that say for *theories* in the social sciences? If we follow Dow and Lawson and presume some kind of necessary correspondence between ontology and theory, then we might make a case that theory in the social sciences should be dualistic as well. Dow's critique of mainstream economics for being dualistic then collapses, because coherent non-mainstream theory must also be dualistic. The route I suggest is to abandon the idea of a necessary correspondence between theory and reality, and to treat theories as knowledge-driven instruments instead. Epistemic or taxonomic non-dualism may then survive, in some instances and manifestations.

In the social sciences, we are confronted with varied, complex and evolving phenomena that often defy simple categorisations. Events are often uncertain, and prediction is beset by the lack of calculable probabilities (Knight, 1921; Keynes, 1936). But the challenge to dualism here is not ontological, but epistemic or taxonomic. It is to the question of taxonomic dualism that we now turn.

A defence of fuzzy taxonomic dualism

Dow (1990, p. 144) argued that a problem with dualism was its assumed 'fixity of meaning of categories'. But while making this warning, Dow did not argue that definitions or categorisations should be entirely abandoned. After all, she accepted that *dualism* was itself a category. Dualism cannot be challenged without a dualist definition of dualism itself. Theoretical approaches must be dualist or non-dualist. Some dualist categorisations must be admitted. Non-dualism requires dualism.

Further difficulties would emerge with a universal rejection of all 'fixity of meaning of categories'. Any universal rule to reject all fixity of meaning would be self-contradictory. It would undermine the universality of that rule. To make sense of anything, some meanings must be fixed, at least for a while. Science is a social process, involving communication of meaning. The fluidity of meanings of words in a language creates difficulties of communication and mutual understanding. Some fixity is required to make adjustment possible.

On the other hand, language and categories evolve, in part to deal with a changing world, in part to rectify conflict or inconsistency and in part to adopt different connotations. Words are borrowed from different contexts or languages. They are sometimes mutated or combined.

Terminological flexibility is inevitable and to some degree necessary, to deal with changing understandings or the changing nature of the world. But at the same time, flexibility can thwart commination and the establishment of shared understanding. Some degree of fixity and flexibility is required. Railing against 'fixity of meaning' overlooks that some fixity is always needed, even in a highly complex and changing world.

Taxonomy is tricky when entities change through time, have fuzzy boundaries, or exhibit wide or complex variation. But some fixity among definitions is essential for analysis and communication. In a 1904 essay, Max Weber (1949, p. 107) argued that conceptual precision was required not despite but because of the changing, tangled and complex nature of socio-economic reality: 'it is *because* the content of historical concepts is necessarily subject to change that they must be formulated precisely and clearly on all occasions'. Real-world muddle is no excuse for a muddled conceptual model. Clear, fixed concepts are necessary to deal with even a messy and changing reality. As Weber (1949, pp. 106–7) argued, the messiness or changeability of reality makes conceptual precision all the more vital. To understand variety or change, we need clear reference points. It is a frequent misconception that a changing or muddled reality must be tackled with changing or muddled concepts.

To suggest that change and complexity disallow 'fixed definitions' may betray a misunderstanding of the nature and purpose of taxonomic definitions. Their primary purpose is to ensure that a community of scientific investigators are talking about the same type of phenomena. This does not mean that they agree on questions of analysis or explanation. It means instead that they are (more or less) engaged with the shared project of understanding a defined set of phenomena. If they are not talking about the same type of thing, then they have little chance of making any progress with the understanding of the phenomena involved. For this reason, taxonomic definitions must be parsimonious, and for a while, fixed. Definitions may be modified later, after understanding improves or when new empirical cases have to be considered (Hodgson, 2019a).

For example, there has been an ongoing debate on the nature or definition of heterodox economics, with no consensus yet appearing (Hodgson, 2019b, ch. 2). In an attempt to deal with the problem, Andrew Mearman (2012) cited Dow's (1990) article. He argued that the attempt to define heterodox economics should be abandoned. For Mearman (2012, p. 407), 'strict, fixed, simple definitions' are unacceptable because they 'suffer from problems of dualism'. Mearman (2012, pp. 408, 414) claimed that attempted definitions of heterodox economics (HE) 'display an unwarranted dualism'. He continued:

> They often create unjustifiably strict distinctions between the categories . . . dualist definitions also tend to become unnecessarily and unjustifiably fixed, mutually exclusive and exhaustive. . . . The main evidence of this problem is the extent of anomalies created by current definitions of HE. In turn, these anomalies result from the simplicity of many definitions of HE, a simplicity which underplays the complexity of HE. . . . Overall, we can see that there are no grounds for treating HE as a fixed object and therefore giving it a fixed definition.

There are several major problems with this argument. First, let us accept with Mearman the possibility that the law of the excluded middle does not apply, and that there are types of economics that do not fit into any reasonable categorisation of orthodox or heterodox: their status is undecided, uncertain or somehow intermediate. This would be an epistemic limitation and a case of epistemic non-dualism. Alongside Mearman, let us also emphasise that both orthodoxy and heterodoxy are in constant development and flux. In other words, they are not fixed objects.

Given these reasonable assumptions, Mearman is still unconvincing. Evidence of 'the extent of anomalies created by current definitions of HE' does not make Mearman's case against definitions as such. It calls for renewed efforts to find a suitable definition. Biologists did not cease to talk about species when it was realised that there was no clear and robust rule that always served to demarcate one species from another. They accepted some fuzzy boundaries and worked both within and around them.

Mearman's claim that 'these anomalies result from the simplicity of many definitions of HE' is also unpersuasive. Simple definitions – such as that of a mammal as an animal that suckles its young – do not necessarily create anomalies, even when the reality is complex and evolving. Further, making definitions more complex could easily create additional anomalies, because of the greater number of criteria involved. Again, there is no necessarily close correspondence between concepts and reality on this issue. Variation, change and complexity in reality does not imply that all concepts and theories have to be equally changeable or complex.

One interpretation of Dow's argument would be that labels or classifications can be acceptable, as long as they are capable of revision, and as long as unwarranted exclusions of undecided, uncertain or hybrid cases are avoided. But accepting that non-dualism itself was a dualistic category, Dow realised that to be effective, any critique of dualism had to be limited rather than universal.

My defence of taxonomic dualism accepts that there are often unclear or apparently arbitrary boundaries. Reality does not always show us sharply where to carve at the joints. The complexity and changeability of the world often thwarts epistemic dualism. But taxonomy requires that we must move forward and identify what we are talking about, and what we are not. Communication must begin among analysts with a common understanding of the type of phenomena under investigation. Shared understanding requires some rough agreement on taxonomic definitions, which are provisionally fixed, maybe to be revised later.

Some conceptual fuzziness is accepted, because boundaries are often changing, arbitrary or difficult to discern. Fuzziness offers some wiggle room in these circumstances. It is tolerated, even embraced. It is not a pretext for protest or exit, or for downing analytical tools. For social scientists to analyse the firm, they do not have to agree upon a sharp boundary between a firm and a non-firm. But they do have to have a rough agreement on what they mean by a firm. Notably, in the 'theory of the firm' in economics, there is not yet any agreement on what economists mean by a firm (Hodgson, 2019a). A taxonomic definition (even if fuzzy) is needed to make progress.

Concluding remarks

Taking stock of the argument, it is important to distinguish between ontological, epistemic and taxonomic (non-) dualism. Ontological non-dualism is a characteristic of the quantum level, but it does not seem to extend anywhere else. It is argued above that cases of continuous variation, hybridity or interaction do not entail ontological non-dualism.

On the other hand, epistemic non-dualism is often wise, as Dow (1990) contended. Complexity and uncertainty mean that we cannot often have enough surety that something is either x or non-x. We should be always aware that some phenomena resist categorisation and ongoing change (especially in open systems, as defined by Bertalanffy (1950) and other systems theorists) means that entities can change form and substance. Epistemically, the uncertain or undetermined middle cannot always be excluded.

While epistemic non-dualism makes taxonomy difficult, it is argued here that the (essential dualist) task of taxonomy cannot be abandoned. It is also a mistake to rail against 'fixed categories' because some fixity is required to communicate meaning. But it must be accepted that labels and meanings are provisional, and they can be changed if required. A (dualist) case for fuzzy taxonomic definitions is made here on these grounds.

With hindsight and with the benefit of later developments in the philosophy of economics, Dow's argument requires some modification, but it retains important insight and value. I have noted here that Dow's (1990) paper does not prefigure the argument by Lawson (1997, 2003) that mathematics is of highly limited use in cases of openness, complexity or uncertainty. Indeed, ontological non-dualism at the quantum level cannot be adequately understood without the use of mathematics. Some problems of categorisation require statistical tools. Dow's (1990) argument does not support Lawson's conclusions concerning the use of mathematics.

But Dow (1990, pp. 146–7) prefigured Lawson's (2003, p. 22) injunction that a good theory must in some way 'correspond' or 'fit' with reality. There is no clear argument in favour of this principle. Indeed, it would be relatively easy to make a case that it is impossible to achieve, at least in the social sciences. A theory can never reflect the teeming, restless complexity of social reality. Instead, it is better to view theories as instruments for understanding and engaging in practice with the real world.

Dow's (1990) paper is a valiant attempt to help identify what is wrong at the core with mainstream economics. It remains pertinent and stimulating. Dow alleged that mainstream theory is dualist. My argument in the present paper suggests that, at best, this allegation is too blunt. Some dualist formulations are unavoidable, as Dow briefly admitted in her paper. We can go further, by examining different meanings and contexts for dualism and non-dualism. But Dow should be given full credit for raising the issue in the first place.

Notes

1 After 30 years have passed, I think that I can now reveal that I was one of the anonymous referees of her 1990 essay for the *Cambridge Journal of Economics*.
2 In addition, following Bhaskar (1975), Lawson (1997, pp. 16–17) adopted an unconventional meaning of *deductivism*, also based on event-level regularities, rather than on the use of axioms and logical deductions (Hodgson, 2019b, pp. 57–58).

References

Archer, Margaret S. (1995) *Realist Social Theory: The Morphogenetic Approach* (Cambridge: Cambridge University Press). https://doi.org/10.1017/CBO9780511557675

Bertalanffy, Ludwig (1950) 'The Theory of Open Systems in Physics and Biology', *Science*, 111, pp. 23–9.

Bhaskar, Roy (1975) *A Realist Theory of Science* (Leeds: Leeds Books).

Chick, Victoria and Dow, Sheila C. (2005) 'The Meaning of Open Systems', *Journal of Economic Methodology*, 13(3), September, pp. 363–81. https://doi.org/10.1080/13501780500223585

Coase, Ronald H. (1937) 'The Nature of the Firm', *Economica*, 4, New Series, November, pp. 386–405. https://doi.org/10.1111/j.1468-0335.1937.tb00002.x

Craib, Ian (1992) Anthony Giddens (London: Routledge).

de Queiroz, Kevin (2005) 'Ernst Mayr and the Modern Concept of Species', *Proceedings of the National Academy of Sciences*, 102 (supplement), May 3, p. 6600. https://doi.org/10.1073/pnas.0502030102

Dewey, John (1910) 'The Short-Cut to Realism Examined', *Journal of Philosophy, Psychology and. Scientific Methods*, 7(20), 29 September, pp. 553–7.

Dewey, John (1938) *Logic: The Theory of Enquiry* (New York: Holt).

Dewey, John and Spaulding, Edward G. (1911) 'Joint Discussion with Articles of Agreement and Disagreement', *Journal of Philosophy, Psychology and Scientific Methods*, 8(21), October 12, pp. 574–9.

Dow, Sheila C. (1985) *Macroeconomic Thought: A Methodological Approach* (Oxford: Basil Blackwell). https://doi.org/10.1017/S0266267100000833

Dow, Sheila C. (1990) 'Beyond Dualism', *Cambridge Journal of Economics*, 14(2), June, pp. 143–57. https://doi.org/10.1093/oxfordjournals.cje.a035123

Dow, Sheila C. (1999) 'Post Keynesianism and Critical Realism: What is the Connection?', *Journal of Post Keynesian Economics*, 22(1), Fall, pp. 15–33. https://doi.org/10.1080/01603477.1999.11490225

Dow, Sheila C. (2002) *Economic Methodology: An Inquiry* (Oxford: Oxford University Press).

Fleetwood, Steve (2017) 'The Critical Realist Conception of Open and Closed Systems', *Journal of Economic Methodology*, 24(1), March, pp. 41–68. https://doi.org/10.1080/1350178X.2016.1218532

Giddens, Anthony (1984) *The Constitution of Society: Outline of the Theory of Structuration* (Cambridge: Polity Press).

Gindis, David (2009) 'From Fictions and Aggregates to Real Entities in the Theory of the Firm', *Journal of Institutional Economics*, 5(1), April, pp. 25–46. https://doi.org/10.1017/S1744137408001203

Gindis, David (2016) 'Legal Personhood and the Firm: Avoiding Anthropomorphism and Equivocation', *Journal of Institutional Economics*, 12(3), September, pp. 499–513. doi:10.1017/S1744137415000235

Hodgson, Geoffrey M. (1984) *The Democratic Economy: A New Look at Planning, Markets and Power* (Harmondsworth: Penguin).

Hodgson, Geoffrey M. (1988) *Economics and Institutions: A Manifesto for a Modern Institutional Economics* (Cambridge and Philadelphia: Polity Press and University of Pennsylvania Press).

Hodgson, Geoffrey M. (2002) 'The Legal Nature of the Firm and the Myth of the Firm-Market Hybrid', *International Journal of the Economics of Business*, 9(1), February, pp. 37–60. https://doi.org/10.1080/13571510110102967

Hodgson, Geoffrey M. (2004) *The Evolution of Institutional Economics: Agency, Structure and Darwinism in American Institutionalism* (London and New York: Routledge).

Hodgson, Geoffrey M. (2015) *Conceptualizing Capitalism: Institutions, Evolution, Future* (Chicago, IL: University of Chicago Press).

Hodgson, Geoffrey M. (2019a) 'Taxonomic Definitions in Social Science, with Firms, Markets and Institutions as Case Studies', *Journal of Institutional Economics*, 15(2), April, pp. 207–33. https://doi.org/10.1017/S1744137418000334

Hodgson, Geoffrey M. (2019b) *Is There a Future for Heterodox Economics? Institutions, Ideology and a Scientific Community* (Cheltenham UK and Northampton MA: Edward Elgar). https://doi.org/10.4337/9781789901597

Keynes, John Maynard (1936) *The General Theory of Employment, Interest and Money* (London: Macmillan).

Knight, Frank H. (1921) *Risk, Uncertainty and Profit* (New York: Houghton Mifflin).

Kuhn, Thomas S. (1962) *The Structure of Scientific Revolutions* (Chicago, IL: University of Chicago Press).

Lawson, Tony (1997) *Economics and Reality* (London and New York: Routledge).

Lawson, Tony (2003) *Reorienting Economics* (London and New York: Routledge).

Mäki, Uskali (1992) 'On the Method of Isolation in Economics', *Poznan Studies in the Philosophy of the Sciences and the Humanities*, 26, pp. 319–54.

Mäki, Uskali (1994) 'Isolation, Idealization and Truth in Economics', *Poznan Studies in the Philosophy of the Sciences and the Humanities*, 38, pp. 147–68.

Mäki, Uskali (ed.) (2001) *The Economic World View: Studies in the Ontology of Economics* (Cambridge: Cambridge University Press).

Mayr, Ernst (1942) *Systematics and the Origin of Species* (New York: Columbia University Press).

Mearman, Andrew (2006) 'Critical Realism in Economics and Open-Systems Ontology: A Critique', *Review of Social Economy*, 64(1), March, pp. 47–75. https://doi.org/10.1080/00346760500529955

Mearman, Andrew (2012) '"Heterodox Economics" and the Problems of Classification', *Journal of Economic Methodology*, 19(4), December, pp. 407–424. https://doi.org/10.1080/1350178X.2012.742201

Ménard, Claude (1996) 'On Clusters, Hybrids, and Other Strange Forms: The Case of the French Poultry Industry', *Journal of Institutional and Theoretical Economics*, 152(1), March, pp. 154–83.

Ménard, Claude (2004) 'The Economics of Hybrid Organizations', *Journal of Institutional and Theoretical Economics*, 160(3), September, pp. 345–76. https://doi.org/10.1628/0932456041960605

Ménard, Claude (2022) 'Hybrids: Where Are We?', *Journal of Institutional Economics*, 18(2), April, forthcoming. https://doi.org/10.1017/S1744137421000230

Pratten, Stephen (2007) 'Realism, Closed Systems and Abstraction', *Journal of Economic Methodology*, 14(4), December, pp. 473–497. https://doi.org/10.1080/13501780701718748

Ridley, Mark (1985) *The Problems of Evolution* (Oxford: Oxford University Press).

Sugden, Robert (2000) 'Credible Worlds: The Status of Theoretical Models in Economics', *Journal of Economic Methodology*, 7(1), March, pp. 1–31.

Weber, Max (1949) *Max Weber on the Methodology of the Social Sciences* (Glencoe, IL: Free Press).

Whitehead, Alfred N. (1929) *Process and Reality: An Essay in Cosmology* (Cambridge: Cambridge University Press).

Whitehead, Alfred N. (1938) *Modes of Thought* (Cambridge: Cambridge University Press).

Williamson, Oliver E. (1975) *Markets and Hierarchies: Analysis and Anti-Trust Implications: A Study. in the Economics of Internal Organization* (New York: Free Press).

Williamson, Oliver E. (1985) *The Economic Institutions of Capitalism: Firms, Markets, Relational Contracting* (London: Macmillan).

Williamson, Oliver E. (1991) 'Comparative Economic Organization: The Analysis of Discrete Structural Alternatives', *Administrative Science Quarterly*, 36(2), pp. 269–96.

5 Naturalism and the new challenge to Sheila Dow's schools-of-thought approach to economics[1]

John Hart

Introduction

Many economic methodologists and philosophers have remarked on the impact of positivism on economics. Boland (1991) described its influence as virtually all-pervasive. Kincaid (1998, p. 559) claimed that positivist ideas 'strongly influenced' the practice of economics. In the 1970s, when positivism came under sustained attack from Kuhn, Lakatos and Feyerabend, heterodox economists believed this spelt the end of positivism and its support for orthodox economics. It was in this atmosphere of the collapse of positivism that Dow (1985) first developed her pluralist schools-of-thought approach to economics.

Hands (2001) pointed out that, in the period following the demise of positivism, a number of competing contenders emerged concerning 'the structure and character of scientific knowledge . . . [so that no] clear replacement' for positivism had (as yet) been found (pp. 4–5). Consequently, in light of this 'philosophically modest, intellectual environment' (p. 327), a 'wide array of broadly methodological topics' was now free to bloom (p. 394).

Against this background, Dow (2021, pp. 49–50) argues that, if there is no 'demonstrably best approach to science' or 'best economic methodology', methodological pluralism should be expected to prevail in economics. That is, alternative (heterodox) approaches, or schools of economic thought, might be expected to 'legitimately coexist' with that of orthodox economics. However, she points out, orthodoxy still tends to dominate economics 'with no acknowledgement of alternatives', particularly with regard to economics education. This is because economics is defined by its method (an 'unexamined acceptance' of 'big-M' Methodology) so that 'anything outside orthodoxy can be classified as not economics'.

If this method is defined by positivism, and if there still has been no clear replacement for positivism since Hands's survey in 2001, then it appears puzzling as to why the news (that there is still no 'best economic methodology') has not yet reached economists continuing to practice 'big-M' Methodology. This is especially the case given that (orthodox) economists are more methodologically aware than earlier and that nowadays some philosophers of science

DOI: 10.4324/9781003142324-6

are to be found in economics departments. The reason orthodoxy still tends to dominate in economics, I suggest, is that gradually, since the 1960s, post-Quinean naturalism has been replacing the defunct positivist view of the scientific method with a scientific approach to philosophy. This has resulted in 'a demonstrably best approach' not to science, but rather to *economic* (and social) science. As the influence of positivism has been declining, 'scientific naturalist' views[2] have been increasingly encouraging the self-image of orthodox economics as a *science* – one that displays the same sort of objectivity as that associated with the natural sciences. While, as Dow rightly says, economics is defined by its method, 'the best economic methodology' today is supported for very different, naturalistic, reasons.[3] If positivism posed the old challenge to Dow's schools-of-thought approach to economics, naturalism poses the new.

In addition to the reasons discussed by Dow (2011, pp. 1162–4) for the dominance of mainstream economics, I add the influence of naturalism. This has taken the place of positivism as the new, increasingly dominant, force in economics and economic methodology. It is amongst the factors that have influenced the empirical turn in economics. In the 1960s and 1970s, according to Backhouse and Cherrier (2017), the abstract pure theory (e.g., the general equilibrium theory, core micro and macro) held the highest status in academic economics. However, by the 1990s, it was applied empirical work that attracted the most esteem. For example, winners of the AEA's Clark Medal now conducted empirical rather than theoretical work. Already in 1993, they note, the notable rise of empirical economics over the past decade drew praise in the citations for the medal. Naturalism's impact has been even greater in economic methodology (e.g., Reiss (2013), Ross (2014)).[4] Boumans (2013) responded to its influence as reflected in Davis and Hands (2011): if the discussion of economics as a science is best done *outside* economic methodology, 'then this volume is ostracizing economic methodology'. Vromen (2021, pp. 27–8) likewise suggests that the fundamental disagreement in today's philosophy of economics relates to naturalists who challenge philosophy's traditional aims, for example, that of 'confronting economists with ideas and insights from philosophy'. He has called for an 'open' and 'public' discussion about the 'pervasive disagreement in current philosophy of economics', namely as to what the philosophy of economics 'is all about, what it should be and what it should do'.

Today, the view that there is no longer justification for a normative economic methodology seems widespread: only a descriptive methodology is appropriate. However, this is a naturalistic view, stemming from its rejection of the positivist attempt to formulate *a priori* general methodological rules that apply normatively to all science, both natural and social. Naturalists argue that we must look instead to *descriptions* of scientific practice to discover how scientific knowledge progresses. However, since scientific naturalists adopt a restrictive view of science, one that limits the concept of science to the natural sciences, they arrive at the *normative* conclusion that the social sciences must follow the approach of the natural sciences. In this way, naturalists have re-established 'the best economic methodology', while denying there is a single best methodology applicable to all science. This helps explain why orthodoxy still tends to dominate in economics despite the collapse of positivism.

Following the demise of positivism, the sociology of scientific knowledge, neo-pragmatism and postmodernism emerged in the 1970s and 1980s and seemed to challenge the status of science and the philosophy of science. These approaches tended to attack the view that science was epistemically privileged compared with other forms of inquiry. At the same time, developments within the philosophy of science had already led to the move away from positivism towards naturalism. Quine (1969), in particular, heralded the 'return' (Kitcher 1992) of a naturalistic approach to the philosophy of science, specifically 'naturalism in its 20th century American incarnation' (Roth 2013, p. 646). The result is that 'philosophical naturalism' has been the 'reigning creed' of analytic philosophy 'for much of the 20th century' (Kim 2003, p. 84).

Especially in the United States, 'the naturalistic conception of philosophy has achieved the status of orthodoxy' (Glock 2008, p. 87); indeed, Keil (2008, p. 254) argues that it 'has become the most forceful meta-philosophical trend of the twentieth century'. From at least the 1980s onwards, the revival of naturalism has not been confined to philosophy. It has increasingly swept aside the challenges posed to the authority of science by sociological and rhetorical studies to become 'the dominant approach among practicing social scientists' (Kincaid 1998, p. 559).

As Kincaid's claim implies, naturalism poses challenges to orthodox economics. However, these challenges are much greater for Dow's pluralist schools-of-thought approach. This is because, besides the mainstream school, the neo-Austrian, Post-Keynesian, and Marxian schools draw more especially on philosophical approaches opposed to naturalism, namely the interpretive and critical traditions in the philosophy of social science.

This chapter is structured as follows: the first section explains the meaning of the term 'scientific naturalism' to which I referred earlier and ends with some observations about naturalism. According to Rosenberg (2016), underlying the central dispute about the correct approach to adopt in studying the social world, 'naturalism versus interpretation' (p. 11), are 'very fundamental issues of philosophy, claims about epistemology, metaphysics, and ethics' (p. 28). The second section uses an example (fortunately supplied by Rosenberg from economics) to introduce economists to this central dispute. 'Fortunately' because 'scholars affiliated with various social science departments' still engage in the philosophy of social science, this is not the case in economics (Mäki 2021, p. 8). The third section builds on this introduction to interpretivism, discussing it more broadly. It then shows how interpretivist influences underlie much of Dow's Post-Keynesian and neo-Austrian schools. The fourth section draws on Braybrooke (1998) to underline how both interpretive and critical social theory are fundamental to Dow's Marxian school.

Scientific naturalism

Since post-Quinean naturalism is a term with a plethora of diverse meanings, brief explanations almost inevitably suffer from vagueness. Fortunately, De Caro and Macarthur (2004) have helped remedy this problem by distinguishing a particular *type* of naturalism, scientific naturalism, which they claim represents 'the current orthodoxy, at least within Anglo-American philosophy' (p. 1). They accurately single out two key characteristic themes of this type (De Caro and Macarthur 2004, 2010; Macarthur 2010).

The first theme concerns the claim that science is the *only* genuine guide for answering ontological questions, that is, what exists in reality. Naturalists are monists for whom nature is the only kind of reality. For scientific naturalists, nature is what natural science, particularly physics, tells us it is. Many adopt physicalism. Mäki (1998, p. 406) explains that physicalist scientific realism 'excludes realism about mental entities and entities dependent on the mental, such as persons, material artifacts, and social institutions construed in a dualist or non-eliminativist physicalist fashion'.[5] Today, the naturalist orthodoxy is a non-reductive (and non-eliminativist) physicalism whereby mental states are said to supervene on physical states, that is, mental states are determined by physical states but are not reducible to them. In other words, although the world might seem to contain 'items of a biological, or psychological, or moral, or social nature . . . [physicalists] insist nevertheless that at the end of the day such items are either physical or supervene on the physical' (Stoljar 2017, p. 1). De Caro and Macarthur (2004, p. 4) contend that the claim that natural science provides the *only* true picture of nature makes this aspect of scientific naturalism a form of scientism. In the past, scientism was viewed as a pejorative term, whereas scientific naturalists today explicitly defend a scientistic perspective (Ladyman and Ross 2007).

The second theme concerns the claim that science is also the *only* genuine guide to answering methodological questions, that is, how we can gain knowledge of reality. Nearly all naturalists deny philosophy the role of an authority that stands before, and can judge, science. Many also deny it a foundational role regarding scientific inquiry. Scientific naturalism goes one step further and denies autonomy to philosophy as in any way separate from science (De Caro and Macarthur 2004, p. 6). In Quine's (1969, p. 126) well-known phrase, 'philosophy is continuous with science', that is, it is entirely encompassed by science. Likewise, Kincaid and Ross (2009, p. v) 'take very seriously the naturalistic insistence that philosophy of science is continuous with science itself'.

It seems it is this orthodoxy of scientific naturalism that Root (1998) has in mind. In a review of Kincaid (1996), he explains that, although today's philosophers of science rest content with describing scientific practice in the natural sciences, 'the story is different with the social sciences; here philosophers continue to say what ought to be done and to prescribe as well as describe scientific practice' (p. 673).[6] Kincaid (1996), he says, is 'prescriptively rich' in the view that the methods of the social sciences ought to be those of the natural sciences.[7] It is in this way that scientific naturalists arrive at their normative conclusion regarding 'the best economic methodology'.

Besides the orthodoxy of scientific naturalism, there are many other varieties and aspects of naturalism. We look at three: the implications of naturalism as a monist doctrine; naturalism from the viewpoint of an extremely broad conception of science; and finally, Quine's reforms of empiricism and post-Quinean reactions to it.

Traditionally, philosophers have supported dualism; here, the view is that there are two kinds of reality. By contrast, naturalism is a monist doctrine, one that entertains a unitary conception of the world, one kind of reality. Naturalists are very fond of presenting themselves as opposed to supernaturalism: 'reality is exhausted by nature, containing nothing "supernatural"' (Papineau 2016, p. 1). By doing so, as Keil (2008, p. 255) observes, they insinuate that any kind of philosophy opposed to naturalism must be obscurantist or involve superstition. However, where non-natural entities are viewed as problematic (i.e., in need of being recast in terms of naturalistic research programs such as behavioral economics), then, Keil insists, naturalism does not compete with the supernatural 'but rather with well-established philosophical theories' (p. 255).

For naturalists, the human-social realm is an example of a problematic entity, in need of naturalization. In the *Methodenstreit*, dualists argued that a dichotomy existed between the reality of the natural world and the social realm. Today, although the notion of a dichotomy is widely rejected, some philosophers continue to argue (with difficulty) for a distinction between the two (Risjord 2016, p. 5). As it stands, the issue remains unresolved: 'is society "natural" or is it "conventional", a historical product of human activities which vary across time and space?' (Manicas 1998, p. 847). Similarly, one might ask whether an economic system, for example the market system, is (spontaneously) natural or conventional (see Mittermaier 2020). According to Andler (2015, pp. 331–2), the naturalistic research program in the social sciences draws on cognitive science and the biological (and cultural) theory of evolution, and it is aimed at 'naturalizing the social sphere'.

Naturalists, in general, argue that it is to science that we must look for answering methodological questions about how to gain knowledge of reality. This appears to place an onus on naturalists to define science. However, it is widely accepted that the collapse of positivist demarcation criteria for science preempts any such attempt. Despite this, as we have seen, scientific naturalists have gone ahead to say that what they mean by science is natural science. Roth (2006, p. 696) criticizes such a move as scientistic. He argues that many naturalists, attempting to explain naturalism, fear that unless they somehow distinguish science in some way, their account will fail to mark off naturalism from alternative approaches. In doing so, he argues, they make a fundamental mistake since naturalism denies 'that one can in principle draw some line between what counts or does not count as science' (p. 696). However, the result of accepting Roth's stance is that the term 'science' has no clear meaning. Consequently, as he says, the notion of science is free to range from physics to history. 'What to call a science can plausibly be said to include all disciplines that seek to provide an integrated and systematic account of their subject matter' (Roth 2013, p. 648). However, Roth (2006, pp. 689–90) argues, far from this being a problem for naturalism, 'liberalizing what to count as science', in particular removing 'the need for invidious distinctions between the natural and social sciences', has made possible its resurgence.

Hands's (2001, p. 129) stance on naturalism appears similar to that of Roth's.[8] From such a standpoint, Hands investigates how the sociology of scientific knowledge affects economics. According to Hausman (2018), researchers in this area are concerned with explaining how non-rational factors (e.g., changes in funding for theoretical economics or political commitments) affect the developments in economic theory. Hausman comments: 'Exactly how, if at all, this work is supposed to bear on questions concerning how well supported are the claims economists make is not clear' (p. 39). Aside from this, the problem is that, in this form, naturalism is limited to descriptive accounts of scientific practice. As Hands (2001, p. 403) acknowledges, his new economic methodology 'does not seem to provide a position from which to *criticize* the practice of economists; [it] appears to have lost its prescriptive bite'.[9]

Naturalists reject the type of empiricism adopted by positivists.[10] In particular, they oppose its reliance on a form of phenomenalism. This idea is that we do not see external material objects directly, but instead experience only sense data, that is, non-physical entities. Naturalists raise various problems with this form of empiricism: it relies on introspection, something outside of natural science; it takes sense data as foundational, that is, as providing knowledge that is certain.

Nevertheless, Quine's (1951) criticism of the two dogmas of positivist empiricism was constructive and aimed at reforming it. His argument against the positivist analytic-synthetic dichotomy concluded that there were no purely analytic or purely synthetic statements. Since this implied that all statements contained an empirical component, they were all open to revision and so did not provide certain, foundational, knowledge. Further, philosophy could no longer be practiced *a priori*, that is, in purely conceptual terms.

From his holistic perspective, Quine argued that, since statements form part of an overall system, or web, of belief, the empirical content of sentences could not be determined individually (as positivists had claimed). Quine radically transformed the nature of empiricism to take 'account of the theoretical as well as the observational facets of science' (Orenstein 1998, p. 3). However, his views, particularly those concerning empiricism, have not been well received by post-Quinean naturalists who remain enthusiastically empiricist, driving the empirical turn in economics.[11] For example, although they agree that observation may be theory-laden, this does not detract from the validity of the normal processes of empirical testing carried out by practicing scientists (Kincaid 2012, p. 6).[12]

An introduction to interpretivism for economists

Rosenberg's (2016) well-known criticisms of economics over many years have been discussed, criticized and dismissed by many, amongst whom have been Kincaid (1996) and Hands (2001). One criticism is that Rosenberg's position represents 'a contemporary version of the [positivist] Received View' (Hands 2001, p. 334). However, this, by itself, does not mean that Rosenberg's position is not broadly naturalist (Ladyman and Ross 2007). Dupré (2003, p. 534) cautions against 'exaggerating the rift in the philosophy of science constituted by the collapse of positivism'. Another criticism is that Rosenberg pays insufficient attention to the social dimensions of scientific knowledge. However, perhaps the main problem that critics have with Rosenberg's stance is that it stymies the project of naturalizing the social sciences.

Notwithstanding these criticisms, Rosenberg's examination of a well-known economic theory provides a unique window for economists to gain insight into the major concerns of both naturalism and interpretivism. As opposed to the naturalist stress on causal explanation, interpretivists emphasize the need for understanding human life 'by means of categories which do not apply to knowledge of the physical world' (Hollis 2002, p. 17). Rosenberg's example casts a spotlight on the role of both naturalism and interpretivism within economics, namely, the reliance by economists on intentional explanation and the denial by naturalists that such explanation is properly causal.[13] Let us proceed to Rosenberg's argument.

Many, if not most, economic methodologists argue that we explain economic action in terms of the desires (preferences) and beliefs (expectations) of individuals. That is, they view preferences and expectations as data, as not only the reasons but also, more fundamentally, the causes of economic action. Economic action is explained as purposeful, intentional, the result of desires and beliefs. This is in line with Max Weber's notion that social, as opposed to natural, science is concerned both with discovering causal laws, regularities or patterns in the data and with interpretive meanings (which are absent from natural science).

Rosenberg (2016) explains why naturalists have a problem with explanations of economic action that adopt this hybridization of the naturalist and interpretive approaches. He claims that the following general statement seems to lie behind such explanations:

> [L] If any person x wants some outcome, *d*, and believes that an action, *a*, is a means to attain *d*, under the circumstances, then x does *a*.
>
> (p. 39)

For most economists, the belief/desire model works because beliefs and desires are *reasons* for actions, that is, they justify (interpret) them and show them to be rationally intelligible in 'the light of the agent's beliefs and desires' (p. 43). He argues that what connects beliefs and desires to actions (and social institutions) is that [L] is interpreted as a *rule*, a social norm or practice and not a causal law. Unlike a causal law, rules can be broken and breaking them leads to punishment (p. 125).

For naturalists, Rosenberg argues, the belief/desire model can work only if beliefs and desires are viewed as causes of, rather than reasons for, behavior: that is, if [L] is interpreted as a causal theory. The problem, Rosenberg says, is that in economics [L] is mistakenly treated as a causal law. However, in a law, the causal links must be contingent: 'when event *a* causes event *b* it must be conceivable for either to have occurred without the other having done so' (p. 58). The causal links must be 'open to rejection as a result of empirical findings about contingent matters of fact' (p. 59). However, in economics, desires, beliefs and actions are logically, not contingently, connected by [L] (p. 57). [L] is, therefore, not an empirical law but merely a principle that reflects our conception of ourselves as rational agents.

Rosenberg's argument clearly reveals the fundamental problem that scientific naturalists have with social sciences. This is that properties and concepts in economics dependent on mental entities, such as belief and desire, are nowhere to be found in the space-time world of natural science. For Rosenberg's critics however, the problem is that the belief/desire model (or folk psychology, the rational choice theory) plays too foundational a role in how most of us think to be cast aside. Consequently, giving it up, as in eliminative materialism, is regarded as too radical. Fortunately, for naturalists, the supervenience formulation of physicalism seemingly allows social scientists to continue using intentional explanations as earlier. This is only apparent, however, because scientific naturalists follow Rosenberg in insisting that such explanations are not proper causal explanations. This is because mental causes are not regarded as 'genuinely additional to the physical cause' (Papineau 2016, p. 13).

Interpretivism and Dow's neo-Austrian and post-Keynesian schools

Following on from the above preview of interpretivism, this section attempts to provide some further insight into its meaning. As we saw in the previous section, interpretivists deny that human life can be fully explained, or explained at all, in naturalist terms. Strict interpretivists, following in the hermeneutic tradition, reject the idea of social inquiry as a science (Hutchinson et al. 2008). Such an idea, they say, represents a misguided attempt to understand human action in terms of its causes. Social inquiry should instead be concerned with 'understanding', or *Verstehen*. This refers to understanding from within via empathy, intuition or imagination, in contrast to understanding from without via observation or calculation. Such understanding does not involve causes at all, or not entirely. This is because the knowledge of such causes alone does not result in understanding. Instead, understanding human action involves looking for its meaning as given in a particular social context. Understanding is provided through interpretation (Rosenberg 2016, p. 27). Consequently, the aim of social inquiry, for strict interpretivists, is to reconstruct, or interpret, the meaning of social contexts or practices.[14]

In what follows, I use the term 'interpretivism' as a bucket-term for the multitude of long-standing philosophical positions opposed in some way to naturalism (including strict interpretivism).[15] In this sense, it can be said that, throughout the history of economic thought, orthodox economics has drawn on both naturalism and interpretivism, despite the (philosophical) irreconcilability of the extreme forms of these doctrines.

One aspect of interpretivism relates to the (naturalist) view that Quine (1951) showed there can be no *a priori* knowledge. Naturalists are fond of describing traditional philosophy as remaining apriorist. However, such a view is mistaken. As Keil (2008, p. 282) points out, criticizing traditional philosophy as apriorist describes only a 'straw man', since almost all philosophers 'subscribe to the demand for including empirical knowledge'. Further, it serves to dismiss the need for conceptual analysis in economics. Fortunately, there are philosophers who oppose such derogation: 'I defend conceptual analysis against the accusation of indulging in a cult of common sense and ordinary use, and I insist, against naturalism, that it is both feasible and necessary to distinguish between factual, conceptual, and moral issues' (Glock 2008, p. 76).[16]

This derogation of the role of conceptual inquiry has impacted orthodox economics, but more severely Dow's Post-Keynesian and neo-Austrian schools. It has led to the evasion of central questions in economics emphasized by these schools. It both prevents conceptual criticism of the fundamental theory that orthodoxy, indeed, continues to rely on and prevents the discussion of the presuppositions upon which heterodox economics depends. For example, core orthodox macroeconomics continues to rely on the grand theoretical presupposition that the framework of supply and demand can be applied to the labor market. However, Post-Keynesians argue that Keynes (1936) replaced this framework with one based on his principle of effective demand. It is this principle, not the labor market, that determines the overall level of output and employment in a modern monetary production economy faced with uncertainty (Torr 1988).

Another aspect of interpretivism denied by naturalists concerns the role of subjective experience in science. Many neo-Austrian economists emphasize – in opposition to naturalists – the importance of intelligibility, or the subjective viewpoint, in understanding economic action (Mittermaier 2020, pp. 167–70). Subjectivism also plays an important role in Keynes's writings. For example, Keynes emphasized the extent to which it is the divergent subjective expectations of bulls and bears that determines the equilibrium price in speculative markets. Interpretivism is usually associated with the idea that human-made rules, rather than natural regularities, explain human action. However, as Braybrooke (1998) points out, interpretivism deals with just *how* the subjective features of human experience relate social phenomena to rules.

He stresses the importance of this concern to social science: 'If social science disregards the subjective forms of experience utterly (as naturalistic inquiries often do), or disregards any of the ways in which their content escapes the study of rules, social science is bound to give an impoverished picture of human life' (p. 842).

'Critical theory' and Dow's Marxian school

In addition to the naturalist and interpretivist approaches, Braybrooke (1998) distinguishes a critical approach within the philosophy of social science (e.g., Habermas 1984). Although it draws on both naturalism and interpretivism, the critical approach makes a distinctive claim, inherited from Marx, that '-so-called social science is in fact an ideological . . . defense of an oppressive social system' (Braybrooke 1987, pp. 17–19).[17] Its concern is that the other approaches may represent societies as harmonious when those societies are, in fact, in difficulty or distress. Alternatively, such distress might be interpreted in a way that is useful to those who benefit from it. Being concerned 'with emancipating people from the oppressions of current society', it denies that any social inquiry can be value-free (Braybrooke 1998, p. 839).

Naturalism challenges not only Dow's Marxian school but also the many other economists who have sympathized with Myrdal's (1958, p. 1) well-known claim: 'Our very concepts are value-loaded . . . they cannot be defined except in terms of political valuations'. Like most heterodox economists, naturalists surprisingly *also* seem to sympathize with Myrdal's claim. Unlike positivists of old, naturalists readily admit that ethical and political values enter into economics. However, they *deny* the heterodox conclusion that economics is not an objective science. They do so by effectively neutralizing the ethical and political values that they accept occur in economics, or in any science.

The notion of science as objective knowledge has recently become a 'hot' topic in naturalism, partly due to the objections of Longino (1996) and others that science reflects a gender bias. This has led to renewed work on the problem of scientific objectivity. Reiss and Sprenger's (2017, p. 17) discussion may be related to distinguishing pre-scientific, scientific and post-scientific (policy) stages of inquiry. They refer to the orthodox economics view, that 'contextual' (i.e., moral and political) values do not inevitably enter into the scientific stage itself, as 'the value-neutrality thesis' (p. 21). In terms of this (well-known) thesis, it is both possible and desirable to separate normative from factual considerations in economics. Both Putnam (2002) and Putnam and Walsh (2012) have challenged this thesis by explaining how values enter into the very heart of science. Despite their arguments, Reiss and Sprenger (2017, pp. 63–4) imply that there are no serious consequences for the objectivity of science. One approach that argues that the intrusion of values into science does not affect scientific objectivity is ethical naturalism.

According to Sturgeon (2006), ethical naturalism is the view that moral properties are natural properties 'of the same general sort as properties investigated by the sciences' (p. 92) or 'the thesis that there is no *is-ought* gap' (p. 103). In naturalistic ethical realism, moral properties supervene on 'the basic physical natures of things' (Copp 2006, p. 8). Consequently, an ethical term such as 'goodness' is exactly like 'healthiness' (Lutz and Lenman 2018, p. 28). It is a complex natural property that, although not directly observable, can cause various effects and also be the effect of various causes. For example, things like pleasure or pain, honesty or untruthfulness contribute or detract from goodness (p. 28). Therefore, for ethical naturalists, the fact that 'contextual values' intrude into the very heart of science has no consequences for the objectivity of science.

Putnam (2002) challenges the value-neutrality thesis. His argument is directed against ethical naturalists who claim that values are factorable into a descriptive and an evaluative component. By contrast, Putnam (2002, pp. 28–45) argues that facts and values are inextricably 'entangled'. For example, he takes issue with Hare (1981, p. 72) who says we do not need to use the 'thick' ethical concept of 'cruel' to describe a cruel action. Instead, 'cruel' can be replaced by a descriptive component ('causing deep suffering') and an evaluative component ('the action is wrong'). But, this 'two-components' approach, Putnam argues, founders on the impossibility of saying what the descriptive meaning of, say, 'cruel' is without using the word 'cruel' or a synonym. For example, 'cruel' does not simply mean 'causing deep suffering'. 'Suffering' does not just mean 'pain' and 'deep' does not just mean 'a lot of'. A surgeon who causes pain is not normally cruel whereas behavior that does not cause pain may be extremely cruel (p. 38). What is characteristic of thick ethical concepts is that to use them with any discrimination one has to be able to identify imaginatively with an evaluative point of view (p. 39). That is why someone who thought that 'brave' simply means 'not afraid to risk life and limb' (descriptive use) would not be able to understand the distinction between rashness or foolhardiness and genuine bravery. The descriptive use of 'brave', therefore, *depends* upon an evaluation of whether the act was rash or not (p. 40).

Naturalists dismiss Putnam's arguments against the value-neutrality thesis for the same reasons that they fail to see norms or values in economics as having any serious consequences for the objectivity of economics.[18] Consequently, the objectivity of science is unaffected regardless of in how many places it can be shown, à la Reiss (2017), that value judgments enter into economics.

Conclusion

According to Newton-Smith (2001, p. 1), '[f]or better or worse, no institution has had more impact on the character of our existence this millennium than science'. In the 1980s and 1990s, the authority of science came under sustained attack and philosophers of science felt the need to defend science (Haack 2003). Unfortunately, the influence of scientific naturalism has turned the defense of science into a defense of scientism. Alarmed by this development, Haack (2012) has provided six signs by which to recognize scientism. Kitcher (2012) also decries the move towards scientism, that is, the 'conviction that science can solve all questions'. Haack (2016) refers to 'the present tidal wave of scientistic philosophy'.

Historically, the methodology of economics has been bound up with the history of economic thought. Work in this tradition generally drew on a detailed and intimate knowledge, not only of (Dow's) major schools of economics, but also of the history of the major debates in economic theory and methodology. Today, the naturalistic approach to economic methodology has no use for such history of economic thought.[19] This is in line with a naturalistic affinity for a Whig interpretation of the history of economics (Freeman et al. 2014). The history of economic thought (as reflected, for example, in Terence Hutchison's many writings) further demonstrates that throughout its history, economics has drawn on both naturalist and interpretivist approaches in the philosophy of social science. Scientific naturalism threatens this longstanding middle-of-the-road approach in economics.

Unlike earlier naturalisms, post-Quinean naturalism in the form of scientific naturalism makes the radical claim that traditional, analytic, philosophy should be replaced by, or made continuous with, natural science. Likewise, both orthodox and heterodox economics as traditionally practiced should be converted (or naturalized) into disciplines that are modeled after the natural sciences. However, scientific naturalists, like the positivists before them, cannot, in principle, demarcate science from non-science. It is better then to follow Roth's view of science as any discipline that attempts a systematic account of its subject matter. In this case, interpretivist views, such as that conceptual analysis and subjectivism are vital to science, can be fully taken on board. This implies a new turn in economics, away from further attempts to model economics after the natural sciences, and towards interpretivism. The need to take the interpretivist approach into account in the practice of economics is, I submit, what underlies Dow's (2021) continued insistence that her pluralistic schools-of-thought approach still applies.[20]

Notes

1 Earlier drafts of this chapter were presented at the 2018 meeting of the Association for Heterodox Economics, De Montfort University, Leicester, UK, and the 2019 meeting of the Economic Society of South Africa held in Johannesburg, South Africa. I would like to thank Chris Torr, Derek Wang, Chad Harris, Duncan Hodge and other members of the Workshop on History and Methodology (WHAM) economics discussion group at the University of the Witwatersrand for helpful feedback on earlier versions of this chapter.

2 Scientific naturalism, as defined by De Caro and Macarthur (2004, 2010), is explained in the next section.

3 Hands (2015, p. 61) acknowledges that economic methodology 'has recently adopted a more naturalistic approach'.

4 See Mireles-Flores (2018) for recent trends in economic methodology.
5 In contrast to scientific realism, Lawson's (1989) critical realism allows for a social ontology separate from the physical realm.
6 Guala (2016) notes that 'the social sciences are ranked low in the pecking order of science'.
7 For Kincaid (1998, p. 559), '[n]aturalism [is] the view that good social science embodies the scientific method common to the natural sciences'.
8 See also Hands (2001, p. 174) where he refers to Roth and suggests that 'one could certainly naturalize on sociology just as easily as behavioral psychology, cognitive science, or evolutionary biology'.
9 Hands (2015, p. 70) accepts that although economic methodology has grown over the years, it has done so in a way that has prevented it from adopting a critical stance towards economics. I argue that this is due to scientific naturalism.
10 Although Lawson (2009) is also critical of (Humean) positivist empiricism, this is for radically different reasons from that of scientific naturalists.
11 By the empirical turn, I mean work in economics where the 'model' ties 'theory' closely and directly to empirical counterparts.
12 In regard to this, Kincaid (2012, p. 6) contends that 'the relationships between theories, applications, and tests propagated by Quine, Kuhn, and Lakatos look like philosophers' fantasies'.
13 In terms of the widely accepted causal closure argument for physicalism (i.e., in terms of a closed versus an open system), 'any mental or biological causes must themselves be physically constituted [e.g. via a supervenience relation] if they are to produce physical effects' (Papineau 2016, p. 8).
14 I am indebted to Robert Kolwalenko, Philosophy, University of the Witwatersrand, for help in understanding this narrow version of interpretivism.
15 See Rosenberg (2016). Many of these positions have their roots in Continental philosophy. Glock (2008, p. 113) notes that although the division between analytic and Continental philosophy has been deplored, 'and may indeed be deplorable, [f]or all that, it remains real'. Both naturalists and interpretivists claim to find support in Kuhn (1962).
16 'To many contemporary philosophers, conceptual analysis is out of date and out of touch with cutting-edge scientific philosophy' (Glock 2008, p. 99).
17 Ross (2012) views criticism of mainstream economics, which draws on the interpretive and critical approaches, as the political ideology of 'anti-economists'.
18 For example, Guala (2016) dismisses Putnam and Walsh (2012) as 'discontented social scientists'.
19 While Hands (2019, p. 11) acknowledges that the relationship 'has weakened during the last two decades', and he suggests that this is due to 'the proliferation of journals in both fields'.
20 Dow's pluralistic approach differs radically from the pluralism of new research fields in economics (e.g., behavioral economics, evolutionary economics, experimental economics and neuroeconomics) influenced by scientific naturalism.

References

Andler, D. (2015) 'Naturalism', in J. D. Wright (ed.) *International Encyclopedia of the Social Behavioral Sciences*, 2nd edn, Amsterdam: Elsevier, vol. 16, pp. 325–33. doi:10.1016/B978-0-08-097086-8.63099-4

Backhouse, R. and Cherrier, B. (2017) 'The age of the applied economist: the transformation of economics since the 1970s', *History of Political Economy* 49 (supplement): 1–33. doi:10.1215/00182702-4166239

Boland, L. (1991) 'Current views on economic positivism', in D. Greenaway, M. Bleaney and I. M. Stewart (eds) *Companion to Contemporary Economic Thought*, London: Routledge, pp. 88–104.

Boumans, M. (2013) 'John B. Davis and D. Wade Hands (eds) The Elgar Companion to Recent Economic Methodology', *Œconomia* 3-2: 319–22. doi:10.4000/oeconomia.307

Braybrooke, D. (1998) 'Contemporary philosophy of social science', in E. Craig (ed.) *The Routledge Encyclopedia of Philosophy*, London and New York: Routledge, vol. 8, pp. 838–47.

Braybrooke, D. (1987) *Philosophy of Social Science*, Englewood Cliffs, NJ: Prentice Hall.

Copp, D. (2006) 'Introduction: metaethics and normative ethics', in D. Copp (ed.) *The Oxford Handbook of Ethical Theory*, Oxford: Oxford University Press, pp. 3–34. doi:10.1093/0195147790.001.0001

Davis, J. B. and Hands, D. W. (eds) (2011) *The Elgar Companion to Recent Economic Methodology*, Cheltenham UK: Edward Elgar.

De Caro, M. and Macarthur, D. (eds) (2010) *Naturalism and Normativity*, New York: Columbia University Press.

De Caro, M. and Macarthur, D. (eds) (2004) *Naturalism in Question*, Cambridge, MA: Harvard University Press.

Dow, S. C. (2021) 'Economic methodology, the philosophy of economics and the economy: another turn?', *Journal of Economic Methodology* 28: 46–53. doi:10.1080/1350178X.2020.1868771

Dow, S. C. (2011) 'Heterodox economics: history and prospects', *Cambridge Journal of Economics* 35: 1151–65. doi:10.1093/cje/ber017

Dow, S. C. (1985) *Macroeconomic Thought: A Methodological Approach*, Oxford: Basil Blackwell.

Dupré, J. (2003) 'Horticultural diversity in the post-positivist garden' (book review of Hands 2001), *Journal of Economic Methodology* 10: 531–5. doi:10.1080/1350178032000130529

Freeman, A., Chick, V. and Kayatekin, S. (2014) 'Samuelson's ghosts: Whig history and the reinterpretation of economic theory', *Cambridge Journal of Economics* 38: 519–29. doi:10.1093/cje/beu017

Glock, H.-J. (2008) 'The development of analytic philosophy: Wittgenstein and after', in D. Moran (ed.) *The Routledge Companion to Twentieth Century Philosophy*, London: Routledge, pp. 76–117.

Guala, F. (2016) 'Review of Mark Risjord (ed.), Normativity and Naturalism in the Philosophy of the Social Sciences', *Notre Dame Philosophical Reviews* 2016.10.14. https://ndpr.nd.edu/reviews/normativity-and-naturalism-in-the-philosophy-of-the-social-sciences/

Haack, S. (2016) *Scientism and Its Discontents*, Rounded Globe. https://roundedglobe.com/books/9935bace-bf5e-459c-80ae-ce42bfa2b589/Scientism%20and%20its%20Discontents/

Haack, S. (2012) 'Six signs of scientism', *Logos & Episteme*, III, 1: 75–95. https://core.ac.uk/download/pdf/131210177.pdf

Haack, S. (2003) *Defending Science – Within Reason: Between Scientism and Cynicism*, Amherst, NY: Prometheus Books.

Habermas, J. (1984) *The Theory of Communicative Action*, vol. 1, trans. T. McCarthy, London: Heinemann.

Hands, D. W. (2019) 'Economic methodology in the twenty-first century (so far): some post-*Reflection* Reflections'. https://ssrn.com/abstract=3464759

Hands, D. W. (2015) 'Orthodox and heterodox economics in recent economic methodology', *Erasmus Journal for Philosophy and Economics* 8: 61–81. http://ejpe.org/pdf/8-1-art-4.pdf

Hands, D. W. (2001) *Reflection without Rules: Economic Methodology and Contemporary Science Theory*, New York: Cambridge University Press.

Hare, R. M. (1981) *Moral Thinking*, Oxford: Clarendon Press.

Hausman, D. (2018) 'Philosophy of economics', in E. N. Zalta (ed.) *The Stanford Encyclopedia of Philosophy* (Fall 2018 edn, PDF version). https://plato.stanford.edu/archives/fall2018/entries/economics

Hollis, M. (2002) *The Philosophy of Social Science*, Cambridge: Cambridge University Press.

Hutchinson, P., Read, R. and Sharrock, W. (2008) *There Is no Such Thing as a Social Science: In Defence of Peter Winch*, Aldershot: Ashgate Publishing Limited.

Keil, G. (2008) 'Naturalism', in D. Moran (ed.) *The Routledge Companion to Twentieth Century Philosophy*, London: Routledge, pp. 254–307.

Keynes, J. M. (1936) *The General Theory of Employment, Interest and Money*, London: Macmillan.

Kim, Jaegwon (2003) 'The American origins of philosophical naturalism', *Journal of Philosophical Research* 28: 83–98 (issue supplement) (APA centennial volume). doi:10.5840/jpr200328Supplement28

Kincaid, H. (2012) 'Introduction', in H. Kincaid (ed.) *The Oxford Handbook of Philosophy of Social Science*, Oxford: Oxford University Press, pp. 3–17.

Kincaid, H. (1998) 'Positivism in the social sciences', in E. Craig (ed.) *The Routledge Encyclopedia of Philosophy*, London and New York: Routledge, vol. 7, pp. 838–47.

Kincaid, H. (1996) *Philosophical Foundations of the Social Sciences*, New York: Cambridge University Press.

Kincaid, H. and Ross, D. (2009) 'Preface', in H. Kincaid and D. Ross (eds) *The Oxford Handbook of Philosophy of Economics*. Oxford: Oxford University Press, pp. i–vi.

Kitcher, P. (2012) 'Seeing Is Unbelieving', *The New York Times Book Review*, March 25, 2012, p. BR31. http://www.nytimes.com/2012/03/25/books/review/alex-rosenbergs-the-atheists-guide-to-reality.html

Kitcher, P. (1992) 'The naturalists return', *Philosophical Review* 101: 53–114. doi:10.2307/2185044

Kuhn, T. S. (1962) *The Structure of Scientific Revolutions*, 1st edn, Chicago, IL: Chicago University Press.

Ladyman, J. and Ross, D. (2007) *Every Thing Must Go: Metaphysics Naturalized*, Oxford: Oxford University Press.

Lawson, T. (1997) *Economics and Reality*, London: Routledge.

Longino, H. (1996) 'Cognitive and non-cognitive values in science: rethinking the dichotomy', in L. H. Nelson and J. Nelson (eds) *Feminism, Science, and the Philosophy of Science*, Dordrecht: Kluwer, pp. 39–58.

Lutz, M. and Lenman, J. (2018) 'Moral naturalism', in E. N. Zalta (ed.) *The Stanford Encyclopedia of Philosophy* (Fall 2018 edn, PDF version). https://plato.stanford.edu/archives/fall2018/entries/naturalism-moral

Macarthur, D. (2010) 'Taking the human sciences seriously', in M. De Caro and D. Macarthur (eds) *Naturalism and Normativity*, New York: Columbia University Press, pp. 123–41.

Mäki, U. (2021) 'The field: tasks, pasts, futures', *Journal of Economic Methodology* 28: 3–13. doi:10.1080/1350178X.2020.1868766
Mäki, U. (1998) 'Realism', in J. B. Davis, D. W. Hands and U. Mäki (eds) *The Handbook of Economic Methodology*, Cheltenham, UK: Edward Elgar, pp. 404–9.
Manicas, P. T. (1998) 'History of philosophy of social science', in E. Craig (ed.) *The Routledge Encyclopedia of Philosophy*, London and New York: Routledge, vol. 8, pp. 847–59.
Mireles-Flores, L. (2018) 'Recent trends in economic methodology: a literature review', *Research in the History of Economic Thought and Methodology* 36A: 93–126. doi:10.1108/S0743-41542018000036A008
Mittermaier, K. (2020) *The Hand Behind the Invisible Hand: Dogmatic and Pragmatic Views on Free Markets and the State of Economic Theory*, Bristol: Bristol University Press. https://library.oapen.org/handle/20.500.12657/40100
Myrdal, G. (ed. P. Streeten) (1958) *Value in Social Theory*, London: Routledge.
Newton-Smith, W. H. (2001) 'Introduction', in W. H. Newton-Smith (ed.) *A Companion to the Philosophy of Science*, Oxford: Blackwell, pp. 1–8.
Orenstein, A. (1998) 'Willard van Orman Quine', in E. Craig (ed.) *The Routledge Encyclopedia of Philosophy*, London and New York: Routledge, vol. 8, pp. 3–14.
Papineau, D. (2016) 'Naturalism', in E. N. Zalta (ed.) *The Stanford Encylopedia of Philosophy* (Winter 2016 edn, PDF version). https://plato.stanford.edu/archives/win2016/entries/naturalism
Putnam, H. (2002) *The Collapse of the Fact/Value Dichotomy*, Cambridge, MA: Harvard University Press.
Putnam, H. and Walsh, V. (eds) (2012) *The End of Value-Free Economics*, London: Routledge.
Quine, W. V. O. (1969) *Ontological Relativity and Other Essays*, New York: Columbia University Press.
Quine, W. V. O. (1951) 'Two dogmas of empiricism', *Philosophical Review* 60: 20–43. https://www.jstor.org/stable/2181906
Reiss, J. (2017) 'Fact-value entanglement in positive economics', *Journal of Economic Methodology* 24: 134–49. doi:10.1080/1350178X.2017.1309749
Reiss, J. (2013) *Philosophy of Economics: A Contemporary Introduction*, Abingdon: Routledge.
Reiss, J. and Sprenger, J. (2017) 'Scientific objectivity', in E. N. Zalta (ed.) *The Stanford Encyclopedia of Philosophy* (Winter 2017 edn, PDF version). https://plato.stanford.edu/archives/win2017/entries/scientific-objectivity
Risjord, M. (2016) 'Introduction', in M. Risjord (ed.) *Normativity and Naturalism in the Philosophy of the Social Sciences*, New York: Routledge, pp. 1–8.
Root, M. (1998) 'Review of Philosophical Foundations of the Social Science by Harold Kincaid', *Mind* 107: 672–5. https://www.jstor.org/stable/2660123
Rosenberg, A. (2016) *Philosophy of Social Science*, 5th edn, Boulder, CO: Westview Press.
Ross, D. (2014) *Philosophy of Economics*, Basingstoke: Palgrave Macmillan.
Ross, D. (2012) 'Economic theory, anti-economics, and political ideology', in U. Mäki (ed.) *Philosophy of Economics, vol. 13 of Handbook of the Philosophy of Science* (eds D. Gabbay, P. Thagard and J. Woods), Amsterdam: Elsevier, pp. 241–85.
Roth, P. A. (2013) 'Naturalized epistemology', in B. Kaldis (ed.) *Encyclopedia of Philosophy and the Social Sciences*, vol. 2, London: Sage Reference, pp. 646–9.

Roth, P. A. (2006) 'Naturalism without fears', in S. Turner and M. Risjord (eds) *Philosophy of Anthropology and Sociology, vol. 15 of Handbook of the Philosophy of Science* (eds D. Gabbay, P. Thagard and J. Woods), Amsterdam: Elsevier, pp. 683–708.

Stoljar, D. (2017) 'Physicalism', in E. N. Zalta (ed.) *The Stanford Encyclopedia of Philosophy* (Winter 2017 edn, PDF version). https://plato.stanford.edu/archives/win2017/entries/physicalism/

Sturgeon, N. L. (2006) 'Ethical naturalism', in D. Copp (ed.) *The Oxford Handbook of Ethical Theory*, Oxford: Oxford University Press, pp. 91–119. doi:10.1093/0195147790.003.0004

Torr, C. S. W. (1988) *Equilibrium, Expectations and Information: A Study of the General Theory and Modern Classical Economics*, Cambridge: Polity Press.

Vromen, J. (2021) 'What are we up to?', *Journal of Economic Methodology* 28: 23–31. doi:10.1080/1350178X.2020.1868768

6 Infinite regress problems and the methodologies of behavioural economics

Peter E. Earl

Introduction

In a paper written as a tribute to the late Mark Blaug, Sheila Dow (2013) opted to go where Blaug had feared to tread, namely, into making a Lakatosian assessment of the methodology of the typical modern behavioural economist. During her exploration of this territory, she considers the legitimacy of interpreting evidence from experiments as implying the existence of systematic tendencies for behaviour to be biased away from optimal choice by heuristics that decision-makers use to reduce cognitive load. She notes (p. 32), via Winter (1964) and Cohen and Dickens (2002), that such interpretations are problematic because optimization is logically impossible owing to a problem of infinite regress: the allocation of resources is a process that entails using some of the resources that the process is intended to allocate, begging the question of what is the optimal allocation of resources to the task of allocating resources, a question whose consideration will itself use some of the resources being allocated, and so on. Modern behavioural economists, thus, seem to be criticizing the rest of the population for not doing something that in reality is impossible, and they fail to see the positive role that heuristics can play in preventing decision paralysis.

This logical objection to the notion of optimization strikes at the hard core of orthodox economics, wherein all choices are viewed as acts of constrained optimization. Hence, it is not surprising that it continues to be ignored within mainstream economics. It is also not surprising that those whose work was the focus of Dow's paper—namely, practitioners of what Sent (2004) has called New Behavioural Economics (NBE)—are also oblivious of it, for they tend not to have received training in what Sent calls Old Behavioural Economics (OBE) or in the modern evolutionary economics that morphed out of OBE via contributions such as Winter's (1964) paper.

Richard Thaler (1987) is the only big-league contributor to NBE to cite Winter's paper (out of the 1,077 citations Google Scholar could find for it at the time of writing [September 2019]). Thaler made no reference to Winter's logical objection to optimization and merely cited the paper as arguing, like Friedman (1953), that competitive pressure will ensure that only the firms

DOI: 10.4324/9781003142324-7

that 'get things right' (Thaler, 1987, p. 123) will survive in the long run. He thereby failed to acknowledge Winter's argument that firms that use fast and frugal decision rules may actually outperform firms that take up time trying to work out optimal responses to changed market conditions. Even Cohen and Dickens's (2002) paper, which is one of only a handful to cite Winter (1964) in a mainstream journal in the past quarter century, has pretty much failed to get economists concerned about the significance of the infinite regress problem for economics: Google Scholar recorded only 38 citations of it by the time of writing this paper.

Undaunted by this, I reconsider here the significance of the infinite regress problem for the methodology of behavioural economics. My focus is different from that of Cohen and Dickens (2002), who raised the infinite regress argument against optimization en route to making a case for building behavioural economics on foundations derived from evolutionary psychology. In essence, their view is that such foundations could be appropriate since, if we accept that optimization is logically impossible and view people as using rules for coping with the resource allocation problem, we need a theory of where these rules come from if we are to prevent our analysis from becoming ad hoc. From the standpoint of evolutionary psychology, modern humans will be prone to achieve needlessly poor outcomes due to having inherited rules and heuristics that gave humans a competitive edge in humanity's long hunter-gatherer era, the only period in human history that is long enough for genetic selection processes to have fine-tuned people for coping with a particular environment. These rules and heuristics may have shortcomings in today's world.

The problem with using evolutionary psychology to explain the origins of the heuristics that underpin NBE is that it leads to a focus on hard-wired heuristics shared by people in general. It diverts attention from the possibility that people will respond differently to identical stimuli because they employ rules that they have created for themselves or picked up in particular cultural settings. This possibility—which may seem analytically inconvenient to economists who habitually work with 'representative agent' models—takes us in the direction of other infinite regress problems, for it begs the question of how people end up adopting the rules and heuristics that make up their distinct identities as individuals.

With this in mind, my objectives in this chapter are, first, to open the Pandora's Box of infinite regress problems that underlie real-world open-ended choice problems, and second, to explore what this implies for behavioural economists who genuinely want to address the human predicament rather than merely pretend to be doing so whilst restricting themselves to situations that they present, explicitly or implicitly, as closed-choice scenarios. The paper points towards a general rules-/heuristics-based view of human behaviour, a view that could provide a basis for 'new' behavioural economists to join forces with those who continue to work in the OBE tradition.

Open-ended choices and the infinite regress problem

The infinite regress argument against optimization can be raised in the context of precisely specified, closed problems, such as those presented to time-constrained subjects in experimental economics laboratories or those that chess players have to address. But real-world problems are often open-ended: rather than always being presented with a problem specification, options, and a set of rules to which we must adhere, we are often in a position to construct our own views of problems and their potential solutions. On such occasions, we have to contend with a richer set of infinite regress problems.

This becomes readily apparent when the 'decision cycle' framework proposed by Dewey (1910) is used for organizing thinking about the analytical and practical challenges that are inherent in open-ended decision problems. In Dewey's framework, choice entails a loop with the following segments: problem recognition; search for alternatives; evaluation of the options that are discovered, in terms of the information that has been discovered about them; ranking of alternatives (choice); implementation (and if this is not possible with plan A, is there an acceptable plan B?); and hindsight review (which could lead to the conclusion that the problem has not been solved, or that attempting to solve it has generated a different problem). Clearly, where decision-makers suffer from bounded rationality and deficient foresight, decision cycles may just keep looping forward in time, as in Bausor's (1982, 1984) helical analysis of choice, rather than ending in an equilibrium that is maintained until there is a shock to the system. But infinite regress problems lurk within any single decision-cycle loop.

The problem of problem recognition

Problem recognition that triggers a process of choice entails choices in its own right. With finite attentive capacity at their disposal, decision-makers have to choose between attending to doing some things and monitoring others. As Berger (1989) has pointed out, this question cannot be answered optimally, as it contains an infinite regress: merely to think about the allocation of attention is itself an act that consumes scarce attentive capacity, begging the question of how much attention we should devote to thinking about the allocation of our attention.

There is also the question of how we should specify whether we have a problem that is worth devoting our attention to solving. The performance of a product or an employee may not be as good as we anticipated but that fact does not of itself imply, we should worry about how to get a better performance: it may be that what we are getting is as good as is possible. But performance that meets expectations may conceal scope for doing better, either because we had set our aspirations needlessly low at the time that we selected the product or employee, or because things have moved on and we could now get better products or more capable employees. Is it worth looking to see whether this is the case? Perhaps the problem is merely a temporary shortfall in performance, but that begs the question of how often we should be checking on performance.

People are beset here with the Duhem–Quine Problem (Duhem, 1906; Quine, 1951), that is, the impossibility of testing one hypothesis without assuming the veracity of other hypotheses. Unexpectedly poor performance may not be caused by the product or the worker in question, but by something else, such as complementary resources not performing as well as we had expected (for example, a 'flat' car battery may not reflect a failure of the battery but be due to a problem with the car's alternator or wiring), or perhaps the measuring device that we are using is defective. Insofar as someone else is supplying information pertinent to judging whether we have a problem, it is possible that we are being given misleading information due to the other party's incompetence or opportunism. However, hiring a third party to audit the second party raises the question of whether we should trust the third-party auditor. For example, in 1997, the New Zealand Government's former Auditor General, Jeff Chapman, was jailed for fraud, and doubts about the integrity of that office resurfaced 2 decades later (see NBR, 2017); note also the collapse of accounting giant Arthur Andersen after its failure to spot what was going on inside Enron.

The decades-long debate about human-induced climate change is a reminder that many of the problems that should concern us lie in the future but may be triggered by causal chains that are taking shape today or that are already underway. The problem here is to know how, and by which method, to try to peer over the horizon in order to detect potential for such problems, even if we accept that the future is inherently unpredictable: perhaps the kind of 'scenario planning' practised by corporations such as Shell is worth trying (see Jefferson, 1983, 2012); perhaps we should heed warnings, or seek advice, from others; or perhaps we should simply wait to see what happens, especially in respect of potential problems that are not of our own making.

Searching for the best search strategy

If we accept that we have a problem that requires attention, the set of potential solutions to it and information about them is something that we have to assemble. Even if there are already potential courses of action 'kicking around', as per Cohen, March and Olsen's (1972) 'garbage can' model of organizational decision-making, we should not presume that these are the only ones to consider. But by which medium should we search (for example, should we search using our social networks, by visiting a store, via the Internet?), how should we specify what we are looking for (e.g., which search terms should we type into Google, if we opt to use Google as a search engine?), and how far should we dig into the set of suggestions that our chosen search method generates? If a few results are elicited by our chosen search questions within our chosen search medium, does this imply that we should try a different search strategy?

It we outsource search via market institutions such as product comparison sites, there is scope for those sites to mislead us due to incompetent construction and incomplete coverage of options (see further Earl, Friesen and Shadforth, 2017) or because they succumb to conflicts of interest. To the extent that such sites differ in what they tell us, there is the question of which ones we should trust. This also applies for comparison sites that claim to find us the best deals from within rival comparison sites (as with trivago.com if one is searching for best-priced hotel accommodation).

Uncertainty about uncertainty at the evaluation stage

To form expectations prior to being able to rank rival courses of action, decision-makers need to assess the information they have gathered about what is available and what consequences could arise as a result of selecting one contender rather than another. Uncertainty is inherent here, and it makes problematic the notion of optimal search: how do we know whether (or the probability that) we have missed possible options and relevant information about these courses of action, and how do we assess the significance of any piece of information? We use our powers of logic and capacities to imagine possibilities when building models of what could happen if we choose a particular option, but the limits to our imagination make it problematic to imagine what we have failed to imagine about what could happen as the sequel to a particular choice. Hence, we should be uncertain about how uncertain we are (cf. Dow, 1995), and any confidence that we feel may simply be the result of our ignorance (Loasby, 1976, p. 158), our lack of knowledge about what we do not know.

As is evident from Shackle (1961), an infinite regress problem also besets us when we attend to the task of figuring out how seriously to take possibilities that we have imagined or are raised in the information we have gathered. For Shackle, a perfect possibility is something for which we can envisage no barrier to its eventuation (which does not mean we should treat it as certain to occur). However, events that look potentially surprising because we can imagine barriers to their eventuation may, nonetheless, take place if other events block the eventuation of the events that we envisage as potential barriers to the outcomes in question—that is, event *A* might be blocked by event *B*, but event *A* could occur if event *B* is blocked by event *C*, but event *C* might itself be blocked by event *D*, allowing event *B* to occur and block event *A*, unless event *D* is blocked, and so on.

Preferences about preferences and other ways of ranking alternatives

In the rational choice model, rankings of rival courses of action are determined—given the expectations that the decision-maker has formed about these options—with the aid of a preference system that is simply assumed to exist in the mind of the decision-maker (and is assumed to obey a particular set of axioms). This view of choice is problematic if we accept Loasby's (1976, p. 6) contention that 'choice is a normative activity': there is scope for the ranking process to be held up if the decision-maker reflects on which preference system or other ranking system (such as a rule or procedure) he or she should use. Such reflection may be concerned with the moral aspect of choice, the relative importance of the ends that are being pursued, or whether a particular system seems to be generating the 'right' ranking in some other sense. Decision-makers would be wise to reflect on whether they should cast a wider net in search of yet more potential ways of arriving at a ranking, for the set of potential preference systems and/or other ranking systems includes those offered by others via the 'market for preferences' (Earl and Potts, 2004), rather than consisting merely of those that decision-makers construct themselves via their limited imaginative capacities. However, to choose between these rival systems requires a preference system or other ranking system, which begs the same question, that is, whether the decision-maker has got an appropriate system for choosing, given his or her expectations about the consequences of choosing each of the options under consideration in the context at hand.

How real-world decision-makers cope in a world of open-ended choices

The infinite regress problems identified in the previous section are circumvented via systems that are based on rules and/or the application of heuristic techniques. These rules/heuristics may be genetically hard-wired, personally created or uploaded/assimilated from social sources. They may be employed unconsciously or consciously, and in many cases they are formally written down, as with constitutional documents or organizational policies and procedures. They may frequently seem highly arbitrary, as they are path-dependent products of complex evolutionary processes and often are organized hierarchically. In some cases, such as legal systems that allow multiple levels of appeal, rule-based systems do not result in definitive verdicts being achieved rapidly, whereas in other cases they make it possible to take decisions instantly in the midst of complex and changing sets of stimuli.

Without these systems there to assist us, the infinite regress problems will render us unable to choose: they are the means by which we replace unanswerable questions with questions that we can answer and that enable us to get through life. Psychologists such as Kahneman (2011, ch. 9) nowadays refer to this question-switching process as 'attribute substitution' or 'the substitution heuristic'. It was a process central to Keynes's analysis of action in the face of fundamental uncertainty (see Koutsobinas, 2014). However, it needs to be pointed out that within psychology there is an extensive literature on attribution that predates Kahneman's contribution and is not based on heuristics. Its potential significance for economics was explored long ago by Rutherford (1988) (see further, Koutsobinas, 2021).

As far as problem-recognition is concerned, these systems of rules include organizational review systems that are routine-based: for example, each department in a university may be required to be assessed in terms of a particular set of criteria at regular intervals. They also include rule-based alarm systems that are triggered when stimuli cross threshold levels on particular variables or are not congruent with other norms (for example, sirens seize our attention because they involve sounds that are at odds with the rules of tonality and musicality). We have context-specific 'ways' of searching for solutions to problems, and they rule out other ways of searching. We also use cognitive rules for appraising the significance of information that we gather. In the face of fundamental uncertainty, we can avoid decision paralysis by having a policy of asking, say, 'What are experts, or people like us, doing in this situation?' and copying their behaviour, rather than trying to assemble probabilistic estimates of inherently dubious relevance. We have value systems that function, like Lakatosian scientific research programmes, by allowing core constructs to rule out accepting some ideas about what is, or will be, a potentially acceptable course of action. These constructs, thus, limit our ranges of choice: in some areas, they will allow substitution but in others they will rule out particular options, deeming them to have 'deal-breaker' shortcomings regardless of their upside aspects. These rules can be changed—and with such changes, our preferences will seem to change—but only along channels deemed acceptable by existing rules that exert ultimate authority. Where we are indifferent between options, this is because choosing one way rather than another clashes with none of our rules.

There are two major implications here for the practice of economics. One is that a key focus of economists should be on identifying the systems of rules and heuristics that drive behaviour and shape responses to changed patterns of incentives in contexts of economic interest. The other is that economists would be wise to study the processes by which these systems of rules and heuristics evolve (cf. Vanberg, 1994), rather than concentrating merely on the significance of a given set of heuristics that seems to be part of Human Nature.

The conventional economist's way of closing open-ended choice problems

It is ironic that the rules by which orthodox economists operate prevent them from taking such a view of economizing activities. Within conventional economic analysis, choices do not run into infinite regress problems because, one way or another, occasions for choice are set up so that they are closed. This has to be done on multiple fronts in order to presume that the decision-makers can find the optimal solution to the problem that he or she faces and verify it as such:

- The problem space in question must be closed, both in terms of the set of available options and information about them, and in the sense that the decision-maker is locked inside this space with no opportunity to consider options that lie outside it.

- If information-processing speeds are finite, there must be no limits on the available time that is necessary for accurately processing the information that is available.
- The decision-maker must possess reliable knowledge about means–end relationships pertaining to what the available options have to offer and the probability distributions of any events that could affect these relationships (for example, the chances that the efficacy of an umbrella will be affected by wind that accompanies rain) or affect the desirability of any of the options (for example, whether there will be rain on particular occasions).
- The decision-maker must have a well-defined objective function/preference ordering in terms of which the available options can be ranked.

If all of these requirements are met, the task of making a decision reduces to that of processing information to arrive at a ranking of rival products or bundles of products. Following this analytical heuristic ensures that the only place for a heuristic inside the model of choice is via the objective function/preference ordering that generates rankings; however, this ranking device is axiom-driven, based on the rules of the rational choice theory rather than based on what is actually known about the ranking systems that real people use.

New behavioural economics

The NBE comes to the aid of conventional economists in situations where they accept that empirical anomalies can be explained on the basis that decisions are driven by heuristics that conflict with those used in the construction of the rational choice theory. Because neither the conventional economists nor those who practice NBE have been willing to grapple with the infinite regress problems that infest resource allocation processes, accepting that heuristics are generating anomalies requires them to see heuristics as being used as a means of dealing with a mismatch between available cognitive capacity and the cognitive capacity that would be necessary for rational choice. Heuristics do, of course, get deployed as means for dealing with inadequate cognitive capacity, but viewing their use solely in these terms misses the bigger point: heuristics *have* to be used for dealing with open-ended problems, because no amount of computing power can get to the bottom of problems that contain any infinite regresses. Failure to appreciate this has resulted in methodological incoherence within NBE. This is a result of the route by which NBE came about, a route whose wellsprings did not entail any substantial grounding in OBE on the part of leaders such as Thaler (as is evident in his 2015 intellectual autobiography).

The heuristics on which attention has been focused within NBE are those that people, in general, seem to use: the implicit presumption (that Cohen and

Dickens, quite reasonably, want to see made explicit) appears to be that these heuristics have become genetically hard-wired as part of Human Nature via evolutionary selection processes. This permits analysis in terms of representative agents rather than leading to a need to follow the approach of marketers, who attempt to segment populations into groups that are characterized by similarities in their personal operating systems. This stands in sharp contrast to the focus within OBE on heuristics that people create for themselves or pick up in a social setting—heuristics that not only make them the individuals that they are but also facilitate coordination within organizations and societies.

The process that resulted in this focus does not appear to have entailed any deep thinking about the philosophical challenges that the theory of choice poses given the nature of the human condition: the only methodological work that Thaler (2015) refers to in his account of how he got started in behavioural economics is Friedman's (1953) famous essay on positive economics. Thaler deployed this when highlighting the predictive shortcomings of the received wisdom and arguing that the established 'as if' theorizing, therefore, cannot be justified on the basis of its predictive success. The key ideas for how to deal with the anomalies that he noticed mainly came from experiments within psychology, particularly those conducted by Kahneman and Tversky, who used some of their findings as the basis for their (1979) Prospect Theory. It is evident from Kahneman's (2011) account of his and Tverky's research programme that these experiments were set up essentially as simple, closed problems, as was the case, for example, with those that examined how the framing of hypothetical lottery choices affected the decisions that subjects made.

The NBE may be said to have begun when Thaler (1980) offered the first application of the Prospect Theory to everyday economic problems after he realized that the theory's S-shaped utility function could be employed in respect of choices in general, if they could be framed in terms of gains and losses relative to a reference point, rather than merely as a better means than the expected utility theory for understanding risk-taking behaviour. Thaler justified his use of the theory not merely in terms of its predictive superiority but also by arguing via Simon (1957, p. 198) that people use decision heuristics as a means of coping with choice problems that would otherwise cause cognitive overload, that is, as a means for dealing with bounded rationality. However, Thaler's appeal to bounded rationality, like that of those who followed his lead, presented a very one-sided view of its significance.

In Simon's view (which earned him the 1978 Alfred Nobel Memorial Prize in Economic Sciences), the decision-maker facing cognitive constraints is trying to operate rationally within these limits by constructing a simple enough model of the choice problem for it to be solvable given these cognitive limits. Simon suggested that the choice procedure that is frequently employed entails taking a satisficing approach and initially searching locally for good-enough solutions. This may sound like a sloppy way of operating and is, hence, consistent with the NBE focus on dysfunctional choices. However, it can actually entail some serious cognitive effort and investment of time if ambitious aspiration levels have been set.

Thaler and those who have followed him did not pick up this point of view and go on to portray decision-makers as actually trying to take good choices, despite being cognitively challenged. Instead, as in the lottery-based experiments conducted by Kahneman and Tversky, the choices that they have analysed in terms of the 'heuristics and biases' perspective typically have been very simple. To practitioners of NBE, people seem as if they cannot be bothered to take the time to take good decisions even where they should be perfectly capable of finding the best choice or, at least, a better choice than the one they make. This way of viewing much of human action is in line with Kahneman's (2011) dual system analysis in which humans often tend to get choices out of the way by 'thinking fast' when they could be doing better in such contexts by 'thinking slow'. It was largely left to consumer researchers in marketing (e.g., Payne, Bettman and Johnson, 1993) to study how increases in cognitive load changed the ways that people chose.

This tendency to portray people as being slack and lazy in their choices has paved the way for the view that consumers could benefit from being 'nudged' (Thaler and Sunstein, 2008) in the right direction via policies that are informed by knowledge of the heuristics that are part of Human Nature. However, practitioners of NBE might have achieved more if they had acknowledged that the use of heuristics can also be an efficient way for time-poor decision-makers to dispose of problems and free up time for enjoying the fruits of their labour. The crucial issue is which heuristics are employed, for the available set of heuristics includes not merely those that are part of Human Nature but also those that are picked up socially (including via the processes of nurturing and education), along with those that we construct for ourselves and test for their reliability. As Winter (1964) and Gigerenzer and his colleagues (Gigerenzer and Goldstein, 1996; Gigerenzer *et al.*, 1999; Gigerenzer and Brighton, 2009) have demonstrated, even in situations where we are prepared to take the time to try hard to avoid needless underachievement, we should not necessarily engage in slow deliberation. Taking time has opportunity costs. Heuristics save time and, indeed, they may result in better outcomes than would have resulted from a detailed examination of alternatives, for taking time can allow opportunities (even lives, if the context is that of a hospital emergency admissions department) to slip away. Moreover, as Heiner (1986) has emphasized, gathering more information can result in more information processing errors.

There is an irony in the focus of NBE on heuristics that 'bias' decisions away from the 'rational' choice: practitioners of NBE have not noticed that using the 'rational choice' reference point has been bias-inducing within economics. It has served to divert NBE from studying what Herbert Simon (1976) called 'procedural rationality', that is, what would constitute 'appropriate deliberation' in the context of interest. Instead, the emphasis is on inappropriate deliberation, studied with the aid of what Rabin (2013) calls 'portable extensions' of existing models. Thus, although Thaler presents himself as a Kuhnian scientific revolutionary, Sheila Dow is right to conclude that NBE is part of the 'protective belt' of the orthodox, rational choice-based economics research programme: its role is to make sense of, and anticipate, choices that are at odds with what the standard theory predicts. By embracing NBE, orthodox economics may give the impression that all bases are covered in the arena of choice. Meanwhile, practitioners of NBE adhere as far as they can to focussing on choices in closed problem spaces with a given set of information (which is viewed as prone to being predictably misused, for example when forming decision weights in the face of uncertainty).

An important aspect of the adherence of NBE to the analytical heuristics of mainstream economics is in its approach to time. Heuristics do not merely save us time that we might otherwise have had to spend thinking about the implications of the information we have for how we rank our options; heuristics may also limit the time we spend gathering information, including the time it takes to receive information that we request from others. In typical NBE contributions, in contrast to those from OBE, the information gathering process is excluded from closed models: heuristics are applied to information that is already at hand. Typically, the closest NBE gets to the possibility of taking time to gather more information is to present a closed choice between taking the default option or some other specific option that could take the form of a specific strategy for gathering information about other options.

Moreover, practitioners of NBE pay little attention to the fact that, if we take decisions in a hurry in one context (for example, by not over-riding the default option for that context), what we are in effect doing is opting to unlock the door of that choice environment to enable us to move on to something else; we deal with life's problems one at a time, not by working out (as in the Arrow–Debreu general equilibrium framework) which is the best affordable bundle of available contingent commodities and without ever needing to make any economic transactions thereafter. Real-world decision-makers have to apply rules to determine which problem to address next and to choose whether to address it via fast and frugal heuristics or in a much more laboured and reflective but ultimately rule-based way. Typically, the problems they have to prioritize are open-ended, so they first have to use heuristics and rules to form conjectures about the relative scale and significance of the problems they have identified.

Conclusion

If we are prepared to take the infinite regress problem as a potential source of decision paralysis, the case that emerges for a heuristics-based view of human action differs sharply from the one found in NBE that is based on limiting cognitive load. Whether fast and frugal or in some sense dysfunctional, and whether employed consciously or unconsciously, heuristics and rules are what humans have to use to avoid decision paralysis and get on with living. To be sure, information overload can prevent us from choosing if we do not use heuristics when we are presented with a wide range of alternatives that differ across many dimensions. However, focussing on the need for heuristics in such situations neglects their necessary role in enabling us to get to that particular choice environment at that point in time, with a particular amount of time to spend there, rather than being paralysed by the infinite regress problems that lurk within the resource allocation problems that we face.

Unlike research subjects in laboratories, real-world decision-makers are mostly dealing with open-ended problems, with discretion regarding whether they even acknowledge they have a problem to solve as well as in respect of how much information they gather and how long they deliberate before reaching a verdict. Moreover, their choice sets are often in a state of flux due to new products continually being introduced. Accepting the necessity of heuristics is a vital step in avoiding misapprehensions that can arise due to treating these open-ended problems 'as if' they are closed puzzles for which equilibrium outcomes must be found.

By recognizing the roles that rules and heuristic play as stopping/closing/switching devices throughout decision cycles, we can seek to analyse such choices as they are and acknowledge that what eventually gets chosen may not produce a state of rest. This was pretty much the practice of OBE, and it does not preclude taking account of the particular heuristics that preoccupy practitioners of NBE and being primed to anticipate lazy or dysfunctional decision-making. So, now that NBE is well entrenched within the economics establishment, is it not time for its practitioners to abandon the rational choice reference point, take infinite regress problems seriously and embrace the wider perspectives of OBE in a genuinely progress research programme, instead of being satisfied with a subservient role within the protective belt of orthodoxy?

References

Bausor, R. (1982). Time and the structure of economic analysis. *Journal of Post Keynesian Economics, 5*(Winter), 163–79. doi: 10.1080/01603477.1982.11489353.

Bausor, R. (1984). Towards a historically dynamic economics: Examples and illustrations. *Journal of Post Keynesian Economics, 6*(Spring), 360–76. doi: 10.1080/01603477.1984.11489446.

Berger, L. A. (1989). Economics and hermeneutics. *Economics and Philosophy, 5*(2, October), 209–34. doi: 10.1017/S026626710000239X.

Cohen, J. L., & Dickens, W. T. (2002). A foundation for behavioral economics. *American Economic Review, 92*(2), 335–8. doi: 10.1257/000282802320191561.

Cohen, M. D., March, J. G., & Olsen, J. P. (1972). A garbage can model of organizational choice. *Administrative Science Quarterly, 17*(1), 1–25. doi: 10.2307/2392088.

Dewey, J. (1910). *How We Think*. New York: D. C. Heath.

Dow, S. C. (1995). Uncertainty about uncertainty. In S. C. Dow & J. Hillard (Eds.), *Keynes, Knowledge and Uncertainty* (pp. 117–27). Aldershot: Edward Elgar.

Dow, S. C. (2013). Formalism, rationality, and evidence: The case of behavioural economics. *Erasmus Journal for Philosophy and Economics, 6*(3, Special Issue), 26–43. doi: 10.23941/ejpe.v6i3.149.

Duhen, P. (1906). *The Aim and Structure of Physical Theory* (translated by P. Weiner). Princeton, NJ: Princeton University Press.

Earl, P. E., Friesen, L., & Shadforth, C. (2017). The efficiency of market-assisted choices: An experimental analysis of mobile phone connection service recommendations. *Journal of Institutional Economics, 13*(4), 849–73. doi: 10.1017/S174413741700011X.

Earl, P. E., & Potts, J. (2004). The market for preferences. *Cambridge Journal of Economics, 28*(4), 619–33. doi: 10.1093/cje/28.4.619.

Gigerenzer, G., & Brighton, H. (2009). Homo Heuristicus: Why biased minds make better inferences. *Topics in Cognitive Sciences I*, 107–43. doi: 10.1111/j.1756-8765.2008.01006.x.

Gigerenzer, G., & Goldstein, D. G. (1996). Reasoning the fast and frugal way: Models of bounded rationality. *Psychological Review, 103*(4), 650–69. doi: 10.1037/0033-295x.103.4.650.

Gigerenzer, G., Todd, P. M., & Group, t. A. R. (1999). *Simple Heuristics that Make Us Smart.* New York: Oxford University Press.

Heiner, R. A. (1986). The economics of information when decisions are imperfect. In A. J. MacFadyen & H. W. MacFadyen (Eds.), *Economic Psychology: Intersection in Theory and Application* (pp. 293–350). Amsterdam: North-Holland.

Jefferson, M. (1983). Economic uncertainty and business decision-making. In J. Wiseman (Ed.), *Beyond Positive Economics? Proceedings of Section F (Economics) of the British Association for the Advancement of Science, York 1981* (pp. 132–59). London: Macmillan.

Jefferson, M. (2012). Shell scenarios: What really happened in the 1970s and what may be learned for current world prospects. *Technological Forecasting and Social Change, 79*, 186–97. doi: 10.1016/j.techfore.2011.08.007.

Kahneman, D. (2011). *Thinking, Fast and Slow.* New York, NY: Farrar, Strauss and Giroux.

Kahneman, D., & Tversky, A. (1979). Prospect theory: An analysis of decision under risk. *Econometrica, 47*(2), 263–91. doi: 0012-9682(197903)47:2<263:PTAAOD>2.0.CO;2-3.

Koutsobinas, T. T. (2014). Keynes as the first behavioral economist: The case of the attribution substitution heuristic. *Journal of Post Keynesian Economics, 37*(2), 337–55. doi: 10.2753/PKE0160-3477370207.

Koutsobinas, T. T. (2021). Attribute substitution, earlier-generation economic approaches and behavioural economics. *Review of Social Economy*, Published online 23 January, doi: 10.1080/00346764.2021.1874498.

Loasby, B. J. (1976). *Choice, Compleitry and Ignorance.* Cambridge: Cambridge University Press.

NBR (2017) 'Cam the Auditor General be trusted to combat corruption in New Zealand?' *National Business Review (New Zealand)*, 22 May. https://www.nbr.co.nz/opinion/nz-politics-daily-can-auditor-general-be-trusted-combat-corruption-new-zealand (viewed 18 September 2019).

Payne, J. W., Bettman, J. R., & Johnson, E. J. (1993). *The Adaptive Decision Maker.* Cambridge: Cambridge University Press.

Quine, W. V. O. (1951). Main trends in recent philosophy: Two dogmas of empiricism. *Philosophical Review, 60*(1), 20–43. doi: 10.2307/2181906.

Rabin, M. (2013). An approach to incorporating psychology into economics. *American Economic Review, 103*(3), 617–622. doi: 10.1257/aer.103.3.617.

Rutherford, M. (1988). Learning and decision-making in economics and psychology: A methodological perspective. In P. E. Earl (Ed.), *Psychological Economics: Development, Tensions, Prospects* (pp. 35–54). Boston, MA: Kluwer Academic Publishers.

Sent, E.-M. (2004). Behavioral economics: How psychology made its (limited) way back into economics. *History of Political Economy, 36*(4), 735–60. doi: 10.1215/00182702-36-4-735.

Shackle, G. L. S. (1961). *Decision, Order and Time in Human Affairs.* Cambridge: Cambridge University Press.

Simon, H. A. (1957). *Models of Man.* New York, NY: Wiley.

Simon, H. A. (1976). From substantive to procedural rationality. In S. J. Latsis (Ed.), *Method and Appraisal in Economics* (pp. 129–48). Cambridge: Cambridge University Press.

Thaler, R. H. (1980). Toward a positive theory of consumer choice. *Journal of Economic Behavior & Organization, 1*(1), 39–60. doi: 1016/0167-2681(80)90051-7.

Thaler, R. H. (1987). The psychology of choice and the assumptions of economics. In A. E. Roth (Ed.), *Laboratory Experiments in Economics: Six Points of View* (pp. 99–130). New York: Cambridge University Press.

Thaler, R. H. (2015). *Misbehaving: The Making of Behavioral Economics.* New York: W. W. Norton.

Thaler, R. H., & Sunstein, C. R. (2008). *Nudge: Improving Decisions about Health, Wealth and Happiness.* New Haven, CT: Yale University Press.

Vanberg, V. (1994) *Rules and Choice in Economics: Essays on Constitutional Political Economy.* London and New York: Routledge.

Winter, S. G. (1964). Economic 'natural selection' and the theory of the firm. *Yale Economic Essays, 4*, 225–272.

7 Should equilibrium be abandoned by heterodox economists?

Victoria Chick

Introduction

Sheila Dow, in her pathbreaking exploration of the role of methodological issues in delineating the borders of schools of economic thought, identifies equilibrium as one of four key areas (Dow 1985, 1996). She identifies equilibrium as a position of rest of the endogenous factors or variables, which she calls 'equilibrium's most general sense' (1996, p. 111). Her case in its favour is that it 'imposes some order . . . even if it is the process itself by which the forces are exerted that are of primary interest, the end point provides a useful reference point' (*Ibid.*).

Her case is convincing. However, many heterodox economists have advocated abandoning the concept. Their reasons are varied, as are their concepts of equilibrium – and these are not always clearly declared. Thus, the literature is something of a mare's nest of disparate meanings and linguistic confusion. In what follows, I shall try to clarify things a bit, though complete clarity is perhaps elusive, and make some judgements about the suitability of equilibrium to heterodox methods and subjects of enquiry.

The chapter proceeds as follows. First, I deal with some problems, which from time to time get in the way of the areas of debate that I think really matter. Then, I look at what is called equilibrium method or equilibrium analysis (Section 'Equilibrium method'). The Section 'Concepts of equilibrium' reviews several concepts of equilibrium. This is not a comprehensive survey: I shall concentrate on those concepts that are most in use in heterodox macroeconomics. My answer to the title's question is not a simple yes or no; there are several answers, depending on the concept of equilibrium in question. These will be given as I proceed. The chapter concludes with a brief final section.

Clearing the ground

Let me start with some points that might be contentious to some, but which will make clear the point of view adopted here and can be quickly dispatched.

DOI: 10.4324/9781003142324-8

Equilibrium and mathematical solutions

It is quite common to call any solution to a system of equations 'equilibrium'. For example, Backhouse (2007) builds his whole argument on the assumption that they are identical (In the same volume, I [Chick 2007] took issue with this assumption, but in quite mild terms.). Many economists further argue that one can *only* study equilibrium, for only equilibrium solutions are intelligible or coherent (e.g., Lucas 1981, p. 226). I think that is also what Joan Robinson meant when she taught that, outside their point of intersection, supply and demand curves 'did not exist' (J. A. Kregel, verbal communication).

There are three things to say about this identification (I would say conflation). The first is that the economy is not a system of simultaneous equations, particularly not a static system. The equations that constitute a model are one way of trying to understand the complex system, that is, the economy; they are an abstraction. Whether they tell us something about the economy depends on that abstraction not doing serious violence to reality, judged in some way. The solution to the model may tell us what the economy or some part of it might look like if the processes underlying the model and encapsulated by the equations were allowed to continue undisturbed by changes in the exogenous variables until they came to a point of rest, if a model is convergent. One would never expect to observe this in the actual economy.

That brings us to the second point: that the processes that lead to equilibrium are often not in the equations but in the 'story' (theory) behind them. Once there are equations, the tendency is for the story to be swept away and with it any possibility of 'reaching equilibrium'. In a static system, the concept of reaching equilibrium has no meaning: one has either been in a position indicated by the mathematical solution 'since the fall of Adam' (Robinson 1978) or one is permanently in some state that renders the system of equations incoherent. The solution of a system of static, simultaneous equations cannot be a point of rest, for there is no motion surrounding it, and one can only distinguish rest by contrast to activity. This is what happened to Marshall's (1961 [1890]) Book V) theory of price and quantity in what his successors labelled a 'perfectly competitive' market, from which, with a boost from Walras (1954 [1926]), equilibrium in economics became identified with market clearing.

The third and most important point is that to call the solution equilibrium may add nothing. The identification with mathematical solutions without an independent definition of equilibrium robs equilibrium of any meaning beyond that of a solution and renders it a redundant word – a word without a concept (Milgate 1987, p. 182, concurs). That the two are not the same should be evident from the fact that, although a mathematical solution is well defined, equilibrium has many interpretations. Vercelli (1991, p. 12) goes further: he points out that *a solution cannot distinguish between equilibrium and disequilibrium*. Any set of values of the endogenous variables outside the solution set simply renders the system internally incompatible; the solution set determines the values of the endogenous variables that make the model coherent; that is all. Consider a 'cobweb' model. At every point in time there is a solution, but only one of these solutions (if the model is convergent) is an equilibrium in the sense of a point of rest.

We believe we have given sufficient reason to reject all definitions of equilibrium that are no more than mathematical solutions – in particular, market clearing.[1] That is not to say that, for example, all static systems must be rejected, as we shall see. There is only one coherent position, the solution set; the question of whether that set is an equilibrium one or not is given, as in Marshall, not by the solution but by the circumstances in which the dynamic interplay of forces that underlie the static system comes to rest. The solution is given by mathematics, but as pointed out earlier, mathematics cannot distinguish between equilibrium and disequilibrium. It is not the job of mathematics. Whether the solution is also an equilibrium is the job of the theorist to define. Equilibrium may coincide with the mathematical solution, but its properties are determined by a completely different sphere of activity,

Equilibrium and the real world

Many would argue that equilibrium is a useless concept, because the real economy is never in equilibrium. Although one can agree wholeheartedly with Lawson's prioritising of ontology (1997, 2003) and to insist on distinguishing the ontic from the theoretic (Lawson 2007), to object to an analytical construct because it does not reflect the real world is to deny the analytical usefulness of abstraction and the possibility of theorising. Lawson is also quite right to censure projecting analytical conclusions onto the real world (especially those arising from theories or models that have paid scant heed to the salient features of that world in their construction) and giving priority to theory ('If what I observe in the world doesn't agree with my theory, it's the world that's wrong'). He is also quite right that equilibrium is not a state that one expects to find in the real world. But these criticisms do not invalidate abstraction and with it the concept of equilibrium. This chapter will treat equilibrium as an analytical construct, not a property of the real world.

General equilibrium

General equilibrium is the subject of two of the best-known critiques of equilibrium: Kaldor (1972) and Kornai (1971). Shackle (1966 [1963], p. 9) had already dismissed it out of hand, because it excludes (Knightian) uncertainty (as opposed to risk). But all equilibria do that. The important point is that general equilibrium precludes the *possibility* of uncertainty *ever* playing a role: everything of relevance is endogenised in a timeless framework (not quite as timeless in Walras's hands as it later became, but still timeless enough). The same stricture may not apply to partial static equilibrium, as we shall see below: it is the generality or completeness of general equilibrium, not its static quality *per se*, that is the problem, and the problem, to my mind, is insuperable. Therefore, I too recommend dismissing general equilibrium, on the grounds that Knightian uncertainty is a core principle of Post-Keynesian economists, and other heterodox schools of thought also embrace it, though they do not make such a fuss about it.

Note that both Kaldor and Kornai use the word 'equilibrium' to *mean* general equilibrium. This to my mind is an abuse of language.[2] Not only does it obscure the distinction between equilibrium as a concept and equilibrium as a method, but it also denies the existence of a rich variety of equilibrium concepts and of methods using those concepts.

Summary of this section

I agree with the critics that general equilibrium is not compatible with heterodox approaches. I also agree that equilibrium is not a property of actual economic systems but reject the conclusion that therefore it should not be used in analysis. And I reject the identification of equilibrium with solutions to mathematical systems, in particular, market clearing, though the two may coincide if equilibrium is defined by a supplementary story of the dynamic interplay of forces leading to that solution.

Clearing away these weeds and undergrowth has been comparatively easy. There remains a forest of ideas whose branches and roots interconnect in complex ways. It is time to try to give a shape to the forest and look at some significant trees. Our first task is to clarify the distinction made earlier between equilibrium as a method and as a concept.

Equilibrium method

The equilibrium method or 'equilibrist method' (Setterfield 1997) is the procedure of finding, in a static model whether partial or general, the solution of the system, ignoring the process that (if the process is convergent) brings the system to rest and simply calling the solution equilibrium without any justification. Chick and Caserta (1997) call this method Equilibrium Theory.[3] Vercelli (1991) calls it the pure equilibrium method. Motion toward that point is not studied, ostensibly because it is 'transitory', whereas equilibrium is 'enduring', a dichotomy brought forward from earlier times to characterise the long run and the short, distinguishing of the operation of the 'fundamentals' – the 'real' forces of productivity and thrift – from monetary forces.

Denis (2007), referring to Lucas's (1987) use of equilibrium, argues that the concept has been hypostasised, that is, the relationships between the elements in equilibrium have been substituted for the whole. The processes that bring those relationships into being are ignored, with, Denis remarks but does not elaborate, 'apologetic results' (p. 261) – see the section on Freeman's critique below. He makes use of Giocoli's (2003) distinction between a system of forces and a system of relationships. Giocoli finds that the emphasis has shifted toward the latter in recent years. Vercelli, after detailing a series of paradoxes thrown up by the pure equilibrium method, concludes that it is not 'fully intelligible unless it is interpreted within a dynamic framework' (1991, p. 22). Freeman (2015, p. 2) contrasts economists' use of this method with its use in the physical sciences, where it is a '*special case* of a temporal argument' embedded in a larger enquiry. For now, it is important to say that this possibility exempts partial static equilibrium from the outright dismissal of general equilibrium, above, but condemns its use in economics when not specifying the larger framework. All three critics make the same point, as do Chick and Caserta in their contrast between Equilibrium Theory and a theory that has an equilibrium. All of us are searching for the right language; there should be better words for this contrast.

To illustrate the point that the equilibrium method can be useful if embedded in a larger, dynamic framework, consider Keynes's *General Theory* (1936), Ch. 3, Section I. Wages are already determined in a bargaining process that has taken place 'offstage', so to speak. Producers know (it is assumed) the total and variable costs of producing various levels of output. They form an expectation of demand and hire the number of workers that can produce the firm's maximum expected profit. Assume that all firms do this at some point in time. The volume of aggregate employment is thereby determined, not necessarily at full employment. That is pure statics – no process, no time.[4] The result is the solution to a maximisation problem. Since it takes place in a static system, one cannot say within this model whether it is an equilibrium or not; it is just the solution.

Despite its static nature, this little model is perfectly acceptable methodologically, first, because everything takes place in the minds of those who hire labour, so there is no need for duration. Second, it is only a small part of a much larger theory full of dynamic processes – a part that is consistent with the larger system. This is what Chick and Dow (2005) mean by a temporary and partial closure within an open system, and it may conform to Freeman's description of the way in which physicists use the static equilibrium method.

In Section II of the Chapter, Keynes foreshadows the place of effective demand in the larger framework to which most of the rest of the book is devoted. There (1936, p. 27) Keynes attaches the word 'equilibrium' to this solution, but note that the context is now the economy as a whole, not only the workings of entrepreneurs' minds: 'It follows, therefore, that, given what we shall call the community's propensity to consume, the equilibrium level of employment . . . will depend on the amount of current investment'. This use of 'equilibrium' is legitimate in the larger context, though not within the confines of the model of Section I, where the term is not used. The Section I model nests inside the larger theory.

In Ch. 5, we return from the big picture to take another small step forward. This chapter gives us the framework in which the economy is imagined moving through time. The subject of Ch. 5 is to ask what happens if producers' expectations of demand are not met. Plainly, since production for the market takes time, expectations are formed at one time and the outturn occurs later[5]; we are no longer in statics but a rather loose kind of period analysis. The main message of Ch. 5 is that a disparity between expectations formed at (a fuzzy) time *t* to apply throughout period t and the outcome at the end of the period cannot affect the volume of employment that was decided at the beginning of *t*, as modelled in Ch. 3: the arrow of time flies in only one direction. But that is not the only message. A disparity may[6] prompt a revision of expectations at the beginning of $t + 1$ and change the amount of employment offered in the new decision-period. A path-dependent system has been set up – one with multiple potential equilibria and no necessary drive toward any particular one – if at all: change and adjustment of expectations could go on indefinitely without ever coming to rest. This temporal framework lies behind the theory of the rest of the book, as adumbrated in Section II of Ch. 3.

Within the temporal framework, rest, in the sense of identical decisions period after period, is only assured if (*inter alia*) expectations are met, whether by a fluke or a convergent learning process. That state of affairs can continue until disturbed by something that changes expectations or outcomes. Of the two, the fluke may be more likely, because in the real world the object of producers' learning would always be in flux. This fact further implies that if some equilibrium is reached, by whatever means, it will not last long. In Keynes's story, equilibrium has been robbed of its status as a state that will endure. Analytically of course, one can stop the economy's restless change to examine the features on an equilibrium configuration. Whether stationary or shifting (Kregel 1979), equilibrium is one of an infinite number of possibilities – perhaps a useful one to single out for study. Once again, the role of abstraction is clearly different from a description of the ways of the world.

History and equilibrium

Setterfield's (1997) critique of equilibrium counterposes equilibrium to path dependency, which he prefers as an organising principle. Path dependency is his version of 'history' in the opposition made famous by Robinson (1974), though she meant something else by 'history'. His 'open-system, *ceteris paribus*' method is Chick and Dow's open system with partial and temporary closures, and Chick and Caserta's provisional equilibrium is his conditional equilibrium (see below). If the above argument is correct, the Robinsonian opposition could be viewed as a false one.[7] One cannot do both sorts of analysis at once, of course, but we have shown that a static system can be nested within a larger system that involves path dependency – as Vercelli and Freeman would have it, a dynamic context. Chapters 3 and 5 illustrate the value of the idea of closed systems nested within open systems.

Caravale (1997) took quite a different view of 'history' in economic analysis, which he regarded as an 'extremely confused notion' not suited to economic theorising: 'The weakness of the atemporal neoclassical conception of equilibrium must not lead us . . . into the unknown (and non-existent) territory of history . . . ' (p. 27). I hope the previous paragraph makes clear what kind of 'history' those cited there are talking about, and I like to think they are making sense.

In his 'Partial defense of equilibrium economics' from its by now traditional opponent, 'history', Backhouse (2004) argues that the omission of processes is a type of *ceteris paribus* theorising. I found this suggestion startling, but Currie and Steedman (1990, p. 19) have found the same idea in Marshall (Book V, Ch. V, Section 4). If it is legitimate to use a static model while keeping the larger model 'in the pound', it would be well to specify the larger model or theory. That would avoid Denis's charge of hypostatisation. Without that larger context, the argument above suggests that calling the method 'equilibrium economics' (or Equilibrium Theory) is not legitimate. Its result is just a mathematical solution.

Freeman's critique

By far the most far-reaching, as well as entertaining, critique comes from Alan Freeman (2007). He takes the above objections to pure static equilibrium, whether general or partial, as his starting point and explains not only why this method persists but also why theories that adopt it are favoured over those that use other methods. He explains the ideological content of static equilibrium. His argument is that static equilibrium serves economics viewed as a religion, whose god is the market. He argues that, by ignoring the path(s) to equilibrium/equilibria, the presumption is established that the market sorts everything out so perfectly that we need not enquire into its workings. He draws a parallel to the Copernican revolution. He points out that Copernicus's findings were known in ancient Greece (discovered by Aristarchus). Why was the pre-Copernican perception kept in place for so long? Because the conception of heaven as perfect (perfect spheres orbiting in perfect circles) is unattainable to mere mortals. 'If the heavens are corrupt, then mere human imperfection requires neither king nor cardinal, emperor nor pope, to right it' (p. 10). Ptolemaic cosmology legitimated papal authority.

Similarly, in economics, the equilibrium-only version of theory is systematically preferred to explorations of processes or adjustment paths. This protects the market from criticism: the god of economics must not be challenged. Whatever allocation the market makes is seen by ordinary human beings as natural and therefore beyond their control; this mind-set protects those who benefit from the workings of the market. More recently, Freeman (forthcoming) has returned to this theme, arguing, further, that a static system precludes endogenous crises.

The odds are stacked against objectors to the equilibrium method, but what can one do? 'The game is rigged. Deal me in' (Leonard Cohen?).

Concepts of equilibrium

Dow proposed that 'rest' was the most general attribute shared by various concepts of equilibrium. What kind of rest? What is it that causes this 'rest' (or, rather, maintains what are seen as the endogenous elements of the economy at the same level of activity)? Caravale's definition of 'neutral equilibrium' is similar but broader: it is an equilibrium 'in which conditions occur that guarantee the "smooth" working of the system either at a single point in time, or through time' (1997, p. 12).

There are many ways that concepts of equilibrium can be categorised, all useful and interesting. We will simply start with the concept with the longest time horizon and proceed in no particular order. This list does not pretend to be complete. It excludes those pertaining mainly to microeconomics, except where there have been repercussions for macroeconomics (i.e., Marshall). And of course, it does not include the concepts of equilibrium that were excluded from consideration in Section 2.0. This includes many modern usages that amount to renaming the solution 'equilibrium' without specifying any independent concept.

Centre of gravitation

Equilibrium as a centre of gravitation is closely associated with the neo-Ricardian or surplus approach. The centre of gravity is a long-run (not a Marshallian long-period) position, an imagined state in which capital is perfectly adapted to the structure and level of demand, such that profit rates are equal across the board. As a 'centre of gravitation' this equilibrium state serves as an attractor, affecting economic decisions in the here and now. This makes sense if interpreted as being in logical time (Caravale 1993, 1997). If understood in historical time, this concept involves the longest time horizon imaginable, a time when the process of accumulation is complete and allocation is perfectly adapted to demand. This concept of equilibrium is teleological: it is difficult to imagine a more complete 'position of rest', as complete an end to history. It compares with the 'attractor' of thermodynamics, universal heat death, for what more is there for the economy to do? And yet this long-run position is described as embodying the dominant, enduring economic forces (*Ibid.*).

Despite his attachment to the neo-Ricardian concept of the long run, Caravale (1993) has made a suggestion that pulls their criterion of equilibrium back from the end of time to the present and made it operational. He suggested substituting for equal profit, equal *expectation* of profit. This fertile suggestion seems not to have been taken up either by neo-Ricardians or by other heterodox economists.[8]

I have two objections to the neo-Ricardian conception of the long run and the characterisation of it as embodying the 'dominant, enduring' forces in the economy. The first is that this imaginary or logical time is then mixed with historical time (when the economy is tending toward the long-run position) but the two are not connected; therefore, there is no way to get from one to the other. I would rather think of a long run that is the culmination of short runs. The second objection is that, surely, the job of theory is to identify and select the 'dominant, enduring' forces in the economy for an analysis. These should be the ontological basis, the starting point, of theory, not a characterisation of its end-point or 'final' equilibrium. They play as important a role in the (Marshallian/Keynesian) short period as in any longer time-frame.

In sum, I find this concept of equilibrium, except as modified by expectations, less than helpful. It is a concept I would abandon.

The concept of gravitation also figures in Marshall, as a 'normal' situation toward which the economy is tending, though in his hands it feels much less sinister: it is his way of making compatible the analytical construct that today we would call equilibrium with the fact that equilibrium is not expected to be found in the real world. When the capital stock is allowed to change (see further, below), industries, though not necessarily individual firms, would earn, on average, 'normal' profits – a level of profit that is just sufficient to keep firms, on average, in business. This is less rigid than equal profits, as normal rates of profit may differ between industries and amongst firms.

Long and short run and period: Marshall and Keynes

For analytical convenience, time can be 'cut up', in a way that is temporally meaningful, to enable partial analysis, as in the long and short periods of Marshall and Keynes (1936), with which the neo-Ricardian concept of the long run position can be contrasted. Time is viewed as a continuum by Marshall, blurring the modern distinction between run (a length of calendar time) and period (an analytical construct).[9] Keynes's interpretation was analytical. For Marshall, though time is continuous, the activities appropriate to each period differ: in the short period, there is no net investment; however, for Keynes, investment demand may be positive, but the new capital is not yet ready to affect the costs of production. Investment is the cut-off point because of its cost, its sporadic nature and the length of time it takes to produce and bring new capital into play.

Equilibrium is defined with respect to the assumptions: Short-period equilibrium is provisional (Chick and Caserta) or conditional (Setterfield), not unique or final: a short-period equilibrium will be disequilibrium when the restrictive assumption is removed. When referred to the real world, the market and short periods must be temporary, as time rolls on inexorably.[10] But in the analytical approach, the forces bringing about market and short-period equilibrium are no less 'dominant' in their time-frame as those in the long period, just restricted by the assumption that the analyst has imposed. And in the analytical device, they are as 'enduring' as it pleases the theorist to maintain the assumption that defines the short period. The bulk of *The General Theory* is concerned with the short period, when the expectations that govern investment are taken as given, as well as the effect of investment on supply conditions. Keynes outlined the effect of investment on demand and the process of adjustment to a one-off change in expenditure on investment – the multiplier.

Changes in supply effected by even a single change in investment are a long-period problem. In the long period, these assumptions are relaxed. We then have what Keynes called 'shifting equilibrium', in which the economy adjusts to changed levels of investment. This is not equilibrium in the sense of rest, as its name indicates. It may be stretching a point to call it equilibrium at all.

The effect of steady accumulation on the marginal efficiency of capital is analysed in Ch. 17. Its probable end-point, a position of unemployment, is not called long-period equilibrium by Keynes, though in my view the label would be appropriate. There is but one explicit reference to long-period *equilibrium* in the book. It is called the long-period equilibrium of employment; however, confusingly, its meaning is quite different, and it is significant that it appears in Ch. 5, not Ch. 3. The long period in this context is defined by assuming 'a state of expectation [of demand for output] to continue for a sufficient length of time for the effect on employment to have worked itself out . . . completely' (p. 48). It has nothing to do with Marshallian periods, still less with the neo-Ricardian conception of the long run. In Marshallian terms, it takes place in the short period: employment decisions are always made in the context of capital stock installed and up and running.

Hahn's criterion

Equilibrium is usually defined by the endogenous variables in question being at a point where their levels do not alter. Frank Hahn (1984 [1973]) proposed the following criterion: 'An economy is in equilibrium when it generates messages which do not cause agents to change the theories which they hold or the policies they pursue' (p. 59).

Although it is refreshing to see human thought and action brought back into economics, on the face of it, this criterion sounds like just another way to define a position of rest, caused by agents not changing their behaviour. But Hahn points out that this criterion is also compatible with moving or shifting equilibria. He also says that it does not require 'exact' market clearing, provided that the deviations from clearing are 'short' enough and 'rare' enough (p. 60). Just what those stipulations mean and why they are necessary is not altogether clear to me – perhaps more persistent or frequent deviations would shake agents' belief in their theories – but the criterion does open up the possibility of underemployment (as long as it does not persist for long). Unemployment is compatible whereas unemployment equilibrium is not.

The uncharacteristic relaxation of precision is welcome, but it is not thoroughgoing. Loasby (1991, pp. 45–8) points out the necessity for all agents to be in this equilibrium state. Loasby also finds the criterion incompatible with new knowledge, but is it not true that all notions of equilibrium keep new knowledge at bay?

Hahn portrays his idea as roughly representing the fluctuations of capitalism. That case seems to me not proven – indeed, I wonder whether any concept of equilibrium can do that or should attempt to do that. Its purpose, when it has one, seems to me to lie elsewhere.

Repetitive time: stationarity

In stationary time, it is imagined as a succession of periods in which various flow variables take place. In stationary time, the arrow of time continues to fly, but since, in equilibrium, nothing changes, time does not really matter. This rather paradoxical situation has made some economists uneasy. Hicks (-see Currie and Steedman, p. 196) calls it an evasion. Shackle's (1972) language is stronger: 'This curious monster (dismissed with gentle scorn by Alfred Marshall) has no claim upon our credulity. It is no more than a timeless system repeating itself along a meaningless dimension' (p. 238). Both Hicks and Shackle prefer 'the purity of argument of the timeless system' (Shackle, *Ibid.*). Shackle compared the time periods over which flows are measured with a string of identical beads: one learns everything from one of them.

Let me put the case in favour of the stationary state. It is a way of squaring the circle when building a theory of an ongoing economy, and one period is insufficient to determine a state of rest (see the argument concerning Keynes's Ch. 3, above). For that you need motion. Marx's reproduction schemes are examples, as is the (remote) possibility of the employment equilibrium in Keynes's Ch. 5 (see above) and the full short-period model assuming expectations are given (see Kregel 1976). In a path-dependent system, in which decision are continually reviewed in the light of past expectations and later outcomes, there is an infinite number of possible paths that the system might take. Stationary equilibrium allows the theorist to say something definite about the relationships that would exist between the elements of the theory in one of those outcomes. There is no implication that that outcome will obtain, but some may agree that it may be useful to understand these relationships.

Conclusion

Mark Setterfield's critique of equilibrium is both subtle and knowledgeable while being enviably clear: there is a straightforward opposition of the Equilibrium Theory and path dependency, of which the latter is preferred. The present paper is more difficult to characterise. Several approaches to the meaning and use of equilibrium are outlined, some are rejected outright, some praised and others saved by their context – one at least to the surprise of the author. There is no simple message. In answer to the question posed by the title, some concepts and methods should be jettisoned, some modified and others rehabilitated or maintained. General equilibrium should go, and with it static equilibrium (because it has no story of process behind it).

With such a story, it is a very useful tool indeed, though its result *should not be called equilibrium*. Neo-Ricardian long-run equilibrium might be useful if modified as by Caravale. The opprobrium cast on stationary equilibrium by Shackle and Hicks – if anyone is still aware of their assessments – needs to be set aside; the stationary state is an essential tool for dealing with an ongoing economy in which flows, of investment, income and the like, are to be analysed. Equilibrium need not mirror the economy: the purpose of abstraction, of theorising, is to find and highlight important features and processes – the map is not the territory. Temporary and partial closures – or the open system, *ceteris paribus* method – permit the use even of pure statics in the context of a wider theory. That is my complex assessment.

Acknowledgements

I am grateful to Jussi Ahokas, Andy Denis, Alan Freeman, Christopher Torr and Alessandro Vercelli for their helpful comments. The usual disclaimer applies.

Notes

1 I would also reject using the word 'equilibrium' for successful profit or utility maximisation. When Hayes (2008, 2020) characterises the point of effective demand as perfectly competitive equilibrium, what he actually means is that Keynes (1936) assumes that firms are able to give effect to their plan to maximise profits, subject to their expectations of demand and provided the planned offers of employment do not exceed full employment.

2 Freeman (2007) narrowly escapes this censure. He says, but only in a footnote (!), 'By the word "equilibrium" I mean general or static equilibrium' (p. 241, n. 1). We take him to mean what Setterfield (1997) calls the equilibrist method.

3 The capital letters were edited out in the original, but they were meant to make a point.

4 It is this model that Mark Hayes (2008, 2020) interprets as representing a perfectly competitive equilibrium. Kregel (1976) states that in the Ch. 3 model short-period expectations (i.e., expectations of demand for output) are assumed to be met. I have in the past agreed with him. Hayes denies that this assumption is at all relevant, and there is some truth in that: since the Ch. 3 model is timeless, expectations and outcomes, which are separated in time by production and marketing processes, cannot be compared. Only expectations figure. But if Ch. 5 is taken into account, the static model is only a first step, a way to make a dramatic cut through the assumption, prevalent among Keynes's colleagues and still in the mainstream today, that equilibrium requires full employment (market clearing). This assumption results from considering the labour 'market' in isolation from the market for output rather than, as in the Principle of Effective Demand, dependent on it.

5 In real life, decisions and outcomes, and their comparison, take place continuously. This is why Keynes rejected working in a formal period framework or using the concepts *ex ante* and *ex post*.

6 May, not will, because it may require several observations to change producers' expectations.

7 See also Chick (1985).

8 The possibility of using it to establish common ground between the modified neo-Ricardian and post-Keynesian concepts was thwarted by Caravale's early death. See Chick (2002).
9 'Term' implies duration or horizon, for example, 'long-term bonds'.
10 Both the 1997 articles avoided 'temporary', in the case of the joint authors because of its association with the classical dichotomy between the 'fundamentals' and monetary factors. Hicks uses 'temporary' in the context of the analytical approach, which I feel is misleading: its duration is under the analyst's control.

References

Backhouse R. E. (2004) 'History and equilibrium: A partial defense of equilibrium economics', *Journal of Economic Methodology*, 11 (3), 291–305. https://doi.org/10.1080/1350178042000252974

Backhouse R. E. (2007) 'Equilibrium and problem solving in economics', in V. Mosini, ed., *Equilibrium in Economics*, London and New York: Routledge.

Caravale, G. (1993) 'Keynes, equilibrium and modern economic systems', in R. F. Herbert, ed., *Perspectives in the History of Economic Thought*, vol. 9, Aldershot: Edward Elgar for the History of Economics Society, pp. 137–54.

Caravale, G. (1997) 'The notion of equilibrium in economic theory', in Caravale, ed., *Equilibrium and Economic Theory*, London and New York: Routledge, pp. 11–35.

Chick, V. (1985) 'Time and the wage-unit in the method of The General Theory: History and Equilibrium', in T. Lawson and H. Pesaran, eds, *Keynes' Economics: Methodological Issues*, Beckinham, Kent: Croom Helm, pp. 196–208.

Chick, V. (2002) 'Reflections on Caravale's contributions relating to equilibrium and their relation to the interpretation of Keynes', in S. Nistico` and D. Tosato, eds, *Competing Economic Theories*, London and New York: Routledge, pp. 167–76.

Chick, V. (2007) 'Equilibrium in economics: some concepts and controversies', in Mosini, ed. (2007), pp. 224–39.

Chick, V. and M. Caserta (1997) 'Provisional equilibrium and macroeconomic theory', in P. Arestis, G. Palma and M. Sawyer, eds, *Markets, Unemployment and Economic Policy*, London and New York: Routledge, pp. 223–37.

Chick, V. and S. C. Dow (2005) 'The meaning of open systems', *Journal of Economic Methodology* 12 (3), 363–81. Reprinted in Dow, *Foundations for New Economic Thinking*, Basingstoke: Palgrave Macmillan, 2012, 178–96. https://doi.org/10.1080/13501780500223585

Denis, A. (2007) 'The hypostatisation of equilibrium in neoclassical economics', in Mosini, ed. (2007), pp. 261–79.

Dow, S. C. (1985) *Macroeconomic Thought: A Methodological Approach*, Cheltenham: Edward Elgar.

Dow, S. C. (1996) *The Methodology of Macroeconomic Thought*, 2nd edn of Dow (1985), Cheltenham: Edward Elgar.

Freeman, A. (2007) 'Heavens above: What equilibrium means for economics', in Mosini, ed. (2007), pp. 240–60.

Freeman, A. (2015) 'Web version of Freeman, A. (2007)'. Online, available at hlttp://-mpra.ub.uni-muenchen.de/65045/

Freeman, A. (forthcoming) 'What was Marx's method, actually?', in J. Jespersen, V. Chick and B. Tieben, eds., *Handbook of Macroeconomic Methodology*, London: Routledge.

Giocoli, N. (2003), *Modeling Rational Agents*, Cheltenham: Edward Elgar.

Hayes, M. (2008) *The Economics of Keynes: A New Guide to the General Theory*, Cheltenham: Edward Elgar.

Hayes, M. (2020) *John Maynard Keynes: The Art of Choosing the Right Model*, Medford, MA: Polity Press.

Kaldor, N. (1972) 'The irrelevance of equilibrium economics', *Economic Journal* 92, 1232–55.

Keynes, J. M. (1936) *The General Theory of Employment, Interest and Money*, London: Macmillan.

Kornai, J. (1971) *Anti-equilibrium*, Amsterdam: North Holland.

Kregel, J. A. (1976) 'Economic theory in the face of uncertainty', *Economic Journal* 86, 209–25.

Lawson, T. (1997) *Economics and Reality*, London and New York: Routledge.

Lawson, T. (2003) *Reorienting Economics*, London and New York: Routledge.

Lawson, T. (2007) 'Tensions in modern economics: The case of equilibrium; analysis', in Mosini, ed. (2007), 133–49.

Lucas, Robert E. Jr (1981) *Studies in Business-Cycle Theory*, Cambridge, MA: The MIT Press.

Lucas, R. E., Jr (1987), *Models of Business Cycles*, Oxford: Blackwell.

Marshall, A. (1961 [1890]) *Principles of Economics*, 9th (variorum) edn (1st edn 1890), London: Macmillan for the Royal Economic Society.

Milgate, M. (1987) 'Equilibrium: Development of the concept', in *The New Palgrave Dictionary of Economics*, London: Palgrave Macmillan, vol II, pp. 1179–73.

Mosini, V., ed. (2007), *Equilibrium in Economics*, London and New York: Routledge.

Robinson, J. (1974) 'History versus equilibrium', Thames Papers in Political Economy, London, Thames Polytechnic. Reprinted in Robinson, *Collected Economic Papers*, vol V, Oxford: Blackwell, 1980, pp. 48–58.

Robinson, J. (1978) 'A Lecture delivered at Oxford by a Cambridge economist', in Robinson, *Contributions to Modern Economics*, Oxford: Blackwell, pp. 137–45. Also reprinted in Robinson, *Collected Economics Papers*, vol. V, Oxford: Blackwell, 1980, pp. 48–58.

Setterfield, M. (1997) 'Should economists dispense with the notion of equilibrium?', *Journal of Post Keynesian Economics* 20 (1), Fall, 47–76. https://doi.org/10.1080/01603477.1997.11490138

Shackle, G. L. S. (1966 [1963]) The Unity of European Economic Thought', reprinted in Shackle, *The Nature of Economic Thought*, Cambridge: Cambridge University Press.

Shackle, G. L. S. (1968) *A Scheme of Economic Theory*, Cambridge: Cambridge University Press.

Shackle, G. L. S. (1972) *Epistemics and Economics*, Cambridge: Cambridge University Press.

Vercelli, A. (1991) *Methodological Foundations of Macroeconomics*, Cambridge: Cambridge University Press.

Walras, L. (1954 [1926]) *Elements of Pure Economics*, tr. William Jaffe, London: George Allen and Unwin.

8 Dow, Keynes and the pragmatic tradition

More in common?

Jennifer Churchill

Introduction

Dow's delineation between schools of thought in macroeconomics rests in part on noting the differing attitudes towards the uncertainty facing the economic theorist. In Dow's own methodological contributions, uncertainty has a central role. Dow's monetary theory also demonstrates an appreciation for, and extension of, Keynes' use of uncertainty as an explanatory factor: our objects of study (economic agents) make decisions in the context of uncertainty – especially in relation to the future – and only by understanding that can we grasp concepts such as liquidity preference.

This chapter focusses on the uncertainty facing the theorist. A further distinction can be drawn between those who emphasise the source of that uncertainty being the nature of inquiry (an epistemic issue) and those who focus more on the idea of uncertainty arising due to the nature of the world (an ontological perspective). The epistemic idea assumes an unassailable gap between subject and object – between ideas and the world. The ontological perspective is an assertion *about* that world. Drawing a clean distinction is not trivial, and yet clearly there is some contention between these two perspectives. The ontologically uncertain will claim that the nature of the world determines the legitimacy of our forms of inquiry, whereas the epistemically uncertain will query the source of the ontologists' assertions about that nature. The current fashion among those who take uncertainty seriously – in the post-Keynesian school at least – is to favor the latter perspective, with Lawson's work on critical realism forming a focal point. Dow has aligned herself with these ideas. Nevertheless, the starting point of this chapter is to note the interest shown by Dow in the epistemic idea of uncertainty. This uncertainty has much in common with the concept of fallibility, something at the heart of pragmatist thought.

In the classical pragmatist tradition, it is thought that our human ideas are bounded by our human faculties and experiences, from which it is impossible to escape. Ascertaining the 'truth' of our ideas, in the strongest sense, asks the impossible – for some objective stance 'outside' ourselves, in the 'real world'. In place of evaluating knowledge claims in terms of their relationship to

DOI: 10.4324/9781003142324-9

an elusive certainty, pragmatist epistemology evaluates claims in accordance with a range of criteria, including alignment with experience, coherence with prior explanation and the logical rigour of the methods used. Scoring higher on one criterion often means scoring lower on another, so we balance according to purpose.

As this evaluation is so important, it is essential to be able to compare and evaluate forms of logic, and to be aware of the strengths and weaknesses of different methods. Keynes' *Treatise on Probability* (2008 [1921]) sought to investigate the nature of inductive logic, and it was, therefore, related to epistemic uncertainty. It can, in my view, be read as part of the pragmatist canon without too gross an intellectual manipulation. Keynes himself referred to the more famous of Charles Sanders Peirce's contributions in the Treatise, and I draw out additional points of seeming alignment in interest from other writings of Peirce as part of the argument of this chapter. Is Dow's work part of the pragmatist canon also? I think there are many aspects of Dow's methodological discussion that have pragmatic echoes, and I will try again to offer some examples here. Dow, however, has taken a conscious decision to avoid any strong claim of alignment – an assertion substantiated below. This decision by Dow aligns with a failure by 'new Keynes scholarship' – a literature devoted to understanding the significance of Keynes' philosophical thought – to pay much heed to the affinities between Keynes' philosophical ideas and those of Peirce.

Dow's dismissal of pragmatism feels significant and worthy of some explanation. Economics already has a school of thought – institutionalist economics – with acknowledged links with pragmatist ideas, which also took/takes uncertainty seriously. Therefore, linking pragmatism with post-Keynesian methodology would be a natural step: It is the similarities between institutionalist and post-Keynesian thinking that is Dow's reason for not covering both schools of thought in her categorisation of the discipline, as we will see below. The consequence of Dow's choice is that the philosophy, vision and ideology – the *mode of thought* – of institutionalist economics is possibly underexplored by some in the post-Keynesian tradition, with the risk that some are accepting an ontological reading of uncertainty mainly through a lack of familiarity with the epistemic alternative.

Pragmatism 101

Pragmatism allows for fallibilism without scepticism where the aim of inquiry is human flourishing (Putnam, 1992; Pihlström, 2004). How can this statement be broken down? We leave the question of the aim of inquiry to begin with and focus on the first half of this description. Take fallibilism: as stated above, at the core of the pragmatic tradition is the belief that there is no process that can take us unquestioningly to truth.[1] As such, all our knowledge is fallible. This should not, however, leave us in despair; the pragmatist tradition has an epistemic outlook that: '[rejects] the Cartesian focus upon the importance of defeating scepticism while endorsing the fallibilist view that any of our beliefs and methods could, in principal, turn out to be flawed' (Legg and Hookway, 2020, section 1). As Russell (1946) argues in his *History of Western Philosophy*: 'To teach how to live without certainty, and yet without being paralysed by hesitation, is perhaps the chief thing that philosophy, in our age, can still do for those who study it' (p. 14, quoted in Dow, 1996, p. 9). My choice of quote is tongue-in-cheek, as Russell would not have enjoyed being associated with pragmatism, and infamously leaves Peirce out of his history.

Accepting fallibility increases the importance of the norms of inquiry. The pragmatist tradition is 'tied to the study of the normative standards we should adopt when carrying out inquiries' (Legg and Hookway, 2020, section 1), on which we see Peirce's pronouncement: 'what is more wholesome than any particular belief is the integrity of belief, and that to avoid looking into the support of any belief from a fear that it may turn out rotten is quite as immoral as it is disadvantageous' (Peirce, 1877, quoted in Menard (ed), 1997, p. 25). There are virtues of inquiry, and the way we discern what is good inquiry in a general sense is to consider the end or purpose of all inquiry, which for Peirce (as we shall see below) is the dispelling of reasonable doubt.

Pragmatism in institutionalist economics

The classical pragmatists – and in their turn, the institutionalists – had more specific views on the scientific method, and many of their writings were imbued with a sense of how important the turn in natural science to dynamic systems with emergent properties would be for the study of economic and social systems (Hodgson, 2004). Veblen thought the marginalist theory would be challenged by this developing understanding. In *The Limitations of Marginal Utility*, Veblen argued, over 100 years ago, that:

> neither Mr. Clark nor any of his associates in this line of research have yet contributed anything at all appreciable to a theory of genesis, growth, sequence, change, process, or the like, in economic life.[. . .]. To the modern scientist the phenomena of growth and change are the most obtrusive and most consequential facts observable in economic life.
>
> (Veblen, 1909, pp. 620–21)

The subject matter of economics, according to Veblen, was material civilisation – a web of dynamic interconnections, processes and institutions that we are socialised into reproducing:

> Material civilization is a scheme of institutions – institutional fabric and institutional growth. But institutions are an outgrowth of habit. The growth of culture is a cumulative sequence of habituation, and the ways

> and means of it are the habitual response of human nature to exigencies that vary incontinently, cumulatively, but with something of a consistent sequence in the cumulative variations that so go forward – incontinently, because each new move creates a new situation which induces a further new variation in the habitual manner of response; cumulatively, because each new situation is a variation of what has gone before it and embodies as causal factors all that has been effected by what went before; consistently, because the underlying traits of human nature (propensities, aptitudes, and what not) by force of which the response takes place, and on the ground of which the habituation takes effect, remain substantially unchanged.
>
> (Veblen, 1909, p. 628)

In Veblen's view, marginalists were hampered by the use of theories created according to the rules of deduction 'instead of being drawn in terms of cause and effect' (Veblen, 1909, p. 625) – they discounted fallible explanations and sought certainties, however empty. Pragmatism offered philosophical support for the pluralist approaches in institutionalist economics, and specifically for an inductive scientific method that was problem-focused and value-laden. It showed the necessity of recognising the habits, conventions and institutions through which economic processes must pass.

Post-Keynesianism has done much to explore and expand our understanding of those economic processes, and these advances complement the institutionalist approach. There are now some theorists using the term PKI – 'Post Keynesian Institutionalists'; Whalen (2011) offers a nice selection and makes a compelling argument: 'Together, Institutionalism and Post Keynesianism provide a formidable alternative to conventional economics: a broader framework for economic analysis and a more secure foundation for exploring and crafting economic policy options' (p. 44).[2] Minsky demonstrated the power of combining post-Keynesian analysis of business and credit cycles with institutional and psychological factors in his financial instability hypothesis and super-cycle. As he notes, the 'actual path an economy traverses depends upon institutions, usages, and policies. In the final analysis, history remains history, although the range of what can happen is limited by basic economic relations' (Minsky, 2008, p. 194).

Dow (and Lawson) on pragmatism and institutionalist economics

In basic terms, the argument of this chapter is that Dow has somehow 'snubbed' the pragmatic tradition despite sharing many of its insights, possibly on flawed grounds, and arguably with negative consequences. Snubbing implies a conscious choice, so this first claim requires considerable substantiation. In *Macroeconomic Thought: A Methodological Approach* (1985), Dow has no separate section for institutionalist economics when detailing the separate schools of thought in macroeconomics, although there is a brief discussion under the heading 'The Marginalist Revolution', where it is presented as a form of the German historical school. There is the following discussion of Veblen's method:

> Veblen's method was multi-disciplinary (see Veblen, 1899c). In particular he brought anthropological and psychological ideas to his analysis of human behaviour; he reacted strongly against the mechanistic behaviour ascribed by the marginalist to 'economics man'. He concluded that individual and group or institutional behaviour are governed by technological conditions; in particular these conditions influenced *both* demand and supply. He foresaw that the attempts by large corporations to maintain profit rates and large unions to maintain wage rates would lead to contraction of output and eventual collapse of the capitalist system. There are strong parallels with Marx's thought in Veblen's analysis.
>
> (Dow, 1985, pp. 54–55)

Dow notes that the tradition lived on, mentioning Commons, Ayers and Mitchell among others, but the section is brief, and Dow does not link the tradition to the classical pragmatic thought of Peirce, James or Dewey. The section finishes with the statement: 'Eclecticism of method, however, has meant that the tradition lacks cohesion' (*Ibid.*, p. 55). This criticism begs the question as to when pluralism in method – seen as positive – crosses the line to become eclecticism in method, and how does the school of post-Keynesian economics avoid the same accusation? An alternative criticism might have been that there was a lack of a consistently-enough organised conceptual framework – a shared view on fundamental economic processes, arguably more present in post-Keynesian (or Kaleckian) economics.[3]

The philosophical journey taken in the chapter 'Methodological Issues and Economics' launches from Russell's previously mentioned quote, traces through the rationalist/empiricist debate, explains and contrasts Dow's famous categories of Cartesian and Babylonian thought, considers the debates within logic regarding deductive and inductive reasoning and finishes with an in-depth discussion of the Kuhnian retort to Popper's views on 'the' scientific method. Kuhn is located as following from Quine and Duhem and followed by the constructive criticism of Lakatos. There is no further relationship drawn between the pragmatic tradition and the work of Quine and Kuhn. Pragmatism is mentioned in parentheses as having 'something in common' with the Babylonian mode of thought (Dow, 1985, p. 14), but the term 'Babylonian' is chosen precisely because it is 'a relatively new term which does not pick up baggage from past debates' (*Ibid.*, p. 15).

In the 1996 update, 'Modes of Thought' gets a devoted chapter and Cartesian and Babylonian thought are demarcated according to the categories of closed versus open systems of thought, atomism versus organism, dualism and finally 'uncertainty, probability and expectations' (Dow, 1996, Ch. 2).

Methodological Issues and Economics is turned into *Methodological Issues in Economics*, and there are added sections on critical realism and pluralism. Pragmatism falls out of the index, although it remains in the equivalent parenthesis (now p. 12). Institutionalist economics gets its own section (4.4) and an update on a recent revival: 'Institutionalist or evolutionary economics, like the Post Keynesian and neo-Austrian schools, has in recent years achieved increasing support . . . [and] . . . achieved a greater degree of coherence' (Dow, 1996, p. 60). There is an acknowledgement of the distinction between old and new institutionalist economics, and a further reflection on Veblen's 'world view' and the interconnections between institutionalist thought and other schools:

> Old Institutionalism, rather, continues in the Veblenian tradition, rejecting methodological individualism and focusing on irreversibilities, in knowledge acquisition and in evolutionary change in institutions and behavior, all analyzed in terms of open system (as theoretical system and as subject matter).
>
> Although institutionalist economics is a distinctive school of thought in terms of understanding of the economic process and theory of knowledge, it has much in common with Post Keynesian economics, and indeed has drawn influences also from neo-Austrian, Marxian and mainstream economics. It is thus an example of a school of thought which has much in common with a range of other schools of thought yet is incommensurate with them. While this is true of all schools of thought, the overlaps in the case of Institutionalist economics are relatively greater. Since the purpose here is to emphasize distinctiveness rather than commonalities, Institutionalism has not been singled out as one of the schools of thought for elaboration of its conceptual foundations. In other words, the selection of schools of thought made here reflects the particular need to illustrate the importance of differences in methodological foundations, rather than to represent macroeconomics in its entirety.
>
> (Dow 1996, pp. 60–1)

Arguably, further important old institutionalist ideas regarding the nature of institutions are included in Dow through references to Lawson. However, aligning with Lawson also induces a movement away from the epistemic uncertainty of pragmatism, towards ontological uncertainty. Dow sees value in the demands of Lawson that social theorists take the methodological requirements drawn from the nature of social reality (social ontology) seriously. Lawson notes that he is at least in part unpacking the ideas already contained in prior economists, specifically Keynes, Marx, Veblen and Hayek (his ordering). For example, Lawson quotes Veblen:

> The growth and mutations of the institutional fabric are an outcome of the conduct of the individual members of the group, since it is out of the experience of the individuals, through the habituation of individuals,

> that institutions arise; and it is in this same experience that these same institutions act to direct and define the aims and ends of conduct.
>
> (Veblen, 1909, p. 243 quoted in Lawson, 1997, p. xiv)

Lawson also quotes Commons:

> The business man who declines to use the banking system which has grown up in the past, the labourer who refuses to come to work when others come, may be industrious, but he cannot live in industrial society. This is familiar enough....But when customs change, or when judges and arbitrators enforce a custom by deciding a dispute, or when labourers or farmers strike in order to modify a custom of business, or when a revolution confiscates slaves or other property of capitalists, or when a statute prohibits a customary mode of living, or when a holding company extends an old custom into new fields – then it is realized that the compulsion of custom has been there all along, but unquestioned and undisturbed.
>
> (Commons, 1934, p. 701 quoted in Lawson, 1997, p. 32)

Apart from drawing on these institutionalist lessons in understanding the processes of transformational social change, Lawson's critical realist position (drawn as it is from the philosophical system of Bhaskar) also contains considerably more, dare I say it, 'baggage' – something that Dow had previously sought to avoid. Despite this baggage, Dow makes an argument regarding the coherence of the 'Babylonian' world view and critical realism (1999) that places emphasis on the shared understanding of open versus closed systems of the 'material' world; Dow is, therefore, clearly siding with Lawson's metaphysical focus, the 'ontological turn'. It may be assumed, therefore, that one implicit concern that Dow has with linking with the pragmatic tradition is that she, like Lawson, links such thinking with the idea of the 'epistemic fallacy', which I would summarise here as the idea that a method can be evaluated prior to (or without ever) ascertaining the 'nature' of the world about which the method seeks to learn. Van Bouwel (2003) offers a full discussion of the epistemic fallacy and finds it wanting. Suffice it to say that pragmatists certainly put the problem the other way round – how is the prior knowledge about the nature of the world ascertained? The nature of theorising is prior to the content of our theory, even theories about existence.

A pragmatic version of Dow would require shifting back towards an epistemic perspective: differences across schools of thought would rest not on greater or less appreciation of the 'openness' of the universe, but due to distinctions regarding the level of critical awareness in the application of closed forms of reasoning such as modelling, when clearly that closedness is an artificially epistemic boundary – a metaphor even. See, for example, Kaldor (1977): '[m]ost abstract economic models postulate a "closed system", but they apply the conclusions reached to open systems, such as national economies, without being fully aware of the inconsistencies involved in this procedure' (Kaldor, 1977, reprinted in Targetti and Thirlwall (eds.), 1989, pp. 426–7). The distinction is subtle, but possibly important.

There is a further reference to pragmatism by Dow in *Economic methodology: an inquiry* (Dow, 2002), under the heading 'Rhetoric'. Here, pragmatism is described as an approach seeking 'a practical (philosophical) resolution to the failure of rationalism to generate truth' (*Ibid*., p. 115). Quine, Dewey and Peirce are named as belonging to the tradition, as is Rorty, and there follows some detail on Rorty's position, which is summarised as stating that 'the value of science-as-a-social-construction lies in its usefulness, since we cannot satisfactorily judge it in terms of how it represents reality' (*Ibid*., p. 115). This argument is then directly tied to Friedman's instrumentalism (although with the caveat that Friedman twists the position to his own taste) prior to a discussion on hermeneutics.

In summary, opportunities to discuss classical pragmatism in depth are not taken. The next section tries to draw out some links between Dow's position and the pragmatic tradition, to give a sense of why such a discussion would have been apt: Dow uses the ideas of Quine and Kuhn as stepping-stones towards her presentation of the modes of thought and the characterisation of schools within macroeconomics, and the possibility of meaningful communication between them, as will be discussed below. There are then other moments of apparent affinity between Dow's contribution and the theories of logic and epistemology from both classical and more modern pragmatism. Dow's categorisation of the modes of thought speaks to Peirce's original critique of Cartesianism. Dow's focus on uncertainty *for the theorist* speaks to the pragmatist focus on fallibility, and there are pragmatic chimes in Dow's discussion of unnecessary dualism (see, for example, Putnam (2002) on the collapsed fact/value dichotomy). The main focus will be on the links with Peirce, as this paves the way to also talk about the relationship between Peirce and Keynes and exposes an argument against pragmatism that may have weighed on the 'new Keynes scholars' and Dow. This argument is challenged in the hope that the links between, in particular, post-Keynesian methodology and the philosophical tradition of pragmatism can be uncovered and strengthened.

Links between Dow and modern pragmatism: overcoming falsificationism

Where precisely are those opportunities to make links with, and to delve deeper into, the pragmatic tradition? Dow's appreciation of the significance of the ideas of not only Kuhn, but also those of Duhem and Quine is one such area. Dow's support for these ideas in how to overcome the naïve falsificationism that emerged from the demarcation debate regarding what is and what is not science is one element of her methodological thought that has a pragmatic flavour.[4] The philosophical flaw with Popper's philosophy of science and the turn to formalism (here meant as a growing dismissiveness of non-deductive methods) was elegantly demonstrated by Quine – ironically through quite formal means – within his writings on the philosophy of language. Quine's paper *Two Dogmas of Empiricism* (1951) set out to achieve a formal analysis of analytical truth. The second of Quine's two dogmas was a form of reductionism regarding the relationship between statements and the world to which they relate:

> The notion lingers that to each statement, or each synthetic statement, there is associated a unique range of possible sensory events such that the occurrence of any of them would add to the likelihood of truth of the statement, and that there is associated also another unique range of sensory events whose occurrence would detract from that likelihood . . . [. . .] . . . The dogma of reductionism survives in the supposition that each statement, taken in isolation from its fellows, can admit of confirmation or infirmation at all. My countersuggestion . . . [. . .] . . . is that our statements about the external world face the tribunal of sense experience not individually but only as a corporate body.
>
> (*Ibid.*, p. 355)

Something closely aligned to this view was put forward earlier by Duhem – hence, the 'Quine-Duhem thesis' label. Quine's argument draws out more clearly some interesting epistemic conclusions:

> The totality of our so-called knowledge or beliefs, from the most casual matters of geography and history to the profoundest laws of atomic physics or even of pure mathematics and logic, is a man-made fabric which impinges on experience only along the edges. Or, to change the figure, total science is a field of force whose boundary conditions are experience (*Ibid.*, p. 356). In other words, the significance of dropping the two dogmas is a blurring of the supposed boundary between speculative metaphysics and natural science. Another effect is a shift towards pragmatism.
>
> (*Ibid.*, p. 340)

Kuhn's contribution to the demarcation debate was an attempt to move away from proscriptions regarding the scientific method, towards describing knowledge growth throughout scientific history. As noted in Balashov and Rosenberg's (2002) anthology of the philosophy of science, '[i]f observational evidence underdetermines theories, we need an explanation of what has determined the succession of theories that characterizes science's history' (p. 407). Kuhn described his approach as a 'historically oriented view of science' (Kuhn, 2012 [1961], p. xliv). Kuhn argued that in the early stages of scientific development, when the body of commonly accepted knowledge from which scientists could draw judgements regarding the plausibility or otherwise of new theories was relatively small, the criteria by which such judgements were made ('judgements' again, remember pragmatism 101) were not limited to experiential fit, or proper application of the 'scientific' method. Conclusions were rather determined by the researcher's 'prior experience in other fields, by accidents of his investigation, and by his own individual makeup' (*Ibid.*, p. 4). Although this is quite obvious when looking far enough back in time, it remains true at all times that an 'apparently arbitrary element, compounded of personal and historical accident, is always a formative ingredient of the beliefs espoused by a given scientific community at a given time' (*Ibid.*, p. 4). Dow notes that specific to economics, and prior to Kuhn, Schumpeter (1954) had spoken of 'vision' as something pre-analytical, grounding decisions regarding the scope and nature of inquiry. One year earlier saw the English language edition of Myrdal pointing to the role of ideology in economic reasoning (Myrdal, 1953). All of these arguments fall within the pragmatism tradition – investigating the methods and norms of inquiry in the context of fallibility.

Back to the classics: Peirce on logic, reasoning and probability

Arguably even more relevant than the post-Popper debates on the method for Dow – and certainly more significant for Keynes – is the work of Peirce. First and foremost a logician (although with contributions ranging across philosophy, particularly notable in relation to the theory of signs and meaning, as well as metaphysics), Peirce worked committedly to delineate and understand the relationships between different forms of reasoning. The discipline of logic, since Aristotle (see Smith, 2018), has included efforts to articulate the rules we follow when reasoning well, and the mistakes, or fallacies that we might commonly make (yet would concede are mistakes were they clearly pointed out to us, and we were *reasonable* people). Through Aristotle to Kant, discussions of logic become more sophisticated, with a particular interest in the 'synthetic' or non-deductive aspects of reasoning. 'Ampliative' logic was a key interest of John Stuart Mill (Robson, 2011), who argued that knowledge even in mathematics ultimately rests on induction, not deduction. Mill also attempted to *describe* causal inference, in particular setting out two methods: The Method of Agreement and the Method of Difference. Both Keynes and Peirce were moved by Mill's efforts, although neither entirely agreed with his conclusions.

Let us recall the earlier attempt to define pragmatism: *Pragmatism allows for fallibilism without scepticism where the aim of inquiry is human flourishing.* To bypass scepticism, Peirce rejected the 'spirit of Cartesianism' in his famous paper of 1878 *How To Make Our Ideas Clear* (reprinted in Houser and Kloesel (eds.), 1992, p. 124). Peirce specifically dismissed the method utilised by Descartes in the *Meditations* – the method of radical doubt. For Peirce, doubt cannot be faked – either you truly doubt something or you do not. One leitmotif throughout the pragmatic tradition is that there must be some level of commitment to descriptive accuracy when it comes to considering how we acquire (and justify) knowledge. Our actual methods of knowledge acquisition have been, over the past few hundred thousand years, phenomenally successful. Methodologies that suggest we should start doing things differently to what comes to us intuitively should be viewed, therefore, with great suspicion – a point key as we saw to the argument of Kuhn.

Doubt, as properly understood, is crucially important when it comes to inquiry, according to Peirce. For Peirce, doubt is the irritation that inspires inquiry. It occurs spontaneously from our practical interaction with the world. There are many things that we do not doubt, not because we have demonstrative truth of their infallibility, but because we have not been offered a reason to doubt them. As Legg and Hookway put it, 'We tend to treat our established beliefs as innocent until "proven guilty"' (Legg and Hookway 2020, section 4.1). See also Menand (1997): 'With the doubt, therefore, the struggle begins and with the cessation of doubt it ends' (Menand, 1997, p. 14). True doubt is the catalyst for inquiry, and inquiry aims at 'fixing belief'. The processes by which we fix belief were considered by Peirce in his 1877 paper *The Fixation of Belief* (reprinted in Houser and Kloesel, 1992, p. 109). There Peirce argued that the proper end of inquiry is the settlement of communal opinion, or at least the potential settlement.

Peirce broke reasoning into three categories: deduction, induction and abduction (Peirce, 1878b, reprinted in Houser and Kloesel (eds.), 1992, p. 186; see also Peirce 1903b, reprinted in Houser et al. (eds.), 1998, p. 226). The term 'abduction' refers to a form of ampliative reasoning, the formation of new theories and hypothesis that have a stab at explaining the world around us, our experience – a model of reasoning that relates to the contemporary notion of 'inference to the best explanation' (Lipton, 2004).[5] In some places, Peirce argued that the processes of inquiry would make use of all three forms of reasoning at different stages; in anticipation of Popper, for example, Peirce saw one process of scientific method as passing from abduction to deduction, and to induction – we imagine a theory, deduce a consequence that should generally hold should that theory be true and test a particular case. However, Peirce continually probed and challenged his own ideas. He was recognisant of a trade-off 'between security and liberty (rich suggestiveness; potency). Deductive reasoning provides the most security, but it is austere and almost entirely without evocative power. Abduction, on the other hand, is abundant in its liberty though nearly devoid of security' (Houser et al. (eds.), 1998, introduction xxxii). In his maturity, Peirce's concern was that he had neglected liberty for security, and narrow interpretations of Peirce and pragmatism certainly read his work in this way, as will be picked up below.

Keynes on logic, probability and reasoning

Keynes wrote on induction and inference in his 'Treatise on Probability' and clearly saw his theory of probabilistic reasoning as being a part of logic: 'If logic investigates the general principles of valid thought, the study of arguments, to which it is rational to attach some weight, is as much a part of it as the study of those which are demonstrative' (Keynes, 2008 [1921], p. 8). From the study of the subset of arguments that leads to certain, demonstrable knowledge, Keynes described his aim as an attempt to re-generalise logic, so that we can consider what it means to be rational in arguments whose conclusions are probable (Keynes, 2008 [1921], chapter II). Formal logic seeks to determine the relations of implication. Keynes' concern was the logic of the relationship of 'inference', a relationship appealed to by the 'everyday' arguments that form the body of science, politics, metaphysics and even rudimentary mathematics (remember Mill's influence). Our inferential arguments make use of natural language and of methods that are familiar and, to an extent, intuitive, such as induction and, more recently, statistical inference – forms of ampliative reasoning. Keynes set out to analyse these methods, and to demonstrate that they are valid. He organised this interest around the question of probability.

Keynes considered probability to be a measure of the degree of rational belief that a conclusion inspires, relative to its argument. Because we are dealing with rational belief, not belief in general, probability is objective, not subjective 'in the sense important to logic' (*Ibid.*, p.4). Probability itself is a relation between two sets of propositions – the first set being the premises of the argument and the second being the set of propositions that form the conclusion: 'Between two sets of propositions, therefore, there exists a relation, in virtue of which, if we know the first, we can attach to the latter some degree of rational belief. This relation is the subject-matter of the logic of probability' (*Ibid.*, p. 6). This is distinct to a thinking of probability as being a property of the event to which the propositions of the conclusion refer. It is this view of probability being a relationship between propositions that gives Keynes' work its logical aspect, rather than a metaphysical one. Keynes is interested in the logical validity of our arguments and is of the view that we can know this without knowing anything about the 'real world'. The truth of our conclusion may depend on something external to us, but the validity of our reasoning stands alone.

An additional idea of Keynes' was the idea that different probability relations could have different weights (*Ibid.*, Chapter IV). The same numerical probability relations could exist between two different sets of arguments and conclusions: however, the first set of arguments could consist of just five propositions, and the second could consist of 50 propositions. Keynes raises the possibility that the second probability relation would, therefore, have more weight. The argument set could differ in quality as well as quantity; for example, we might have differing levels of confidence in the truth of our premises We may feel differently about the conclusion drawn from a small set of premises about which we feel confident than a conclusion drawn from a large set of premises whose truth is highly questionable.

Under the influence of Russell and Moore, Keynes argues that objective probability relationships are known through intuition – our knowledge of them is something immediate, direct (as in Russell's knowledge by acquaintance) and/or irreducible (as in Moore's conception of simple terms such as 'good'). Keynes' assertion that probability relations are known intuitively is contentious and was publicly repudiated by Keynes a few years after publication (see, for example, Gillies, 2000, Chapter 3). However, Keynes' interest in the processes of inferential reason, and in 'ordinary discourse logic' are still interesting, and are reason, no less, to place Keynes himself in the pragmatist tradition.

In the Treatise, Keynes refers to Peirce's *Theory of Probable Inference* and *On an Improvement in Boole's Calculus of Logic*. Also of relevance for Keynes' philosophical interests would have been *The Probability of Induction*, where Peirce puts forward his own argument about the importance of evidential 'weight' in probabilistic argument: 'our belief ought to be proportional to the weight of evidence, in this sense, that two arguments which are entirely independent, neither weakening nor strengthening each other, ought, when they concur, to produce a belief equal to the sum of the intensities of belief which either would produce separately' (Peirce, 1878, reprinted in Houser and Kloesel (eds.), 1992, p. 159; see also Kasser, 2016 on this topic).

Peirce's categorisation of *The Three Normative Sciences* (Peirce 1903b, in Houser et al. (eds.), 1998, p. 196) might also have appealed: Peirce was referring to logic, ethics and esthetics (sic). Modern textbooks insist that students are clear on the distinction between normative and positive statements and refrain from the former in their economic science. Keynes, however, referred to economics, in the Cambridge tradition, as a 'moral science' (Davis, 1991, in Bateman and Davis (eds.), 1991). This reminds us again of the opening definition of the pragmatic tradition: pragmatism allows for fallibilism without scepticism, *where the aim of inquiry is human flourishing*. Pragmatism stands against any suggestion that the normative and positive can be clearly separated in inquiry. The contemporary pragmatist debate regarding the collapse of the fact/value dichotomy (see Putnam, 2002) is arguably one dual worthy of more consideration by Dow. The unapologetic *purpose* of institutionalist economics draws deeply on the influence of Dewey, even today. Compare, for example, the criticism aimed at Keynesian policy urging a magnitude of investment but not a direction, with the institutionalist Kapp (2011) arguing that '[i]nvestments and production will have to be guided by substantive human needs' (p. 96), and noting that, in principle, it is scientifically possible to determine and define such social minima 'not only in respect to elemental biological requirements but also to the psychological, safety, and aspirational needs' (p. 92).[6] Here is a vision of economic moral science: guided by ethical purpose, that itself has scientific foundations.[7]

Carabelli's interpretation of Keynes' philosophy

Following the work of Carabelli (1988), Keynes is understood to have put forward a coherent philosophical framework incorporating probability, intuition and judgement. Further, this Keynesian philosophy is deemed to offer a sound and fecund epistemological foundation for a post-Keynesian economic 'vision'. In the decades following Carabelli's work, there were a number of other important publications: 1989 saw O'Donnell's *Keynes, Philosophy, Politics and Economics*; 1994 saw Davis' *Keynes's Philosophical Development*; and 1996 saw Bateman's *Keynes's Uncertain Revolution* and Coates' *The claims of common-sense Moore, Wittgenstein, Keynes and the social sciences* in 2004. This literature was largely favourable to Keynes' philosophical thought and supportive of the suggestion that this thought underlies his economic theory in an essential way. This body of work was later referred to collectively by Lord Skidelsky as 'the new Keynes scholarship' (2003).

One interesting argument made by Carabelli and picked up in particular by Coates (2004) was that there was an important influence of the later Wittgenstein on Keynes – or if not an influence, then an affinity. An argument suggesting the former, that is, retrospectively justifying Keynes' work from the prospective of post-analytic philosophy, requires arguing that Keynes was not simply philosophically aware, but was a philosophical visionary, which is a tall order. As there is no reference to Wittgenstein in the index of the Treatise, the latter argument is really the most that can be hoped for. But of more interest for our purpose is the question of why instead (or as well) did not Carabelli and the other 'new Scholars' not more closely link Keynes to Peirce and the pragmatist tradition?

My impression is that Carabelli seems to reject Dewey's focus on purpose as offering support for instrumentalism (the idea that theory is good if it enables prediction, regardless of its relation to meaning) – we saw above the same argument being made by Dow in relation to pragmatism more broadly. Purpose is here being understood in too narrow a sense. Purpose should be understood as moral purpose, as much if not more than as 'use'. There is also a sense that for Carabelli and for Dow, pragmatism leads to narrow views of science, such as verificationism. In this, they are not alone: 'From the perspective of the logical empiricists, the pragmatic thinkers were viewed as having seen through a glass darkly what was now seen much more clearly. The myth developed (and unfortunately became entrenched) that pragmatism was primarily an anticipation of logical positivism, in particular, the positivist's verifiability criterion of meaning' (Bernstein, 1992, p. 817). It is not difficult to see where the idea comes from. Peirce put forward a number of pragmatic 'maxims', and the narrower of these (those pulling towards security, and away from uberty) could clearly be read in this way. See, for example, the following passage from *Pragmatism as the Logic of Abduction* that clearly suggests a pathway towards the verificationist principle of Ayer:

> Admitting, then, that the question of pragmatism is the question of Abduction, let us consider it under that form. What is good abduction? What should an explanatory hypothesis be to be worthy to rank as a hypothesis? Of course, it must explain the facts. But what other conditions ought it

> to fulfil to be good? The question of the goodness of anything is whether that thing fulfils its end. What, then, is the end of an explanatory hypothesis? Its end is, through subjection to the test of experiment, to lead to the avoidance of all surprise and to the establishment of a habit of positive expectation that shall not be disappointed. Any hypothesis, therefore, may be admissible, in the absence of any special reasons to the contrary, provided it be capable of experimental verification, and only in so far as it is capable of such verification. This is approximately the doctrine of pragmatism.
> (Peirce, 1903b, in Houser et al. (ed.), Vol. II, p. 235)

However, the quote does not end at that point, and neither should our judgement of Peirce's idea. Peirce continues: 'But just here a broad question opens out before us. What are we to understand by experimental verification?' Peirce most certainly did not have a narrow meaning in mind, that is, something to do with labs and controlled conditions. A wider reading involves some sense of the pragmatist view of our transactional relationship with the world. Also, here again an explanation is good that improves our ability to successfully achieve our purpose, but our purpose can just as likely be moral or aesthetic as it can be in some way practical.

Conclusion

There are clear echoes of pragmatist themes in the work of both Keynes and Dow. Pragmatist epistemology leads to conclusions similar to those carefully and powerfully made by Dow: that underdetermination in theory does not mean that we are reduced in methodology to description, or to relativism. Pragmatists have long argued that it is still possible to articulate what makes good theory, by pointing to the range of criteria that seem important (or reasonable) – explanatory reach, internal consistency, tractability, usefulness, etc. There will always be trade-offs, such as between stability and liberty. No one theory will be superior on all counts; the pluralism of theory is, therefore, a strength. Acknowledgement that no one method will be superior on all counts leads to the same conclusion regarding the pluralism of method. The norms of inquiry are important, as is the purpose of inquiry. If the reasons I have uncovered in this chapter – chiefly, too narrow a reading of pragmatist ideas – are what stand in the way of the pragmatic tradition being taken as seriously by Dow and the post-Keynesians as by the institutionalists, then I think they should be reconsidered. A more thorough grounding in the tradition could avoid the risk that its insights be needlessly re-discovered, or worse, put forward in less convincing, more superficial ways.

Notes

1 There are, in fact, pragmatist theories of truth, all of which object to a naïve correspondence theory.
2 Interestingly, none of the contributors reference Lawson or critical realism.

3 Morgan and Rutherford (eds.) (1998) offer an excellent range of views on the determinants behind the demise of institutionalist influence in the interwar period.
4 See, for example, Wade Hands (2004) for a full discussion on the links between Deweyan pragmatic philosophy and contemporary economic methodology.
5 Lawson acknowledges Peirce's efforts in a footnote: 'This (Aristotelian) mode of inference is interpreted as retroduction by, for example, Peirce (1867), Hanson (1958), Bhaskar (1978), McMullin (1984) and as abduction by Peirce (1867) and various Institutionalist economists. Peirce is probably the most important contributor here' (Lawson, 1997, 294 (footnote)).
6 Disappointingly, Kapp's subchapter 'The American Influence: Pragmatism, Darwinism, Brook Adams' of 'Intellectual Antecedents of Institutional Economics' is missing (Berger and Steppacher 2011, p. 11, editorial introduction).
7 With thanks to Sebastian Berger for introducing me to Kapp, and to this debate.

References

Balashov, Y. and Rosenberg, A. (eds.) (2002). *Philosophy of Science Contemporary Readings* Abingdon: Routledge.

Bateman, B. and Davis, J.B., (eds) (1991). *Keynes and Philosophy: Essays on the Origins of Keynes's Thought.* Aldershot: Edward Elgar Publishing.

Bernstein, R.J., (1992, Winter). 'The Resurgence of Pragmatism', *Social Research,* Vol. 59, No. 4, pp. 813–40. http://www.jstor.org/stable/40970721

Carabelli, A.M., (1988). *On Keynes's Method.* Basingstoke and London: Macmillan Press Ltd. https://doi.org/10.1007/978-1-349-19414-8

Coates, J., (2004). *The Claims of Common Sense: Moore, Wittgenstein, Keynes and the Social Sciences.* Cambridge: Cambridge University Press. https://doi.org/10.1017/CBO9780511520020

Davis, J.B., (1991). 'Keynes's View of Economics as a Moral Science', in *Keynes and Philosophy: Essays on the Origins of Keynes's Thought.* Eds. Bradley W. Bateman and John B. Davis. Aldershot: Edward Elgar Publishing, pp. 89–103.

Davis, J.B., (1994). *Keynes's Philosophical Development.* Cambridge: Cambridge University Press.

Dow, S.C., (1985). *Macroeconomic Thought: A Methodological Approach* Oxford: Basil Blackwell Ltd.

Dow, S.C., (1996). *The Methodology of Macroeconomic Thought: A Conceptual Analysis of Schools of Thought in Economics.* Cheltenham and Northampton, MA: Edward Elgar.

Dow, S.C., (1999, Autumn). 'Post Keynesianism and Critical Realism: What Is the Connection?', *Journal of Post Keynesian Economics,* Vol. 22, No. 1, pp. 15–33. https://doi.org/10.1080/01603477.1999.11490225

Dow, S.C., (2002). *Economic Methodology: An Inquiry.* Oxford: Oxford University Press.

Gillies, D., (2000). *Philosophical Theories of Probability.* Abingdon: Routledge https://doi.org/10.4324/9780203132241

Hodgson, G.M., (2004). *The Evolution of Institutional Economic Agency, Structure and Darwinism in American Institutionalism.* London and New York: Routledge. https://doi.org/10.4324/9780203300350

Houser, N. and Kloesel, C., (eds) (1992). *The Essential Peirce: Selected Philosophical Writings, Volume 1 (1867–1893).* Bloomington: Indiana University Press. https://doi.org/10.2307/j.ctvpwhg1z

Houser, N., Eller, J.R., Lewis, A.C., De Tiene, A., Clark, C.L., and Bront Davis, D., (1998). *The Essential Peirce: Selected Philosophical Writings, Volume 2 (1893–1913),* Bloomington: Indiana University Press.

Kaldor, N. (1977) 'Equilibrium Theory and Growth Theory', originally published in M.Boskin (ed.) *Economics and Human Welfare: Essays in Honour of Tibor Scitovsky.* Academic Press, 1997.

Kapp, K.W. [Berger, S and Steppacher, R (eds.)] (2011). *The Foundations of Institutional Economics.* London and New York: Routledge. https://doi.org/10.4324/9780203827864

Kasser, J. (2016). 'Two Conceptions of Weight of Evidence in Peirce's Illustrations of the Logic of Science', *Erkenn* Vol. 81, pp. 629–48. https://doi.org/10.1007/s10670-015-9759-5

Keynes, J.M., (2008 [1921]). *A Treatise on Probability:* BN Publishing, reprint of Keynes, J.M. (1978) Johnson E. and Moggridge, D. (eds) *The Collected Writings of John Maynard Keynes.* Royal Economic Society.

Kuhn, T.S., (2012 [1961]). *The Structure of Scientific Revolutions.* 4th ed. Chicago, IL and London: The University of Chicago Press.

Lawson, T., (1997). *Economics & Reality.* Abingdon, UK: Routledge. https://doi.org/10.4324/9780203195390

Legg, C. and Hookway, C., (2020). "Pragmatism", *The Stanford Encyclopedia of Philosophy* (Fall 2020 Edition), Edward N. Zalta (ed.), https://plato.stanford.edu/archives/fall2020/entries/pragmatism/ [accessed 31 March 2020].

Lipton, P., (2004). *Inference to the Best Explanation.* 2nd ed. London and New York: Routledge.

Menard, L., (ed) (1997). *Pragmatism: A Reader.* New York: Vintage.

Minsky, H., (2008). *Stabilizing an Unstable Economy.* New York: McGraw Hill.

Morgan, M.S. and Rutherford, M. eds. (1998). 'From Interwar Pluralism to Postwar Neoclassicism', Annual Supplement to Volume 30 *History of Political Economy.* Durham, NC and London: Duke University Press.

Myrdal, G., (1953). *The Political Element in the Development of Economic Theory.* London: Routledge & Kegan Paul Ltd.

O'Donnell, R.M. (1989). *Keynes: Philosophy, Economics and Politics.* Basingstoke and London: Macmillan Press Ltd. https://doi.org/10.1007/978-1-349-07027-5

Peirce, C.S. (1877). 'The Fixation of Belief', in Houser, N and Kloesel, C. (eds) (1992) *The Essential Peirce: Selected Philosophical Writings, Volume 1 (1867–1893).* Bloomington: Indiana University Press. https://doi.org/10.2307/j.ctvpwhg1z

Peirce, C.S. (1878a). 'How to Make Our Ideas Clear', in Houser, N and Kloesel, C. (eds) *The Essential Peirce: Selected Philosophical Writings, Volume 1 (1867–1893).* Bloomington: Indiana University Press. https://doi.org/10.2307/j.ctvpwhg1z

Peirce, C.S. (1878b). 'Deduction, Induction, and Hypothesis', in Houser, N and Kloesel, C. (eds) *The Essential Peirce: Selected Philosophical Writings, Volume 1 (1867–1893).* Bloomington: Indiana University Press. https://doi.org/10.2307/j.ctvpwhg1z

Peirce, C.S. (1903a). 'The Three Normative Sciences', in Houser, N., Eller, J.R., Lewis, A.C., De Tiene, A., Clark, C.L. and Bront Davis, D. (eds) *The Essential Peirce: Selected Philosophical Writings, Volume 2 (1893–1913).* Bloomington: Indiana University Press.

Peirce, C.S. (1903b). 'Pragmatism as the Logic of Abduction', in Houser, N., Eller, J.R., Lewis, A.C., De Tiene, A., Clark, C.L. and Bront Davis, D. (eds) *The Essential*

Peirce: Selected Philosophical Writings, Volume 2 (1893–1913). Bloomington: Indiana University Press.

Peirce, C.S. (1903c). 'The Nature of Meaning', in Houser, N., Eller, J.R., Lewis, A.C., De Tiene, A., Clark, C.L. and Bront Davis, D. (eds) *The Essential Peirce: Selected Philosophical Writings, Volume 2 (1893–1913)*, Bloomington: Indiana University Press.

Pihlström, S., (2004). 'Putnam and Rorty on Their Pragmatist Heritage: Re-Reading James and Dewey', in Khalil, E.L. (ed.) *Dewey, Pragmatism and Economic Methodology*. Abington: Routledge. Cp. 3. https://doi.org/10.4324/9780203799901

Putnam, H. (Conant, J. (ed)) (1992) *Realism with a Human Face Cambridge*, Massachusetts, and London: Harvard University Press.

Putnam, H., (2002). *The Collapse of the Fact/Value Dichotomy and Other Essays*. Cambridge, MA, and London, England: Harvard University Press.

Quine, W.V., (1951, January). 'Main Trends in Recent Philosophy: Two Dogmas of Empiricism', *The Philosophical Review*, Vol. 60, No. 1, pp. 20–43, reprinted in Balashov and Rosenberg (eds.) (2002) *Philosophy of science contemporary readings*. Abingdon: Routledge.

Robson, J.M. (ed.) (2011) *Collected Works of John Stuart Mill: VII. System of Logic: Ratiocinative and Inductive*. Abington: Routledge.

Russell, B. (2004)[1946]) *History of Western Philosophy*, Oxford U.K. and New York, U.S.A., Routledge.

Rutherford, M., (2011). *The Institutionalist Movement in American Economics, 1918–1947: Science and Social Control*. Cambridge and New York: Cambridge University Press.

Schumpeter, Joseph A. (1954). *History of economic analysis*. London: Allen & Unwin. Edited from a manuscript by Elizabeth Boody Schumpeter.

Skidelsky, R., (2003). *John Maynard Keynes 1883–1946: Economist, Philosopher, Statesman*. Basingstoke and London: Macmillan.

Smith, R., (2018). 'Aristotle's Logic', in Zalta, E.N. (ed.) *The Stanford Encyclopedia of Philosophy*, Spring 2018 Edition. https://plato.stanford.edu/archives/spr2018/entries/aristotle-logic/ (accessed 15 September 2018).

Targetti, F. and Thirlwall, A.P., (1989), *The Essential Kaldor*. London: Duckworth.

Veblen, T., (1909, November) 'The limitations of marginal utility', *Journal of Political Economy*, Vol. 17, No. 9, pp. 620–36.

Van Bouwel, J., (2003). 'When Unveiling the Epistemic Fallacy Ends with Committing the Ontological Fallacy. On the Contribution of Critical Realism to the Social Scientific Explanatory Practice', *Philosophica*, Vol. 71, pp. 81–98.

Wade Hands, D., (2004). 'Pragmatism, Knowledge, and Economic Science: Deweyan Pragmatic Philosophy, and Contemporary Economic Methodology', in: Khalil, E.L. (ed.) *Dewey, Pragmatism and Economic Methodology*. Abington: Routledge. https://doi.org/10.4324/9780203799901

Whalen, C.J., (ed.) (2011). *Financial Instability and Economic Security after the Great Recession*. Cheltenham, UK and Northampton, MA: Edward Elgar. https://doi.org/10.4337/9780857934840

9 Keynes in transition

'The Economic Possibilities for Our Grandchildren'[1]

Jesper Jespersen

Introduction

J. M. Keynes is known for his contribution to macroeconomic theory and methodology. A realistic analysis of 'The economy as a whole' to sustain a 'good society' was his ambition from a very early stage of his academic life. In fact, while being a student at Cambridge University, 1902–05 he studied philosophy and mathematics and wrote essays on themes like 'ethics, beauty, virtue, happiness and egoism'; see, among others, O'Donnell (1989), Carabelli (2021), and Fitzigibbons (1988). His fellowship-dissertation for King's College focused on the probability-theory: how to make rational decisions in a (partly) unknown and unknowable environment. These human aspects of understanding social processes were constantly on his mind during his academic work on (macro)economics.

Many scholars have discussed the development in Keynes's (macro)economic thinking and his transformation from a rather conventional neoclassical economist accepting and teaching the 'Quantity Theory of Money and Prices' into the genuine original macroeconomist of *The General Theory*. They have also discussed whether this transformation occurred abruptly or as a more continued exercise digging deeper into the methodological challenges of understanding 'the economic society in which we actually live' (*GT*, p. 3). I have no definitive answer to this question. But after studying *The Economic possibilities for our grandchildren* (Keynes, 1930b) in its historical context[2], I am inclined to say that this essay belongs to the beginning of the gradual process of Keynes's continuous challenges to neoclassical economics[3]: a process that came to a dramatic change when the economic consequences of the economic slump (of the early 1930s) became apparent. He could no longer defend neoclassical economics as a 'moral science'[4], see also Skidelsky and Skidelsky (2012).

Keynes characterised his intellectual path to *The General Theory* as 'a struggle of escape from habitual modes of thought and expression' (*GT*, p. viii). This transformation in his mind from a description of a closed non-monetary economy to an open system expressed in his essay *A Monetary Theory of Production* (1933) was, indeed, remarkable for so many reasons. As we shall see,

DOI: 10.4324/9781003142324-10

the '*Economic possibilities for our Grandchildren*' represents an important steppingstone guiding Keynes towards a macroeconomic methodology of relevance for 'real world phenomena' and the foundation of a good society'.

Hence, in the essay, we find Keynes 'midstream' – halfway out of neoclassical macroeconomic, but less than halfway into *The General Theory*. One should keep in mind that in October 1930 he had just published *A Treatise on Money*, which was an attempt to elaborate on the 'Quantity Theory of Money and Prices'.

Further, in this essay, he adopted an unconventional long-term view: '[T]ake wings into the future. What can we reasonably expect . . . hundred years hence?' Nothing could, of course, be said, definitively, but we see that Keynes's mind had started working within an open (macroeconomic) system. Anything could happen, depending on external, unforeseeable events and political decisions. The long-term outcome of the course taken by the macroeconomic system, what he later called the *Quaesitum*, was not predetermined.[5] This argument runs counter to neoclassical general equilibrium economics. Hereby, Keynes demonstrated that he was prepared to envision long-term challenges to society with respect to, for instance, technology, demography and in today's world: climate changes. Government cannot know the future with any kind of certainty; however, it can reduce its possible individual and social costs by precaution and protection to reduce the potentially disastrous and irreversible consequences of uncertain events.

As we shall see, Keynes was caught in 1930 in the middle of an intellectual sloughing from the neoclassical straight-jacket of *A Treaty of Money* into the open-system analysis of *The General Theory*. In this essay, Keynes argued that the future is open. He concludes the essay in the following manner: 'chiefly, do not let us overestimate the importance of the economic problem, or sacrifice to its supposed necessities other matters of greater and more permanent significance' (*Ibid.*, p. 332). Obviously, he was searching the economics for a 'good society', where 'love, truth and beauty could be our guiding motives'.

Background for '*Economic Possibilities for Our Grandchildren*'

The essay '*Economic Possibilities for Our Grandchildren*' should be read and interpreted in the above presented perspective of Keynes being 'mid-stream' in his (macro)economic and social thinking. This essay was originally given as a lecture for undergraduates in 1928 – before the slump initiated. But Keynes did publish it in a slightly edited form in the Autumn of 1930 in the weekly *Nation and Atheneum* and finally, after some further editing, he did include it in his book, *Essays in Persuasion*, published in late 1931. So, this essay must be taken seriously as a steppingstone in Keynes's continuous attempts to reconcile his philosophical vision of 'a good life' and his macroeconomic thinking partly inherited from his mentor Alfred Marshall.

In retrospect, one can see, as mentioned, that this reconciliation was a lifelong process, which involved some fundamental thinking about the methodology of macroeconomics and individual behaviour in the perspective of uncertainty. On the one hand, Keynes seemed to stay loyal to the fundamental principles of his utopian vision of a 'good society' developed within the 'Apostle Society' in Cambridge and debated at length with the participants of the Bloomsbury circles.[6] On the other hand, this vision was increasingly on a collision course with the foundation of neoclassical economics based on individual optimisation of utility and profit and a perfect market economic system. He had learned an economic theory while sitting at the feet of Alfred Marshall, but increasingly at odds with the real-world economic outcome.

This essay takes a very long-term perspective, two generations or even longer. Keynes reveals himself as being concerned with the consequences of a process of continuous technological progress leading to an ever-enlarging capacity of producing material goods. A quadrupling of the economic possibilities for our grandchildren, but for what use, when all the basic needs are more than fulfilled? Keynes did wonder. Material output is, of course, a necessary means to achieving a certain standard of living to get a 'good life'; however, it could not and should not be an end by itself. Traditional (and often dirty and hard) work in agriculture and manufacturing could never be a goal by itself.

> But beware! The time for all this is not yet" – he wrote in 1930 and continued: "For at least another hundred years we must pretend to ourselves and to everyone that fair is foul and foul is useful and fair is not. Avarice and usury and precaution must be our gods for a little longer. For only they can lead us out of the tunnel of economic necessity into daylight
> (CWK IX, p. 331).

So, by November 1931, the dating of the Preface to his volume of *Essays in Persuasion* in which the essay on the economic possibilities for our grandchildren was included, Keynes was still in a sense arguing as a neoclassical economist. Without hesitation, he claimed that savings, even in the form of 'love of money' are 'tremendously useful in promoting the accumulation of capital . . . which within hundred years will make us reach our destination of economic bliss' (*Ibid.*, p. 329). Not until the marginal utility of an extra unit of output (for ourselves) has become zero will mankind be released from the chains of perceived economic necessity. According to neoclassical economic utilitarian philosophy, human wants are unlimited. Enough will never become enough, at least, according to neoclassical economics, until the economic problem has been solved for the individuals. So, the bliss of the transcendence of these loathsome premises will never happen in our lifetime. Capitalism will generate new demand for material and positional goods (and services). But Keynes, being a sceptic towards calculated utilitarianism, had to hesitate: could it be right to let this immoral economic practice go on for another 100 years at the expense of real human values like 'love, beauty and truth'?

In addition, following the neoclassical dictum could cause a Faustian temptation, which Keynes sees as a likely consequence of the neoclassical ethical support of 'avarice, usury and love of money'. He asked himself (and the reader): will it be possible after another 100 years, where people have been told that 'foul is useful and fair is not' for them to make a psychological turn around? When goods no longer are scarce and 'enough has (at last) become enough', what should people then do? Are they mentally able to make such a change of priorities, after they for more than two generations have accepted that Mammon is the superior God?[7]

In the early 1930s, Keynes was facing an existential transformation in his intellectual life. He wanted to liberate himself from the neoclassical strait-jacket of analyzing the economy as a whole within a deterministic/closed market model guided by immoral individual behaviour. The defining moment of this existential intellectual transformation came, when he admitted that the adherents of the mainstream neoclassical paradigm had no method for the analysis of open-system macroeconomics.[8]

He was under his way of merging his vision for a 'good society' with a relevant and therefore realistic macroeconomic theory. This challenge had in many ways made him a methodological driver all his intellectual life, where he had gone all the way from G. E. Moore's lectures on philosophy, while being a student in Cambridge, via *Treatise on Probability* and *A Treatise on Money*. In 1930, he was obviously still not satisfied, so the 'long struggle' had to go on leading towards *The General Theory* (1936) and later on to *How to pay for the War* (1940) with a summing up on philosophy and economics for a 'good society' in *My early Beliefs*[9] (Keynes, 1946).

When reading the essay 'The Economic possibilities for Our Grandchildren', one should keep in mind that back in 1930 Keynes was less than halfway through his methodological transformation of his macroeconomic analysis (but one should be aware that the word 'possibilities' indicates that he was dealing with an open-system analysis); that the economic outcome was not predetermined, especially not in the very long run. Obviously, he was still struggling with the methodology of the intermediate period: when the tempest/crisis is over after say 3 to 5 years, what could be said? He was in doubt without, yet, a theoretical alternative. As we shall see, in this 1930-essay, he is surprisingly neoclassical when looking at the medium run, even though it caused him strong moral distaste. He had to be loyal to his (inherited) understanding of medium run economics, where 'avarice and usury and precaution must be our gods for a little longer' (*Ibid.*, p. 331). It took him another 6 years to elaborate his fundamentally new methodology based on his understanding of 'uncertainty' and rational *social* behaviour of individuals and the government. In 1936, he could, at last, abandon the belief that the 'morbidities of greed and avarice' were needed for solving the economic problems of mankind.

Fortunately, shortly after the publication of *A Treatise on Money* in 1930, the deepening of the economic crisis made Keynes increasingly dissatisfied with the (macro)economic analysis within that book. In this process, he was supported by a very inspiring dialogue with his young colleagues in Cambridge, known as the Circus; see Kahn, 1987. But, it was not until the Michaelmas Term of 1932 that Keynes changed the title (and content) of his lecture plan. For years, the course had been announced as 'The Pure Theory of Money and Prices' based on the 'Quantitative Theory of Money and Prices' in perspective of the 'fundamental equation developed in *A Treatise on Money*'. In 1932, the content of the course was changed and was called 'A Monetary Theory of Production'. Here, it was demonstrated as to how 'aggregate demand' could play an active role shaping the future of (macro)economic development. At last, he was able to reconcile his vision of a good society with solid (to say the least) macroeconomic arguments, and ethically respectable individual behaviour, which made him able to write rather affirmatively in 1942: 'In the long run almost anything is possible' (CWK, XXV, pp. 264–70).

Hence, one of the steppingstones for his transformation from *A Treatise on Money* (1930) to *The General Theory* (1936) may have been his re-writing of *The Economic Possibilities for our Grandchildren* for the *Essays in Persuasion*, 1931. This essay operates with the very long-term view, where, as mentioned, Keynes reconciled his Utopian view for a good society with a morally respectable macroeconomic theory for the long run, although he was still surprisingly neoclassical in his medium-term economic analysis.

A closer look at the arguments within the 'economic possibilities for our grandchildren'

Within the essay, Keynes really takes a long-run view on society, where economics should be considered as an instrument to realise a 'good life for everyone' but should never be considered as a goal by itself. This is a remarkable vision presented in the middle of the early 1930s where the slump dominated. He even dared to conclude: 'it is a wildly mistaken interpretation . . . that a decline in prosperity is more likely than an improvement in the decade ahead of us' (*Ibid.*, p. 321).

Why? Let me explain: If capital increases, say, by 2% per annum, then the capital equipment will have increased by one half in 20 years, and seven and a half times in 100 years. 'At the same time technical improvements in manufacture and transport have been proceeding at a greater rate in the last ten years than ever before in history' (*Ibid.*, p. 325).

However, Keynes was still only halfway out of the neoclassical grip, so he did not (yet) worry about 'aggregate demand'. This worry had to wait *for The General Theory*. However, it is interesting that Keynes sees the present (1930-slump) in this essay as caused by 'a new disease of which some readers may not yet have heard – namely, *technological unemployment* . . . the use of labour outrunning the pace at which we can find new uses for labour' (*Ibid.*, p. 325).

'All this means in the long run *that mankind is solving its economic problem* . . . - but not *the permanent problem of the human race*' (*Ibid.*, p. 326) (my emphasis)

This prophecy about the possible increase in production within 100 years seems, by and large, to have held true. On the other hand, his vision, that this huge expansion of gross domestic product (GDP)/capita in the industrialised countries would create a material saturation, did not materialise. The idea of abundancy that 'this is enough' has definitely not showed up as a dominant political argument. In some way, Keynes was also here more of a prophet than he would have liked himself to be, when he wrote, 'we have been trained too long to strive and not to enjoy. To judge from the behaviour and the achievements of the wealthy classes today . . . the outlook is very depressing!' (*Ibid.*, p. 328).

But Keynes was an optimist at least regarding the 'possibilities', because if production was distributed more equally (fairly!) then there was no reason to let all technological advances be transformed into increased material production. Keynes played with the idea of splitting the continuous productivity increases into, on the one hand, a doubling of production and, on the other hand, a halving of the need to work: 'Three-hour shifts [a day] or a fifteen-hours week . . . is quite enough to satisfy the old Adam in most of us!' (*Ibid.*, p. 329). Working is a necessity, but not the meaning of life. Keynes quoted an old epitaph of a charwoman: 'Don't mourn for me . . . For I'm going to do nothing for ever and ever' (*Ibid.*, p. 327).

Unfortunately, Keynes's optimism was reversed less than half a page later in the essays for at least two reasons: one microeconomic: people's changed psychology, and one macroeconomic: the neoclassical analysis of economic growth.

Faustian temptation

Keynes is sceptical towards the 'possibility' of a transition of the human nature and behaviour from greed to 'love, beauty and truth' even when the economic problems are solved. For thousands of years, human beings have been struggling to get enough material goods to survive and to protect themselves towards uncertain events. As Keynes could have said: 'about the future we simply don't know'. So, to protect yourself and your family, the 'rational' behaviour is to accumulate – especially in societies with little or no welfare state.

This behaviour of selfishness has an outcome in an unregulated market system: some families will be (much) more successful than others. There will be an elite of wealthy people, who have a trend-setting material living standard. What the elite gets as a 'normal' living standard, the masses will aspire for, especially in a society with a liberal ideology where everyone is his own 'wheel of fortune'. The social hamster-wheel of work, greed and envy is driving the economic system along. If everyone were more equally wealthy – and the economic consequences of the uncertain future would be more equally shared – there would be less inclination to acquire more and more richness.

But even if this desire of 'getting as rich as the other' were reduced, then another psychological problem emerges, Keynes warned: what to do (meaningfully) when the working load is reduced and free time increased? For more than 200 years, the accumulation of private wealth has been the social norm. We have been taught by neoclassical economists that the objective of rational, social and ethically correct behaviour was to strive for increased money-income. Accordingly, if the economic problems are solved, mankind will be deprived of its traditional purpose.

Unfortunately, this 'rational' behaviour of striving for money-income has for now been promoted for such a long time, that it is considered the only way to behave while being a respectable family father (and even citizen). These norms of 'purposiveness' (Victorian) duties (which Keynes calls 'the old Adam') are built into our social norms and morals by the (protestant) religion (Max Weber and others).

On the other hand, if the economic system really does deliver an abundance of material goods, by the time our grandchildren are living, there will be no reason to continue acting according to what Keynes called pseudo-moral principles: the love of money as a passion. Such behaviour should rather be recognised as a 'disgusting morbidity, one of those semi-criminal, semi-pathological propensities' (*Ibid.*, p. 329). Keynes concluded this section of the essay:

> I see us free, therefore, to return to some of the most sure and certain principles of religion and traditional virtue – that avarice is a vice, that the extraction of usury is a misdemeanour and the love of money is detestable, that those walk most truly in the paths of virtue and sane wisdom who take least thought for the morrow.
>
> (*Ibid.*, pp. 330–31)

Neoclassical analytical resistance

Two sentences later, Keynes demonstrated how deeply rooted his macroeconomic analysis still was in neoclassical logic and its acceptance – even recommendation – of immoral behaviour like 'avarice, usury and love of money' to overcome the material needs for ordinary people. This was a seemingly blind belief in the neoclassical 'trickle down' effect.

He felt himself committed, therefore, to give intellectual support to an economic behaviour, of which he has just expressed his deepest human distaste. Here, we find Keynes caught between ethics and academic integrity. He was trapped between the rather conventional (macro)economic analysis in the *Treatise on Money* and his ethics expressed clearly while being a student and reiterated in his self-biographical essay 'My Early Beliefs' from 1937. In 1930, he was not (yet) able to present an alternative macroeconomic theory to overturn the neoclassical medium-term analysis of economic growth presented within *A Treatise on Money.*

Therefore, Keynes did not dare to scrap the neoclassical (macro)theory in the medium-term analysis. It would have been like throwing the baby with the bath-water, because he was not yet ready with a substituting macro-theory.

Keynes had to be loyal to his *magnus opus* published contemporary with the essay on 'Economic Possibilities of our Grandchildren'.

So, to be academically consistent, Keynes had to write (although with some unease):

> Be aware! The time for all this is not yet. For at least another hundred years we must pretend to ourselves and to everyone that fair is foul and foul is fair; for foul is useful and fair is not. Avarice, usury, and precaution must be our gods for a little longer still. For only they can lead us out of the tunnel of economic necessity into daylight.
>
> (*Ibid.*, p. 331)

While Keynes was writing *A Treatise on Money* during the second half of the 1920s, neoclassical theory held that the market economic system will after a while adjust to full employment equilibrium. Keynes's aim in this book was to explain that in the short run obstacles to this adjustment process could be coherent with the neoclassical medium-term theory of market equilibrium. On the other hand, looking at the real economic development during the 1920s, it was obvious that it had taken some time, to say the least, for the economy to adjust, if at all? In fact, high unemployment had prevailed in Great Britain all way through the 1920s.

By Autumn 1929, the economy fell apart once again; however, the *Treatise on Money* was nearly finished (especially the theoretical vol. 1). Keynes had a problem maintaining that it was only short-term maladjustment, which prevented the macroeconomic system from adjusting to full equilibrium by following the path plotted by his novelty the 'fundamental equation' (an elaboration of the 'Quantity Theory of Money and Prices'). Even though many short-term obstacles to market equilibrium were suggested and analysed by Keynes on the trajectory of the fundamental equation, he did not challenge that the adjustment process would converge into full employment sooner or later. So, only avarice and usury 'can lead us out of the tunnel of economic necessity into daylight' (*Ibid.*, p. 331).

Neoclassical theory is, according to Keynes in 1930, theoretically correct in the intermediate run. Although the fundamental individual psychological premises were ethically detestable/disgusting to him, he recognised that they needed to be our gods as long as there is a material necessity and thereby a need for an increased production (and real income). It was necessary for savings to be transferred (by the rich people mainly) into real productive equipment and by that to increase the amount of real capital and, hence, productive capacity.

Concluding remarks

Nearly 100 years have passed. Keynes was alarmingly right in his worries that the Faustian Challenge of not being able to change human behaviour away from focusing on 'avarice, greed and love of money' has come true, even though we (the grandchildren) have (more) than enough. We have lost our ethical compass in our pursuit of wealth, where growth in GDP has become our new religion.

He was equally right when he in the preface to *The General Theory* wrote about his colleagues that they 'will fluctuate between a belief that I am quite wrong and a belief that I am saying nothing new' (GT, p. xxi). Although money-income has doubled more than eight times in the meantime, economic growth in money terms has still the highest priority by politicians and is endorsed by mainstream economists. In addition, the economic policy is also (nearly) unchanged and still supported by the (lack of) ethics within mainstream (neoclassical) economics. All macroeconomic models in use by governments and international institutions are neoclassical general equilibrium models, and textbooks at almost all universities are of the utilitarian type.

From Keynes's 1936 and today's Post-Keynesian point of view, this state of art would have been/is, of course, very disappointing. Keynes was in the middle of a fundamental sea change in these early years of the 1930s. He struggled with the increasing divergence between economic theory and 'how to live a good life' in reality. While writing the essay, more than 10 years had passed since the end of WWI and unemployment was still high and inequality profound in Britain. Hence, to Keynes it became increasingly unbearable to accept the neoclassical theory of a self-adjusting macroeconomic system that could be called anything like a 'good society'.

What Post-Keynesian scholars claim today, and Keynes had realised in the early years of 1930s, the missing link of a macroeconomic analysis was *effective demand.* This concept was unfolded in *The General Theory and* based on a theory that could be supported by fair and just social behaviour, especially when uncertainty prevails. It is the effective demand decided by firms and governmental institutions, which together could set the tracks of the economic development leading towards a good society for 'our grandchildren'. *The principle of effective demand* (Ch. 3 of *GT*) gave him, at last, the arguments of how to merge a morally acceptable economic behaviour (of 'being good') with a prosperous economic and good society (see chapter 24 of *GT* with the title: 'The Concluding notes on the Social Philosophy towards which the General Theory might lead'). In fact, his new macroeconomic theory made him even more optimistic. In the 1930-essay, he mentioned that it might take 100 years to saturate people's material needs – within *The General Theory,* where the redistribution of income and wealth was recommended, the time-span until saturation was dramatically reduced to 25 years (see Chick & Freeman, 2018, p. 156).

As we can see, Keynes's ambition throughout his life was to give his economic colleagues, especially those who gave policy advice, an ethical, acceptable and realistic economic theoretical foundation, to promote a 'good society'.

When Keynes stepped down as editor of the *Economic Journal* in 1945, he expressed his firm confidence in his general theory, which made him appeal to his colleagues while offering a toast to

> . . . economics and economists who are the trustees, not of civilisation, but the possibilities of civilisation.
>
> (Harrod, 1951, pp. 193–4)

Notice that Keynes once again used the word 'possibilities', because nothing is certain regarding the future. He felt for good reason after the war that he had been rather successful not only in fulfilling the ambition of setting up an analytical framework for establishing a 'good society', but also for making a significant contribution toward making the British economy reasonably safe (from an economic point of view) through the WWII[10] Now, it would be up to his successors in Cambridge, Whitehall and Westminster to teach, administer and realise the *economic possibilities* for our grandchildren within a good society.

It had not been an easy route for Keynes to combine his juvenile vision of a good society with a realistic macroeconomic theory and even more difficult to practice it during the war. The preparation for this success had been a long intellectual journey with a number of (theoretical) steppingstones, of which the essay 'The economic possibilities for our grandchildren' was just one. His procedure was all the way to combine (and adjust) his theoretical work with practical experiences from being a civil servant in the India Office, special advisor to the Treasury during WWI and WWII and bursar at King's College without losing his ethical compass.

This is really an exercise in how macroeconomics should (and could) progress with relevance for how to confront the challenges of rising inequality and emerging climate crisis, which are threatening our civilisation. Allow me, therefore, to pose a final question to the dominant economic profession: why did Keynes's method of combining a vision for a *good society* with a *realistic* macroeconomic theory not penetrate the mainstream economics of today? If Keynes's vision had been understood and then practised, the life prospects for our children and grandchildren would have been much brighter.

Notes

1 I have benefitted from profound comments on an earlier version from Roy Rotheim and Victoria Chick, of course, without any commitments to them.
2 See Skidelsky (1983, 1992).
3 It is remarkable that none of the contributors to Boldrine and Levine (eds) (2008) takes up the methodological and theoretical question, which Keynes was struggling with in the early 1930s, that the neoclassical model could not explain that the economic possibilities were not realized!
4 'I also want to emphasise strongly the point about economics being a moral science. I mentioned before that it deals with introspection and with values. I might

have added that it deals with motives, expectations, psychological uncertainties', Keynes in a letter to R. Harrod, 1938 (CWK XIV, p. 296) (Jespersen, 2009).

5 Further, this long-run view is also a fundamental change from his defeatist 1923-statement: *In the long run we are all dead.* The aim of this essay is nearly the opposite: to prepare the future economy for the coming generations!

6 See *My early beliefs*, 1937 a short biographical note (CWK, vol. X, pp. 433–51).

7 Recall Michael Douglas in the movie 'Wall Street' (1987) exclaiming 'Greed is Good!'

8 A critique Keynes developed in the early 1930s, see especially three essays published: *A Monetary Theory of Production*, CWK XIII, pp. 408–11; *The Means to Prosperity* (*CWK IX*, pp. 335–66) and *National Self-Sufficiency,* The Yale Review, Vol. 22, no. 4 (June 1933), pp. 755–69.

9 Published post-hum.

10 A view that was developed and supported in his BBC-lecture on *post-war planning*, April 1942 'How much does Finance matter?' Here, he concluded:

> Anything we can actually do we can afford. Once done it is there. . . . We shall, in very fact, have built our New Jerusalem out of the labour which in our former vain folly we were keeping unused and unhappy in enforced idleness.

Supported by, *In the long run almost anything is possible*, Keynes, 1942, in Moggridge (ed.), pp. 220, 224.

References

Boldrin, M. and David K. Levine (2008), All the Interesting Questions, Almost All the Wrong Reasons, in Lorenzo Pecchi and Gustavo Piga (eds), *Revisiting Keynes: Economic Possibilities for Our Grandchildren*, Cambridge, MA: MIT Press, pp. 161–78. https://doi.org/10.7551/mitpress/9780262162494.001.0001

Carabelli, A. (2021), *Keynes on Uncertainty and Tragic Happiness*, London: Palgrave/Macmillan. https://doi.org/10.1007/978-3-030-75665-9

Chick, V. (1983), *Macroeconomics after Keynes: A Reconsideration of the General Theory*, Cambridge, MA: MIT Press.

Chick, V. and A. Freeman (2018), The Economics of Enough: A Future for Capitalism or a New Way of Living?, in S. Dow et al. (eds), *Money, Method and Contemporary Post-Keynesian Economics*, Cheltenham and Northampton, MA: Edward Elgar, pp. 148–59. https://doi.org/10.4337/9781786439864

Fitzgibbons, A. (1988), *Keynes's Vision: A New Political Economy*, Oxford: Clarendon Press. https://doi.org/10.1093/0198283202.001.0001

Harrod, R. (1951), *The Life of John Maynard Keynes*, London: Macmillan.

Jespersen, J. (2009), *Macroeconomic Methodology: A Post-Keynesian Perspective*, Cheltenham, UK and Northampton, MA: Edward Elgar.

Johnson, E. and D. Moggridge (eds) (1972–89), *The Collected Writings of John Maynard Keynes*, 30 vol., London: Macmillan and Cambridge University Press.

Keynes, J.M. (1930a), A Treatise on Money, in E. Johnson and D. Moggridge (eds), *The Collected Writings of John Maynard Keynes*, vols V and VI, London: Macmillan and Cambridge University Press.

Keynes, J.M. (1930b), Economic Possibilities for our Grandchildren, in E. Johnson and D. Moggridge (eds), *The Collected Writings of John Maynard Keynes*, vol. IX, London: Macmillan and Cambridge University Press, pp. 321–32.

Keynes, J.M. (1936), The General Theory of Employment, Interest and Money, in E. Johnson and D. Moggridge (eds), *The Collected Writings of John Maynard Keynes*, vol. VII, London: Macmillan and Cambridge University Press.
Keynes, J.M. (1883–1946), in G. Foccarelli and H. Kurz (eds), *Handbook of Economic Analysis*, vol 1, Cheltenham: Edward Elgar, pp. 468–483.
Keynes, J.M. (1949), My Early Beliefs, in E. Johnson and D. Moggridge (eds), *The Collected Writings of John Maynard Keynes*, vol. X, London: Macmillan and Cambridge University Press, pp. 433–51.
Moggridge, D. (ed.), (2010), *Keynes on the Wireless*, London: Palgrave/Macmillan.
O'Donnell, R. (1989), *Keynes, Philosophy, Economics and Politics*, London: Macmillan. https://doi.org/10.1007/978-1-349-07027-5
Skidelsky, R. (1983), *Keynes, Hopes Betrayed*, London: Macmillan.
Skidelsky, R. (1992), *Keynes, as Saviour*, London: Macmillan.
Skidelsky, R. and E. Skidelsky (2012), *How Much Is Enough? The Love of Money and the Case for the Good Life*, London: Allen Lane.

10 Ethical practice in economics

Research, policy advice and education

Paul Dalziel

Introduction

Keynes ended his famous essay on economic possibilities for our grandchildren with his often-quoted aspiration for the economics discipline: 'If economists could manage to get themselves thought of as humble, competent people, on a level with dentists, that would be splendid'! (Keynes, 1930, p. 332). A feature of dentistry, of course, is that dental professionals must meet professional standards of conduct, performance and ethics. Thus, the General Dental Council in the United Kingdom pursues three statutory objectives: '(a) to protect, promote and maintain the health, safety and well-being of the public; (b) to promote and maintain public confidence in the professions regulated under this Act; and (c) to promote and maintain proper professional standards and conduct for members of those professions'.[1] There is no similar oversight of economists in the United Kingdom. From its earliest days, for example, the Royal Economic Society has been an open society (Coats, 1968, p. 359); that is, membership is available to anyone who shares the aims and objectives of the society, without requiring adherence to any public set of professional standards.[2] A similar situation prevailed for many decades in the American Economic Association (AEA) (Coats, 1985), until its Executive Committee adopted the AEA Code of Professional Conduct on 20 April 2018.[3]

Recently, a body of research has advocated greater attention to professional ethics for guiding the behaviour of economists. Important examples are the articles by DeMartino (2005, 2009) and the chapter by Bartlett (2009). An early synthesis was DeMartino's (2011) book, *The economist's oath*, with a further impetus provided by the essays in *The Oxford handbook of professional economic ethics*, edited by DeMartino and McCloskey (2016). Both books received mixed reactions from economists. Two reviews in the *Journal of Economic Literature* (JEL) were critical: Oster (2011) welcomed the former book's stimulus to thought but found the applied chapters and other parts 'unconvincing', whereas Krueger (2017, p. 216) concluded her review by associating the epithet 'windbags' with the contributors to the latter book (see DeMartino and McCloskey, 2018, for a polite but forceful reply). Other reviewers were enthusiastic. Ianole (2013, p. 277), for example, praised the 'masterly crafted

DOI: 10.4324/9781003142324-11

central argument' of DeMartino's book, whereas Negru (2019, p. 131) described the *Handbook* as 'a pioneering work'.

Sheila Dow has made important contributions to this literature. This includes not only a chapter in the *Handbook* itself (Dow, 2016a), but also her analysis of economics and ethics in Dow (2013, 2015a, 2015b, 2016b). Further, Dow's wider research programme has presented valuable insights on ethical standards in the practice of economics in her work on the Scottish political economy tradition (for example, Dow, 1987, 1997a; Dow, Dow and Hutton, 1997, 2000) and on methodology (for example, Dow, 1985, 1990, 1997b, 2002, 2007).

Dow observes that the Scottish Enlightenment was distinctive 'for its historically contingent view of knowledge creation, given the intrinsic human incapacity to identify truth (or at least to know that it has been identified)' (Dow, 1997a, p. 468). Given that knowledge is contingent and fundamentally uncertain, Dow (2015c, p. 41) suggests that 'the study of economics can be understood therefore as an attempt to reduce our uncertainty about the economy'. That study depends on conventions accepted by scientists, acknowledging that 'these conventions can be more or less successful' (*Ibid.*, p. 469). Conventions are themselves contingent, of course, and contested, as Dow explains (*Ibid.*):

> To think, as we have done here, of economic methodology in terms of conventions for coping with uncertainty is to reflect the conclusions from the philosophy of science that there is no demonstrably best methodology of science. Rather, communities of scientists develop methodologies which make most sense to them in relation to the way they understand the subject matter (their ontology), perpetuate it through 'normal science' and propagate it through education. Non-mainstream approaches to economics, which have different ontologies, have therefore developed different conventions from mainstream economics.

This diversity leads Dow to argue that 'a cautious approach should be taken to putting together a code of ethics on the grounds that any code might lead to further discrimination against pluralist economics if interpreted from a monist perspective' (Dow, 2013, p. 21; see also Dow, 2016a). Dow (1980) describes, for example, how 'methodological morality' influenced the outcome of the Cambridge controversies on capital theory, where that concept referred to the mainstream convention that 'all forms of analysis other than technical formalism are regarded as, if not illegitimate, then morally inferior' (*Ibid.*, p. 379). Agreeing with DeMartino (2011), Dow (2015b, p. 128) has expressed her views as follows:

> A code is a clear set of rules. But professional ethics for economists are anything but simple, and do not lend themselves to strict rules. Within

> a pluralist environment, for example, each school of thought has its own understanding of the subject matter and how to build knowledge about it. The onus is on the economist to explain and make the case for, not only particular policy advice, but also the perspective and framework that generated it. It is so much more simple, and yet unjustifiable, to assert one best approach that is beyond discussion.

This does not imply tolerance for 'anything goes' in economic methodology; instead, Dow (2016a, p. 760) observes that 'knowledge activities are pursued within knowledge communities' and so pluralist economics can be 'structured roughly (and provisionally) around a range of such communities'. The objective of ethical self-reflection is to assist in developing good practice. As the opening chapter of *The Oxford handbook of professional economic ethics* argues, professional ethics 'is a conversation rather than constraint, a dance rather than a pose' (DeMartino and McCloskey, 2016, p. 5). It continues (*Ibid.*):

> Professional ethics refers to a *tradition of critical inquiry* into the myriad questions that surround professional engagement. It entails reflection and debate, literatures, curriculum, texts, journals, and bulletins probing the nature of professional practice for its ethical substance. Professional ethics is intended to assist well-meaning professionals, and the profession as a whole, to do good – not to prevent charlatans from doing harm.
>
> (DeMartino, 2011)

In that spirit, this chapter aims at contributing to the ongoing conversation about ethical practice in economics. Echoing Keynes's (1930) aspiration begins with the standards of conduct, performance and ethics that govern dental professionals in the United Kingdom (GDC, 2013), discussing what economists might learn from that framework for our own ethical practice.[4] The chapter then considers the AEA Code of Professional Conduct adopted by the AEA in April 2018; this is done in the light of Sheila Dow's analysis of pluralism in economics. The third section argues that the education of economists should include opportunities to study professional ethics (Dolfsma and Negru, 2019), based on the movement in economic policy from an emphasis on increasing economic production towards increasing the well-being of people (Dalziel, Saunders and Saunders, 2018). This is reinforced by the observation that economists typically work in organisations that have formal codes of conduct (in research and in the civil service, for example). The chapter ends with a brief conclusion.

Ethical standards for United Kingdom dental professionals

Recall from the chapter's opening paragraph that the General Dental Council in the United Kingdom has three statutory purposes, the first of which is 'to protect, promote and maintain the health, safety and well-being of the public'. Some of the motivation for a code of professional standards for economists comes from claims of important episodes where economic policies have resulted in significant harm to public well-being. Indeed, DeMartino (2016a, 2016b) has coined the term *econogenic harm* for such episodes. He argues that econogenic harm is ubiquitous (see DeMartino, 2011), raising ethical questions that economists must address. The editor of the *Challenge* journal has suggested the failures of the profession to anticipate the global financial crisis of 2008: 'invite analysis of the objectivity of economic research and policy advice – and indeed these may ultimately be ethical questions' (Madrick, 2009, p. 3). Dow (2015a) herself has analysed how austerity policies implemented in response to the global financial crisis depended on mainstream 'beliefs' that raise important issues of ideology, power and ethics.

This argument does not suggest that all economic policies are harmful; nor does it suggest that the economic profession causes more harm than good. Rather, the argument is that econogenic harm occurs on a sufficient scale to warrant public policy 'to protect, promote and maintain the health, safety and wellbeing of the public', and that a contribution to that goal would be to require members of the economic profession to meet certain ethical standards. DeMartino (2016a, p. 49) explains as follows:

> The transformation of medical ethics is relevant for economics. Economists today occupy the privileged position of the medical expert prior to the emergence of the idea of patient rights. Their authority, stemming from their presumed expertise, creates in their own minds and even in the minds of those affected by their decisions the right to do what they deem best.

The analogy, however, is not straightforward. A named medical practitioner may meet with a named patient at a particular time. Based on the practitioner's expertise and information provided, the patient may consent to a specific medical treatment. After the event, it is reasonable to suggest that peers can judge the claimed expertise of the medical practitioner and the quality of the information provided before the patient's consent. A committee of peers could investigate whether the patient did, indeed, provide informed consent to the actual treatment carried out by the medical practitioner. None of these fits easily with the way in which economists typically contribute to economic policy formation.

First, economists are typically policy advisors rather than policy decision-makers. Second, it is rare for one economist to have sole responsibility for providing that advice. Third, in a well-functioning democracy, there is typically a range of voices supporting or opposing particular proposals for policy change. Fourth, it is rare for a policy problem to involve a clear diagnosis and a simple treatment; policymakers are typically grappling with problems that have multiple causes where any number of outside shocks might interfere with the effectiveness of any policy response. Thus, even if is possible to identify harm resulting from a particular policy, it is not obvious that this will have been the result of ethical misbehaviour by an individual named economist.

Consider, for example, a major example highlighted by DeMartino (2011, chapter 9); namely, the widespread adoption by economists of the Washington Consensus to advise governments to embrace reforms based on rapid privatisation, market deregulation and economic freedom. Much can be criticised about the Washington Consensus. Oster (2011, p. 721), for example, accepts one might argue there were underestimates of the difficulty of moving to a market economy, underestimates of the expected dislocations at the bottom end of the income distribution, naïvety in ignoring the likelihood of corruption in state property disposals, and overconfidence in our economic models. All these are serious problems, but the question is whether the resulting outcomes would have been different if economists advising governments had been accountable to articulated professional standards of ethical behaviour. Following the medical practitioner example above, could peers reasonably judge that an individual economist had behaved unethically when his or her advice was based on a framework so widely accepted in the profession that it had earned the label of 'Washington Consensus'? I would suggest the answer is no. There are deeper social forces at play.

Insight into these deeper social forces can be found in chapter 12 of *The general theory of employment, interest and money*, which analyses the state of long-term expectations. Keynes observes that investment decisions depend on the state of long-term expectations and the state of confidence that we have in those expectations (Keynes, 1936, p. 148). Keynes continues, 'the outstanding fact is the extreme precariousness of the basis of knowledge on which our estimates of prospective yield have to be made' (*Ibid.*, p. 149). Indeed, 'if human nature felt no temptation to take a chance, no satisfaction (profit apart) in constructing a factory, a railway, a mine or a farm, there might not be much investment merely as a result of cold calculation' (*Ibid.*, p. 150). Consequently, 'in practice, we have tacitly agreed, as a rule, to fall back on what is, in truth, a *convention*' (*Ibid.*, p. 152, emphasis in the original).

This relates to Sheila Dow's (2015c) analysis about the importance of conventions in different schools of economic methodology. Conventions are also important for users of economic analysis. Adapting the language of Keynes, given the extreme precariousness of the basis of knowledge about the future, the state of confidence in economic policy decisions depends on a widely accepted *convention* that economists can design good policies reflecting a trusted professional consensus summarised in publications such as OECD (2019) and World Bank (2019). Episodes of econogenic harm should weaken that confidence, but Dow (2015a) has documented how the global financial crisis did not weaken conventional beliefs in the ability of economists to design the austerity policies in response.

In that light, consider the second statutory objective of the General Dental Council: 'to promote and maintain public confidence in the professions regulated under this Act'. If the arguments just discussed are accepted, this is the opposite of what would help reduce econogenic harm. The issue is not that individual economists behaving badly are damaging the reputation of the wider profession. Rather, the issue is that current convention gives too much confidence in a profession that has, inter alia, underestimated the difficulty of moving to a market economy, underestimated the expected dislocations at the bottom end of the income distribution, been naïve in ignoring the likelihood of corruption in state property disposals, and been overconfident in its models (Oster, 2011, p. 721). Indeed, Colander (2016) argues that the more serious ethical problem of economics has to do with a lack of humility.

The third statutory objective of the General Dental Council is 'to promote and maintain proper professional standards and conduct'. The council lists nine principles that registered dental professionals must keep to at all times (GDC, 2013, p. 4):

1 Put patients' interests first
2 Communicate effectively with patients
3 Obtain valid consent
4 Maintain and protect patients' information
5 Have a clear and effective complaints procedure
6 Work with colleagues in a manner that is in patients' best interests
7 Maintain, develop and work within your professional knowledge and skills
8 Raise concerns if patients are at risk
9 Make sure your personal behaviour maintains patients' confidence in you and the dental profession

Each principle has a set of standards that dental professionals must observe to remain registered, with published guidance on how to meet the standards. The underlying assumption is that the profession is able to set accepted standards (for example, about how to place patients' interests first) and is then able to judge whether an individual member of the profession has departed from a standard. It does not address the possibility that the profession in general might be failing in some ethical matter. The AEA Code of Professional Conduct does address this possibility.

The AEA code of professional conduct for economists

At the time of preparing *The Oxford handbook of professional economic ethics*, the editors could make the following observation: 'Since its founding 1885 and up to the present, the American Economic Association (AEA – perhaps the most influential professional association of economists in the world – has never cultivated enquiry into professional ethics' (DeMartino and McCloskey, 2016, p. 3). That history changed in October 2017, when the AEA Executive Committee created an ad hoc committee to consider a code of professional conduct (Campbell et al., 2018a, p. 1).[5] The Committee began with the AEA mission 'to promote the advancement of knowledge about economics' (*Ibid.*):

> The Committee believes that the AEA's mission is best achieved, and ought to be achieved, in an environment that encourages free expression and exchange of ideas evaluated solely on scientific merit. In particular, the AEA should aspire to a professional environment that promotes equal opportunity and equal treatment for all economists, regardless of age, gender, race, ethnicity, national origin, religion, sexual orientation, disability, health condition, marital status, parental status, genetic information, professional status, or personal connections. Moreover, the Committee believes that the AEA mission can only be fulfilled if economists adhere to the highest level of honesty and integrity in all aspects of their work.

The Committee acknowledged that recent events had raised concerns about systematic deviations for those ideals, accepting that 'in the economics profession as in society at large, it has become apparent that unacceptable behaviour has been allowed to continue through tacit toleration' (*Ibid.*). Note that the references to 'systematic deviations' and 'tacit toleration' are statements about the profession in general. The Committee recommended a Code of Professional Conduct (*Ibid.*, p. 2). It circulated a draft to AEA members, and it made several revisions in response to comments received (Campbell et al., 2018b, p. 1). The AEA Executive Committee voted to adopt the revised Code on 20 April 2018 (AEA, 2018).

The Code consists of six short paragraphs reproduced in Box 1. The Code sets out broad principles rather that detailed standards. Further, the Code does not use the word 'ethics', but it recognises that the principles are requirements for 'encouragement of economic research' and 'perfect freedom of economic discussion'. The Code not only demands individual responsibility for personal conduct, but also insists on collective responsibility for developing institutional arrangements and a professional environment that promote free expression concerning economics.

Recall Sheila Dow's argument cited earlier in this chapter: 'that a cautious approach should be taken to putting together a code of ethics on the grounds that any code might lead to further discrimination against pluralist economics if interpreted from a monist perspective' (Dow, 2013, p. 21). The AEA Code of Professional Conduct actively seeks to promote freedom of economic discussion, to create a professional environment with equal opportunity and fair treatment for all economists, and to support participation and advancement in the profession by individuals from all backgrounds. Further, the AEA Leadership has published an open letter to members acknowledging

BOX 1 AEA CODE OF PROFESSIONAL CONDUCT, ADOPTED APRIL 20, 2018

The AEA holds that the principles of professional conduct should guide economists in academia, government, nonprofit organisations and the private sector.

The AEA's founding purpose of 'the encouragement of economic research' requires intellectual and professional integrity. Integrity demands honesty, care and transparency in conducting and presenting research; disinterested assessment of ideas; acknowledgement of the limits of expertise; and disclosure of real and perceived conflicts of interest.

The AEA encourages the 'perfect freedom of economic discussion'. This goal requires an environment where all can freely participate and where each idea is considered on its own merits. Economists have a professional obligation to conduct civil and respectful discourse in all forums, including those that allow confidential or anonymous participation.

The AEA seeks to create a professional environment with equal opportunity and fair treatment for all economists, regardless of age, sex, gender identity and expression, race, ethnicity, national origin, religion, sexual orientation, disability, health condition, marital status, parental status, genetic information, political affiliation, professional status, or personal connections.

Economists have both an individual responsibility for their own conduct and a collective responsibility to promote professional conduct. These responsibilities include developing institutional arrangements and a professional environment that promote free expression concerning economics. These responsibilities also include supporting participation and advancement in the economics profession by individuals from all backgrounds, including particularly those who have been historically underrepresented.

The AEA strives to promote these principles through its activities.

Source: https://www.aeaweb.org/about-aea/code-of-conduct.

some longstanding problems in the profession after a survey on the professional climate in economics (Blanchard, Bernanke and Yellen, 2019):

> Although a full analysis of the survey results remains to be done, it is evident from the findings released today that many members of the profession have suffered harassment and discrimination during their careers, including both overt acts of abuse and more subtle forms of

> marginalization. This is unacceptable. Excluding or marginalizing people based on their gender, race, or other personal characteristics is not only deeply unfair to those who are excluded, it damages the field as a whole by limiting the diversity of perspectives and dissuading talented people from becoming economists. It is striking that, in an era when women and members of under-represented minority groups have entered so-called STEM fields at increasing rates, the low rates of participation and advancement of women and minorities in economics have changed little in recent decades.

Consistent with Dow's analysis, that statement recognises the damage done to economics when the diversity of perspectives is limited. Following Dow's lead, however, we should also recognise that the damage is not limited to the profession. It extends to everyone who has suffered econogenic harm from economic policies – such as the austerity programmes in the United Kingdom (Dow, 2015a) – created from a monist perspective.

To illustrate how deeply embedded monism is within the profession, consider the JEL classification system for economic research maintained by the AEA. As Dalziel and Saunders (2019, p. 142) point out, the JEL system maintains a category for 'feminist economics', which it lists as a subset of the field B5: Current Heterodox Approaches. The International Association for Feminist Economics (IAFE) is founded on a common cause 'to further gender-aware and inclusive economic inquiry and policy analysis with the goal of enhancing the well-being of children, women and men in local, national, and transnational communities' (IAFE, 2019). By what criteria could such a mission be categorised as a *heterodox approach*? Feminist scholarship has transformed many disciplines of scientific enquiry, but the economics profession continues to consign feminism to its own box, placed outside the mainstream.

Consequently, the AEA Code of Ethics is a step, but only a step, towards meeting the concerns of Dow and others for a more pluralist profession. The Code's call, for example, for an environment where 'each idea is considered on its own merits' does not address the questions raised by Dow (2013, 2015a, 2015b, 2015c, 2016a, 2016b) about the validity of the conventions that currently guide the evaluations of merit within the discipline.

Ethical standards and the education of economists

In 1948, Paul Samuelson published the first edition of his famous textbook that 'dominated the college classrooms for two generations' (Skousen, 1997, p. 137). Indeed, Stanley Fischer has suggested that '*Economics* must be one of the great achievements of economics, and indeed I would guess of any field' (Samuelson et al., 1999, p. 363). Chapter 2 introduced three central problems of every economic society that framed the book: what to produce, how to produce and for whom to produce. On the third question, Samuelson (1948, p. 14) made the following observation:

> When we come to the third question of the desirable distribution of wealth and income between individuals, we leave the field of science altogether. *De gustibus non est disputandum:* there is no disputing (scientifically!) tastes; and the same goes for ethics. We must leave the definition of social *ends* to the philosopher, the theologian, the statesman, and to public opinion.

Thus, Samuelson's textbook treated ethics as outside the discipline of economics (and therefore not required in the education of economists), on the basis that economics is concerned with technocratic questions concerning the efficient organisation of production. This is consistent with a more general distinction often made between positive science and normative ethics, going back in economics at least to Keynes (1890). Dow (1987, p. 341, emphasis added), however, reminds us that the Scottish political economy tradition 'developed as a *moral* science'. She explains this was unsurprising, given that the degree structure in Scottish universities at the time included moral philosophy among a set range of subjects. Dow further observes that the moral principles of Scottish jurisprudence had a profound influence on how the founders of the Scottish political economy tradition depicted human behaviour (*Ibid.*):

> . . . man was not viewed as an isolated atom, but as a political being or a social being. … Thus Hume would refer to "society" rather than individuals, and Smith would discuss the tempering effect of social pressures on individual greed. It was this view of individuals as members of society, rather than isolated atoms, which provided the basic principles underlying Scottish political economy, differentiating it from formal utilitarianism.

More recently, modern-day economists have criticised the preoccupation of economics with the issues of production that framed Samuelson's economic problems of what, how and for whom. There is a strong movement shifting focus to the well-being of people. This chapter, for example, has already cited the goal of the IAFE (formally incorporated in 1992) to enhance the well-being of children, women and men in local, national and transnational communities. In a similar vein, the Commission on the Measurement of Economic Performance and Social Progress published an influential report that described its unifying theme using these words: 'the time is ripe for our measurement system to shift emphasis from measuring economic production to measuring people's well-being' (Stiglitz, Sen and Fitoussi, 2009, p. 12). Although this report focused on measurement issues, there is now a trend in policy making that is shifting emphasis from promoting the growth of economic production *per se* to providing much greater attention to trends in personal and community well-being within each country (see, for example, Dalziel, Saunders and Saunders, 2018). In New Zealand, in 2019, this trend led to the creation of the world's first 'wellbeing budget' (Dalziel, 2019; Robertson, 2019).

Since economists recognise that our work affects the well-being of people and communities, ethical considerations are inevitable. What is the duty of care of an economist who is engaged in his or her professional activities? What are the responsibilities of economists when politicians propose policies that the profession considers would be generally harmful to the well-being of identifiable groups of people? How should office-bearers of the profession respond after episodes of significant econogenic harm? These questions go well beyond the principles of the AEA Code of Professional Conduct, with its relatively narrow focus on encouraging economic research and promoting perfect freedom of economic discussion.

Further, the AEA Code recognises that economists work in a range of institutions, including academia, government, non-profit organisations and the private sector. Consequently, a great many economists must consider some formal statement of ethical standards in performing their work. In the United Kingdom, for example, the UK Research Integrity Office has published a code of practice that aims 'to encourage all involved in research to consider the wider consequences of their work and to engage critically with the practical, ethical and intellectual challenges that are inherent in the conduct of high - quality research' (UKRIO, 2009, p. 7). The code sets out seven principles that are described as: excellence, honesty, integrity, co-operation, accountability, training and skills, and safety (*Ibid.*, pp. 7–8). The Civil Service Code expects civil servants to carry out their role with dedication and a commitment to the Civil Service and its core values of integrity, honesty, objectivity and impartiality. It sets standards of behaviour under each of those headings plus a further section on political impartiality.[6]

Hence, economic professionals need understanding of how to address ethical issues in economics. Consequently, an important project for the profession to reflect on is 'what it means to train and educate an ethical economist and what is needed for economics to become an ethical profession' (Dolfsma and Negru, 2019, p. 4). Following DeMartino (2019, p. 9), a simple introduction to what might be considered unacceptable behaviours by an economist is not sufficient. Rather, genuine education in ethics is required so that students can develop the necessary skills to engage with 'critical inquiry into the myriad ethical questions that arise in the context of and as a consequence of economic practice' (*Ibid.*).

Conclusion

Throughout her career, Sheila Dow has made impressive contributions to the economics literature across a broad range of subjects. This chapter has focused on her contributions to research questions concerning ethical considerations to guide the professional work of economists and how best to express generally accepted conventions of ethical behaviour. The chapter has noted Dow's research on the ethical foundations of the Scottish political economy tradition, her analysis of the importance of conventions in the face of fundamental uncertainty, her commitment to pluralism within economics research and her concerns that a formal code of ethics could constrain pluralism.

The chapter concludes by stating that economic professionals need to understand better how to address ethical issues in economics. This view comes from a recognition that the professional work of economists affects people's well-being, for better or for worse. Any impact on human well-being inevitably raises ethical considerations. The AEA's Code of Professional Conduct is a positive step, but this chapter has noted that the Code has a relatively narrow focus on encouraging economic research and promoting perfect freedom of economic discussion. Crucial though these goals are for supporting pluralism in the profession, other important ethical questions need further attention, such as the role of individual economists in causing econogenic harm to identified groups of people, as well as the role of leadership in the profession in responding to such episodes. Sheila Dow's research, including the lessons she has highlighted from the founders of the Scottish political economy tradition, provides a solid foundation for the ongoing self-reflection and actions that are required.

Notes

1 Dentists Act 1984, accessed 30 July 2019 at https://www.legislation.gov.uk/ukpga/1984/24. There are criticisms of the ways in which these standards are enforced; see, for example, Kelleher (2017), who refers to 'state-sponsored dental terrorism', and Renshaw (2018), who refers to 'serious concerns'.
2 Note, however, that the Society's strategy for the period 2019–23 includes a commitment to 'review the role it can play in promoting good professional conduct in the discipline'; see https://www.res.org.uk/about/our-strategy.html (accessed 30 July 2019).
3 See https://www.aeaweb.org/about-aea/code-of-conduct (accessed 30 July 2019).
4 Colander (2016, p. 749) has made a similar connection between Keynes's allusion to dentists and the code of ethics issues, but argues that economists might adopt a variation of the code of ethics prepared by the National Society of Professional Engineers.
5 DeMartino (2019, pp. 7–8) discusses this 'about-face' by the AEA.
6 Statutory guidance on the Civil Service code, accessed 2 August 2019 at https://www.gov.uk/government/publications/civil-service-code/the-civil-service-code.

References

AEA. (2018) *AEA Code of Professional Conduct.* American Economic Association. https://www.aeaweb.org/about-aea/code-of-conduct [Accessed 10 February 2022].

Bartlett, R. L. (2009) Code of ethics for economists. In: Pel, J. & van Staveren, I. (eds.) *Handbook of economics and ethics.* Cheltenham: Edward Elgar, pp. 54–61. https://doi.org/10.4337/9781848449305.00015.

Blanchard, O., Bernanke, B. & Yellen, J. (2019) *A message from the AEA leadership on the professional climate in economics*. American Economic Association. https://www.aeaweb.org/news/member-announcements-mar-18–2019 [Accessed 10 February 2022].

Campbell, J., Bertrand, M., Dupas, P., Edelman, B. & Shapiro, M. D. (2018a) *Ad hoc committee to consider a code of professional conduct: Interim report*. American Economic Association. https://www.aeaweb.org/about-aea/code-of-conduct [Accessed 10 February 2022].

Campbell, J., Bertrand, M., Dupas, P., Edelman, B. & Shapiro, M. D. (2018b) *Ad hoc committee to consider a code of professional conduct: Final report*. American Economic Association. https://www.aeaweb.org/about-aea/code-of-conduct [Accessed 10 February 2022].

Coats, A. W. (1968) The origins and early development of The Royal Economic Society. *Economic Journal*, 78(310), 349–71. https://doi.org/10.2307/2229470.

Coats, A. W. (1985) The American Economic Association and the economics profession. *Journal of Economic Literature,* 23(4), 1697–727. http://www.jstor.org/stable/2725706.

Colander, D. (2016) Creating humble economists: A code of ethics for economists. In: DeMartino, G. F. & McCloskey, D. N. (eds.) *The Oxford handbook of professional economic ethics*. Oxford: Oxford University Press, pp. 737–49. https://doi.org/10.1093/oxfordhb/9780199766635.013.040.

Dalziel, P. (2019) Wellbeing economics in public policy: A distinctive Australasian contribution. *Economic and Labour Relations Review*, 30(4), 478–97. https://doi.org/10.1177/1035304619879808.

Dalziel, P. & Saunders, C. (2019) Gendered innovations in economics: Marilyn Waring's approach to social science research. *Women's Studies International Forum*, 72, 137–43. https://doi.org/10.1016/j.wsif.2018.05.004.

Dalziel, P., Saunders, C. & Saunders, J. (2018) *Wellbeing economics: The capabilities approach to prosperity*. London: Palgrave Macmillan. https://doi.org/10.1007/978-3-319–93194-4.

DeMartino, G. F. (2005) A professional ethics code for economists. *Challenge*, 48(4), 88–104. https://doi.org/10.1080/05775132.2005.11034308.

DeMartino, G. F. (2009) On the need for professional economic ethics. *Challenge*, 52(4), 6–15. https://doi.org/10.2753/0577-5132520401.

DeMartino, G. F. (2011) *The economist's oath: On the need for and content of professional economic ethics*. Oxford: Oxford University Press. https://doi.org/10.1093/acprof:oso/9780199730568.001.0001.

DeMartino, G. F. (2016a) *The economist's oath*: On economic agency, economic theory, pluralism, and econogenic harm. *Rethinking Marxism*, 28(1), 47–56. https://doi.org/10.1080/08935696.2015.1123016.

DeMartino, G. F. (2016b) "Econogenic harm": On the nature of and responsibility for the harm economists do as they try to do good. In: DeMartino, G. F. & McCloskey, D. N. (eds.) *The Oxford handbook of professional economic ethics*. Oxford: Oxford University Press, pp. 71–97. https://doi.org/10.1093/oxfordhb/9780199766635.013.005.

DeMartino, G. F. (2019) Training the 'ethical economist'. In: Dolfsma, W. & Negru, I. (eds.) *The ethical formation of economists*. Abingdon: Routledge, pp. 7–23. https://doi.org/10.1093/acprof:oso/9780199730568.003.0012.

DeMartino, G. F. & McCloskey, D. N., eds. (2016) *The Oxford handbook of professional economic ethics.* Oxford: Oxford University Press. https://doi.org/10.1093/oxfordhb/9780199766635.001.0001.

DeMartino, G. F. & McCloskey D. N. (2018) Professional ethics 101: A reply to Anne Krueger's review of *The Oxford handbook of professional economic ethics. Econ Journal Watch*, 15(1), 4–19.

Dolfsma, W. & Negru, I., eds. (2019) *The ethical formation of economists.* London: Routledge. https://doi.org/10.4324/9781351043809.

Dow, A., Dow, S. C. & Hutton, A. (1997) The Scottish political economy tradition and modern economics. *Scottish Journal of Political Economy*, 44(4), 368–83. https://doi.org/10.1111/1467-9485.00065.

Dow, A., Dow, S. C. & Hutton, A. (2000) Applied economics in a political economy tradition: The case of Scotland from the 1890s to the 1950s. *History of Political Economy*, 32(Suppl_1), 177–98. https://doi.org/10.1215/00182702-32-Suppl_1-177.

Dow, S. C. (1980) Methodological morality in the Cambridge controversies. *Journal of Post Keynesian Economics*, 2(3), 368–80. https://doi.org/10.1080/01603477.1980.11489168.

Dow, S. C. (1985) *Macroeconomic thought: A methodological approach.* Oxford: Blackwell.

Dow, S. C. (1987) The Scottish political economy tradition. *Scottish Journal of Political Economy*, 34(4), 335–48. https://doi.org/10.1111/j.1467-9485.1987.tb00291.x.

Dow, S. C. (1990) Beyond dualism. *Cambridge Journal of Economics*, 14(2), pp. 143–57. https://doi.org/10.1093/oxfordjournals.cje.a035123.

Dow, S. C. (1997a) Economics and religion. In: Arestis, P., Palma, G. & Sawyer, M. (eds.) *Capital controversy, post-Keynesian economics and the history of economics: Essays in honour of Geoff Harcourt, Volume 1.* London: Routledge, pp. 466–73. https://doi.org/10.4324/9780203983294.

Dow, S. C. (1997b) Mainstream economic methodology. *Cambridge Journal of Economics*, 21(1), 73–93. https://doi.org/10.1093/oxfordjournals.cje.a013660.

Dow, S. C. (2002) *Economic methodology: An inquiry.* Oxford: Oxford University Press.

Dow, S. C. (2007) Variety of methodological approach in economics. *Journal of Economic Surveys*, 21(3), 447–65. https://doi.org/10.1111/j.1467-6419.2007.00510.x.

Dow, S. C. (2013) Codes of ethics for economists: A pluralist view. *Economic Thought*, 2(1), 20–29.

Dow, S. C. (2015a) The role of belief in the case for austerity policies. *Economic and Labour Relations Review*, 26(1), 29–42. https://doi.org/10.1177/1035304614567262.

Dow, S. C. (2015b) The economist's oath: A review essay. *International Review of Applied Economics*, 29(1), 125–28. https://doi.org/10.1080/02692171.2014.983732.

Dow, S. C. (2015c) Addressing uncertainty in economics and the economy. *Cambridge Journal of Economics*, 39(1), 33–47. https://doi.org/10.1093/cje/beu022.

Dow, S. C. (2016a) Codes of ethics for economists, pluralism, and the nature of economic knowledge. In: DeMartino, G. F. & McCloskey, D. N. (eds.) *The Oxford handbook of professional economic ethics.* Oxford: Oxford University Press, pp. 750–63. https://doi.org/10.1093/oxfordhb/9780199766635.013.041.

Dow, S. C. (2016b) Economics and ethics. In: Kiddey, R. (ed.) *The ethical is the social: ISRF Bulletin Issue XI.* London: Independent Social Research Foundation, pp. 10–14.

GDC (2013) *Standards for the Dental Team.* London: General Dental Council. https://www.gdc-uk.org/information-standards-guidance/standards-and-guidance/standards-for-the-dental-team [Accessed 10 February 2022].

IAFE (2019) *Mission statement.* International Association for Feminist Economics. http://www.iaffe.org/pages/about-iaffe/miss/ [Accessed 10 February 2022].

Ianole, R. (2013) Review of *The economist's oath: On the need for and content of professional economic ethics* by George F. DeMartino. *Review of Social Economy*, 71(2), 277–80. https://doi.org/10.1080/00346764.2013.800307.

Kelleher, M. (2017) State-sponsored dental terrorism? *British Dental Journal*, 223(10), 759–64. https://doi.org/10.1038/sj.bdj.2017.983.

Keynes, J. M. (1930) Economic possibilities for our grandchildren. Reprinted in and cited from: Johnson, E. & Moggridge, D. (eds.) *The collected writings of John Maynard Keynes. Volume IX: Essays in persuasion.* London: Macmillan, 1978, pp. 321–32. https://doi.org/10.1017/UPO9781139524162.

Keynes, J. M. (1936) *The general theory of employment, interest and money.* London: Macmillan. https://doi.org/10.1007/978-3-319-70344-2.

Keynes, J. N. (1890) *The scope and method of political economy.* London: Macmillan. https://doi.org/10.1017/CBO9781139170116.004.

Krueger, A. O. (2017) Review of *The Oxford handbook of professional economic ethics* edited by George F. DeMartino and Deirdre N. McCloskey. *Journal of Economic Literature*, 55(1), 209–16. https://doi.org/10.1257/jel.55.1.209.

Madrick, J. (2009) Letter from the editor. *Challenge*, 52(4), 3–5. https://doi.org/10.2753/0577-5132520400.

Negru, I. (2019) Review of *The Oxford handbook of professional economic ethics* edited by George F. DeMartino and Deirdre N. McCloskey. *Review of Political Economy*, 31(1), 131–34. https://doi.org/10.1080/09538259.2019.1591772.

OECD (2019) *Economic policy reforms 2019: Going for growth.* Paris: OECD Publishing. https://doi.org/10.1787/aec5b059-en.

Oster, S. (2011) Review of *The economist's oath: On the need for and content of professional economic ethics* by George F. DeMartino. *Journal of Economic Literature*, 49(3), 719–22. https://doi.org/10.1257/jel.49.3.719.

Renshaw, J. (2018) Serious concerns about the General Dental Council's performance and its direction of travel. *British Dental Journal*, 224(4), 213–14. https://doi.org/10.1038/sj.bdj.2018.80.

Robertson, G. (2019) *The wellbeing budget.* Wellington: New Zealand Government. https://www.treasury.govt.nz/publications/wellbeing-budget/wellbeing-budget-2019 [Accessed 10 February 2022].

Samuelson, P. (1948) *Economics*, 1st Edition. New York: McGraw Hill.

Samuelson, P. A., McGraw Jr., H. W., Nordhaus, W. D., Ashenfelter, O., Solow, R. M. & Fischer, S. (1999) Samuelson's *Economics* at fifty: Remarks on the occasion of the anniversary of publication. *Journal of Economic Education*, 30(4), 352–63. https://doi.org/10.1080/00220489909596092.

Skousen, M. (1997) The perseverance of Paul Samuelson's *Economics. Journal of Economic Perspectives*, 11(2), 137–52. https://doi.org/10.1257/jep.11.2.137.

Stiglitz, J., Sen, A. & Fitoussi, J-P. (2009) *Report by the Commission on the Measurement of Economic Performance and Social Progress.* https://www.insee.fr/en/information/2662494 [Accessed 10 February 2022].

UKRIO (2009) *Code of practice for research: Promoting good practice and preventing misconduct.* London: UK Research Integrity Office. https://ukrio.org/publications/-code-of-practice-for-research/ [Accessed 10 February 2022].

World Bank (2019) *World development report 2019: The Changing Nature of Work.* Washington: World Bank. https://www.worldbank.org/en/publication/wdr2019 [Accessed 10 February 2022].

11 Sheila Dow as historian of economic thought

The Scottish political economy tradition

Robert McMaster

Introduction

Sheila Dow has accomplished much during her illustrious career. She is perhaps most notable for her contributions to Post-Keynesian economics, particularly (but by no means exclusively) central banking, the methodology of economics, especially around her work on Babylonianism and together with Vicky Chick (Chick and Dow, 2005), and her contribution to open systems reasoning. Dow has also made incisive contributions in the history of economic thought, and in this chapter, I focus on an aspect of her work in this area. On this, I believe that Dow's thinking has been shaped by a tradition that has influenced her approach in the other areas of her analysis. Moreover, she has been at the forefront of studying the enduring influence of this tradition on notable figures in economics. Dow's scholarship in this area deserves to receive as much attention as her work in other fields.

Of course, I refer to what Dow terms as the "Scottish political economy tradition." There is extensive literature on the Scottish Enlightenment (for example, Broadie, 1990, 2003; Herman, 2003; Munck, 2000), and on individuals', chiefly Adam Smith and David Hume, inspiration in developing economic thought; however, there has been relatively little scholarship on the Scottish political economy tradition as a whole. For Dow, both in an individual capacity and together with her husband Alexander (Alistair) and other scholars formerly based at Glasgow Caledonian University – principally Alan Hutton and Michael Keaney – the Scottish political economy represents a distinct tradition that influenced important aspects of 20th-century economic thought (Dow *et al.*, 1997, 1998a).[1] Obviously, there are key figures in this tradition, such as Hume and Smith, but the intellectual context in which their ideas developed is important in apprehending the nature of their thinking. Dow's pioneering work on this enables us to appreciate the philosophical currents that shaped the development and evolution of substantial areas of political economy and latterly, economics. The influence of this tradition may have waned of late, but it, nonetheless, still echoes in some schools of thought and retains the potential to inform the future evolution of economics.

DOI: 10.4324/9781003142324-12

In this chapter, I attempt to outline the basis of Dow's argument about the importance of the Scottish political economy tradition, and its continuing relevance despite the hostility of the prevailing academic environment in economics. In doing so, I argue that Dow's work represents a modern embodiment of this tradition. Finally, I argue that Dow overlooks some potentially interesting dimensions in Scottish political economy, especially Smith's references to social provisioning and care that anticipate and could theoretically inform a rejuvenated political economy.

The remainder of the chapter is structured as follows: the next section provides a brief outline of the salient aspects of the Scottish Enlightenment. I then consider Dow *et al.*'s analysis of Scottish political economy, and Dow's references to "tradition" in economic thought. The next section identifies the potential of Smith's references to social provisioning and care. This is followed by a brief conclusion.

The Scottish enlightenment

The Enlightenment was an 18th-century European phenomenon that heralded a new era of scientific discovery, and in doing so contested the role of the Christian church as the dominant source of knowledge. In Hegelian or Kuhnian terms, the Enlightenment can be viewed as epoch, or paradigm, changing, as the thesis presented by the Church – chiefly the Catholic variant of Christianity – was challenged by the power of ideas (and values) generated across Europe. As such, the Enlightenment possessed an important emancipatory dynamic, which extended beyond the elite to reach all parts of European societies (Munck, 2000).[2]

Briefly, European Enlightenment philosophy represented new ways of thinking about reality and thereby generated scientific insights. As Dow and Dow (2013, 2014) and Dow *et al.* (1997) recognise, the emergence and dissemination of the Enlightenment in Europe adopted different forms and evolved in distinctive ways. For instance, in France there was emphasis on Cartesian rationality and deductive reasoning. Other central figures included Montesquieu, especially on the constitutional separation of powers, Voltaire and his advocacy of the separation of Church and State, Jean-Jacques Rousseau on the notion of a social contract, and Denis Diderot's opposition to slavery and torture (see, for example, Munck, 2000). In England, following Francis Bacon and Isaac Newton, empiricism dominated (Dow and Dow, 2014). By contrast, in Scotland, knowledge was said to emerge from experience, and "with the aid of imagination and reason it could be systematised and communicated for more general, albeit *provisional*, application" (Dow and Dow, 2013: 7, emphasis added). Moreover, historical and social context matter in apprehending meaning. This provisional nature of knowledge and emphasis on historical context perhaps anticipates the later pragmatist tradition that influenced the likes of Thorstein Veblen and the original institutionalists.

Dow (2002a, 2009a, 2009b) develops her argument by identifying four philosophical strands in the Scottish Enlightenment: natural law philosophy, historical approach to analysis, "common-sense" philosophy, and "moderate" scepticism.

Natural law philosophy in the Scottish Enlightenment is associated with Francis Hutcheson, who argued that nature is governed by causal forces. Dow notes how this was especially influential in the development of David Hume's *Treatise of Human Nature*. This is accompanied by a recognition of historical contingency, and therefore how evidential properties require to be considered over different historical periods. From here, Dow considers that Scottish Enlightenment writers, such as Hume, not only adopted a historical sensitive approach, but also socially grounded their reasoning, such as with regard to the effect of social change in northern rural Scotland, while acknowledging transcendental features. Finally, Dow detects a mild fallibilism (moderate scepticism) in respect to knowledge in that there was a consensus over the limitations of human knowledge, which encouraged the reflection over transcendental knowledge claims.

The Enlightenment in Scotland was influenced by mainland Europe[3] as well as by England, and partly as a consequence a distinctive approach emerged. Dow and Dow (2013, 2014) and Dow *et al.* (1997, 2000) further argue that the characteristics of the Scottish Enlightenment were also shaped by the unique institutional context of 18th-century Scotland. During this period, the country experienced the profound transformation on which Smith and others wrote extensively. Political union with England (and Wales) entailed the suspension of Scotland's parliament, rendering it a "stateless nation" (McCrone, 1992). For Dow and Dow (2014: 39), this shifted "the focus for public debate . . . away from politics and more towards issues concerning religion and moral issues more widely." The dynamic of such discourse was shaped by continuing independent Scottish institutions: the dominant Presbyterian church, the Roman law-based legal framework, and the national education system, which was based on a platform of general literacy. Accordingly, higher education was more readily available in Scotland than in many other parts of Europe at the time. It was partly through education and cultural links with mainland Europe that Continental currents influenced the Enlightenment in Scotland (Dow and Dow, 2014). Moreover, the social order in Scotland, or at least the central lowlands was transforming from a largely agrarian social order to what Smith in *The Wealth of Nations* termed as a "commercial society."

On this, Herman (2003: 11) observes:

> Fundamental to the Scottish notion of history is the idea of progress. The Scots argued that societies, like individuals, grow and improve over time. They acquire new skills, new attitudes and a new understanding of what individuals can do and what they should be free to do.

For Dow, these aspects reveal a defining aspect of the Scottish Enlightenment: its concern with practical issues in a historical context. Indeed, many figures in the Scottish Enlightenment devoted attention to what they considered to be the relatively slow development of the Highlands and Islands. According to Dow (2009b), Enlightenment figures were sympathetic to the possibilities that "lagged commercialisation" may be (at least partly) due to cultural differences with the rest of Scotland; specifically, that the Highlands and Islands remained a "gift society" (Dow, 2009a). For example, Dow reports how Hume adopted a sensitive and open-minded approach in his analysis of the Highlands, especially in respect of its dominant Gaelic culture after the 1745 Jacobite Rebellion. Dow (2009b: 7) writes:

> Hume, along with others, took a constructive approach to the post-Rebellion situation by considering methods of economic improvement in the Highlands. This humanist effort, another indicator of the increasing entrenchment of the classical episteme, encouraged some to advocate dramatic change in land use and economic organisation. But Hume was more cautious, paying attention to the particularities of Highland and Island culture as well as economic conditions.

Unfortunately, Hume's sensitivity did not feature largely in the authorities' approach, and the region was subjected to a period of sustained ethnic cleansing, depopulation, and transformed land use. This is a legacy that resonates to this day.

Hume's and others' work on the Highlands reveals how they conceived of material economic progress and social development as intertwined. In her own analysis on the Enlightenment, Dow argues that this is a distinguishing feature of the Scottish contribution. She identifies Adam Ferguson's respect for the moral legitimacy of "savage" societies (for example, Dow and Dow, 2014). There was explicit recognition and concern about how the development to a "commercial" society could impact the existing value structure of society. In particular, both Hume and Smith were alert to the dangers of specialisation through the division of labour, acknowledging, in particular, the potential impact on workers' mental well-being. Ferguson, Hume, and Smith were among those who advocated universal education, ensured by the state to provide a means of addressing the numbing effects of repetitive working. Nonetheless, Hume emphasised that employment in the new industrial age offered many benefits, both material and cultural.

The progression of society to a "commercial" state reflects the stage view of history advocated by prominent figures in the Enlightenment. Although the stadial theory of historical development may be an intellectual reverberation of the *Auld Alliance*,[4] Dow and Dow (2014) observe that in the French variant, particularly associated with the likes of Turgot, developmental stages centre on the relations around sustenance and agriculture. Turgot explicitly identified three stages of development and hinted at a fourth (Meek,

1971). Hunting, pasturage, and agriculture were explicitly defined, with clearly demarked distinctions in each stage around property, social surplus, government, and the like. Steuart and Smith expressed similar ideas, with Smith famously defining four stages (Meek, 1971; Milonakis and Fine, 2009; Samuels, 1977, 1993). As with Turgot, Smith's focus for the first three stages (savagery; barbarism; civilisation) corresponds with the emergence of increasingly advanced means of food production. For instance, with barbarism, the pastoral organisation of animals succeeded simple hunter-gathering, and barbarism itself was succeeded by propertied agriculture. For Smith, the final stage – commercial society – was the ultimate in societal development and one in which Smith contended that the focus would be growing prosperity and wealth (the plutology of Classical political economy).

The stadial approach was highly influential in the political economy, with thinking evolving to the notion of a stationary state through Ricardo and Mill (Milonakis and Fine, 2009), and forming an important aspect of Marx's dialectical approach, and later Marxist accounts (for example, Laibman, 2010; cf. Samuels, 1993). These approaches challenge Smith's contention that commercial society represented the final stage of human progress, and the echo of this has persisted through the likes of Francis Fukuyama's (1992) assertion of the *End of History*. Indeed, in the *General Theory*, Keynes explicitly acknowledged the stationary state in terms of abundance in which the nature of "commercial society" would change for the better.[5]

The analysis of the transformation of society was also reflected in an interest in demographic change, which as Dow and Dow (2014) highlight is exemplified by Hume's concern for the depopulation of the Highlands and Islands.

The other areas of contribution identified by Dow emphasise the theories and notions that have shaped the emergence of economics in the late 19th century and into the 20th century. They include a theory of value, a strong advocacy of free trade, and Smith's metaphor of the "invisible hand."

The theory of value, Dow and Dow (2013; 2014) argue, that emerged from the Scottish Enlightenment was encouraged by the morality of the transformation to commercialism and "more practical" thinking of just or fair price reflecting efforts and resources in the production process. Dow and Dow observe that Adam Smith's approach to pricing, centering on prices oscillating around a "natural price" was influenced by Hutcheson's natural law philosophy.

On the promotion of free trade, both Hume and Smith were partly prompted in their criticisms of Mercantilist self-interest in favour of what they saw as an important means to expand markets and therefore material wealth and productive capability. Undoubtedly, Smith's notion of the limits of markets was also influential in shaping this view.

Relatedly, Dow (2002a, b, 2009a, b, 2010), Dow and Dow (2006, 2013, 2014), and Dow *et al.* (1998a, 2000) powerfully argue that important attributes of the legacy of the Scottish Enlightenment remain influential, but mistakenly so. In particular, in her work, Dow focusses on two aspects: Hume's philosophy (2002a, b, 2009a, 2009b) and Smith's "invisible hand" (Dow, 2010; Dow and Dow, 2014).

In a series of articles, Dow (2002a, b, 2009a, 2009b) argues that Hume's philosophy has been misinterpreted, especially by critical realists. Hume is frequently – and erroneously according to Dow – confined to a logical positivist position through his empiricism. However, Dow contends that Hume's embrace of the Scottish Enlightenment approaches to issues of a historical and social context and fallibilism suggests an affinity with much of the foundations of the critical realist argument (Dow, 2002a).

Finally, for Dow (see, for example, Dow, 2010; Dow and Dow, 2013; 2014), Smith's much quoted reference to the "invisible hand" does not, as the Chicago School would have us believe, demonstrate Smith's affinity to, and endorsement of, *laissez faire*. Rather, Smith was sensitive to the potential for markets to reduce monopoly, and to the risks to social well-being that may arise from selfishness. Accordingly, the "invisible hand" was a testament to a set of specific circumstances as opposed to a general phenomenon (Dow and Dow, 2014; see also Evensky, 2005; Samuels *et al.*, 2011).

The significance of these two aspects cannot be understated for Dow. Scottish political economy emerges from the Enlightenment and is reflective of its philosophy and methods. I now turn to Dow's observations on this.

Dow on the Scottish political economy tradition

Dow's analysis of the Scottish political economy tradition commences with a discussion of the notion of "tradition." In various works, Dow and colleagues (in particular, Dow, 1987; Dow *et al.*, 1997, 1998a, 1998b, 2000) identify the distinctions between "paradigms," "schools of thought," "research programmes," and "traditions" as modes of classification. Indeed, the boundaries are vague and permeable between each. Nonetheless, for Dow and Dow *et al.*, it is possible to provide a delineation. For instance, Dow *et al.* (1998b) observe that "school of thought" frequently refers to a group of economists who are broadly contemporaries or who may be similarly geographically located, such as the Austrian, Chicago, and German Historical schools. Today, with the advent of enhanced communications, scholars following a particular school of thought are more likely to be spatially dispersed than earlier.

The Kuhnian concept of paradigm refers to a particular world view – it is the lenses that we use to see (Kuhn, 1996). They involve the adherence to a set of central tenets around which scientific communities are organised and evolve. Thus, according to Dow paradigms – unlike schools of thought – they persist over generations. Paradigms and traditions demonstrate similarities in that knowledge emerges in communities with shared philosophical views. However, paradigms are identifiable by a distinctive world view ontologically, whereas traditions need not (Dow *et al.*, 1997). Indeed, more than one paradigm may emerge from a tradition (Dow and Dow, 2006):

> The concept of tradition refers to a community of customs, thought and practices. In other words, it extends beyond specific theories to encompass what might be called an 'approach' to the subject matter . . . What is being suggested, then, is that the Scottish tradition [of political economy] encapsulated a specific view of scientific knowledge, its relation to reality and its role in society that generated a particular approach to economics.
> (Dow *et al.*, 1997: 370)

This is a significant point, as Dow *et al.*'s position is such that scientific knowledge is embedded in broader society, and therefore the customs, practices, and values of that society are, to some extent, reflected in scientific communities. Of course, as society reproduces and evolves, so does science.

In the case of a Scottish tradition in political economy, focussing on Hume and Smith, in particular,[6] Dow and her colleagues identify a series of features, which together they claim delineate a particular Scottish approach. This is summarised in Table 11.1.

For Dow, tradition does not refer to theoretical content, but to an "approach," and hence a method. This is clear from Table 11.1. Taking the case of attitude towards the individual, there is extensive evidence from the writings of Hume and Smith that they conceived the individual as primarily influenced by "sentiment" and "passions" and thereafter "reason." This distances both from the standard economic notion of *homo economicus*, which, of course, stresses rationality in decision-making. Again, criticisms of the Chicago School variant of Smith resonate.

Over the course of various publications, Dow and colleagues argue that as political economy "emerged as a practical application of moral philosophy" (Dow *et al.*, 1997: 373), its analytical entry point are real-world issues, such

Table 11.1 The features of the Scottish political economy tradition

Aspect of the tradition	*Description*
Theoretical approach	Preference for arguing from first principles; Concern with practical issues; Preferences for breadth of understanding of background to these issues; Acknowledgement of sociological and psychological aspects of theory appraisal
Epistemological approach	Fallibilism – Acceptance of the limitations of theory
Attitude to the role of history	Preference for approaching first principles through their historical development
Attitude to the individual	Specification of first principles through non-individualistic representation of human nature; emphasis on "conventional behaviour," such as sentiment and passion; Individuals understood as social beings

Adapted from: Dow (1987); Dow *et al.* (1997, 2000).

as those alluded to earlier in respect to the transformation of Highland and Island society in 18th-century Scotland (for example, Dow and Dow, 2013). As a pre-requisite to apprehending the nature of these issues, there has to be some understanding of historical context and other background factors, such as prevailing customs and social organisation. On this, history is recognised as irreversible (Dow *et al.*, 2000). Again, the contrast with the mechanistic and time reversible approach of much of the standard economic theory is worthy of note.

The limitations of theory as the epistemological approach of Scottish Enlightenment thought fosters what Dow *et al.* (1997) refer to as open systems. Dow is noted for her contribution to the development of open systems methodology in economics (for example, Chick and Dow, 2005; Dow, 2002c), and others (for example, Davis, this volume) provide an insightful analysis. My point here is that Dow traces her open systems reasoning to the Scottish political economy.

Concisely, for Dow, open systems do not have predetermined boundaries and are, therefore, subject to varying degrees of uncertainty. More precisely, variables cannot be designated as either exogenous or endogenous, and, indeed, it may not be possible to identify all variables in a system. The relationships between variables are not completely known, and interrelationships may change, such that structure and agency are interdependent (see Davis, this volume; Dow, 2002c).[7]

The Influence of the Scottish political economy approach especially as embodied by Smith on later Classical political economists, such as Marx is well known (Dow *et al.*, 1998a; Milonakis and Fine 2009). This also extends to Institutional economics and Post-Keynesianism (Dow *et al.*, 1998b). Indeed, Hayek's views on knowledge were influenced by Scottish Enlightenment scholars, such as Ferguson, Hume, and Smith. Similarly, Keynes' views on uncertainty were influenced by the Enlightenment epistemological approach (Dow *et al.*, 1998a).

Of course, much has been made of mainstream economics association with Smith, with general equilibrium seen as a development of Smithian thinking (for a critique, see Evensky, 2005). On this, Dow *et al.* write:

> [General equilibrium] . . . is a continuation in the sense that the questions Smith posed in terms of the Scottish political economy approach have been posed again within the quite different approach of general equilibrium theory . . . the way in which questions and theories are understood is coloured fundamentally by approach, which contributes to the different interpretations of Smith.
>
> (1998: 377)

In other words, although standard economics may share similar interests in the issues and phenomena as Smith (and others), there are pronounced differences in approach between the political economy of the Scottish tradition and more recent mainstream economics. Smith may be considered as the father of political economy, much less so of modern standard economics.

There is a literature examining the transformation of political economy into economics (for example, Milonakis and Fine, 2009). A particular manifestation of this lies in the investigation of teaching in universities. As part of their examination of the emergence and decline of the Scottish political economy, Dow and her colleagues discuss the evolution of teaching in Scottish universities.

Following the Treaty of Union between England and Scotland in 1707, the education system in the latter retained its autonomy. In the "ancient" Scottish universities – Aberdeen, Edinburgh, Glasgow, and St Andrews – undergraduate provision reflected the more general school education in Scotland, and typically degree programmes over the past four years (as opposed to 3 years in many other systems). Until fairly recently, Arts degrees carried a philosophical core, and this was reflected in the teaching of political economy and then economics.

Dow *et al.* (1998a, 2000) and Alastair Dow and Hutton (2006) provide accounts of the emergence and evolution of the teaching of economics in Scottish universities. Dow and Hutton contrast early university teaching of economics in England and Scotland, reflecting that in England from 1900 onwards, there were aspects to curriculum design: theory, applied studies, and history. Theory dominated and led to an increasingly abstract approach following Alfred Marshall's influence, which became ever more divorced from history. In Scotland, theory was intertwined with history and philosophy, with a relatively less emphasis given to deductive reasoning than the nascent neoclassicism. This persisted into the 1950s, when university education in Scotland increasingly came to resemble that of elsewhere, especially the United States and England.[8] Hutton (2006) viewed this as the "analytical" turn in the approach to economics teaching, resonant of the evolution of political economy into economics, and part of the process of increasing internationalisation of the academy. For Dow and Hutton, and Hutton, the Scottish political economy tradition endured in university teaching over the first half of the 20th century, in part due to particular institutional arrangements, such as the emphasis on philosophy and history in the wider educational approach and the influence of a relatively small number of academics in the four ancient universities. With the increasing dominance of neoclassical economics and the retirement of those key individuals in Scottish universities, the economics curriculum aligned more closely to an Anglo-American one from the 1950s onwards (Hutton, 2006).

As is argued elsewhere in this volume, Dow's emphasis on open systems reasoning (for example, Chick and Dow, 2005), the importance of uncertainty (for example, Dow *et al.*, 2018), the role of history (for example, Dow, 2002c), and her promotion of pluralism in economic reasoning (for example, Dow, 2004) mark her as an outstanding economist of our time, and one who has been central to the development of Post-Keynesianism, the history of economic thought, and the methodology of economics. More than this, Sheila Dow can be seen as a prominent and gifted advocate for the Scottish political economy tradition. Her work not only has an affinity with this tradition, but it also represents a development of it. However, there are areas where this tradition may provide further illumination, and augment Dow's case and analysis. In the following section, I argue that, in particular, Adam Smith's recognition of individuals as social beings provides a platform for the study of the economy as processes of social provisioning and within this an appreciation of the significance of care.

Scottish political economy and social provisioning

A row may be added to Table 11.1, which augments and strengthens Dow's argument. It is the view of the economy, and its function. This is an area that Dow under-explores in her analysis. It has potentially profound implications for the conceptualisation of the economy. In the Scottish political economy, the economy is not isolated from the rest of society, and it is to some degree reflected in Smith's allusion to provisioning. In *Wealth of Nations* (*WN*, 1997), Smith identifies a hierarchy of human wants:

> After food, clothing and lodging are the two great wants of mankind.
>
> (Smith, 1997 [1776]: 266)

Steuart also discusses provisioning as an *aim* of political economy:

> The principal aim of [political economy] is to secure a certain fund of subsistence for all ... inhabitants, to obviate every circumstance which may render it precarious; to provide everything necessary for supplying the wants of society . . .
>
> (1767: Book 1)

This is in contrast to the standard economic account where all goods are essentially morally equivalent in a market exchange system typified by unlimited wants and scarcity. Smith and Steuart offer a hierarchical perspective on apprehending the satisfaction of wants. The first concerns the provisioning of society, which commences with the production of food (hence the interest and debate in food-related issues, such as the Corn Laws in Classical political economy). The second relates to other goods that are not as important in ensuring the satisfaction of basic requirements. For Boulding (1986), mainstream economics has lost this central insight. In doing so, it also fails to examine the ecology of the economy. He argues,

> Modern economics has gone wholly towards the view of economic life as society organized by exchange, and has largely lost the sense of it

being a process of provisioning of the human race, or even of the whole biosphere.

(Boulding, 1986: 10)

Beyond Kenneth Boulding, arguably, feminist economics has been the most alert body of scholars in developing the notion of social provisioning. In particular, Marilyn Power (2004) is prominent in discussing the importance of social provisioning specifically to feminist economics. In doing so, she discusses the concept in terms of social processes that emphasise the interdependence of individuals in organising to address their needs, wants and to socially reproduce. For Power, social provisioning has five dimensions:

1 Care, especially caring and unpaid labour, which Power describes as "fundamental," and should be valued in accordance with its centrality to social reproduction.
2 An assessment of human well-being that goes beyond standard national income accounting. Power alludes to the capabilities approach, and there is a certain resonance with Steuart's original incantation.
3 An acknowledgement of the influence of social norms and power relations on socio-economic processes and outcomes.
4 Economic processes are goal directed and value laden.
5 The organisation of social provisioning is influenced by race, class, gender, and other group characteristics.

Power (2004: 7) is explicit in observing that as a conceptualisation, social provisioning is "classical" rather than "neoclassical." In analysing the history of care in economic thought, Davis and McMaster (2020) argue that standard economics does not, or at least inadequately incorporates (1), (3), (4), or (5), and (2) is confined by a utilitarian calculus. This appears in juxtaposition to the Scottish political economy approach examined by Dow and her colleagues.

Taking Power's "fundamental" first point, following Davis and McMaster (2017, 2020) and Terjesen (2011), there is substantial evidence that Adam Smith acknowledged the importance of care.

In a series of publications, Davis (for example, 2003, 2011) and others convincingly argue that the mainstream economics conceptualises an asocial and atomistic model of the individual. This is a marked departure from the Scottish Enlightenment thought and Scottish political economy tradition, at least as evident in Hume and Smith. In both *The Theory of Moral Sentiments* (*TMS*, 2000) and *WN*, Smith develops a sophisticated analysis of human behaviour and relations. Sympathy is at the centre of Smith's analysis in *TMS*.[9] Smith's use of sympathy refers to "fellow feeling" (Terjesen, 2011). Accordingly, individuals are not atomistic entities, but are socially situated. Moreover, this reflects Enlightenment thinking that morality is intrinsic to all human activities (Evensky, 2005; Garnett, 2019). Indeed, Garnett (2019) compellingly argues that Smith's use of "self-love" in *WN* differs significantly from *homo economicus*. Instead, the socially embedded individual's references are influenced by what is deemed to be culturally acceptable. On this, in the Smithian sense, "self-love" means what a socially habituated individual's appeal to what an "impartial spectator" would approve satisfies their sense of self-approval (Garnett, 2019).

At several points in *TMS*, Smith appears to anticipate later contributions to the theorising of care (Davis and McMaster, 2020). Care is essential to the functioning and reproduction of society (for example, Engster, 2005; Tronto, 2013). The literature on care identifies three dimensions: psychological (through emotional attachments and motivations), labour (through the functional delivery of care activities), and philosophical (through ethical considerations), and it is profoundly relational (Tronto, 2013). Smith recognises at least two of the dimensions. The pivotal role of sympathy in *TMS* emphasises the connectedness and relatedness between individuals (Terjesen, 2011), and hence our mutual inter-dependencies. This lies at the centre of care and caring (Engster, 2005).

In *TMS*, Smith makes explicit reference to care in the title of Chapter 1 of Section 2. As Davis and McMaster (2020) note, in discussing virtue in Part 5, Smith represents care in terms of concentric rings: "Every man, as the Stoics used to say, is first and principally recommended to his own care" (2000 [1759]: 321). Care extends from the individual and then to the immediate family, and then to familiar others. Hume's contention that moral obligation diminishes with distance (for example, Dow, 2002a) influences Smith's framing of care. However, the two-part parable of the Chinese earthquake suggests that the potential for personal influence shapes the moral obligation to care. In *TMS*, Smith invites us to consider the morality of an individual ("a man of humanity in Europe," 2000 [1759]: 136). In the first case, the man, who has no connection with China or its people, is untroubled by a devastating earthquake. Indeed, according to Smith, he would "snore with the most profound security over the ruin of a hundred million of his brethren" (*Ibid.*). However, if this man were to lose a small finger the next day, he could not sleep. For Smith, the former represents a catastrophe and the latter a matter of comparatively little consequence.

In the second case, again the European has no association with China, but in this scenario the man could – for whatever reason – prevent the disaster through the sacrifice of a pinkie. Smith asks whether the individual would make this sacrifice. Smith answers that he would.

So why the difference, Smith inquires. In the first case, the individual's self-interest and distance from the tragedy signals an utter indifference. However, in the second case, the same individual appears to demonstrate considerable beneficence. This seems a remarkable change in the man's character. This is not the case according to Smith. Instead, the man acts out of a sense of duty motivated by self-love as self-approval. As Garnett (2019: 132) observes:

> The difference between the two cases is not the man's character . . . but the price of self-approval: the price he must pay (the sacrifice he must incur) in order to earn the approval of his impartial spectator.

In both scenarios, the individual's behaviour is morally defensible. In the first case, the individual is powerless. In the second, he is not, and is therefore morally compelled to act. On this, Smith connects acts of care with duty:

> When the happiness or misery of others depends in any respect upon our conduct, we dare not, as self-love might suggest to us, prefer the interest of one to that of many. The man within immediately calls to us, that we value ourselves too much and other people too little, and that, by doing so, we render ourselves the proper object of the contempt and indignation of our brethren.
>
> (Smith, 1759, cited in Garnett, 2019: 133)

Smith appears aware of the sophisticated nature of care. It can be bound up with affection, sympathy, duty, and virtue. Care can be associated with beneficence and personal ties, and vice versa. Here, Smith suggests a virtuous cycle, and importantly that the well-being of individuals is predicated on their sociality. However, in the Chinese earthquake parable, Smith recognises that circumstances may dictate that even in the absence of personal ties, there is a responsibility to care by virtue of a shared humanity. On this, people are profoundly sociable, and therefore, care is instinctive, certainly to those with whom we have bonds, and yet there is also a duty of care in Smith's argument. These insights may be traced to Smith's, and other Enlightenment writers' approach to the economy as embedded in society and as a means of provisioning. This certainly resonates with the stadial understanding of development and assists in the framing of practical issues – a focus of the Scottish political economy.

On this basis, as noted, Table 11.2 may be extended to include social provisioning.

Of course, this interpretation underlies the potential affinities between the Scottish political economy and the capabilities approach usually associated with Martha Nussbaum and Amartya Sen, but that is beyond the boundaries of the present argument. Seen here, Dow's insights into the nature and relevance of the Scottish Enlightenment and political economy may be augmented through the lens of social provisioning.

A brief conclusion

Sheila Dow is probably most noted for her cutting-edge contributions to the methodology of economics, Post-Keynesian macroeconomic theory, and central banking. However, throughout her career, Dow both in an individual capacity and in collaboration with scholar husband Alexander (Alistair) and

Table 11.2 The features of the Scottish political economy tradition (extended version)

Aspect of the tradition	*Description*
Theoretical approach	Preference for arguing from first principles; Concern with practical issues; Preferences for breadth of understanding of background to these issues; Acknowledgement of sociological and psychological aspects of theory appraisal
Epistemological approach	Fallibilism – Acceptance of the limitations of theory
Attitude to the role of history	Preference for approaching first principles through their historical development
Attitude to the individual	Specification of first principles through non-individualistic representation of human nature; emphasis on "conventional behaviour," such as sentiment and passion; Individuals understood as social beings
View of the economy	Embedded in wider society and a means of provisioning; providing every member of society with sufficient means to live a flourishing life

Adapted from: Dow (1987); Dow *et al.* (1997, 2000).

others, such as Alan Hutton and Michael Keeney, provides notable insights into important aspects of the history of economic thought, principally centering on what she terms the "Scottish political economy tradition." Along with her colleagues, she argues that a distinctive Scottish political economy tradition can be traced to the Enlightenment, where Hume and Smith were pioneering advocates and system builders. Among the features of this approach, she identifies a concern for practical matters, preferences for moral philosophy, multi-disciplinarity, and history, among others. Dow observes that from the middle of the 20th century onward this tradition declined as neoclassical and mainstream economics emerged to dominate the discipline.

Dow's work in this area is incredibly valuable in that she demonstrates that the Scottish political economy tradition retains a salience for modern economics, especially as the mainstream is subject to on-going critique from both within and beyond the academy. Indeed, Dow is perhaps the modern embodiment of this tradition in her advocacy of pluralism, open systems thinking, the relevance of history to theory, and the history of economic thought. It is difficult to see a finer proponent of the Scottish political economy than Sheila Dow. However, in saying this, Dow's analysis could be augmented by the recognition of the economy as a source of social provisioning, and accordingly that individuals are socially embedded. Arguably, there is evidence to the effect that Adam Smith (among others) predicated their work on this insight. If, indeed, this is the case, there is then an argument that Smith's approach placed care as a significant attribute in the morally driven behaviour of people in the economy and wider society.

I hope that in the future, Sheila Dow as the foremost modern Scottish political economist will find the opportunity to turn her attention to exploring this possibility and develop further insights into the potential directions for economic thought in these challenging times.

Notes

1 For example, Dow identifies the influence of David Hume on Keynes and Hayek (Dow, 2002a, 2009a; Dow and Dow, 2013).

2 Parallels may be drawn with the dogmatic resistance of the Church to the Copernican revolution, where the prevailing Ptolemaic contention of the Earth as the centre of the universe was challenged by the Copernican inspired heliocentric view of the Sun as the centre of the Solar System. The latter threatened the role of the (Catholic) Church, which assumed the Earth as the centre of the Universe and the Church as at the centre of Earth with Divine authority invested in the Pope. Scotland, of course, experienced a Protestant Reformation in the 16th century in a way that France did not. Presbyterianism came to dominate religious life in Scotland, whereas Catholicism remained dominant in France.

3 Key figures in the Scottish Enlightenment, such as Hume and Smith, spent significant periods of time in France and elsewhere on mainland Europe.

4 The *Auld Alliance* was an arrangement between France and Scotland dating from the 13th century until the Treaty of Edinburgh in 1560. The specific purpose of the Alliance was to limit the political and military ambitions of England during the period.

5 Keynes, for example, states:

> If I am right in supposing it to be comparatively easy to make capital-goods so abundant . . . this may be the most sensible way of gradually getting rid of many of the objectionable features of capitalism. A little reflection will show what enormous social changes would result from a gradual disappearance of a rate of return on accumulated wealth. A man would still be free to accumulate his earned income with a view to spending it at a later date. But his accumulation would not grow. He would simply be in a position of Pope's father, who, when he retired from business, carried a chest of guineas with him to his villa at Twickenham and met his household expenses from it as require.
>
> (1936: 221)

6 This is by no means an exclusive focus. Dow and her colleagues acknowledge the influential roles of other Scottish Enlightenment figures. For instance, Dow, *et al* (1998b) contributed to an edited volume on John Rae, and Dow and Dow (2006) edited a volume that explores the contributions of numerous writers, such as James Steuart, Francis Hutchison, Thomas Chalmers, etc.

7 Dow likens this to Babylonian thought, which stresses that under uncertainty there can be no way to reason from a single approach. Accordingly, we should be open to multiple possible explanations, where "weight of argument" (for example, Dow *et al.*, 2018) assists in attempts to apprehend reality.

8 Dow and Hutton emphasise that the university economics education in Scotland was not unique. They identify similarities with Oxford and the Politics, Philosophy, and Economics (PPE) curriculum.

9 Samuels (1977) identifies four domains to Smith's approach to moral philosophy: natural theology, ethics, justice, and concern for wealth (expediency). *TMS* explored ethics and *WN* plutology.

References

Boulding, K. E. (1986) What went wrong with economics? *The American Economist*, 30: 5–12: https://doi.org/10.1177/056943458603000101

Broadie, A. (1990) *The Tradition of Scottish Philosophy: A New Perspective on the Enlightenment*, Rowman and Littlefield: Edinburgh.

Broadie, A. (ed) (2003) *The Cambridge Companion to the Scottish Enlightenment*, Cambridge University Press: Cambridge.

Chick, V. and Dow, S. C. (2005) The meaning of open systems, *Journal of Economic Methodology*, 12: 363–81: https://doi.org/10.1080/13501780500223585

Davis, J. B. (2003) *The Theory of the Individual in Economics: Identity and Value*, Routledge: London

Davis, J. B. (2011) *The Individual and Identity in Economics*, Cambridge University Press: Cambridge.

Davis, J. B. (this volume) Sheila Dow's open systems methodology, in *Economic Methodology, History and Pluralism*, Negru, I. and Hawkins, P. (eds), Routledge: London.

Davis, J. B. and McMaster, R. (2017) *Health* Care *Economics*, Routledge: London.

Davis, J. B. and McMaster, R. (2020) A road not taken? A brief history of care in economic thought, *European Journal of the History of Economic Thought*, 27: 209–29: https://doi.org/10.1080/09672567.2020.1720767

Dow A. and Hutton, A. (2006) Economics in the Scottish universities from the late nineteenth century, in Dow, A. and Dow, S. C. (eds) *A History of Scottish Economic Thought*, Routledge: London.

Dow, A. and Dow, S. C. (eds) (2006) *A History of Scottish Economic Thought*, Routledge: London.

Dow, A. and Dow, S. C. (2013) Economic development in the Scottish enlightenment: Ideas as cause and effect, in *Development and Economic Reform in Emerging Economies*, Ruzlev, K. and Perdikis, N. (eds), SCEME Studies in Economic Methodology, 2, Pickering and Chatto: London (7–22).

Dow, A. and Dow, S. C. (2014) Scotland, in *Routledge Handbook of the History of Global Economic Thought*, Barnett, V. (ed), Routledge: London.

Dow, A., Dow, S. C. and Hutton, A. (1997) The Scottish political economy tradition and modern economics, *Scottish Journal of Political Economy*, 44: 368–83: https://doi.org/10.1111/1467–9485.00065

Dow, A., Dow, S. C., Hutton, A. and Keaney, M. (1998a) Traditions in thought: The case of Scottish political economy, *New Political Economy*, 3: 45–58.

Dow, A., Dow, S. C., Hutton, A. and Keaney, M. (1998b) Rae and the tradition of Scottish political economy, in *The Economics of John Rae*, Hamouda, O. F., Lee, C. H., and Mair, D. (eds), Routledge: London (245–260).

Dow, A., Dow, S. C. and Hutton, A. (2000) Applied economics in a political economy tradition: The case of Scotland from the 1890s to the 1950s, *History of Political Economy*, 32 (suppl 1): 177–98.

Dow, S. C. (1987) The Scottish political economy tradition, *Scottish Journal of Political Economy*, 34: 335–48: https://doi.org/10.1111/1467–9485.00065

Dow, S. C. (2002a) Historical reference: Hume and critical realism, *Cambridge Journal of Economics*, 26: 683–95: https://doi.org/10.1093/cje/26.6.683

Dow, S. C. (2002b) Interpretation: The case of Hume, *History of Political Economy*, 34: 399–420.

Dow, S. C. (2002c) *Economic Methodology: An Inquiry*, Oxford University Press: Oxford.

Dow, S. C. (2004) Structured pluralism, *Journal of Economic Methodology*, 11: 275–90: https://doi.org/10.1080/1350178042000252965

Dow, S. C. (2009a) David Hume and modern economics, *Capitalism and Society*, 4: 1–29: https://doi.org/10.2202/1932-0213.1049

Dow, S. C. (2009b) Hume and the Scottish enlightenment: Two cultures, *Revista de Economia*, 35: 7–20.

Dow, S. C. (2010) Smith's philosophy and economic methodology, in *Elgar Companion to Adam Smith*, Young, J. T. (ed), Edward Elgar: Cheltenham (100–11).

Dow, S. C., McMaster, R. and Cumbers, A. (2018) *Sine Praejudicio*? Economics and the 2014 Scottish independence referendum, *Cambridge Journal of Economics*, 42: 597–615: https://doi.org/10.1093/cje/bex091

Engster, D. (2005) Rethinking care theory: The practice of caring and the obligation to care, *Hypatia*, 20: 50–74: https://doi.org/10.1111/j.1527-2001.2005.tb00486.x

Evensky, J. (2005) "Chicago Smith" versus "Kirkaldy (sic) Smith", *History of Political Economy*, 37: 197–203.

Fukuyama, F. (1992) *The End of History and the Last Man*, Free Press: New York.

Garnett, R. (2019) Smith after Samuelson: Care and harm in a socially entangled world, *Forum for Social Economics*, 48: 125–36: https://doi.org/10.1080/07360932.2019.1601122

Herman, A. (2003) *The Scottish Enlightenment: The Scots' Invention of the Modern World*, Fourth Estate: London.

Hutton, A. (2006) A Scottish tradition of applied economics in the twentieth century, in *A History of Scottish Economic Thought*, Dow, A. and Dow, S. C. (eds), Routledge: London (228–244).

Keynes, J. M. (1936) *The General Theory of Employment, Interest and Money*, Macmillan: London.

Kuhn, T. S. (1996) *The Structure of Scientific Revolutions*, (Third Edition), University of Chicago Press: Chicago, IL.

Laibman, D. (2010) Capitalism: Some theoretical reconsiderations, *World Review of Political Economy*, 1: 23–50: https://doi.org/10.2307/41931865

McCrone, D. (1992) *Understanding Scotland: The Sociology of a Stateless Nation*, Routledge: London.

Meek, R. L. (1971) Smith, Turgot, and the 'four stages' theory, *History of Political Economy*, 3: 9–27: https://doi.org/10.1215/00182702-3-1-9

Milonakis, D. and Fine, B. (2009) *From Political Economy to Economics: Method, the Social and the Historical in the Evolution of Economic Theory*, Routledge: London.

Munck, T. (2000) *The Enlightenment: A Comparative Social History 1721–1794*, Arnold: London.

Power, M. (2004) Social provisioning as a starting point for feminist economics, *Feminist Economics*, 10: 3–19: https://doi.org/10.1080/1354570042000267608

Samuels, W. J. (1977) The political economy of Adam Smith, *Ethics*, 87: 189–207: https://doi.org/10.1007/978-1-349–12266-0_5.

Samuels, W. J. (1993) Adam Smith as social constructivist and dialectician: Aspects of intergenerational intellectual relations, *History of Economic Ideas*, 1: 171–92.

Samuels, W. J. with Johnson, M. F. and Perry, W. H. (2011) *Erasing the Invisible Hand: Essays on an Elusive and Misused Concept in Economics*, Cambridge University Press: Cambridge.

Smith, A. (2000 [1759]) *The Theory of Moral Sentiments*, Prometheus Books: Amherst, MA.

Smith, A. (1997 [1776]) *An Inquiry into the Nature and Causes of the Wealth of Nations*, Penguin: London.

Steuart, J. (1767) *An Inquiry into the Principles of Political Economy*, https://www.marxists.org/reference/subject/economics/steuart/book1.htm

Terjesen, A. (2011) Adam Smith cared, so why can't modern economics? The foundations of care ethics in early economic theory, in *Applying Care Ethics to Business*, Hamington, M. and Sander-Staudt, M. (eds), Issues in Business Ethics (34), Springer: New York (55–72).

Tronto, J. C. (2013) *Caring Democracy: Markets, Equality, and Justice*, New York University Press: New York.

12 The conditions under which Adam Smith's invisible hand operates

Christopher Torr

Introduction

In her distinguished career, Sheila Dow has contributed greatly to our knowledge in fields such as macroeconomics, methodology, monetary theory, and the history of economic thought. It is a great honour to be part of a venture that celebrates her achievements. Her research into the Scottish Enlightenment and the work of Adam Smith is particularly insightful, and in what follows certain of her observations on Adam Smith's invisible hand provide a springboard for further analysis.

We start off by examining how Smith presented the notion of an invisible hand. He commences with a general statement on how individual endeavours benefit society, whereafter he imposes two conditions on the general argument. Both conditions appear to involve what we would today consider as involving national accounting considerations. Once these conditions are in place, Smith makes his one and only invisible hand declaration in the book. We also examine national accounting features to understand the conditions that Smith imposed on his general statement. Smith's attacks directed against the merchants and manufacturers are also discussed. Before the conclusion, we examine Mittermaier's insistence that we identify the environment in which societal gains can be expected to follow from the economic pursuits of the otherwise reviled merchants and manufacturers.

How Smith presents the notion of an invisible hand in chapter ii of Book IV of *The Wealth of Nations*

Smith presents his invisible hand argument in paragraphs 4–9 of chapter ii of Book IV of *The Wealth of Nations*. From the outset, it is apparent that the distinction between foreign and domestic sectors is going to dominate the proceedings. It is no coincidence that the terms 'foreign countries' and 'home' appear in the title of the chapter.

To anybody brought up on the idea that the invisible hand is about individuals pursuing their own gain and at the same time benefitting society, paragraph 4 should contain no great surprises. Here, we find the following:

DOI: 10.4324/9781003142324-13

> Paragraph 4 Every individual is continually exerting himself to find out the most advantageous employment for whatever capital he can command. It is his own advantage, indeed, and not that of the society, which he has in view. But the study of his own advantage naturally, or rather necessarily, leads him to prefer that employment which is most advantageous to the society.

Nevertheless, this general statement does contain a small surprise. It contains no mention of an invisible hand. Smith wants to present two conditions that apply to paragraph 4 before he plays this card. Without categorising under what heading the conditions might fall, he commences paragraph 5 with the word *First* and he commences paragraph 7 with the word *Secondly*. *First* has to do with whether the employment of capital is going to involve domestic or foreign activity, and *Secondly* has to do with an aggregation issue. With the benefit of hindsight, we are tempted to interpret such conditions in terms of national accounting concepts. Before we get to that, let us see what Smith includes under *First* and *Secondly*.

The following sections are taken from paragraphs 5–9. It must be emphasised that they are extracts from a fuller text and that emphasis has been added. The purpose of presenting the extracts is to reveal Smith's insistence on the conditions imposed:

> Paragraph 5 First, every individual endeavours to employ his capital **as near home** as he can, and consequently as much as he can in the support of **domestic industry** . . .
>
> Paragraph 6 . . . every wholesale merchant naturally prefers the **home trade**
>
> Paragraph 6 **Home** is in this manner the centre, if I may say so, round which the capitals of the inhabitants of every country are continually circulating
>
> Paragraph 6 But a capital employed in **the home trade**, it has already been shown, necessarily puts into motion a greater quantity of **domestic industry**, and gives revenue and employment to a greater number of **the inhabitants of the country**, than an equal capital employed in the **foreign trade** of consumption
>
> Paragraph 6 . . . every individual naturally inclines to employ his capital in the manner in which it is likely to afford the greatest support to **domestic industry**, and to give revenue and employment to the greatest number of **people of his own country**.
>
> Paragraph 7 Secondly, every individual who employs his capital in the support of **domestic industry**, necessarily endeavours so to direct that industry that its produce may be of the greatest possible value.
>
> Paragraph 9 As every individual, therefore, endeavors as much as he can both to employ his capital in the support of **domestic industry**, and so to direct that industry that its produce may be of the greatest value;

every individual necessarily labours to render the annual revenue of the society as great as he can.

Paragraph 9 By preferring the support of **domestic to that of foreign industry**, he intends only his own security; and by directing that industry in such a manner as its produce may be of the greatest value, he intends only his own gain, and he is in this, as in many other cases, led by an invisible hand . . .

The sections in bold type reflect Smith's insistence that the individuals involved are employing capital locally. By the time we get to the end of paragraph 9, we may be forgiven for wondering what an invisible hand is, but there can surely be no doubt that what comes with the territory is the domestic environment. An invisible hand operates in an environment in which each manufacturer employs his or her capital domestically. Smith refers to this issue eight times in the space of the four paragraphs listed above.

Over and above the repetition of the domestic argument, the underlined sections reveal how often Smith employs the term <u>every individual</u> here. From the *Secondly* paragraph onwards, he introduces the condition that every individual is trying to direct industry so that its produce may be of the greatest value. The word counts are provided to give some insight into the concepts preoccupying Smith's mind as he presented his invisible hand argument. Here are some more figures before we move on to other matters:

every individual – mentioned seven times in paragraphs 1–11
society – mentioned 14 times in paragraphs 1–11
domestic – mentioned 10 times in paragraphs 1–10
home – mentioned 16 times in paragraphs 1–10
foreign – mentioned 17 times in paragraphs 1–10

The link between the general statement of paragraph 4 (in which an invisible hand is not mentioned) and paragraph 9 (in which it is) has to do with the verb *leads/led*. In the last sentence of paragraph 4, we observe an individual studying his own advantage. By way of a more colloquial expression, we can observe that the individual has done his or her homework on the basis of which a business decision can be made. In paragraph 9, Smith is talking about an individual – having done his or her homework – who is being *led* by an invisible hand. If we combine the two images, we have a situation in which homework-cum-appraisal places an individual in a position to select the appropriate employment of capital. Viewed in this way, the individual is not being informed and led by an outside entity. It is the homework-cum-appraisal exercise that leads the entrepreneur to her employment-of-capital decision. In a nutshell, she is leading herself on. In paragraphs 5–9, Smith sets his analysis up in a way that confines the ventures to domestic ones.

With the First and Secondly conditions in place, Smith presents a modified version of paragraph 4 as an invisible hand explanation. In today's terminology, we might say that he is confining himself to operations that do not involve foreign domestic investment (FDI). In other words, Smith is saying that on the understanding that no FDI is involved, every individual seeking his or her gain is following a path that will benefit everybody.

Smith's insistence on the domestic nature of every individual's employment-of-capital decision has implications for the society implied by the proceedings. So far, we know that FDI is being left out of the story.

The society that emerges from Smith's account of an invisible hand is a domestic society

The unit that Smith investigates in his invisible hand argument is 'every individual' and every such individual is employing his or her capital. The unrestricted version of an invisible hand argument (paragraph 4) specifies that the pursuit of individual gain benefits society without the society concerned being specified. Smith might be referring to the society of England, France or Germany, for example. He could also be referring to the combined societies of England, Scotland, France and Germany. With the elimination of FDI, an invisible hand is leading individuals in England to employ capital in England, while at the same time leading individuals in Germany to employ capital in Germany, and so on. Whether or not we agree with Smith's argument, we have to admit that it greatly simplifies matters for him. By his removing FDI from the proceeds, we can conceive of paragraph 4 as follows:

> Every individual is continually exerting himself to find out the most advantageous employment for whatever capital he can command. It is his own advantage, indeed, and not that of the society [inside the geographical confines of England] which he has in view. But the study of his own advantage naturally, or rather necessarily, leads him to prefer that employment which is most advantageous to this society [in England].

With English manufacturers employing capital domestically, Smith can devote his attention to the benefits accruing to groups of individuals in England. These may, of course, include French citizens. We might wish to say, therefore, that Smith is concerned with the domestic rather than the national product. In a more complete analysis, of course, we would have to consider that Rebecca, opening up a pin factory in the United Kingdom, might have to import raw materials from Scandinavia and the 'annual revenue of society' (paragraph 7) would thereby be reduced, with the benefits accruing to the Scandinavian society. In today's system of national accounts, imports and exports do not include net income from abroad. In the current account figures, the items included under foreign trade do include the incomes of (say) British citizens working abroad, from which we must subtract the incomes of foreigners working in the United Kingdom in order to arrive at the net income from abroad. In the process, we can reconcile the national accounts figures with the current account figures. With Smith arguing that the individuals employ capital domestically, there is no need to consider the income they earn abroad because they do not. And if there are British citizens earning an income by teaching in foreign countries, they are, by definition, not part of the society within the geographical confines of England. The actual calculation, of course, would once again depend on how we interpret Smith's 'annual revenue of society' and whether or not he presupposes the annual revenue of society within the geographical confines of England.

By confining attention to the home industry, the society in question is presumably the society living within the geographical confines of England. It could be a section of society in Britain – in Wales, for example. Whatever it is, however, its members exclude those living on the continent or further abroad. He is consequently taking a domestic rather than a national view of annual revenue. In linking the welfare of society to annual revenue, he is adopting what we today might specify as a gross domestic product (GDP) view on the welfare of society in the sense that society benefits when annual revenue increases. There would be many, of course, who would not consider either GDP, gross national product (GNP), annual income, or annual revenue as an accurate barometer of welfare. In terms of climate change, one might argue that Smith's invisible hand involves the measures of production rather than the measures of welfare.

On another issue that can be conceived of as a national accounting one, Smith's approach provides no clear indication as to how he is handling what we today call the issue of double counting. It is not altogether clear whether the annual revenue he refers to in paragraph 9, or the benefits accruing to society in paragraph 4, includes or excludes intermediate goods. We find divergent views on this in the literature – Blaug (1978, chapter 2), for example, argues that Smith's approach excludes intermediate goods, whereas O'Donnell (1990, 30) indicates that it does not.

Suppose Rebecca's homework has taken into account the possibility of setting up a factory in Paris. She homes in on London for security/management reasons, even if the projected returns for Paris are a bit higher. Her homework could also have revealed that a London venture appears to offer a better rate of profit than a butchery in Birmingham, a bakery in Bristol or a pin factory in Portsmouth.

Her decision would, under today's considerations, be classified under private investment and, hence, GDP (or expenditure) in the national accounts. If her homework had led her to take up the Paris option, there would be no investment entry in the national accounts, but rather an entry in the balance of payments reflecting the flow of funds to France. Or to put matters more precisely, the selection of the Paris option would have led to either foreign direct investment (FDI) or foreign portfolio investment (FPI). So, if she chooses Paris, her actions would not have troubled the local national accounts scoreboard. At a later stage, of course, there may be a repatriation of earnings. This would appear in the figures of the balance of payments, but such an item is not included in the net exports falling under GDP.

To sum up, her homework points towards the London venture and let us suppose her estimates point towards a 3% rate of profit. This then is the most advantageous employment for the capital that she can command, and the capital amount involved represents a benefit to British society as long the annual revenue that Smith is talking about is an accurate reflection of welfare.

Let us suppose that it is 1789 and that Rebecca has become aware of the volatile political climate emerging in France. Even if the estimated rate of returns on a Paris factory is 10%, Rebecca will baulk at the prospect, over and above her inclination to want to keep a close eye on the factory proceedings. If the political situation had been the other way around, Rebecca might very well regard the overseas venture as the more advantageous, in which case Smith could hardly claim that the study of her own advantage leads her to prefer that employment that is the most advantageous to British society. Keeping investment local facilitates Smith's welfare calculations even if he is ostensibly arguing that it is easier to keep an eye on a pin factory in Kirkcaldy than it is to keep an eye on one in Paris. We can, nevertheless, conceive of a situation in which Rebecca's homework leads her to prefer that employment that is the more advantageous to French society than it is to British society. Smith's approach rules FDI out of court. He thereby forges a link that runs from private gain to public benefit (in terms of production). In the process, he avoids having to consider the benefits accruing to French society. As Dow (2009, 17) has indicated, the term 'invisible hand' can refer 'to the unintended consequences of bias in favour of domestic over foreign direct investment'. Persky (1989: 198) notes that Smith's argument is 'limited to domestic industry, because if capital was employed outside the nation, it wasn't obvious that this would do much good for the domestic economy'.

During the decades wherein globalisation was on the increase, attempts to leave FDI out of the proceedings would appear counterintuitive. Suppose Rebecca's homework leads her to proceed with a pin factory in Paris. Her actions that might otherwise have been benefitting people in Kirkcaldy would now be benefitting a portion of French society. It is understandable that somebody like Alan Greenspan would have been seen fit to analyse events during his watch as an extension of Smith's argument. On at least five occasions in *The age of turbulence*, Greenspan (2007) seeks to extend Smith's analysis from a domestic to an international context (pages 15, 248, 262, 367 and 488). On page 262, for example, we find:

> The expression 'invisible hand' does not seem to have been very important to Smith; in all his writings, he used it only three times. The effect it describes, however, is something he discerns at every level of society, from the great flows of goods and commodities between nations to everyday neighbourhood transactions . . .
>
> (Greenspan, 2007, 262)

In his age of turbulence, which also represents an age of globalisation, Greenspan is both allowing for the presence of FDI and bringing the societies of different nations into the picture.

Merchants and manufacturers – villains or heroes?

Towards the end of Book 1, Smith divides the revenue of society into three parts, namely the 'rent of land, the wages of labour, and the profits of stock' with the people involved in the three orders being landlords, labourers and what we might today refer to as businessmen or businesswomen. In Smith's approach, the third group consists for the most part of merchants and manufacturers (*WN*, I.xi.6) – see Rothschild and Sen (2006: 327–3) for more on this issue.

Smith asserts that the interests of the landlords are 'strictly and inseparably connected with the general interest of the society' (*WN*, I.xi.7). In the next paragraph, he adds, 'The interest of the second order, that of those who live by wages, is as strictly connected with the interest of the society as that of the first'.

A different picture emerges with regard to the third order. We find him referring to:

> . . . an order of men whose interest is never exactly the same with that of the public, who have generally an interest to deceive and even to oppress the public, and who accordingly have, upon many occasions, both deceived and oppressed it.
>
> (*WN*, I.xi.9)

How is such wickedness reconciled with the beneficial role played by individuals in the invisible hand explanation?

Mittermaier (2020: 41) notes that Smith 'reserved the only invective in the book for merchants and manufacturers', and Bishop (1995: 7) reminds us that it is the 'aggregated interests of the merchants and manufacturers which he [Smith] says oppresses society'.

Blaug (1978, 37) is referring to the *Wealth of Nations*, IV, chapter iii, part ii, paragraph 9 when he writes:

> The whole book is directed against 'the mean rapacity, the monopolizing spirit of merchants and manufacturers, who neither are, nor ought to be, the rulers of mankind.' The merchants and master-manufacturers are the architects of the hated Mercantile system . . .

The potential for conflict emerging from these brief accounts of M&M behaviour seems strangely at odds with the benefits dished out to society every time an M or an M takes it upon himself or herself to engage in the pursuit of economic gain. We return to this in the following section.

The type of environment in which societal benefits follow from individual pursuits

The system of national accounts in place today has been in existence for some 80 years. When reading Smith, we often have to guess what aggregation procedure he might have had in mind – some 250 years ago. A first-year economics student is today taught that somebody investing £10 million in a domestic venture is simultaneously contributing £10 million to GDP. This kind of reasoning might very well have been less clear in Smith's circles circa 1776 and it does not seem untoward that Smith would find it necessary to specify that a measure of the private economic amount involved amounted to an equivalent addition to annual revenue even if today it seems as something of a tautology. In the paragraphs where Smith presents his invisible hand explanation, he indicates that the benefits accruing to society *necessarily follow* from the employment of capital by the individual participants. The word *necessarily* appears five times in paragraphs 4–9 of chapter ii of Book IV. Sometimes, Smith seems to want to go further than simply note that one amount is simply equal to another:

> But the annual revenue of every society is always precisely equal to the exchangeable value of the whole annual produce of its industry, or rather is precisely the same thing with that exchangeable value.
>
> (*WN*, IV.ii.9)

Kennedy (2017: 92) uses the term 'simultaneously and inescapably' when he discusses the process whereby the merchant's action adds an equivalent amount of domestic revenue. Mittermaier (2019, 140) notes that Smith's arguments come across as little more than a 'seemingly trivial logical necessity'. He notes elsewhere that:

> Far from being about a grand harmony of interests, the invisible-hand argument is seemingly quite trivial. The product/revenue of society is the aggregate of what individuals produce. Where all are striving to produce more, all are striving to increase the product/revenue of society and that is by definition advantageous to society or in the public interest.
>
> (Mittermaier, 2020, 63)

Smith's invisible hand presentation presents us with at least two puzzles. Our knowledge of national accounts leads us to understand that an investment of £10 million by an individual can simultaneously mean the addition of £10 million to the annual revenue of the domestic society. Why should we want to classify such a process as an invisible hand argument if it simply amounts to national accounting conventions? And how are we to reconcile the villainous roles of M&Ms with the benefits they are serving up to the local community?

In his reinterpretation of Smith's contribution, Mittermaier (2020) provides an eloquent answer to such questions. He identifies the need to spell out the conditions necessary for an invisible hand explanation to operate. What kind of an environment does it require? What institutions are necessary for individual endeavours to translate into societal benefits? What makes villains heroes?

To illustrate how Smith deals with such conflicting notions, let us imagine adding a third paragraph, appropriately titled *Thirdly* to the *First* and *Secondly* paragraphs discussed in Section 1.

To recap Smith's arguments, recall the general statement (*WN*, IV, ii, paragraph 4) that Smith presents to illustrate that the pursuit of gain by 'every individual' leads, of necessity, to societal gain.

This is followed by the paragraph headed *First* in which Smith seeks to keep all employment of capital local.

Next comes paragraph 7, which is headed *Secondly* in which societal benefits are held to be commensurate with the employment of capital by M&Ms.

We now imagine a paragraph headed *Thirdly* in which further conditions necessary for societal gains to follow from private pursuits are considered.

The essence of Mittermaier's considerable contribution is his emphasis on the need to specify the environment in which Smith's invisible hand can be expected to operate (Mittermaier, 2020, 17). The requisite institutions need to be specified, and on top of that we need to consider whether such institutions would emerge of their own accord or whether deliberate action needs to be taken to ensure that they do come into existence. Those who believe that the requisite institutions will come into play of their own accord are classified as dogmatic free marketeers, whereas those who argue that deliberate planning has to be undertaken to ensure their existence are regarded as pragmatic free marketeers.

In brief, Mittermaier asks us to consider the idea that there is a hand behind the invisible hand. He thereupon asks you if you envisage the H behind the IH as invisible. If you answer yes, he classifies you as entertaining a dogmatic view on free markets. If you answer no, the hand you envisage behind the invisible hand is a visible one, and you are regarded as entertaining a pragmatic view on free markets (Mittermaier, 2020, 17).

As noted above, Smith's main target in the *Wealth of Nations* are the merchants and manufacturers and they are singled out for their 'monopolizing spirit'. A particular feature of the institutional environment in which an invisible hand is supposed to operate is the legal infrastructure. If the laws and customs of society are not there to guard against monopolistic practices, individuals pursuing their own ends will not generate societal benefit. Mittermaier ask us to consider whether an appropriate legal structure will come into effect on its own accord, or whether it has to be deliberately planned. An invisible hand argument requires appropriate competitive behaviour on the part of merchants and manufacturers. The benefits to society will not accrue if the system allows monopolistic practices. When viewed in such a light, the invisible hand argument offered in chapter ii of Book IV appears as more of an ideal type of organisation to be striven for, than as an actual description of the status quo in England in the run up to the Industrial Revolution.

Conclusion

Smith's account of an invisible hand argument has been presented first as a general statement of the idea that the striving for gain on the part of individuals leads to societal benefits. Smith thereafter modifies his argument by ruling FDI out of court and by specifying a particular aggregating procedure that appears to amount to a tautology. With these modifications in place, he brings an invisible hand into the argument. The merchants and manufacturers who are engaged in investment ventures emerge as the societal benefactors, even though they are singled out as the villains of the peace elsewhere in the book. Mittermaier's novel approach to reconcile such views is investigated. He posits a hand behind the invisible hand and raises the question of whether that hand is also invisible. He thereby introduces a scheme whereby we can analyse whether or not the institutions required for an invisible hand to operate have to be deliberately planned.

References

Bishop, J.D. (1995) Adam Smith's invisible hand argument. *Journal of Business Ethics*, Vol. 14 (3), 1–16. https://www.jstor.org/stable/25072635

Blaug, M. (1978) *Economic theory in retrospect*, Third edition. Cambridge: Cambridge University Press.

Dow, S.C (2009) Knowledge, communication and the Scottish enlightenment. *Review of Philosophical Economics*, Vol. 10 (2), 3–23. https://doi.org/10.3917/rpec.102.0003

Greenspan, A. (2007) *The age of turbulence*. New York: Penguin Press.

Kennedy, G. (2017) *An authentic account of Adam Smith*. Palgrave Macmillan.

Mittermaier, K.H.M. (2019) The invisible hand and some thoughts on the non-existent in what we study. *Journal of Contextual Economics*, Vol. 139, 135–58. https://doi.org/10.3790/schm.139.1.135

Mittermaier, K.H.M. (2020) *The hand behind the invisible hand. Dogmatic and pragmatic views on free markets and the state of economic theory*. Bristol: Bristol University Press. https://library.oapen.org/handle/20.500.12657/40100

O'Donnell, R. (1990) *Adam Smith's theory of value and distribution*. New York: St Martin's Press.

Persky, J. (1989) Adam Smith's invisible hands. *Journal of Economic Perspectives*, Vol. 3(4), 195–201. https://www.jstor.org/stable/1942919

Rothschild, E. and Sen, A. (2006) Adam Smith's economics. In K. Haakonssen (ed.), *The Cambridge Companion to Adam Smith*. Cambridge University Press, 319–65.

Smith, A. (1776 [1982]) *An inquiry into the nature and causes of the wealth of nations*. Glasgow edition.

13 Mary Theresa Rankin

A monetary economist in the Scottish tradition of political economy

Robert W. Dimand

Introduction

Mary Theresa Rankin was a pioneering woman among the economists in Scotland (see Dow and Dow, eds., *A History of Scottish Economic Thought*, 2006, on Scottish economists) and an active participant in monetary economics in the time of Keynes. Isabel Frances Grant, Rankin's junior by 5 years and an innovative economic historian of Scotland, followed a non-academic path as founder of the Highland Folk Museum (see Grant 1930, 1934 on Scottish economic history and her contributions to the *Economic History* supplement to the *Economic Journal*), whereas Rankin achieved an academic career, earning a DPhil at Oxford in 1919 (a year before women who had earned Oxford degrees were allowed to receive them) and teaching at the University of Edinburgh from 1921 to 1953 as assistant lecturer, lecturer, and senior lecturer (and also lectured at what was then Herriot-Watt College). The 108 founding members of the Scottish Society of Economists in 1897 were all male, and the society remained all-male until four women joined in 1905, but, male or female, "Few of these early members would have accepted the designation of an economist as a professional designation"[1] (Campbell 1997, p. 359, see also Rankin 1954); however, Rankin clearly established herself as a female professional economist in Scotland. In addition to writing three books about wage-setting through conciliation and arbitration (Rankin 1916, 1931a, 1931b), Rankin upheld the classical monetary views of her mentor Joseph Shield Nicholson, notably in her collection of reprinted articles and lectures, *Monetary Opinions and Policy, 1924–34* (Rankin 1935) and in her contributions to *The Scotsman*. Like Nicholson (see his introductory essay and notes to Adam Smith 1884), Rankin identified strongly with the Scottish tradition of political economy and applied economics stemming from David Hume, Adam Smith, Sir James Steuart, and Adam Ferguson (see Dow 1987; Dow, Dow and Hutton 1997; Dow and Dow, eds., 2006 on that tradition[2]). Writing Rankin's obituary for the *Scottish Journal of Political Economy*, Alan Thompson (1964, pp. 80, 81) stressed Rankin's "directness and simplicity of style, matched by a capacity for thorough and fruitful research which made her so much an economist in the Scottish tradition" and called

DOI: 10.4324/9781003142324-14

her "a disciple of Adam Smith." Although Rankin's focus on monetary economics, her commitment to the Scottish political economy tradition, and her pathbreaking role as an eminent female economist in Scotland parallel Sheila Dow's intellectual interests and career, and her study and celebration of the Scottish tradition, there is one crucial divergence: as Nicholson's intellectual heir defending classical monetary economics, Rankin's "hostility to Keynes was always marked" (Thompson 1964, p. 80), in sharp contrast to Sheila Dow's affinity to Keynes and Post-Keynesian monetary economics.

Mary T. Rankin was born in 1882 to a Presbyterian minister and his wife in Lanarkshire, in a family that stressed education and service (her brothers became Chief Justice of Calcutta and Professor of Old Testament History at Edinburgh University, her sister Medical Officer of Health for Lancaster). She received her MA with first-class honors in economic science from the University of Edinburgh in 1910. She studied there and came under the lasting influence of Joseph Shield Nicholson, professor of political economy and mercantile law at Edinburgh from 1880 to 1925 and founding president of the Scottish Society of Economists from 1897 to 1903 (see Rankin 1927, her obituary of Nicholson in the *University of Edinburgh Journal*, and Rankin 1954 on the Scottish Society of Economists). Rankin's first book, on *Arbitration and Conciliation in Australasia: The Legal Wage in Victoria and New Zealand* (Rankin 1916), sponsored by the Carnegie Trust for Scottish Universities, was published with an enthusiastic introduction by Nicholson, who had supervised the study. She continued to write on the arbitration and conciliation of industrial disputes in Australia and New Zealand (Rankin 1931a) and in Britain (Rankin 1931b, 1955), publishing her last article on the subject after she had, at the age of 70, retired from teaching. She became recognized as an authority on the organization of the labor market, a subject on which she published four book reviews in the *Economic Journal* in 1929 alone. Her thorough empirical treatment of industrial disputes was accepted as politically neutral, unlike Nicholson's hostility to trade unions as a form of monopoly, which led him to complain to the Edinburgh Chamber of Commerce that "It is not pleasant for a man at my time of life to be accused of being reactionary, old-fashioned and fossilized" (Nicholson 1894, quoted by Scott, revised by Maloney, 2004).

Shield Nicholson and the Scottish tradition of political economy

Nicholson had been one of Alfred Marshall's earliest students at Cambridge (before Marshall succeeded Henry Fawcett as professor in 1885), bracketed second for the first-class honors degree in moral sciences in 1876, and won the Cambridge Cobden Club's triennial essay competition in 1877 (with his close friend John Neville Keynes as runner-up) and again in 1880, the first two times the prize was offered. His first winning Cobden essay gained him a Cambridge ScD and was published as *The Effects of Machinery on Wages* (Nicholson 1878; see Groenewegen 2011), and he wrote a pathbreaking article on human capital in the inaugural issue of the *Economic Journal* (Nicholson 1891). W. R. Scott described Nicholson as "for the most part . . . a conciliatory bimetallist, a moderate under-consumptionist, a pragmatic free-trader, and a subtle defender of the quantity theory of money" (Scott, revised by Maloney, 2004 – see Scott 1927, Nicholson 1886, 1887a, 1887b, 1888a, pamphlets issued by the Bimetallic League and reprinted both in his 1888 *Essays on Present Monetary Problems* and among the essays added to Nicholson's *Treatise of Money*, 1888b).[3] Nicholson upheld Adam Smith's tradition in Scottish political economy, editing a new edition of *The Wealth of Nations* (Smith 1884)[4]; wrote regularly in support of classical principles in *The Scotsman* as J. R. McCulloch had done before him and Rankin did afterward; and in 1903, joined with Charles Bastable and Francis Y. Edgeworth to organize the manifesto of the economics professors defending free trade against Joseph Chamberlain's "Tariff Reform" agitation (Groenewegen 2011). While a private tutor in Cambridge prior to winning, before turning 30, the chair at Edinburgh (where had studied in 1872–73), Nicholson lectured on political economy for the Association for the Higher Education of Women from 1878 to 1880, displaying an attitude toward opening universities to women and this was reflected in his support for Rankin's career. Relations between Marshall and Nicholson cooled after Nicholson and Marshall differed over bimetallism and the quantity theory of money in papers for the Gold and Silver Commission (Nicholson, "Causes of Movements in General Prices," in Nicholson, 1888b, pp. 342–79, and Marshall 1888), and Nicholson's review in *The Scotsman* of the first edition of Marshall's *Principles* found Marshall's handling of economic history inadequate (in Groenewegen 1998, Vol. I, pp. 166–8). Marshall refused to speak to Nicholson after Nicholson voted for H. S. Foxwell rather than A. C. Pigou to succeed to Marshall's chair at Cambridge (Groenewegen 2011). In contrast to his break with Marshall, Nicholson remained close to John Neville Keynes, who checked the proofs of all three volumes of Nicholson's *Principles of Political Economy* (1893, 1897, 1901).[5] Neville Keynes's son John Maynard Keynes invited Nicholson (1914) to write a substantial review article in the *Economic Journal* on the report of the Royal Commission on Indian Currency and Finance, a report largely drafted by Maynard Keynes.

Rankin's *Monetary Opinions* in the Edinburgh tradition

Rankin's *Monetary Opinions and Policy 1924–34* (1935, p. v) carried a foreword from F. W. (later Sir Frederick) Ogilvie, then President and Vice-Chancellor of Queen's University, Belfast, but until the previous year Nicholson's successor in the chair of political economy in Edinburgh. The pioneer of the economics of tourism (Ogilvie 1933), he was later the second director-general of the BBC and then the principal of Jesus College, Oxford. Ogilvie emphasized Rankin's worthy place in the distinctive tradition in political economy at the University of Edinburgh, going back to Dugald Stewart's lectures in 1800 ("the first public course specifically on political economy to be given in any British university") but given vitality by Nicholson, that "efforts should be made from time to time to bring the results of economic analysis before wider audiences, and to offer to the public careful and disinterested guidance on some of the major economic issues of the day" (see Dow 1987; Dow, Dow and Hutton 1997; Hutton 2006). Ogilvie held (p. vi) that, although Rankin's papers were written for particular occasions over 11 years,

> so little were they influenced in their composition by things ephemeral that they can stand erect now, to be both a history of monetary problems in this period and a most valuable exposition, in non-technical terms, of some of the main principles of the theory of money.

Rankin spoke to such professional but non-academic audiences as the Insurance Society of Edinburgh ("Problems of Currency and Exchange," March 1929, in Rankin 1935, pp. 27–51) and the Chartered Institute of Secretaries, meeting in Edinburgh in November 1931 ("The Economic Position," Rankin 1935, pp. 52–65). Her "Post-War Changes in Banking Function" (1935, pp. 93–115) was the opening address to the Institute of Bankers in Scotland, delivered over 2 days (October 25 and 26, 1932) in Edinburgh and Glasgow. The *Edinburgh Evening News* (October 26, 1932) reported that Rankin was "the first woman who has addressed the Institute of Bankers in Scotland" at all, let alone a two-evening opening lecture. Her opening remarks show clearly why she was welcomed by such audiences:

> Needless to say, I am not this evening going to lead you into the dark night of the monetary theorists. My view on the subject of banking is severely practical and not at all mystical – and my sympathy in these controversies is entirely with the bankers.
>
> (1935, pp. 93–94)

None of the papers in Rankin (1935) had appeared in a scholarly journal.

Rankin (1935, p. 8) insisted in 1924 that some price fluctuations

> are necessary to healthy economic conditions and to the promotion of social welfare. It is useless to say that the proposal is to stabilize general prices, but in no way to interfere with relative prices. It has yet to be shown that this is not impossible. Mr. Hawtrey acknowledges this to be a fundamental difficulty. To Mr. Keynes [1923] its importance is so slight that it passes unnoticed.

Contrary to Hawtrey and Keynes, Rankin (1935, pp. 10–12) held that monetary factors were only secondary in driving the trade cycle, insisting that

> Everyone [!] will admit that the cycle originates with a rise in demand for specific articles leading to a rise in price, which in turn leads to

> competition for a not unlimited market, and consequently to temporary over-production at the high level of prices.

The remedy would be to "check purely speculative borrowing . . . This, however, is more likely to be effectively accomplished by a more complete adoption of the gold standard throughout the world than in reality existed before the war, than by abandoning the standard."

Reviewing the Macmillan Report before the Scottish Society of Economists in March 1932, Rankin (1935, p. 90) held that

> To raise international prices by monetary manipulation to the level of 1928, as is usually suggested, would be to invite a repetition of the sad history of prices since that period. In no official record or index of production is it denied that the origin of the disastrous fall in prices in 1929 was the over-production of primary commodities, and the final breakdown of pools and monopolies, which had attempted to keep up prices in face of improved processes of production and an over-abundant supply.

Over-production of primary commodities seemed to her so obviously the culprit for the Great Depression that she saw no reason to mention the 1929 Wall Street stock market crash or fiscal and monetary policies that might have translated such a shock into a contraction of demand.

In *The Scotsman* (April 29, 1932, Rankin 1935, pp. 86–92), Rankin considered "The Price Level: Should it be Raised?" She found that "perhaps the most useful result of the Macmillan Committee was the clarity with which it demonstrated" that the higher price level that would benefit Britain and the world was not a higher British price level but higher prices elsewhere, especially in "the gold-hoarding countries, France and America." Britain's abandonment in August and September 1931 of a fixed parity between sterling and gold had lowered the gold price of British goods compared with the price levels of those countries that remained on the gold standard exchange standard. Rather than seeing a floating exchange rate as providing an opportunity for domestic monetary expansion, she focused exclusively on net exports, where a domestic price increase would offset the gains from exchange depreciation:

> Impassioned appeals for this policy [of higher prices] should first be addressed to France and America, whose hearts of gold will, doubtless, be touched by the sad spectacle of the British Empire sinking, for lack of specie and a fillip to price, into the abyss.
>
> (1935, p. 89)

"No clever financial theories should be allowed to hide from the British trader that he must bring down his costs," warned Rankin (1935, p. 92). Rankin (1935, pp. 91–2) had no sympathy for the concern of Irving Fisher

(1932, 1933) and of Keynes (1936, Chapter 19) that deflation, by raising the real value of inside debt, is contractionary and imposes real costs by raising risk premiums and the probability of bankruptcy and default:

> So far as prices and debt are concerned, a rise in price would doubtless enable industry to carry with less difficulty the burden of debt, public and industrial. But a great deal of the industrial debt should never have been incurred, and should no longer be carried. A fall in price which led to the excision of this debt would perform a more useful function. The immediate evil of the agitation for a price-raising policy is not that it is likely to be carried into effect, but that false hopes based upon it may retard this excision and lead to further misdirection of capital.

Rankin's essays robustly clash with the suggestion that Keynesians were constructing straw men or Aunt Sallies (depending on which side of the Atlantic the suggestion was made) in attributing such views to anti-Keynesian economists between the wars. Rankin emphatically endorsed adjusting debt levels by bankruptcy, repudiation, and cost-cutting, not by raising the price level to ease the burden of debt.

Writing a year later in *The Scotsman* (April 8, 1933, Rankin 1935, pp. 131–7) in response to Keynes's March 1933 articles in *The Times* reprinted as *The Means to Prosperity* (Keynes 1933), Rankin (1935, p. 137) warned that "Government expenditure based on borrowing will encourage and increase the dislocation between wholesale and retail prices [and] encourage expenditure on consumers' goods and hinder it on producers' goods, on which the real prosperity of the country depends." Invoking the authority of Adam Smith in her 1932 address to the Institute of Bankers, Rankin (1935, p. 114) observed,

> A popular view of internal debt since the war, but one which was already time-worn in Adam Smith's day, is that the internal debt is no burden on a nation; it merely means, as it were, 'the right hand paying the left,' the amount of wealth within the country being unaffected by these payments. Adam Smith thought very poorly of that argument. He pointed out that the payment of debt interest meant drawing wealth away from the more productive sources of the country to the less productive – the dislocation caused thereby depending on the amount so drawn.

Rankin stressed, decades before it became a commonplace of macroeconomics, credible commitment to a policy:

> Sir Charles Addis is of opinion that once it is realized that the Government is firmly resolved to resist further inflation, and that it regards itself as committed to the policy of the Cunliffe Report, traders will settle

> down to the new condition of things, and be content with the smaller margin of profit.
>
> ([1924] 1935, p. 35, citing an address by Addis to a joint meeting of the Institute of Bankers in Scotland and the Society of Accountants, published in the *Accountants Magazine*)

Rankin did not endorse the gold exchange standard in all circumstances. Her article in *Scotsman* about "British and American Monetary Plans" (1943) would have been much more welcome to Keynes than her interwar essays, for Rankin (1943) endorsed the British monetary proposal (the Keynes Plan) and its advocacy of an international money of account (to be called bancor) with a gold value that would vary from time to time. In contrast, the White Plan, devised by Harry Dexter White of the US Treasury, proposed an international money of account (to be called unitas), equal to "the existing legal gold content of ten American dollars" so that "the value of all currencies will be tied to a fixed quantity of gold," removing a means of adjusting payments imbalances. She concluded that

> In the British plan any variations in the value of gold may be offset by a change in the gold content of 'bancor' – in other words, the values of currencies need not vary with the value of gold nor with the value of any one currency; but in the American plan they would. The real point of the objection is not that the paper currencies would be tied to gold but that, because of the concentration of gold in America, they would in effect be tied to one particular currency. Fixed exchange rates in these circumstances involve a risk to other countries' price structure which it may be found difficult to accept. Here, and not in the more technical provisions, lies the main difference between the plans.

As Rankin (1943) summarized the difference,

> The British plan [the Keynes Plan] poses the question: How can matters be arranged so that a country shall have no difficulty in making international payments? The American plan [the White Plan]: How can matters be arranged so as to ensure international payments being made?

Since "There is no doubt that at the end of the war Britain will be, at least for some, among the 'deficit countries' on current trade account, and the United States the chief creditor or 'surplus country,'" the Keynes Plan wished surplus countries to share the burden of balance of payments adjustment, unlike the White Plan. Rankin's sympathy was with the unsuccessful struggle that Keynes waged for the British Plan at the Dumbarton Oaks and Bretton Woods conferences, in contrast to her disdain a decade earlier for Keynes's contribution on monetary policy and price-level stabilization in the Macmillan Report.[6]

From the Scottish Society of Economists to the Scottish Economic Society

Two chapters of Rankin (1935) had been read to the Scottish Society of Economists, "The Policy of Monetary Stabilisation" (pp. 1–26) in 1924 and her critique of the Macmillan Report in 1932 (Rankin 1935, pp. 66–85). Despite Rankin's continued active participation, Alec Cairncross (1954, p. 1), president of the newly-established Scottish Economic Society and the first editor of the *Scottish Journal of Political Economy*, reported that "After the death of Shield Nicholson, however, the [Scottish] Society [of Economists] languished and for the past twenty years it has ceased to meet." But, as R. H. Campbell (1997, pp. 360–1) remarked,

> That the old society had followed such good economic principles that it still had funds in hand made the continuity even more attractive to the new impecunious body.[7] The chief negotiator of the linkage, and one of the few who was a member of both, was Mary Rankine [*sic*]. Appropriately, she became one of the first vice-presidents of the reconstituted society and continued to play an active part in its affairs until her death.

Reception and marginalization

H. W. M.[8] (1935, p. 734), reviewing Rankin (1935) in the *Journal of the Royal Statistical Society*, was willing to "cordially endorse" F. W. Ogilvie's evaluation of Rankin as "one of Nicholson's most distinguished pupils and afterwards his colleague" who had "worthily upheld the tradition which she inherited." The reviewer added that

> It is not necessary to share all Dr. Rankin's views in order to appreciate the value of her lectures. She appears to be a firm believer in the old monetary creeds and has little respect for the modern mystics – say for Mr. Keynes or President Roosevelt – while even the Macmillan Report is criticized somewhat petulantly. Nevertheless, her sturdy conservatism is not only respectable but to be respected.

In *International Affairs*, Lord Meston (1935) agreed that

> A disciple of the late Shield Nicholson, Dr. Rankin carries his tradition of common-sense conservatism in economics. The essays which she collects in this little book are running comments on the movements of the last ten years, and bring with a breeze of refreshing candour, as well as a welcome freedom from jargon. She is no respecter of persons.[9]

Only Claude Guillebaud (1935, p. 637), nephew of Alfred Marshall and future editor of the variorum edition of Marshall's *Principles*, continued the hostilities between Marshall (1980) and his former student Nicholson, curtly dismissing the book by Nicholson's disciple in a short paragraph in a review of six books on money:

> Dr. Rankin is a resolute opponent of all measures or policies, directed to extracting the world from its economic difficulties, which diverge from the straight and narrow path of the reduction of costs and financial orthodoxy. As a whole these essays are rather slight and scarcely stand up to the test of publication in book form.

Apart from the Mary T. Rankin Prize awarded each year to the best final-year undergraduate economics student at the University of Edinburgh, Rankin is little remembered (although her career and 1935 collection are noted in Dimand 2014). Within the history of economic thought and especially the history of interwar British monetary economics, she has been marginalized as a woman in an era when economics was even more male-dominated than in recent years; as an economist at a Scottish university when the history of British economics focuses on Cambridge, Oxford, and LSE; and as an upholder of an earlier economic orthodoxy who was critical of the monetary theories and stabilization policies advanced by Keynes and Hawtrey. The history of the Scottish tradition in political economy has emphasized the 18th century, the glorious era of Hume, Steuart, and Smith, and secondarily the first half of the 19th century, the era of McCulloch (Dow 1987; Dow, Dow and Hutton 1997; Dow and Dow, eds., 2006 – but see Hutton 2006 on applied economics in 20th-century Scotland, in Dow and Dow, eds., 2006). However, although she has been neglected in the history of that tradition, Rankin was noteworthy for achieving a successful academic career as a pioneering woman in economics in Scotland in the first half of the 20th century; as a key player in the formation of the Scottish Economic Society; as continuing the distinctive Edinburgh tradition of Dugald Stewart, McCulloch, Nicholson, and Ogilvie of bringing the classical principles of political economy to wider audiences; and as an articulate participant in monetary debates, whose writings vividly show what Keynes (1933, 1936) was arguing against and refute the common claim that Keynes was arguing against views that no one defended. Within Scotland she held the attention of professional societies of bankers, insurers, and corporate secretaries and, like McCulloch and Nicholson, the readers of *The Scotsman*, forums for the discussion of monetary analysis and policy generally neglected in the histories of monetary economics. As a woman in Scottish economics, as an upholder of the Scottish tradition of political economy, and as a monetary economist in Scotland, Rankin's career displayed parallels with the career and contributions of Sheila Dow although taking an utterly different attitude to Keynes's revolution in monetary economics. As Ogilvie said in his foreword to Rankin (1935), Mary Theresa Rankin was "one of Nicholson's most distinguished pupils" and "worthily upheld the tradition which she inherited."

Acknowledgments

I am grateful to Chantal Mundell, a Brock graduate now with the Canadian Imperial Bank of Commerce, for her able research assistance about Mary T. Rankin.

Notes

1 Campbell (1997, p. 359) observed that although the society's founding president, Nicholson, was a professor of political economy (and of law), "Three lawyers, an accountant and an actuary followed Nicholson as president."

2 The history of political economy in Scotland can be traced back at least two and a half centuries before Hume and Smith (the starting point of Dow and Dow, eds., 2006): see Raymond De Roover (1970) on the economic thought of Jean Mair (or John Major), who lived from 1469 to 1550. Mair, a professor at the Sorbonne and at St. Andrew's (where he was one of John Knox's teachers), was hailed by Hugh Trevor-Roper (2008, p. 21) as "the most interesting intellectual figure – and the most radical social and political thinker – who had yet appeared in Scotland . . . If Major was the last of the Scottish Schoolmen, he was also the first Scottish critical historian." However, De Roover (1970, p. 68) reports that, in his own time, Mair "was ridiculed by Rabelais in one of the most scabrous and scatological chapters of *Gargantua*" and that Erasmus expressed aversion to Mair.

3 In a lecture on *Irregularity of Employment and Fluctuations of Prices* given and published in Edinburgh, Cambridge economist Herbert Somerton Foxwell (1886, p. 53) declared: "You will find an excellent and clear exposition of the whole matter [of bimetallism] by Professor Nicholson in his pamphlet on *The Silver Question*, with the general."

4 Although originally from Lincolnshire and, apart from a year at the University of Edinburgh, educated at Trinity College, Cambridge, at King's College, London (BA 1870 in logic and metaphysics, MA and Gerstenberg Prize for Political Economy 1877), and in law at Heidelberg, Nicholson integrated into the Scottish tradition of political economy: "When Nicholson died, *The Times* [13 May 1927] wrote that 'he knew his *Wealth of Nations* as thoroughly as the Scottish peasant knows his Bible, and believed in it almost as thoroughly'" (Scott, revised by Maloney, 2004). In 1885, Nicholson marred Jeannie, daughter of William Ballantyne Hodgson, his predecessor in the professorship.

5 In contrast to his reservations about Marshall's (1980) presentation of economic history, Nicholson admired the exposition of theory in Marshall's *Principles* and considered it the right book for honors students. Nicholson's *Principles of Political Economy* was written for pass students, hence, presumably, "its omission of the marginal principle" (Scott, revised by Maloney, 2004).

6 "But Mr. Keynes, who is here refusing to countenance any fall of costs which means a fall in the *price* of factors, is consistent with the fundamental assumption with which he started – the policy of stabilization – which is that adjustment must not take place through price – except, curiously enough, by a rise (which in itself betrays the inflationary nature of the policy). . . . The alternative method to having our prices brought down to the world level is, the Report then tells us, to have the world level raised to our prices (a truly British outlook)" (Rankin 1935, pp. 77–8).

7 According to Cairncross (1954, p. 1), "After a short wooing, the dowager Society agreed to the match, throwing in a small dowry to show that the change of title was entirely acceptable," the new title being "less suggestive of exclusiveness and

professional mysteries" even though, according to Campbell (1997, p. 359), the older society "was not a society of economists in spite of its name but a society drawn from those in professional ranks of Edinburgh who happened to have an interest in economic questions." A further complication was that, according to Campbell (1997, p. 362), "the conference of economists in the Scottish universities, which had started in 1951, and from which much of the initiative for the revival of the Society had come, still went on" and did not merge with the annual conferences of the Scottish Economic Society when those began in 1982.

8 The review was signed only with the reviewer's initials, as was then customary for reviews in that journal.

9 See, for example, Rankin (1935, pp. 22, 26), addressing the Scottish Society of Economists in 1924 on proposals for monetary stabilization (including Keynes 1923): "Mr. Keynes' criticism of Professor Irving Fisher's scheme – viz."

References

Campbell, R. H. (1997) "The Scottish Society of Economists – The Scottish Economic Society, 1897–1997," *Scottish Journal of Political Economy* 44(4), 359–67. https://doi.org/10.1111/1467–9485.00064

Cairncross, Alexander K. (1954) "The Scottish Economic Society," *Scottish Journal of Political Economy* 1(1), 1–6. https://doi.org/10.1111/j.1467–9485.1954.tb00692.x

De Roover, Raymond (1970) "La Pensée économique de Jean Mair, professeur à la Sorbonne et à l'Université de Saint-André en Ecosse (début du XVIe siècle)," *Journal des Savants* 1970(2), 65–81. https://doi.org/10.346/jds.1970.1217

Dimand, Robert W. (2014) "Presidential Address: The Global Economic Crisis in Light of the History of Interwar Monetary Economics," *Journal of the History of Economic Thought* 36(1), 3–21. https://doi.org/10.1017/S105383721300045X

Dow, Alexander, and Sheila Dow, eds. (2006) *A History of Scottish Economic Thought.* London and New York: Routledge.

Dow, Alexander, Sheila Dow, and Alan Hutton (1997) "The Scottish Political Economy Tradition and Modern Economics," *Scottish Journal of Political Economy* 44(4), 368–83. https://doi.org/10.1111/1467–9485.00065

Dow, Sheila (1987) "The Scottish Political Economy Tradition," *Scottish Journal of Political Economy* 34(4), 335–48. https://doi.org/j.1467–9485.1987.tb00291.x

Fisher, Irving (1932) *Booms and Depressions.* New York: Adelphi.

Fisher, Irving (1933) "The Debt-Deflation Theory of Great Depressions," *Econometrica* 1(3), 337–57. https://doi.org/10.2307/1907327

Foxwell, Herbert Somerton (1886) *Irregularity of Employment and Fluctuations of Prices.* Edinburgh: Co-Operative Printing Company Ltd.

Grant, Isabel Frances (1930) *The Social and Economic Development of Scotland before 1603.* Edinburgh: Oliver and Boyd; reprinted Westport, CT: Greenwood Press, and London: Shepheard-Walwyn, 1971.

Grant, Isabel Frances (1934) *The Economic History of Scotland.* London and New York: Longmans, Green; reprinted New York: AMS Press, 1976, Westport, CT: Greenwood Press, 1979.

Groenewegen, Peter, ed. (1998) *Alfred Marshall: Critical Responses*, 2 volumes. London: Routledge.

Groenewegen, Peter (2011) *The Minor Marshallians and Alfred Marshall: An Evaluation.* London and New York: Routledge.

Guillebaud, Claude W. (1935) "Review (of Rankin 1935 and Five Other Books on Money)," *Economic Journal* 45(178), 366–9. https://doi.org/10.2307/2224664

Hutton, Alan (2006) "A Scottish Tradition of Applied Economics in the Twentieth Century," in Dow and Dow, eds. (2006).

Keynes, John Maynard (1923) *A Tract on Monetary Reform*. London: Macmillan.

Keynes, John Maynard (1933) *The Means to Prosperity*. New York: Harcourt Brace.

Keynes, John Maynard (1936) *The General Theory of Employment, Interest and Money*. London: Macmillan.

M., H. W. (1935) "Review (of Rankin 1935 and of *The Price of Gold* by I. Shrigley)," *Journal of the Royal Statistical Society* 98(4), 734–5. https://doi.org/10.2307/2342315

Marshall, Alfred (1888) "Note on Professor Nicholson's Paper for the Gold and Silver Commission," in Peter Groenewegen, ed., *Official Papers of Alfred Marshall: A Supplement*, Cambridge, UK: Cambridge University Press, 1996, pp. 65–80.

Marshall, Alfred (1890) *Principles of Economics*. London: Macmillan, 8th ed., 1920; variorum, ed. C. W. Guillebaud for the Royal Economic Society, 1961.

Meston, [Lord] (1935) Review (of Rankin 1935). *International Affairs* 14(5), 713–714. https://doi.org/10.2307/2601860

Nicholson, Joseph Shield (1878) *The Effects of Machinery on Wages*. London: Swann Sonnenschein & Co., 2nd ed. 1892; New York: Arno Press, 1972.

Nicholson, Joseph Shield (1886) *The Silver Question*. London: Bimetallic League.

Nicholson, Joseph Shield (1887a) *The Stability of a Fixed Ratio between Gold and Silver under International Bimetallism*. London: Bimetallic League.

Nicholson, Joseph Shield (1887b) *Bimetallism for Practical Men*. London: Bimetallic League.

Nicholson, Joseph Shield (1888a) *The Joint Standard Consistent with Sound Political Economy*. Manchester: Bimetallic League.

Nicholson, Joseph Shield (1888b) *Treatise of Money and Essays on Monetary Problems*. London: Adam and Charles Black, 5th ed. 1901.

Nicholson, Joseph Shield (1891) "The Living Capital of the United Kingdom," *Economic Journal* 1(1), 95–107. https://doi.org/10.2307/2955843

Nicholson, Joseph Shield (1893, 1897, 1901) *Principles of Political Economy*, 3 volumes. London: Adam and Charles Black.

Nicholson, Joseph Shield (1894) *Strikes and a Living Wage: A Lecture to the Edinburgh Chamber of Commerce on 20th December 1893*. Edinburgh: Chamber of Commerce.

Nicholson, Joseph Shield (1914) "The Report on Indian Currency and Finance in Relation to the Gold Exchange Standard," *Economic Journal* 24(94), 236–47. https://doi.org/10.2307/2222423

Ogilvie, Frederick W. (1933) *The Tourist Movement: An Economic Study*. London: P. S. King & Son; London: Staples Press, 1945.

Rankin, Mary Theresa (1916) *Arbitration and Conciliation in Australasia: The Legal Wage in Victoria and New Zealand*, with an introduction by J. Shield Nicholson. London: George Allen & Unwin.

Rankin, Mary Theresa [as M.T.R.] (1927) *Joseph Shield Nicholson*. Edinburgh: Oliver and Boyd, reprinted from *University of Edinburgh Journal* 2 (Autumn 1927).

Rankin, Mary Theresa (1931a) *Industrial Conciliation and Arbitration in Australasia*. London: P. S. King & Son.

Rankin, Mary Theresa (1931b) *Arbitration Principles and the Industrial Court: An Analysis of Decisions, 1919–1929*. London: P. S. King & Son.

Rankin, Mary Theresa (1935) *Monetary Opinions and Policy, 1924–34*, with a foreword by F. W. Ogilvie. London: P. S. King & Son.
Rankin, Mary Theresa (1943) "British and American Monetary Plans," *The Scotsman*, May 29.
Rankin, Mary Theresa (1954) "The Scottish Society of Economists," *Scottish Journal of Political Economy* 1(1), 7–8. https://doi.org/10.1111/j.1467–9485.1954.tb00693.x
Rankin, Mary Theresa (1955) "The Scottish Cases Before the Industrial Disputes Tribunal, 1951–53," *Scottish Journal of Political Economy* 2(2), 218–30. https://doi.org/10.1111/j.1467–9485.1955.tb00731.x
Scott, W. R. (1927) "Joseph Shield Nicholson, 1850–1927," *Proceedings of the British Academy* 13, 346–67.
Scott, W. R., rev. by John Maloney (2004) "Nicholson, Joseph Shield (1850–1927)," *Oxford Dictionary of National Biography*. https://doi.org/10.1093/ref:odnb/35229.
Smith, Adam (1884) *An Inquiry into the Nature and Causes of the Wealth of Nations*, with introductory essay and notes by J. Shield Nicholson. London: T. Nelson & Sons.
Thompson, Alan (1964) "Obituary: Mary Rankin," *Scottish Journal of Political Economy* 11(1), 80–83. https://doi.org/10.1111/j.1467-9485.1964.tb00961.x
Trevor-Roper, Hugh (2008) *The Invention of Scotland: Myth and History*. New Haven, CT: Yale University Press.

14 David Hume as a Scottish political economist

Maria Pia Paganelli

Introduction

David Hume is often seen as a precursor of modern monetary theories, so much so that two Nobel Laureates in Economics, Milton Friedman and Robert Lucas, cite him as an earlier supporter of their (different) monetary theories. Friedman (1987) claims that Hume is a proto-monetarist, since he too suggests that the 'good policy of the magistrate is to keep [money] still increasing' (Hume [1752] 1985, 288). Lucas (1996) claims that Hume is a proto-promoter of money neutrality, because he claims that an increase in money will be reduced to just an increase in nominal prices (Hume [1752] 1985, 285), and if it occasionally seems otherwise, this is just because Hume was confused by his lack of technical skills. Being considered a precursor implies being an early step in the development of a theory, which has since progressed and improved over time. It also implies that the context in which a theory is discovered is irrelevant to its justification, because the modern theory incorporates what was correct in the precursor theory, shedding what was not correct (Dow 1987).

Sheila Dow (2002a) offers an account of the importance of recognizing an author's context, especially when there are charges of inconsistencies. She recognizes both the 18th century and the Scottishness of David Hume (Harris 2015). His political economy is, thus, a Scottish political economy (Dow and Dow 2015). Dow briefly mentions the different possible interpretations of Hume's monetary views when his context is taken into serious consideration (Dow 2009). I will elaborate on her claim and show how Hume fits in his 18th-century Scottish context in a more consistent manner than in a 20th (or 21st) century one.

Context matters

Hume lives in a time of major changes. Scotland is going through a massive economic and cultural expansion (Broadie 2007; Rutherford 2012). Hume sees the benefits of the increased commercialization of his society and writes in defense of it (Berry 1994). Commerce needs to be defended, because, at the same time, Hume's world is a world where special interests ask for privileges

DOI: 10.4324/9781003142324-15

and obtain them in the name of enriching a country. When trade is considered a zero-sum game, others become enemies, and we are consumed by a "jealousy of trade" (Hont 2005). We want to be richer than our neighbors, so we impose trade restrictions with the assumption that in this way we are able to stimulate domestic industries (Viner 1930).

But Hume does not buy into the idea that trade restrictions stimulate economic growth. Commerce is a positive sum game. It is trade, and only trade that allows societies to grow, both economically and in all other aspects. Indeed, "industry, knowledge, and humanity are linked together by an indissoluble chain, and found, from experience as well as reason, to be peculiar to the more polished, and what are commonly denominated, the more luxurious ages" (Hume [1752] 1985, 271): luxury is almost synonymous with commerce.

Once we are exposed to luxuries that we do not have, Hume's story goes, we are motivated to be more industrious so that we can acquire these fancy things to show off among our peers (*Ibid.*). This implies that it is demand that drives industry, not money (Paganelli 2006). Money simply follows the "manners and customs of the people" (Hume [1752] 1985, 290). Where commerce is scarce, money is scarce too as it is not needed. When commerce develops, more money will enter into circulation to exchange the new goods. So, money is an effect of wealth and commerce, not its cause (*Ibid.*, pp. 291–3).

Hume embeds the idea that money follows trade, or the industry of a people, in the so-called price-specie flow mechanism (Berdell 1995). If we artificially "multiply" money, we will experience higher domestic prices, which induce us to buy imports, since they are cheaper than what we produce at home. And to pay for those imports, our multiplied money will leave the country, thus resulting in the level of money going back to being proportionate to the industry of the people. Similarly, according to Hume, if we "annihilate" money, then the prices of domestic products will drop. Lower domestic prices will attract foreign buyers, so our exports will increase, and money will come back and re-establish itself to the level proportionate to the industry of the people (Hume [1752] 1985, 311).

However, Hume does tell us that the good policy of the magistrate is to keep money "still encreasing." And here is where context plays the most fundamental role. His price-specie flow mechanism, Hume tells us, can be short-circuited in two ways: with the introduction of paper money and with hoarding. These are Hume's words:

> Our modern politics embrace the only method of banishing money, the use of paper-credit; they reject the only way of amassing it, the practice of hoarding.
>
> (*Ibid.*, p. 24)

So, the only way to keep money "still encreasing," in Hume's view, is deflation via hoarding.

Throughout the economic essays, Hume tells us that an (exogenous) increase in money supply is a *disadvantage*:

> it is certain that, since the discovery of the mines in AMERICA, industry has encreased in all the nations of EUROPE, except in the possessors of those mines; and this may be justly ascribed, amongst other reasons, to the encrease of gold and silver.
>
> (*Ibid.*, p. 286)

This is because by increasing prices, it discourages exports and thus the domestic industry

> the dearness of every thing, from plenty of money, is a disadvantage, which attends an established commerce, and sets bounds to it in every country, by enabling the poorer states to undersell the richer in all foreign markets.
>
> (*Ibid.*, p. 284)

This fits his price-specie flow mechanism but not Friedman's reading of Hume as a proto-monetarist.

The passage that Friedman cites is one where Hume claims that the good policy of the magistrate is to keep money increasing. But in Hume's context, this is achieved not by a central bank increasing money supply at a constant rate, but by *decreasing* the quantity of money in circulation via hoarding. Remember how the price-specie mechanism works: by "annihilating" money, prices decrease, making domestic products competitive in the international market, thus stimulating the exports of goods and thus money inflows as a payment for those exports. But this inflow of money would bring prices back up, leaving us with only a temporary benefit. Thus, we should keep prices "sinking." And to keep prices "sinking," money needs to be continually "annihilated."

So, one way to short-circuit the price-specie flow mechanism is through the continuous annihilation of money. Hume tells us that his preferred method involves making hoarding possible through the alternative uses of gold and silver (see quotation below). Commodity money can be used as a commodity after all. So, hoarding gold and silver by using them to decorate palaces and churches or to make silverware is Hume's suggested "monetary policy." For Hume, this is achieved indirectly, by trying to influence the fashion and habits of using precious metals as commodities, rather than money (Paganelli 2007). This long quotation encapsulates Hume's policy prescription and can be unpacked only when his context is carefully analyzed:

> In France many have large sums in their coffers: Great quantities of plate are used in private houses and all the churches are full of it. By this means, provisions and labor still remain cheaper among them, than in nations that are not half so rich in gold and silver. The advantages of

> this situation, in point of trade as well as in great public emergencies, are too evident to be disputed. The same fashion a few years ago prevailed in GENOA, which still has place in ENGLAND and HOLLAND, of using services of CHINA-ware instead of plate; but the senate foreseeing the consequence, prohibited the use of that brittle commodity beyond a certain extent; while the use of silver-plate was left unlimited. And I suppose, in their later distress, they felt the good effect of this ordinance. Our tax on plate is, perhaps, in this view, somewhat impolitic.
>
> (*Ibid.*, pp. 317–8)

The good policy of the magistrate, thus, seems to prohibit the use of china-ware to encourage the use of silverware and the gold decoration of homes and churches.

According to Hume, another way in which we can decrease money supply so that prices could be kept low, exports high, and money flowing in is by having a public treasure. Whatever money flows in is hoarded in the treasure, so prices remain low. Hoarding money is useful in times of war as it makes it easier to pay for troops; however, it can be dangerous in times of peace because it may attract either enemies or overly ambitious government plans (Paganelli 2012).

So, we can increase the industry of a country and thus the quantity of money in it by taking some money out of circulation and waiting for the price-specie flow mechanism to do its magic. On the other hand, we can decrease the industry, and thus the quantity of money, with a multiplication of money, that is with inflation. And inflation for Hume is achieved with the introduction and presence of paper money.

Hume regards paper money as "counterfeited money" (*Ibid.*, p. 284), because it is not universally accepted (as opposed to gold and silver, which are money because they are universally accepted). Paper is accepted as money only domestically but not by foreigners. So, an increase in paper money will increase domestic prices, dampen exports and thus production. Imports will be cheaper and thus their consumption will increase. Imports will be paid with gold and silver, as paper money does not go abroad. This leaves a weaker economy and a less safe economy. If a war should occur, the country will have problems defending itself since soldiers required payment in gold and silver.

Hume's conviction that an increase in money supply (via paper in particular) would cripple both the economy and the safety of a country is what makes him propose the abolition of private banks (*Ibid.*, pp. 284–5). He instead favors one single national bank holding 100% reserves and thus not increasing money supply with what we would today call a "money multiplier" (Paganelli 2014):

> No bank could be more advantageous, than such a one as locked up all the money it received, and never augmented the circulating coin, as is usual, by returning part of its treasure into commerce.
>
> (*Ibid.*, p. 284)

> The bank should be funded by taxpayers. Its costs would be significantly less than its benefits, in terms of avoided disruptions.
>
> (*Ibid.*, p. 285)

Conclusions

Seen within an 18th-century Scottish context, Hume's perception of money is significantly different from the 20th-century context-free interpretations. If Friedman believes that a constant 3% increase in money supply achieved by a rule-based central bank is the optimal policy, then Hume believes that hoarding gold and silver is the appropriate mechanism to generate a trade-based stimulus of the economy.

Similarly, if Lucas believes that money is neutral because people rationally expect changes in policies and incorporate them into their actions, then Hume believes that money is neutral but only in its function of unit of account. And rather than seeing an individual as having rational expectations, Hume believes that "Mankind are, in all ages, caught by the same baits: The same tricks, played over and over again, still trepan them" (Hume [1752] 1985, 363). His conclusions may not overlap with those of Lucas, not only because Hume knows less mathematics than Lucas, but also because Hume works and lives in an actual and intellectual context that is very different from that of Lucas.

The context in which Hume writes is a context of mercantilist policies that restricted trade and limited commerce under the pretense of economic growth. Hume instead believes in positive sum games of trade and in the fact that only trade could increase prosperity in a country. His encouragement of hoarding and of the abolition of the fractional reserve system of banking are measures, in his view, that are used to stimulate growth via increasing trade.

As Sheila Dow claims, context matters. Context matters in the formation of someone's ideas. Context matters in the interpretation of someone else's ideas (Dow 2002b). The case of David Hume is a case in point. Taking part of a work out of its original context and insert it into a different context will inevitably generate different interpretations. And when Hume is placed back into a Scottish political economy context, as Sheila Dow recognizes, one may claim that he fits less inconsistently there than in a 20th-century money neutrality or monetarist context.

References

Berdell, John F. (1995). 'The present relevance of hume's open-economy monetary dynamics', *Economic Journal*, 105: 1205–17. https://doi.org/10.2307/2235412

Berry, Christopher J. (1994). *The idea of luxury: A conceptual and historical investigation* (Cambridge University Press: Cambridge).

Broadie, Alexander. (2007). *Scottish enlightenment* (Birlinn Limited: Edinburgh).

Dow, Alexander; Dow, Sheila. (2015). 'Economic development in the Scottish enlightenment: Ideas as cause and effect.' In Ruziev, K.; Perdikis, N. (eds), *Development and financial reform in emerging economies*. (Pickering and Chatto: London).

Dow, Sheila C. (1987). 'The Scottish political economy tradition', *Scottish Journal of Political Economy*, 34: 335–48. https://doi.org/10.1111/j.1467-9485.1987.tb00291.x

Dow, Sheila C. (2002a). 'Historical reference: Hume and critical realism', *Cambridge Journal of Economics*, 26: 683–95. https://doi.org/10.1093/cje/26.6.683

Dow, Sheila C. (2002b). 'Interpretation: The case of David Hume', *History of Political Economy*, 34: 399–420. https://doi.org/10.1215/00182702-34-2-399

Dow, Sheila. (2009). 'Hume and the Scottish enlightenment: Two cultures', *Revista de Economia*, 35: 7–20. https://doi.org/10.5380/re.v35i3.16948

Friedman, Milton. (1987). 'Quantity theory of money.' In John E.; Murray M.; and Peter N. (eds), *The new Palgrave dictionary of economics*, vol. 4, pp. 3–20 (New York: Stockton Press; and London: Macmillan).

Harris, James. (2015). *An intellectual biography of David Hume* (Cambridge University Press: Cambridge).

Hont, Istvan. (2005). *Jealousy of trade: International competition and the nation state in historical perspective* (Belknap Press of Harvard University Press: Cambridge, MA).

Hume, David. ([1752] 1985). *Essays, moral, political, and literary* (Liberty Fund: Indianapolis, IN).

Lucas, Robert E., Jr. (1996). 'Nobel lecture: Monetary neutrality', *Journal of Political Economy*, 104: 661–82. https://doi.org/10.1086/262037

Paganelli, Maria Pia. (2006). 'Hume and endogenous money', *Eastern Economic Journal*, 32: 533–47.

Paganelli, Maria Pia. (2007). '"The good policy of the magistrate": Deflation as a policy option in David Hume's economic essays', *History of Economic Ideas*, 15: 9–25.

Paganelli, Maria Pia. (2012). 'David Hume on public credit', *History of Economic Idea*, 20: 31–43.

Paganelli, Maria Pia. (2014). 'David Hume on banking and hoarding', *Southern Economic Journal*, 80: 968–80. https://doi.org/10.4284/0038-4038-2013.163

Rutherford, Donald. (2012). *In the shadow of Adam Smith: Founders of Scottish economics, 1700–1900* (Palgrave Macmillan: New York).

Viner, Jacob. (1930). 'English theories of foreign trade before Adam Smith', *The Journal of Political Economy*, 38(3): 249–301 and 38(4): 404–57. https://doi.org/10.1086/254107 and https://doi.org/10.1086/254122

Sheila Dow's body of work

Publications from 1980 to 2022

Authored books

with P E Earl, *Money Matters: A Keynesian Approach to Monetary Economics*, Martin Robertson, 1982, p.270

Macroeconomic Thought: A Methodological Approach, Basil Blackwell, 1985, p.278

Financial Markets and Regional Economic Development: The Canadian Experience, Gower, 1990, p.188

Macroeconomic Thought: A Methodological Approach – Japanese translation, Nihon Keizai Hyeronsh, 1991, p.350

Money and the Economic Process, Elgar, 1993, p.219

The Methodology of Macroeconomic Thought, Elgar, 1996, pp.255. Reprinted and issued in paperback 1998.

Economic Methodology: An Inquiry Oxford: Oxford University Press 2002, p.216. Chinese translation published in 2004 by Shanghai University of Finance & Economics Press.

Foundations for New Economic Thinking: A Collection of Essays. London: Palgrave Macmillan, 2012.

Edited books

with P Arestis, *Money, Method and Keynes: Selected Essays by Victoria Chick*, Macmillan, 1992. Portuguese translation 2010.

with J Hillard, *Keynes, Knowledge and Uncertainty*, Elgar, 1995.

with P E Earl, *Economic Organisation and Economic Knowledge: Essays in Honour of Brian JLoasby* Vol 1, Aldershot: Elgar, 1999.

with P E Earl, *Contingency, Complexity and the Theory of the Firm: Essays in Honour of Brian J Loasby* Vol 11, Aldershot: Elgar, 1999.

with P Arestis and M Desai, *Money, Macroeconomics and Keynes*, Routledge, 2002.

with P Arestis and M Desai, *Methodology, Microeconomics and Keynes*, Routledge, 2002.

with J Hillard, *Post Keynesian Econometrics, Microeconomics and the Theory of the Firm: Beyond Keynes* vol I, Cheltenham: Elgar, 2002.

with J Hillard, *Keynes, Uncertainty and the Global Economy: Beyond Keynes* vol II:, Cheltenham: Elgar, 2002.

With A C Dow, A *History of Scottish Economic Thought.* London: Routledge, 2006; paperback edition published 2009.

With R Arena and M Klaes (eds), *Open Economics: Economics in Relation to Other Disciplines,* Routledge, 2009.

S Dow, J Jespersen and G Tily (eds), *The General Theory and Keynes for the 21st Century.* Cheltenham: Edward Elgar, 2018.

S Dow, J Jespersen and G Tily (eds), *Money, Method and Post-Keynesian Economics for the 21st Century'* Cheltenham: Edward Elgar, 2018.

Refereed academic journal papers

Methodological Morality in the Cambridge Controversies, *Journal of Post Keynesian Economics*, 2.3. 368–80, 1980 http://hdl.handle.net/1893/22744

Weintraub and Wiles: The Methodological Basis of Policy Conflict, *Journal of Post Keynesian Economics*, 3:3. 325–39, 1981 http://hdl.handle.net/1893/22738

The Regional Composition of the Money Multiplier Process, *Scottish Journal of Political Economy*, 29.1. 22–44, 1982

Schools of Thought in Macroeconomics: The Method is the Message, *Australian Economic Papers*, 22.2. 30–47, 1983 http://hdl.handle.net/1893/25151

Methodology and the Analysis of a Monetary Economy, *Economies et Societes, Monnaie et Production*, 18.1. 7–35, 1984

with P E Earl, Methodology and Orthodox Monetary Policy, *Economie Appliquee*, 37.1. 143–63, 1984

Microfoundations: A Diversity of Treatments, *Eastern Economic Journal*, 1.4. 342–60, 1984

The Capital Account and Regional Balance of Payments Problems, *Urban Studies*, 23.3. 173–84, 1986. http://hdl.handle.net/1893/26289

Speculation and the Monetary Circuit: with particular attention to the Euro-currency market, *Economies et Societes, Monnaie et Production*, 20.3. 95–109, 1986

Post Keynesian Monetary Theory for an Open Economy, *Journal of Post Keynesian Economics*, 9.2.237–59, 1986–87. http://hdl.handle.net/1893/22745

The Treatment of Money in Regional Economics, *Journal of Regional Science*, 27.1. 13–24. 1987. http://hdl.handle.net/1893/25160

Money and Regional Development, *Studies in Political Economy*, 23.1. 73–94, 1987. http://hdl.handle.net/1893/25175

Banking and Regional Development in Canada, *British Journal of Canadian Studies*, 21.1. 16–40, 1987

The Scottish Political Economy Tradition, *Scottish Journal of Political Economy*, 34.4. 335–48, 1987

with V Chick, A Post Keynesian Perspective on Banking and Regional Development, *Thames Papers*, Spring 1–22, 1988. http://hdl.handle.net/1893/22686

Money Supply Endogeneity, *Economie Appliquee*, 41.1. 19–39, 1988

with A C Dow, Idle Balances in Keynesian Theory, *Scottish Journal of Political Economy*, 35.3. 193–207, 1988. http://hdl.handle.net/1893/25174

Incorporating Money in Regional Economic Models, *London Papers in Regional Science*: Recent Advances in Regional Economic Modelling, 19. 208–18, 1988

Post Keynesian Economics: Conceptual Underpinnings, *British Review of Economic Issues*, 10.3. 1–18, 1988

Beyond Dualism, *Cambridge Journal of Economics*, 14.2. 143–58, 1990. http://hdl.handle.net/1893/22693

Post Keynesianism as Political Economy: A Methodological Discussion, *Review of Political Economy*, 2.3. 345–58, 1990. http://hdl.handle.net/1893/25152

Are There Any Signs of Postmodernism within Economics? *Methodus*, 3.1. 81–5, 1991

Money, Finance and the Role of the State, *Journal of Economic Surveys*, 6.2. 195–200, 1992. http://hdl.handle.net/1893/25156

The Regional Financial Sector: A Scottish Case Study, *Regional Studies*, 26.7. 619–31, 1992. http://hdl.handle.net/1893/25161

with J Smithin, Free Banking in Scotland, 1695–1845, *Scottish Journal of Political Economy*, 39.4. 374–90, 1992. http://hdl.handle.net/1893/22740

with DNF Bell, Economic Policy Options for a Scottish Parliament, *Scottish Affairs*, 13.Autumn, 42–67, 1995

The Appeal of Neo-classical Economics: Some Insights from Keynes's Epistemology, *Cambridge Journal of Economics*, 19.6. 715–34, 1995. http://hdl.handle.net/1893/22683

Why the Banking System Should be Regulated, *Economic Journal*, 104.436. 698–707, 1996. http://hdl.handle.net/1893/25153

Horizontalism: A Critique, *Cambridge Journal of Economics*, 20.4. 497–508, 1996. http://hdl.handle.net/1893/22694

with V Chick, Regulation and Differences in Financial Institutions, *Journal of Economic Issues*, 30.2. 517–23, 1996. http://hdl.handle.net/1893/25155

Mainstream Economic Methodology, *Cambridge Journal of Economics*, 21.1. 73–93, 1997. http://hdl.handle.net/1893/22692

with A Dow and A Hutton, Scottish Political Economy and Modern Economics, *Scottish Journal of Political Economy*, 44.4. 368–83, September 1997. http://hdl.handle.net/1893/25162

with C Rodriguez Fuentes, Regional Finance: A Survey, *Regional Studies*, 31.9. 903–20, December 1997. http://hdl.handle.net/1893/22700

The Exogenous Money Supply Assumption in Monetary Theory and Policy, *Archives of Economic History*, 8.1–2. 7–36, December 1997

with A Dow, A Hutton, and M Keaney, Traditions in Economics: The Case of Scottish Political Economy, *New Political Economy* 3.1. 45–58, 1998. http://hdl.handle.net/1893/22746

Monetary Interpretations of the Great Depression: A Review Essay, *Research in the History of Economic Thought and Methodology*, 16. 257–62, 1998.

with J Smithin, Change in Financial Markets and the First Principles of Monetary Economics *Scottish Journal of Political Economy*, 46.1. 72–90, February 1999. http://hdl.handle.net/1893/25163

Post Keynesianism and Critical Realism: What is the Connection? *Journal of Post Keynesian Economics*, 22.1. 15–33, 1999. http://hdl.handle.net/1893/22747

Prospects for the Progress of Heterodox Economics, *Journal of the History of Economic Thought*, 22.2. 157–70. 2000. http://hdl.handle.net/1893/24906

With C Rodriguez Fuentes, Integracion monetaria y estructura financiera. Implicaciones para los mercados regionales de credito. *Información Comercial Española*, 785. 133–45. 2000.

with A C Dow and A Hutton, Applied Economics in a Political Economy Tradition: The Case of Scotland from the 1890s to the 1950s, *History of Political Economy*, 32.Annual Supplement. 177–98, 2000. http://hdl.handle.net/1893/25164

with V Chick, Financial Integration in Europe: A Post Keynesian Perspective, *Archives in Economic History*, 11.1–2. 21–40, 2000. http://hdl.handle.net/1893/25154

Methodology in a Pluralist Environment, *Journal of Economic Methodology*, 8.1. 33–40, 2001. http://hdl.handle.net/1893/22762

with V Chick, Formalism, Logic and Reality: A Keynesian Analysis, *Cambridge Journal of Economics*, 25.6. 705–22, 2001, reprinted in G M Hodgson (ed.), *Mathematics and Modern Economics*. Cheltenham: Edward Elgar, 2012. http://hdl.handle.net/1893/22690

Interpretation: The Case of Hume, *History of Political Economy*, 34.2. 399–420, 2002. http://hdl.handle.net/1893/22689

With V Chick, Monetary Policy with Endogenous Money and Liquidity Preference: A Nondualistic Treatment, *Journal of Post Keynesian Economics*, 24.4. 587–608, 2002. http://hdl.handle.net/1893/22763

Postmodernism and Analysis of the Development Process, *International Journal of Development Issues*, 1.1. 27–34, 2002. http://hdl.handle.net/1893/22768

Historical Reference: Hume and Critical Realism, *Cambridge Journal of Economics*, 26.6. 683–97, Nov 2002. http://hdl.handle.net/1893/22701

History of Economic Thought in the Post Keynesian Tradition, *History of Political Economy*, 34.Annual Supplement. 319–36, 2002. http://hdl.handle.net/1893/22764

The Relationship between Mathematics and Economics, *Journal of Post Keynesian Economics*. 25.4. 545–8, 2003. http://hdl.handle.net/1893/22765

'The Prospects Facing an Independent Scotland in the Euro-zone Alongside the Rest of the UK', *Scottish Affairs* 45.Autumn. 60–71, 2003. http://hdl.handle.net/1893/22685

With C Rodriguez Fuentes, 'EMU and the Regional Impact of Monetary Policy', *Regional Studies* 37.9. 969–80, 2003. http://hdl.handle.net/1893/22703

'Uncertainty and Monetary Policy', *Oxford Economic Papers*, 56. 539–61. 2004. http://hdl.handle.net/1893/22684

'*Reorienting Economics*: Some Epistemological Issues', *Journal of Economic Methodology*, 11.3. 307–12, 2004. http://hdl.handle.net/1893/22703

'Structured Pluralism', *Journal of Economic Methodology*, 11.3. 275–90, 2004. reprinted in W Olsen (ed.), *Realist Methodology*, Sage, 2010. http://hdl.handle.net/1893/22704

'Knowledge, Information and Credit Creation: The Impact of Monetary Policy', *Papales de Economía Española*, (special issue on Money, Financial System and Economic Growth) 101. 99–113, 2004. http://hdl.handle.net/1893/22769

With V Chick, 'The Meaning of Open Systems', *Journal of Economic Methodology*, 12.3. 363–81, 2005. http://hdl.handle.net/1893/22766

With A Dow, 'The Application of Development Economics: General Principles and Context Specificity', *Cambridge Journal of Economics*, 29. 1129–43, 2005. [http://hdl.handle.net/1893/22670] http://hdl.handle.net/1893/22688

Why the Banking System Should be Regulated, republished in Chinese, *Investment Order Review*.

Mathematics in Economic Theory: Historical and Methodological Analysis, translated into Russian, *Voprosy Ekonomiki*. No.7, 2006.

'Variety of Methodological Approach in Economics', *Journal of Economic Surveys* 21.3. 447–19, 2007. http://hdl.handle.net/1893/592

With K Ruziev and D Ghosh, 'The Uzbek Puzzle Revisited: Analysis of Economic Performance in Uzbekistan Since 1991', *Central Asian Survey* 26.1. 7–30, 2007. http://hdl.handle.net/1893/650

With A Montagnoli, 'The Regional Transmission of UK Monetary Policy', *Regional Studies* 41.6. 797–808, 2007. http://hdl.handle.net/1893/594

'Mainstream Methodology, Financial Markets and Global Political Economy', *Contributions to Political Economy* 27. 13–29, 2008. http://hdl.handle.net/1893/595

'Plurality in Orthodox and Heterodox Economics', *Journal of Philosophical Economics* 1.2. 73–96, 2008. http://hdl.handle.net/1893/1090

With D Ghosh and K Ruziev, 'A Stages Approach to Banking in Transition Economies', *Journal of Post Keynesian Economics* 31.1. 3–34, 2008. http://hdl.handle.net/1893/989

With D Ghosh, 'Fuzzy Logic and Keynes's Speculative Demand for Money', *Journal of Economic Methodology* 16.1. 57–69, 2009. http://hdl.handle.net/1893/983

With M Klaes and A Montagnoli, 'Risk and Uncertainty in Central Bank Signals: An analysis of Monetary Policy Committee Minutes', *Metroeconomica* 60.2. 584–618, 2009. http://hdl.handle.net/1893/9209

'David Hume and Modern Economics', *Capitalism and Society*, 4.1, Article 1, 2009. http://www.bepress.com/cas/vol4/iss1/art1

'History of Thought and Methodology in Pluralist Economics Education', *International Review of Economics Education* 8.2. 41–57, 2009. http://hdl.handle.net/1893/3038

'Knowledge, Communication and the Scottish Enlightenment', *Revue de Philosophie Economique/Review of Philosophical Economics* 10.2. 3–23, 2009. http://hdl.handle.net/1893/3126

'Psikhologiya finansovykh rynkov: Keynes, Minski i povedencheskiye finansy' ('Psychology of Financial Markets: Keynes, Minsky and Emotional Finance'), in Russian translation, *Voprosy Economiki* 1. 99–113, 2010.

'Hume and the Scottish Enlightenment – Two Cultures', *Revista de Economia* 35.3. 7–20, 2009. http://hdl.handle.net/1893/3168

'Cognition, Sentiment and Financial Instability: Psychology in a Minsky Framework', *Cambridge Journal of Economics* 35.2. 233–50, 2011. http://hdl.handle.net/1893/3059

'Heterodox Economics: History and Prospects', *Cambridge Journal of Economics* 35.6. 1151–66, 2011. http://hdl.handle.net/1893/3578

With A Dow, 'Animal Spirits Revisited', *Capitalism and Society* 6.2, article 1, 2011, at http://www.bepress.com/cas/vol6/iss2/art1/. http://hdl.handle.net/1893/3643

'Policy in the Wake of the Banking Crisis: Taking Pluralism Seriously', *International Review of Applied Economics* 26.2. 161–75, 2012. http://hdl.handle.net/1893/22625

'What are Banks and Bank Regulation For? A Consideration of the Foundations for Reform', *European Journal of Economics and Economic Policies: Intervention* 9.1. 39–56, 2012. http://hdl.handle.net/1893/22594

With V Chick, 'On Causes and Outcomes of the European Crisis: Ideas, Institutions and Reality', *Contributions to Political Economy* 31.1. 51–66, 2012. http://hdl.handle.net/1893/10324

with A Montagnoli and O Napolitano, 'Interest Rates and Convergence Across Italian Regions', *Regional Studies* 46.7. 893–905, 2012. http://hdl.handle.net/1893/22641

'Different Approaches to the Economic Crisis', *Economic Thought: History, Philosophy and Methodology* 1.1, 2012. http://et.worldeconomicsassociation.org/index

'Andrew Skinner 1935–2011', *History of Political Economy* 44.4. 583–94, 2012. http://hdl.handle.net/1893/15922

'Codes of Ethics for Economists: A Pluralist View', *Economic Thought* 2.1, 2013, http://et.worldeconomicsassociation.org/article/view/65

With A Dow, 'Economic History and Economic Theory: The Staples Approach to Economic Development', *Cambridge Journal of Economics* 38.6. 1339–54, 2014. https://doi.org/10.1093/cje/bet021, online 5 June 2013. http://hdl.handle.net/1893/18208

With V Chick and C Rodriguez Fuentes, 'Good Banks and Bad Banks, Centralised Banks and Local Banks and Economic Growth', *Ekonomiaz* 84.3. 110–27, 2013. http://hdl.handle.net/1893/18209

With V Chick, 'Keynes, the Long Run and the Present Crisis', *International Journal of Political Economy* 42.1. 13–25, 2013. http://hdl.handle.net/1893/22638

'Formalism, Rationality and Evidence: The Case of Behavioural Economics', *Erasmus Journal for Philosophy and Economics*, 6.3. 26–43, 2013. http://ejpe.org/pdf/6-3-art-2.pdf/http://hdl.handle.net/1893/19497

'Addressing Uncertainty in Economics and in the Economy', *Cambridge Journal of Economics* 39.1. 33–48, 2015. https://doi.org/10.1093/cje/beu022, online 7/7/14 http://hdl.handle.net/1893/21040

'Animal Spirits and Organization', *Journal of Post Keynesian Economics* 37.2. 211–32, 2014. http://hdl.handle.net/1893/21330

'The Role of Belief in the Case for Austerity Policies', *Economic and Labour Relations Review* 26.March. 29–42, 2015. https://doi.org/10.1177/1035304614567262 online 7 January 2015 http://hdl.handle.net/1893/21626

'The Economist's Oath: A Review Essay', *International Review of Applied Economics* 29.1. 125–8, 2015. http://hdl.handle.net/1893/22503

'Ontology and Theory for a Redesign of European Monetary Union', *World Economic Review*, 6. 1–11, 2016. http://hdl.handle.net/1893/23630

'Uncertainty: A Diagrammatic Treatment', *Economics: The Open-Access, Open-Assessment E-Journal* 10. 1–25, 2016. http://doi.org/10.5018/economics-ejournal.ja.2016-3 http://hdl.handle.net/1893/22811

'The Political Economy of Monetary Reform', *Cambridge Journal of Economics* 40.5. 1363–76, 2016. https://doi.org/10.1093/cje/bew013 Advance Access publication 26 April http://hdl.handle.net/1893/23503

'Framing Financial Markets: A Methodological Account', *Brazilian Keynesian Review* 2.2. 160–73, 2016. http://hdl.handle.net/1893/25144

'Central Banking in the 21st Century', *Cambridge Journal of Economics* 41.6. 1539–57, 2017. https://doi.org/10.1093/cje/bex051 http://hdl.handle.net/1893/25767

'Keynes and Gesell: Political and Social Philosophy, Epistemology and Monetary Reform', *Annals of the Fondazione Luigi Einaudi* 1.1. 77–92, 2017. http://hdl.handle.net/1893/27245

'Global Currency Reform: A Proposal', *Journal of King Abdulaziz University: Islamic Economics* 30.2. 79–82. https://doi.org/10.4197

With R McMaster and A Cumbers, '*Sine praejudicio*? Economics and the 2014 Scottish independence referendum', *Cambridge Journal of Economics*, https://doi.org/10.1093/cje/bex091, online 24 January 2018. http://hdl.handle.net/1893/26951

'Monetary Reform, Central Banks and Digital Currencies', *International Journal of Political Economy*, 48.2. 153–73.

'Gender and the Future of Macroeconomics: An Evolutionary Approach', *Review of Evolutionary Political Economy* 1.1. 55–66, 2020.

with C Rodriguez-Fuentes, 'The Role of Credit in Regional Divergence: Spanish Regions and Eurozone Countries', *Brazilian Journal of Political Economy/Revista de Economia Politica* 40.4. 712–27.

'Endogenous Money and Ideas for Monetary Reform', *European Journal of Economics and Economic Policies: Intervention* 17.3. 367–80.

'Scottish Enlightenment Historical Epistemology and Modern Challenges for Economic Thought', *Review of Economic Philosophy* 22.1. 17–38, 2021.

'A Deeper Struggle for the Soul of Economics', *Journal of Economic Methodology*. https://doi.org/10.1080/1350178X.2021.2010282; online 16 Dec 2021

'The Pursuit of Coherence in Mainstream Macroeconomic Methodology', *Capitalism and Society* 15.1, article 3, 2021.

'Economic Methodology, the Philosophy of Economics and the Economy: Another Turn?' *Journal of Economic Methodology* 28.1. 46–53. https://doi.org/10.1080/1350178X.2020.1868771, published online 15 Jan 2021.

'Endogenising Uncertainty', *Journal of New Economics*, 2021.

Forthcoming

'Alfred Marshall, Evolutionary Economics and Climate Change', *Review of Political Economy*, July 2022. https://doi.org/10.1080/09538259.2021.1987088.

With A C Dow, 'Coase and the Scottish enlightenment', *Journal of the Aurora Philosophy Institute.*

'Comment on John Davis's "A methodological perspective on economic modelling and the global pandemic: Commentary"', *Economic Thought: History, Philosophy, and Methodology.*

Contributions to edited works

Substantive Mountains and Methodological Molehills: A Rejoinder, in B J Caldwell (ed), *Appraisal and Criticism in Economics*, Allen and Unwin, 1984, 433–7

with P E Earl, Monetary Policy in a Speculative Environment, in P Hare and M Kirby (eds), *An Introduction to British Economic Policy*, Wheatsheaf, 1984, 61–75

with A C Dow, Animal Spirits and Rationality, in T Lawson and H Pesaran (eds), *Keynes' Economics: Methodological Issues*, Croom Helm, 1985, 46–65

What Happened to Keynes' Economics, in O Hamouda and J Smithin (eds), *Keynes and Public Policy After Fifty Years*, Vol. I, Edward Elgar, 1988, 101–10

with V Chick, A Post Keynesian Perspective on Banking and Regional Development, in P Arestis (ed), *Post Keynesian Monetary Economics*, Edward Elgar, 1988, 219–50

with A C Dow, Endogenous Money Creation and Idle Balances, in J Pheby (ed.), *New Directions in Post Keynesian Economics*, Edward Elgar, 1989, 147–64

Comment on Goodhart, C A E, Keynes, Money and Monetarism, in R Hill (ed.), *Proceedings of Eighth Keynes Seminar*, Macmillan, 1989, 129–30

Hermeneutics, Subjectivity and the Lester/Machlup Debate: A Comment, in W J Samuels (ed), *Economics as Discourse*, Kluwer, 1990, 185–7

The Scottish Political Economy Tradition, in D Mair (ed), *The Scottish Contribution to Modern Economic Thought*, Aberdeen University Press, 1990, 19–32

Keynes's Epistemology and Economic Methodology, in R O'Donnell (ed), *Keynes as Philosopher - Economist*, Macmillan, 1991, 144–67. http://hdl.handle.net/1893/25147

The Post Keynesian School, in D Mair and A Millar (eds), *A Modern Guide to Economic Thought*, Elgar, 1991, 176–206

The Scottish Political Economy Tradition as a Mode of Thought, *Economic History and Economic Theory: Festschrift in Honour of L Humanidis*, University of Piraeus, 1991, 94–107

The Scottish Political Economy Tradition, in M Blaug (ed), *William Whewell (1794–1866), Dionysius Lardner (1793–1859), William Lloyd (1795–1852) and Charles Babbage (1792–1871), Pioneers in Economics* Section II, Vol 19, Elgar, 1991

with A C Dow, Idle Balances in Keynesian Theory, in M Blaug (ed), *John Maynard Keynes (1883–1946), Pioneers in Economics Section IV, Vol 48:2*, Elgar, 1991

Postmodernism and Economics, E Graham, J Doherty and M Malek (eds), *Postmodernism and the Social Sciences*, Macmillan, 1992

Monetary Theory, in G Hodgson, W Samuels & M Tool (eds), *Elgar Companion to Institutional and Evolutionary Economics*, Elgar, 1994

European Monetary Integration and the Distribution of Credit Availability, in S. Corbridge, R. Martin and N Thrift (eds), *Money, Power and Space*, Blackwell, 1993

Uncertainty, *Elgar Companion to Radical Political Economy*, in P Arestis and M Sawyer (eds), Elgar, 1994

The Religious Content of Economics, in H G Brennan and A M C Waterman (eds), *Economics and Religion*, Kluwer, 1994, 215–28

Uncertainty about Uncertainty, in S C Dow and J Hillard (eds), *Keynes, Knowledge and Uncertainty*, Elgar, 1995, 117–36.

with V Chick, Wettewerb und die Zukunft des europäischen Banken- und Finanzsystems, in C Thomasberger (ed), *Europäische Geldpolitik zwischen Marktzwängen und neuen institutionellen Regelungen*, Metropolis-Verlag, 1995

Liquidity Preference in International Finance: The Case of Developing Countries, in P Wells (ed), *Post Keynesian Economic Theory*, Kluwer, 1995, 1–16. http://hdl.handle.net/1893/26297

with A C Dow, Endogenous Money Creation and Idle Balances, in M Musella and C Panico (eds), *The Supply of Money in the Economic Process: A Post Keynesian Perspective*, Elgar, 1995, 473–90

European Monetary Integration, Endogenous Credit Creation and Regional Economic Development, in X Vence-Deza and J S Metcalfe (eds), *Wealth from Diversity: Innovation and Structural Change and Finance for Regional Development in Europe,* Kluwer, 1996, 293–306

Keynes's Philosophy and Post Keynesian Monetary Theory, in P Arestis (ed.*), Keynes, Money and the Open Economy: Essays in Honour of Paul Davidson,* vol.I, Elgar, 1996, 34–49

Economics and Religion, in P Arestis, G Palma and M Sawyer (eds), *Capital Controversy, Post-Keynesian Economics and the History of Economics: Essays in Honour of Geoff Harcourt* vol. 1, Elgar, 1996, 466–73.

Methodological Pluralism and Pluralism of Method', in Salanti, A and E Screpanti (eds), *Pluralism in Economics: Theory, History and Methodology*, Elgar, 1997, 89–99. http://hdl.handle.net/1893/25157

Endogenous Money, in G C Harcourt and P Riach (eds), *The Second Edition of the General Theory*, Vol. 2, Routledge, 1997, 61–78

with V Chick, Competition and Integration in European Banking, in A Cohen, Hagemann, H and J Smithin (eds), *Money, Financial Institutions and Macroeconomics*, Kluwer, 1997, 253–70

Scottish Devolution and the Financial Sector, in M Danson, S Hill and G Lloyd (eds), *Regional Governance and Economic Development, European Research in Regional Science* Vol 7, 1997, 229–241. http://hdl.handle.net/1893/25158

Rationalisation in Economics, in K Dennis (ed.), *Rationality in Economics: Alternative Perspectives,* Kluwer, 1998, 5–16. http://hdl.handle.net/1893/25173

Knowledge, Information and Credit Creation, in R Rotheim (ed), *New Keynesian Economics,* Routledge. 1998, 214–26.

Post Keynesian Methodology, in T B Davis et al (eds), *The Handbook of Economic Methodology,* Elgar, 1998, 378–82.

With A Dow, A Hutton, and M Keaney, John Rae and the Tradition of Scottish Political Economy, in O F Hamouda, C Lee and D Mair (eds), *The Economics of John Rae,* Routledge, 243–58, 1998 http://hdl.handle.net/1893/25172

Financial Structure and the Economic Performance of Peripheral Economies: the Case of Europe, in S Hill and B Morgan (eds), *Inward Investment, Business Finance and Regional Development.* London: Macmillan, 1998, 170–85.

with Carlos Rodriguez Fuentes, The Political Economy of Monetary Policy, in P Arestis and M C Sawyer (eds), *The Political Economy of Central Banking,* Elgar, 1998, 1–19.

Economics, Ethics and Knowledge, in J Dean and A Waterman (eds), *Economics and Religion: Normative Social Theory.* Boston: Kluwer, 1999, 123–30. http://hdl.handle.net/1893/25179

Stages of Banking Development and the Spatial Development of Financial Systems, R Martin (ed.), *Money and the Space Economy,* Wiley, 1999, 31–48.

Keynesian Monetary Theory and the Debt Crisis, in O Hamouda and B Price (eds), *Keynesianism and the Keynesian Revolution in America,* Elgar, 1999, 103–15.

International Liquidity Preference and Endogenous Credit Creation, in J Deprez and J Harvey (eds), *Foundations of International Economics.* London: Routledge, 153–70, 1999. http://hdl.handle.net/1893/25159

Rationality and Rhetoric in Smith and Keynes, in R Rossini, G Sandri and R Scazzieri (eds), *Incommensurability and Translation.* Aldershot: Elgar, 1999, 189–200. http://hdl.handle.net/1893/22699

With D N F Bell, The Financial Powers of the Parliament, I G Hassan and C Warhurst (eds), *The New Scottish Politics.* The Stationary Office, 2000, 93–97.

Hume: A Re-assessment, in P L Porta, R Scazzieri, and A S Skinner (eds), *Knowledge, Division of Labour and Social Institutions,* Elgar, 2001, 75–92.

With C J Rodriguez Fuentes, Desregulacion Financiera y Competencia Bancaria: Implicaciones para el Desarrollo Regional, in F Calero Garcia, R Lorenzo Alegria and S Morini Marrero (eds), *Economia y Finanzas,* Gobierno de Canarias, S/C de Tenerife.

Modernism and Postmodernism: A Dialectical Process, in S Cullenberg, J Amariglio and D F Ruccio, eds), *Postmodernism, Economics and Knowledge,* Routledge, 2001, 61–76. Japanese language edition, Ochanomizu Shobo

The ECB, Banking, Monetary Policy, and Unemployment, in L Magnusson and B Stråth (eds), *From the Werner Plan to EMU: In Search of a Political Economy for Europe, Presses Universitaires Europeennes,* 2001, 179–92.

Post Keynesian Methodology, in R Holt and S Pressman (eds) *A New Guide to Post Keynesian Economics,* Routledge, 2001, 11–20.

Liquidity Preference in International Finance: The Case of Developing Countries, in P Wells (ed), *Post Keynesian Economic Theory.* New edition in Chinese, 2001.

with A C Dow, The Relevance of Historical Experience for Economics, in P Arestis, M Desai and S C Dow (eds) *Methodology, Microeconomics and Keynes,* London: Routledge, 2002, 39–50.

Keynes, The Post Keynesians and Methodology, in Dow, S and Hillard, J (eds), *Beyond Keynes: Post Keynesian Econometrics, Microeconomics and the Theory of the Firm,* Aldershot: Elgar, 2002, 162–75.

Methodological Pluralism and Pluralism of Method, in G M Hodgson (ed.), *A Modern Reader in Institutional and Evolutionary Economics: Key Concepts*. Cheltenham: Elgar, 2002, 136–46.

with A C Dow and A Hutton, Thomas Chalmers and the Economics and Religion Debate, in D Hum (ed.), *Faith, Reason and Economics*. Winnipeg: St John's College Press, 2003, 47–58.

'The Relevance of Controversies for Practice as well as Teaching', in E Fullbrook (ed.), *The Crisis in Economics: The Post-Autistic Economics Movement: The first 600 days*, London: Routledge, 2003, 132–4.

Economists' Knowledge and the Knowledge of Economic Actors, J Runde and S Mizuhara (eds), *Perspectives on the Philosophy of Keynes's Economics: Probability, Uncertainty and Convention*. London: Routledge, 2003.

Postwar Heterodox Economics: Post Keynesian, in J Biddle, J B Davis and W Samuels (eds), *The Blackwell Companion to the History of Economic Thought*, Oxford: Blackwell, 2003: 471–8.

'Critical Realism and Economics', in P Downward (ed.), *Applied Economics and the Critical Realist Critique*, London: Routledge, 2003, 12–26. http://hdl.handle.net/1893/25182

'A teoria monetária pós-keynesiana para uma economia aberta' ('Post Keynesian Monetary Theory for an Open Economy'), in F Ferrari-Filho and L F de Paulo (eds), *Globalizacao Financeira: ensaios de macroeconomia aberta* (*Financial Globalisation: Essays on Open Macroeconomics)*, Petropolis: Editora Vozes, 2004, 78–105.

'The Issue of Uncertainty in Economics', in P Mooslechner, H Schuberth and M Schuerz (eds), *Economic Policy-making under Uncertainty: The Role of Truth and Accountability in Policy Advice*. Cheltenham: Edward Elgar, 2005, 191–203. http://hdl.handle.net/1893/25184

with A C Dow, 'The Importance of Context for Economic Policy: The Case of Scotland', in A Haroon Akram-Lodhi, R Chernomas and A Sepheri (eds), Globalization: *Neoconservative Failure and the Democratic Alternatives*. Winnipeg: Arbeiter Ring, 2005, 287–302. http://hdl.handle.net/1893/25183

'Beyond Dualism', in J B Davis (ed.), *Recent Developments in Economic Methodology*. Vol II. Cheltenham: Edward Elgar, 2006, pp. 261–75.

With C. Rodriguez-Fuentes, 'Um "survey" da literatura de finanças regionais', in Crocco, M. and Jayme Júnior, F. (eds), *Moeda e Território: uma interpretação da dinâmica regional brasileira* (*Money and Territory: an interpretation of the Brazilian regional dynamics*). Editora Autêntica: Belo Horizonte, 2006.

'Endogenous Money: Structuralist', P Arestis and M Sawyer (eds), *Handbook of Alternative Monetary Economics*. Cheltenham: Edward Elgar, 2006, 35–51. http://www.e-elgar.co.uk/bookentry_main.lasso?id=3506

'Heterodox Economics: A Common Challenge to Mainstream Economics?', in E. Hein and A. Truger (eds), *Money, Distribution and Economic Policy – Alternatives to Orthodox Macroeconomics*. Cheltenham: Elgar, 2007, pp. 31–46. http://hdl.handle.net/1893/22619

'Pluralism in Economics', in J Groenewegen (ed.), *Teaching Pluralism in Economics*. Cheltenham: Edward Elgar, 2007. http://hdl.handle.net/1893/22644

With M Klaes and A Montagnoli, 'Monetary Policy by Signal', in D G Mayes and J Toporowski (eds), *Open Market Operations and the Financial Markets*. London: Routledge, 2007. http://hdl.handle.net/1893/22632

With A C Dow, 'History for Economics: Learning from the Past', in P E Earl and B Littleboy (eds), *Regarding the Past*. Brisbane: University of Queensland, pp. 1–8, 2008.

With A Dow, 'Theories of Economic Development in the Scottish Enlightenment', in P E Earl and B Littleboy (eds), *Regarding the Past*. Brisbane: University of Queensland, pp. 9–24, 2008.

'The Future of Schools of Thought within Pluralist Economics', in J T Harvey and R F Garnett (eds), *Future Directions for Heterodox Economics*. Ann Arbor: University of Michigan Press, 2008, pp. 9–26. http://hdl.handle.net/1893/22642

'Monetary Policy', in J B Davis and W Dolfsma (eds) *The Elgar Companion to Socio-Economics*. Cheltenham: Edward Elgar, 2008, 463–77. Reprinted in W Dolfsma, M White, D Figart, E Mutari and R McMaster (eds), *Social Economics: Critical Concepts in Economics*. London: Routledge, 2016. http://hdl.handle.net/1893/22650

'History of Thought, Methodology and Pluralism', in Jack Reardon (ed.), *A Pluralist Handbook for Economics Education*, London: Routledge, 2009, 43–53. http://hdl.handle.net/1893/22643

With M Klaes and A Montagnoli, 'Variety of Economic Judgement and Monetary Policy-making by Committee', in E Hein, T Niechij and E Stockhammer (eds), *Macroeconomic Policies on Shaky Foundations: Whither Mainstream Economics?* Marburg: Metropolis-Verlag, 2009, 33–50. http://hdl.handle.net/1893/22633

'Smith's Philosophy and Economic Methodology', in J T Young (ed.), *Elgar Companion to Adam Smith*. Cheltenham: Edward Elgar, 2009: 100–11. http://hdl.handle.net/1893/22651

'Was there a (Methodological) Keynesian Revolution?', in B Dimand, R Mundell and A Vercelli (eds), *Keynes's General Theory After Seventy Years*. London: Palgrave Macmillan for the International Economic Association, 2010, pp. 268–86. http://hdl.handle.net/1893/22645

'Psychology of Financial Markets: Keynes, Minsky and Emotional Finance', in D B Papadimitriou and L R Wray (eds), *The Elgar Companion to Hyman Minsky*, Cheltenham: Elgar, 2010. http://hdl.handle.net/1893/22646

'Economics and Moral Sentiments: The Case of Moral Hazard', in J C Caldas and V Neves (eds), *Facts, Values and Objectivity*'. London: Routledge, 2012, pp. 17–32. http://hdl.handle.net/1893/22634

with P E Earl, J Foster, G C Harcourt, G M Hodgson, J Metcalfe, P Ormerod, B Rosewell, M C Sawyer and A Tylecote (2009), 'Letter to the Queen, 10 August', reprinted in G M Hodgson (ed.), *Mathematics and Modern Economics*. Cheltenham: Edward Elgar, 2012.

'Monetary policy and regulation of financial markets – a Keynesian view', in G Chaloupek and M Marterbauer (eds), '75 Jahre *General Theory of Employment, Interest and Money*', *Wirtschaftswissenschaftliche Tagungen der AK-Wien*, reihe bd. 17, pp. 43–60, 2012. http://hdl.handle.net/1893/22640

'The Methodology of Finance' in J Michell and J Toporowski (eds), *The Handbook of Critical Issues in Finance*. Cheltenham: Edward Elgar, 2012, 218–24. http://hdl.handle.net/1893/22630

With P E Earl, J Foster, G C Harcourt, G M Hodgson, J S Metcalfe, P Ormerod, B Rosewell, M C Sawyer and A Tylecote, 'Letter to the Queen, 10 August', 2009, reprinted in G M Hodgson (ed), *Mathematics and Modern Economics*. Cheltenham: Edward Elgar, 2012.

'Keynes on Knowledge, Expectations and Rationality', in E S Phelps and R Frydman (eds), *Rethinking Expectations: the Way Forward for Macroeconomics.* Princeton NJ: Princeton University Press, 2013. http://hdl.handle.net/1893/10280

'Policy in the Wake of the Banking Crisis: Taking Pluralism Seriously', in P Arestis and M Sawyer (eds), *Economic Policies of the New Thinking in Economics.* London: Routledge, 2013. http://hdl.handle.net/1893/22627

'Teaching Open System Economics', in J Jespersen and M O Madsen (eds), *Teaching Post-Keynesian Economics.* Cheltenham: Edward Elgar, 2013, pp. 73–87. (http://hdl.handle.net/1893/18211

With V Chick, 'Financial Institutions and The State: A Re-examination', in L-P Rochon and M Seccareccia (eds), *Monetary Economics of Production: Banking and Financial Circuits and the role of the State.* Cheltenham: Edward Elgar, pp. 99–111, 2013. http://hdl.handle.net/1893/22628

'The Real (social?) Experience of Monetary Policy', in J Pixley and G C Harcourt (eds), *Financial crises and the nature of capitalist money: Mutual developments from the work of Geoffrey Ingham.* London: Palgrave Macmillan, pp. 178–95, 2013. (http://hdl.handle.net/1893/18212

With V Chick, 'Post Keynesian Theories of Money and Credit: Conflicts and (Some) Resolutions', in G C Harcourt and P Kriesler (eds) *Handbook of Post-Keynesian Economics.* Oxford: Oxford University Press, 2013. http://hdl.handle.net/1893/22629

'Methodology and Post-Keynesian Economics', in G C Harcourt and P Kriesler (eds) *Handbook of Post-Keynesian Economics.* Oxford: Oxford University Press, 2013. http://hdl.handle.net/1893/18210

'Codes of Ethics for Economists, Pluralism, and the Nature of Economic Knowledge', in G DeMartino and D N McCloskey (eds), *Handbook on Professional Economic Ethics.* Oxford: Oxford University Press. Published online March 2014 oxfordhandbooks.com

With A Dow, 'The Staples Approach and the Financial Crisis', in J Stanford (ed.), *The Staples Approach @ 50: Reflections on the lasting significance of Mel Watkins' "A Staple Theory of Economic Growth".* Toronto: CEPA, 2014, pp. 114–7.

With A Dow, 'Scotland', in V Barnett (ed.), *The Routledge Handbook to the History of Global Economic Thought.* London: Routledge, 2014, pp. 38–47. http://hdl.handle.net/1893/21077

'The Role of Methodology in the Economics Curriculum', in M A Madi and J Reardon (eds), *The economics curriculum: towards a radical reformulation.* London: College Publications, in collaboration with the WEA, 2014, pp. 53–60. http://hdl.handle.net/1893/21335

'The relationship between central banks and governments: what are central banks for?', in C Goodhart, D Gabor, I Ertürk and J Vestergaard (eds), *Central Banking at a Crossroads: Europe and Beyond.* London, New York and Delhi: Anthem Press, 2014, pp. 229–43. http://hdl.handle.net/1893/22508

With A Dow, 'Economic Development in the Scottish Enlightenment: Ideas as Cause and Effect', in N Perdikis and K Ruziev (eds), *Development and Financial Reform in Emerging Economies.* London: Pickering and Chatto, 2015, pp. 7–22. http://hdl.handle.net/1893/21334

with K Ruziev, 'A Re-evaluation of Banking Sector Reforms in Transition Economies: Intentions and Unintended Consequences', in N Perdikis and K Ruziev (eds), *Development and Financial Reform in Emerging Economies.* London: Pickering and Chatto, 2015, pp. 81–98. http://hdl.handle.net/1893/21333

'Money, Banking and Deficits', in T Ali and D Ashiagbor (eds), *The Case for Full Employment*. London: Work Forum Press, 2015. http://hdl.handle.net/1893/22504

'Monetary Policy', in J B Davis and W Dolfsma (eds), *The Elgar Handbook of Socio-Economics* (second edition). Cheltenham: Edward Elgar, 2015, pp. 533–47. http://hdl.handle.net/1893/22506

'Neoclassicism, critical realism and the Cambridge methodological tradition', in J Morgan (ed.), *What is Neoclassical Economics?* London: Routledge, pp. 102–18, 2015 [http://hdl.handle.net/1893/22677] http://hdl.handle.net/1893/22695

'Consistency in Pluralism and Microfoundations', in J Courvisanos, J Doughney and A Millmow (eds), *Reclaiming Pluralism in Economics*. London: Routledge, 2016, pp. 32–46. ISBN 978-1-138-95176-1. http://hdl.handle.net/1893/23344

'Cambridge's contribution to methodology in economics' in R Cord (ed.), *The Palgrave Companion to Cambridge Economics*. London: Palgrave Macmillan, 2017, pp. 27–49. ISBN 978-1-137-41232-4. http://hdl.handle.net/1893/25165

'Post Keynesian Economics: Conceptual Underpinnings', *British Review of Economic Issues*, 10.3.1–18, 1988, reprinted in L-P Rochon and S Rossi (eds), *Post-Keynesian Economics*. Cheltenham: Edward Elgar.

'Post Keynesianism as Political Economy: A Methodological Discussion', *Review of Political Economy*, 2.3.345–58, 1990, reprinted in L-P Rochon and S Rossi (eds), *Post-Keynesian Economics*. Cheltenham: Edward Elgar.

'Horizontalism: A Critique', *Cambridge Journal of Economics*, 20.4.497–508, 1996, reprinted in L-P Rochon and S Rossi (eds), *Post-Keynesian Economics*. Cheltenham: Edward Elgar, 2017.

'Post Keynesianism and Critical Realism: What is the Connection?' *Journal of Post Keynesian Economics,* 22.1.15–33, 1999, reprinted in L-P Rochon and S Rossi (eds), *Post-Keynesian Economics*. Cheltenham: Edward Elgar, 2017.

'Keynes on Domestic and International Monetary Reform', in S Dow, J Jespersen and G Tily (eds), The General Theory and Keynes for the 21st Century. Cheltenham: Edward Elgar, pp. 132–44, 2018.

'Pluralist economics: is it scientific?', in S Decker, W Elsner and S Flechtner (eds), *Advancing Pluralism in Teaching Economics: international perspectives on a textbook science*. London: Routledge, pp. 13–30, 2018.

'Why regulate the financial system?', in L A Lindman, M Storlie and A Crawford (eds), *Rethinking Finance*. Oslo: Rethinking Economics Norway, pp. 36–44, 2018.

'Geoff Hodgson on Pluralism and Historical Specificity', in F Gagliardi and D Gindis (eds), *Institutions and Evolution of Capitalism: Essays in Honour of Geoffrey M. Hodgson*. Cheltenham: Edward Elgar, 2019, pp. 14–28.

'Risk and Uncertainty', in R Dimand and H Hagemann (eds), *The Elgar Companion to John Maynard Keynes*. Cheltenham: Edward Elgar, 2019, pp. 255–62.

'Opportunities and challenges for Post-Keynesian economics?', in J Jespersen and F Oleson (eds), *Progressive Post-Keynesian Economics: dealing with reality*. Cheltenham: Edward Elgar, pp. 1–15, 2019.

'Forward' to P Armstrong, Can Heterodox Economists Make a Difference? *Conversations with Key Thinkers*. Cheltenham: Edward Elgar, 2020, pp. xxi-xxii. **ISBN:** 978 1 80037 088 3

Interview in P Armstrong, Can Heterodox Economists Make a Difference? *Conversations with Key Thinkers*. Cheltenham: Edward Elgar, 2020, pp. 302–15. **ISBN:** 978 1 80037 088 3

'Money, Finance and the Role of the State', in B Dunn (ed.), *A Research Agenda for Critical Political Economy*. Cheltenham: Edward Elgar, 2020.

'The methodological role of the history of economic thought', in G Deleplace, M C Marcuzzo and P Paesani (eds), *New Perspectives on Political Economy and Its History*. London: Palgrave Macmillan, 2020, pp. 21–38.

'Financialization, money and the state', in P Mader, D Mertens and N van der Zwan (eds), *International Handbook of Financialization*. London: Routledge, 2020, pp. 56–67.

'Is Macro in Crisis?' in H Bougrine and L-P Rochon (eds), *Money and Crises in Post-Keynesian Economics: Essays in honour of Marc Lavoie and Mario Seccareccia*, vol. 1, Cheltenham: Edward Elgar, pp. 231–45, 2020. **ISBN:** 978 1 78643 954 3

'Pluralism and Heterodox Economics', in A Hermann and S Mouatt (eds), *Contemporary Issues of Heterodox Economics: Implications for Theory and Policy Action*. London: Routledge, 2020, pp. 275–81.

'Preface' to J Robinson, *Economic Philosophy*. London: Routledge, 2021, pp. viii–xvi.

With A Dimmelmeier, 'Paradigms and research programmes', in *J-F* Morin, C. Olsson and E. Ozlem Atikcan (eds), *Key Concepts in Research Methods*. Oxford: Oxford University Press, pp. 209–13.

Review essay on M Schabas and C Wennerlind, *A Philosopher's Economist: Hume and the Rise of Capitalism, Œconomia – History / Methodology / Philosophy*. https://journals.openedition.org/oeconomia/11048

Forthcoming

'Unification and Pluralism', in B Caldwell, J Davis, U Mäki, and E-M Sent (eds), *Methodology and History of Economics: Reflections with and without Rules. Essays in Honour of D. Wade Hands*. London: Routledge, 2022.

'Uncertainty and Macroeconomic Methodology', in V Chick and J Jespersen (eds), *Handbook of Macroeconomic Methodology*.

'Economics, the Plastic Arts and Social Transformation', in C Repapis and S Myrogiannis (eds), *Economics and Art Theory*. London: Routledge.

'Marshallian', in B Haddad and B D Solomon (eds), *Dictionary of Ecological Economics*, Cheltenham: Edward Elgar.

Encyclopaedia/dictionary entries

Geoff Harcourt, in T Cate, et al (eds), *Encyclopedia of Keynesian Economics*, Elgar, 1997, 226–9. 2nd edition 2009/10.

Liquidity Preference, in P O'Hara, et al (eds), *Encyclopedic Dictionary of Political Economy*, London: Routledge, 1999, 670–3.

Money Supply: Endogenous or Exogenous?, in H Vane and B Snowdon (eds), *An Encyclopedia of Macroeconomics*, Elgar, 2002, 500–3.

The Babylonian Mode of Thought, in J King (ed.), *The Elgar Companion to Post Keynesian Economics*, Cheltenham: Elgar, 2003, 11–15.

'David Hume', in J McCusker (ed.), *Encyclopaedia of World Trade since 1450*. Farmington Mills, MI: Macmillan, 2005.

'Pluralism', in S Durlauf and L Blume (eds), *The New Palgrave Dictionary of Economics*, 2nd edition. London: Macmillan, 2008.

'Economic Methodology' in *The International Encyclopedia of the Social Sciences*, 2nd edition. London: Macmillan Reference/Thomson, 2008.

'The Babylonian Mode of Thought', in J King (ed.), *The Elgar Companion to Post Keynesian Economics*, 2nd edition, Cheltenham: Edward Elgar, 2012. http://hdl.handle.net/1893/22647

With V Chick, 'Choice Under Uncertainty', in J King (ed.), *The Elgar Companion to Post Keynesian Economics*, Cheltenham: Edward Elgar, 2012. http://hdl.handle.net/1893/22617

'The Liquidity Trap', in L-P Rochon and S Rossi (eds) *Encyclopedia of Central Banking*. Cheltenham: Edward Elgar, 2015, 300–2. http://hdl.handle.net/1893/22505

'Regional Finance', *The International Encyclopedia of Geography: People, the Earth, Environment and Technology*, Wiley-AAG, http://onlinelibrary.wiley.com/doi/10.1002/9781118786352.wbieg0472/pdf. http://hdl.handle.net/1893/23502

'Animal Spirits', in L-P Rochon and S Rossi (eds) *Encyclopedia of Post-Keynesian Economics*. Cheltenham: Edward Elgar.

'Methodology', in L-P Rochon and S Rossi (eds) *Encyclopedia of Post-Keynesian Economics*. Cheltenham: Edward Elgar.

Popular journal/website paper

with A C Dow, The Balance of Payments and Economic Policy, *Canadian Forum,* 59.5.20–23, 1979

A Finance Policy for Scotland, *Fraser of Allander Quarterly Economic Commentary*, 17.2. 61–3, 1991

The Relevance of Controversies for Practice as well as Teaching, *PAE Newsletter,* 6.6–8, 2001.

'The Forces Driving the Scottish Economy', *Perspectives*, Spring 2003.

'Redesigning global financial institutions', *Perspectives*, Winter 2008.

'Economics for the Future', *RSA Journal*, 24–7, Winter 2010.

'Time to accept economic known unknowns? The case for "pluralism"', *Conversation* 26 November 2011. http://hdl.handle.net/1893/23492

'Policy in the Wake of the Banking Crisis', *Australian Options*, 22–3, summer 2011/12.

'Economic Thinking', www.usilive.org/economic-thinking/, April 2012

'Perspectives on the Global Financial Crisis', *QFinance,* fifth edition. London: Bloomsbury 2014.

'The Culture of Expertise in Macreconomics', Rebuilding Macro blog 7 January 2018, https://www.rebuildingmacroeconomics.ac.uk/culture-expertise-macroeconomics/.

Journal letters/notes/short papers/abstracts (in refereed academic journals)

Reply: Neoclassical Tautologies and the Cambridge Controversies, *Journal of Post Keynesian Economics*, 5.1.132–4, 1982

Substantive Mountains and Methodological Molehills: A Rejoinder, *Journal of Post Keynesian Economics*, 5.2.304–8, 1982–83

'*On Keynes's Method*, Anna Carabelli and *Keynes: Philosophy, Economics and Politics*, R M O'Donnell: Review Essay, April 1991. http://hdl.handle.net/1893/26298

Post-Keynesian Methodology: A Comment, *Review of Political Economy*, 4.1.11–3, 1992

Scottish Business Affairs: A Comment, *Scottish Affairs*, 1.157–8, 1992

Kuhn's Paradigms and Neo-Classical Economics: A Comment, *Economics and Philosophy*, 28.2.221–2, Spring 1994

Comment on Kloten paper, in S Frowen and J Holscher (eds), *The German Currency Union of 1990: A Critical Assessment*, Macmillan, 1997, 200–202.

Editorial Note for Controversy on Formalism in Economics, *Economic Journal*, 108.451.1826–8, 1998

The Foundations of Economics, Review article, *Economic Issues* 3.1.81–4, 1998.

Brown Comment: A Reply, *Journal of Post Keynesian Economics*, 23.2.357–60, 2000–1.

Science Studies: An Exemplar, *Journal of Economic Methodology*, 8.3.423–8, 2001.

'Axioms and Babylonian Thought: A Reply', *Journal of Post Keynesian Economics*, 27.3.383–9, 2005. http://hdl.handle.net/1893/25177

'Transforming Economics through Critical Realism', *Journal of Critical Realism*, 5.1. 151–8, 167–8, 2006.

'Introduction: The Methodology of Development Economics', *Journal of Economic Methodology*, 14.1.1–4.

'Addressing the Psychology of Financial Markets: Comment', *Economics*, posted online 25/09/09.

'Economics and Ethics', *ISRF Bulletin* XI.10–14.

'People have had enough of experts', INET Symposium on Experts, February 2017. https://www.ineteconomics.org/perspectives/blog/people-have-had-enough-of-experts http://hdl.handle.net/1893/25180

Index

Note: **Bold** page numbers refer to tables; Page numbers followed by "n" denote endnotes